ON
SRI CHINMOY'S SUNLIT PATH

STORIES BY DISCIPLES OF SRI CHINMOY

All drawings by Sri Chinmoy

Cover photo:
Sri Chinmoy, August 7th, 1976 *The Golden Boat*, NY, USA

Text and artwork copyright © 2015 Sri Chinmoy Centre
All rights reserved

No portion of this book may be reproduced in any form
without express written permission from the publisher:
The Golden Shore Verlagsges.mbH, Germany

ISBN: 978-0-9933080-9-3

CONTENTS

INTRODUCTION 7

I FIRST STEPS ON THE SUNLIT PATH
1 JOINING THE SRI CHINMOY CENTRE 11

II EXPERIENCES WITH SRI CHINMOY
2 IN THE MASTER'S PRESENCE 225
3 INNER COMMUNICATION 311
4 LIFE AND DEATH 337

III LIVING AS A DISCIPLE OF SRI CHINMOY
5 THE ETERNAL JOURNEY 365
6 AN INNER CONNECTION 391
7 SERVICE 417
8 SELF-TRANSCENDENCE 455
9 MEDITATION AND TRANSFORMATION 503

GLOSSARY 535

INTRODUCTION

Sri Chinmoy was born in 1931, to a spiritual family in East Bengal. At the age of twelve he joined his elder brothers and sisters at the Sri Aurobindo Ashram in Pondicherry, where he meditated many hours a day, and attained the state of God-realisation. Following an inner calling, he came to the West in 1964, and spent the rest of his life in service to humanity.

As a spiritual Master, Sri Chinmoy made himself remarkably available to those sincerely wanting to learn from him. He was also remarkably active and creative. Not only a teacher of silent meditation, but also a musician, sportsman, writer, artist and humanitarian, he demonstrated that the inner depths and ancient wisdom of the East can be effectively combined with the dynamism and modernity of the West.

From 1970, Sri Chinmoy offered twice-weekly peace meditations at the United Nations Headquarters, and he held the opening meditation at the World Parliament of Religions in its centenary year of 1993. In his 43 years of service, he offered over 700 meditative concerts, composed over 22,000 songs, created over 140,000 abstract paintings, and has over 1,600 published books.

A sprinter in his youth, Sri Chinmoy became a prolific runner of longer distances, and in later life achieved many extraordinary feats in weightlifting. In sport, as in all his activities, he taught the ideal of self-transcendence: reaching beyond one's own perceived limitations, and

 competing with oneself rather than with others.

Since his Mahasamadhi in 2007, we naturally speak of Sri Chinmoy's outer life in the past tense, but his inner presence lives on, perhaps yet more tangibly. His teachings and artistic works also continue to offer their illumination and inspiration. In Sri Chinmoy's words, "The Guru is not the body. The Guru is the revelation and manifestation of a divine Power upon earth."

Sri Chinmoy demonstrated that each soul is unique, and taught through his own example the oneness of all humanity. He honoured all religions, and accepted thousands of disciples from all walks of life. The worldwide Sri Chinmoy Centre continues to flourish as a spiritual community.

As Sri Chinmoy's disciples, while we have in common our meditation practice, each of us will come with a different set of experiences, gifts and challenges. We are athletes, writers, artists and musicians, according to our capacity and inspiration. We strive to be of service by offering Sri Chinmoy's teachings, by performing his songs and plays, staging races, owning and working in shops or restaurants.

In this volume, we tell the stories of how Sri Chinmoy came to be our Guru. We share our memories of the Master, describe the ways his teachings have enriched our lives, and celebrate the abundant diversity of our spiritual path – in Sri Chinmoy's words, 'the sunlit path'.

PART I

FIRST STEPS ON THE SUNLIT PATH

CHAPTER 1

JOINING THE SRI CHINMOY CENTRE

*The Guru is both vision and reality.
Through meditation we realise
The vision of the Guru.
Through dedication we manifest
The reality of the Guru.*

– Sri Chinmoy

ABHINABHA
Amsterdam, The Netherlands

When I was nineteen years old one day I discovered that I was no longer happy. It was a revealing, somewhat shocking discovery. The childhood behind me had been full of happiness. I was a lucky kid: plenty of friends, loving parents, a happy childhood. Even now you could safely say I was fortunate. I studied something I liked, I lived in Amsterdam, an exciting and 'happening' place, I had enough friends. All the ingredients for a happy life were there, you might say. Yet I was not really happy.

There was a persistent superficiality about my life, which I was dreading more with every passing day. Conversations were always about the same kind of topics. Life revolved around studying, going to the theatre and hanging out in bars to talk and drink. It felt like a record playing the same tune over and over again. I was missing something, although I couldn't really put my finger on it. I guess I hungered for a deeper profundity than could be scraped from the daily grind of student life. I guess you could say I was spiritually hungry. At the time I was already meditating, just by myself. It was nice, but nothing special. The meditation practice was very separate from my daily dealings in the university.

It was during this period that I attended a lecture given by the Sri Chinmoy Centre in Amsterdam. How I got to that lecture in the first place is a funny story. At the university I had heard about an Indian Guru who was supposed to give a lecture in a well-known church.

It triggered an immediate response. This was what I was looking for, I thought, and decided to go. The lecture started at seven but for some reason I could not find the church, which was really weird because I was sure I had seen it many times. It was already past seven and I was still circling around on my bicycle. Suddenly a tiny poster caught my attention. The poster was hanging on the iron grating of a city park entrance. On it was a small picture of a friendly Indian man and a short poem about inner peace. The name underneath the picture read 'Sri Chinmoy'. It advertised a meditation lecture, although not the one I had planned to attend. Cool, I thought, another Indian Guru giving a lecture in town. I looked at the information underneath. The lecture was starting at seven thirty, about half an hour from now. The venue was nearby. "All right, then let me just go there," I thought. I jumped on my bike and pedaled my way over to the venue, which I had no trouble at all to find. I arrived well in time. There were only a handful of people there. Flute music played and incense wafted. It was very low key, you could say. That lecture changed my life.

Sri Chinmoy wasn't there, which disappointed me a little at the start. The speaker was a Belgian man of about forty years, exuding a marked inner poise. As soon as he started speaking my disappointment vanished. He talked about a spiritual life, a life of peace, love and happiness and the ways to bring these qualities to the fore through meditation. The man was very nice, humble and likeable. And his words were like music to my ears.

I left the lecture feeling a deep sense of peace and a joyful, exuberant feeling in my heart. This really was what I had been looking for! It was as if a curtain was drawn from my eyes and suddenly there was this beautiful view on a new and promising future. It felt natural and totally right. I guess it was destiny.

During a couple of months I followed the meditation class offered by the Sri Chinmoy Centre. Gradually I became more inspired and enthusiastic about Sri Chinmoy's philosophy. What really appealed to me was the combination of a profound and soulful inner life with a dynamic and versatile outer life.

I also had my doubts. I was only twenty years old at the time. Was I ready to become a spiritual person, a modern monk so to speak? My heart was definitely telling me to jump into the spiritual life, but a more conservative part was holding me back. It took me a while to decide. And I would have lingered on even longer if it wasn't for two dreams I had in which Sri Chinmoy vividly appeared. In the first dream he was teaching his students songs and I was listening in. In the second dream Sri Chinmoy was in a Dutch town called Leiden, but in my dream it was spelled 'Lijden', which is the Dutch word for suffering. It was totally symbolic. Sri Chinmoy was there and I remember he shook my hand and smiled at me, as if to say, "I can take all of your suffering away." When I awoke I felt a very spiritual energy and I knew I had to become his student. So I did. It turned out to be the best decision of my life. But I guess it was destiny.

ADARINI & LÁZSLÓ
Geneva, Switzerland

Often I would call my Dad 'Guru' and Guru 'Dad'. It used to bother me that my tongue would play this type of trick. So one day, in a sweet, relaxed moment while chatting with my Guru, Sri Chinmoy, I casually asked him why this was happening to me. Guru gently replied, "It is quite normal. Your father brought you to me, so he was your first Guru."

This is why this story is mostly about how my father became Guru's disciple, and why I will be eternally grateful to him.

Many years before this incarnation of mine, my father was having a rough time in Hungary. His father had died of poisonous water during the Second World War. At that time my father was four years old. But before that, something unusual had already happened. At the time of my father's birth, my grandfather found a Guru and became vegetarian, which was very unusual at that time in a goulash-lovers' country. My father maintained that diet in a fanatical manner even during his orphanage years.

Now we jump forward to when my father was 15 years of age. Being in a Communist country, the advantage was that playing sports was free. My father did judo and gymnastics as extracurricular activities. One day during recreation, my father helped a boy who had been beaten up by five bigger boys. In those days, fights among classmates were quite brutal. At the end of that one they were asking "to whom this ear belongs". You can imagine wartime must have been awful. My Dad, despite having grown up without any religious background, made a deal with the Supreme: if the Supreme helped him escape from Communism, he would go and light a candle in the church every day.

Then and there my father started planning his escape. Skipping a few incredible details, I will go straight to the juicy story. At that time he was 20 years old and the Hungarian Revolution had just started. The escape agent had been caught right in front of my father by the Hungarian military. Now my father was lost in the forest and started walking aimlessly, looking for a way out, when suddenly a light came straight out of his heart, guiding him out of the forest. It must have been amazing not knowing anything about spirituality, trusting basically the only thing that shone on earth at this moment of despair.

After many other quite unusual episodes, my Dad then boarded a truck with other escaping Hungarians. He was hoping for the final crossing to the other side, the 'free world'. This was when something more amazing happened – something that really shows that, when the Supreme wants you somewhere, He will find His instrument anywhere. The story goes something like this. The truck in which my father was hiding got pulled over by the Hungarian military and all the refugees were held at gunpoint outside the truck – except my father, who was the last one to exit the truck. He was held back with a rifle pointed at him. His first thought was, "That's it, he's going to shoot." But you will not believe what happened. Remember the boy that my father helped in a fight when he was 15 years old. Well, yes – it was him! He recognised my father and let him pass through the border.

On the Austrian side, all the refugees had to wait for the proper papers and a country of adoption. My father's first choice was Sweden, but fate chose otherwise. In the office that helped all the exiled Hungarians was a man whom my father knew. He was in charge of sending people to Switzerland. So, within a very short time my father was sent to Winterthur, a Swiss city. This was another miracle, as some of the other refugees had to wait a very long time to get a country of adoption.

As promised, my father's quest for spirituality got really intense – or rather, the Supreme's promise to guide my father to Guru was fulfilled in October 1971. In a violent dream involving being shot at by arrows, my father ran to escape the arrows. Then, suddenly, a brick wall appeared with an image of a face on it. This was where my father took the ultimate leap of faith. He jumped into the face and woke up. Six months later, in March of 1972 on a poster on a Geneva wall, my father recognised the same face he had seen in his dream. And this was how I became at the age of 7 a devoted, loving disciple of my beloved Guru.

My father passed away in September 2003. During his years as a disciple he had many incredible inner experiences that only an Avatar such as our Guru can reveal to his student. Going through my father's collection of photos and poems of Guru, I discovered the poster that 'found' my father on a Geneva street. The face on it was none other than the Transcendental Picture.

In March 1972 a meditation class was given by a Japanese disciple living in England (according to my research). In those days, to be accepted by Guru you just had to send a letter and a photo directly to Guru's house. Guru would respond himself with a letter. And lucky for my Dad! Guru actually came in June of the same year to Geneva and again in the summer of 1973. My father had organised a conference for Guru. All my family went to wait for Guru at the airport. We then invited our beloved Guru to our small apartment to have tea and some delicious pink cake that my mother had specially made. We had photos of Guru on the wall and to us, the kids, Guru was our uncle.

I remember Guru touching our heads, my sister, my brother and me. This was my first conscious blessing. Even though on the outer plane I had no idea what was going on, I loved my 'uncle'; he was so beautiful. We also had a lovely boat trip with Guru. I think my first surrender-moment was when we were asked to sit next to Guru for a photo. I remember being squished under Guru's arm next to my brother. I could not even lift my head, so tightly was I held there. What a blessing I got! But back then I was probably wondering how I could escape. That evening Guru wanted my mother to come to the conference, so Guru requested Kailash to babysit us. I don't remember how we behaved and I hope he has forgotten – we the little monsters! We also had a picnic in a park where I was wondering why people were sitting so far away from Guru. He was all alone under a tree, writing. He looked so beautiful.

So this is the story of how my father and I became disciples. Since then it has been transformation at the speed of a bullet – even though I know that many opportunities were missed that could have made us fly much faster. But our Guru will never give up. He gives and gives and gives, even when our head hits the wall. My gratitude to my beloved Guru is measureless for Eternity.

ADESH
Zurich, Switzerland

It was 1986, ten years after meeting Abarita outside Ravi Shankar's concert. I remembered that Abarita was dealing with Indian instruments, so I called him and asked whether he had a tamboura for me to buy. In the meantime, Abarita had set up his tofu factory and no longer had anything to do with Indian instruments. But he gave me the phone number of someone in Madal Bal, who agreed to purchase a tamboura for me. I was to pick it up from the Madal Bal health food store at the Kreuzplatz in Zurich on January 2nd, 1987. (Later I learned that this arrangement had been organised from Minati's store Sangit Sushama in Heidelberg.) On this day, January 2nd, Ajita and I were still living in Appenzell, about 120 km away from Zurich. Our whole family, with Anupama two years old and Bandhavi six months old, travelled by train to Zurich to visit the shop at the Kreuzplatz. Gunthita was working in the shop. The tamboura was sitting there in one corner. I picked up the instrument and tried to tune it, but somehow I was not able to. I wondered what could possibly be wrong, as tuning the tamboura should not have been a problem for me. However, I simply could not tune it. I thought, well and good, let's do it in the Indian way and give it a little time. So I placed it back in the corner and looked around the tiny shop.

There were many pictures of Guru, but one picture immediately struck me. Guru looked so happy in this picture and this immediately made me jealous. Here was definitely somebody who had really found his goal, who was satisfaction incarnate. And I wasn't!

A recording of Gunthita's music group (named 'Fountain Light' at that time) was playing in the shop. I went back to the tamboura, and gave it to Ajita to try, but lo and behold, it was in tune. It was exactly in tune with the music that was playing. At that point I knew something was happening. I felt a new sensation in my heart, it was like a tiny candle flame, such a nice, warm, loving feeling. We bought two of Guru's books and asked Gunthita how to become disciples. She explained that we would have to send in our photos. After leaving the shop, I still felt Guru's light warming my heart. Back home I sent my picture to Madal Bal, and about a month later, I got a call from Kailash saying that I was accepted as Guru's disciple.

From the very first moment I became Guru's disciple I had this sensation in the middle of my chest where the spiritual heart is located. It is like a tiny flame, like a candle flame peacefully, steadily burning in my chest, my heart. It is also like a little inner cry, like a little pain, crying constantly. And at the same time it is joy, peace, light and, most importantly, the feeling of constant gratitude. It is the presence of Guru's loving concern, Guru's constant guidance, assurance that I would eternally be Guru's child. In short, it is God's living presence in my heart, planted and raised gently by Guru's loving care, eternal friendship and oneness.

As our family lived close to Appenzell in a mountain range east of Switzerland, and the Centre was about 100 km away in Zurich, we could not attend the twice-weekly Centre meditations regularly. So Ajita and I took turns and each of us went every fortnight to Zurich to attend the meditations on Wednesdays. I will never forget the lonely train rides late in the night in the small rattling, shaking, loud, last night train through the hills of Appenzell, in a state of being uncomfortably half asleep on the wooden benches, but still full of an inner joy and satisfaction I had never experienced before. About once a month on a Sunday our whole family made the trip to Zurich to attend the Centre meditations; I do not quite remember how we managed with the children as they could not sit still for more than two minutes, especially Bandhavi who was hardly one year old, still a real baby. The first very significant experience I had was after such a Sunday meditation, when Abarita gave us a ride to the railway station in Zurich. When we got out of the car, the presence of Guru's candle flame in my heart suddenly had left me. It was the shock of my life. I felt an unbearable void as though the real in me were dying, already dead. I was in a panic. I felt, "No – please – do not leave me alone. I will never survive." Ajita looked at me and saw that something was very wrong. She asked me why I was so pale. And just then the feeling came back, Guru's presence was there again and has never left me since. It is as if Guru wanted to show me that his presence within my heart cannot be taken for granted – he can withdraw at any time. When I think back I cannot imagine how I lived before, without this wonderful feeling in my heart. Nevertheless I always felt a special guidance in my life and I always had the strong feeling that I was on earth for something special. How could I know that I was meant to become a disciple of the greatest Avatar that had ever lived on earth?

My meditation times in the beginning were very irregular. I meditated every day in the morning though, but not at a fixed time as we should do. I meditated at whatever time I felt was right. As I actually did not know how to meditate, I just looked at Guru's Transcendental Picture and listened, listened to the sounds around me, listened to my heartbeat. What also helped me very much was that I felt that Guru's face on the Transcendental Picture was the most relaxed face I had ever seen. So I also tried to relax my face as much as possible. What made it easy was Guru's presence in my heart, which I always felt and could always get back to when I got lost in thoughts and daydreams.

The Centre meditations I felt to be very long (and sometimes I still feel that way!). In the beginning I imagined all sorts of faces or images in the Transcendental Picture, like a small child. I definitely had no idea how to meditate. But just looking at Guru's Transcendental Picture was enough for Guru to mould and shape me and my life. The first song I came to know was 'Amal Dhabal Pal Tuleche', and I liked it very much. So, at one Wednesday meditation, where we usually sing a few songs after the Invocation, I prayed, or rather in a way forcefully hoped, that this song would be sung. And 'Amal Dhabal Pal Tuleche' was really sung. Instead of feeling gratitude I felt very proud that my wish was fulfilled, I even had the feeling that it was my force that made Kailash sing the song. What a fool I was (or still am?). Poor Guru, he fulfils a wish and then gets undivine pride instead of soulful gratitude in return.

AJITA
Zurich, Switzerland

The whole family travelled to Zurich to go to the health food store to buy a tamboura for Adesh's experiment with the children at his work. Yet the tamboura's biggest boon was that it was to be the instrument to bring us in contact with Guru.

As we entered the health food store I saw Guru's smiling photographs, and I thought that this smile could not be real. I had never seen anyone smiling so brightly. I was both confused and thrilled. Up to now my mind had always found some faults when I wanted to become familiar with a new path or a Master. My feelings had no place in my decisions. But this time I told my mind to shut up. From somewhere deep inside I felt that this was to be the right path for me. Through the shop window I could see Guru's weightlifting picture, which also bewildered me. What on earth had this to do with spirituality? But again I felt it to be right and told my mind to wait and see.

As Adesh could somehow not tune the tamboura we wanted to buy, we put it under Guru's picture. In the meantime, going through the books in the store, I picked the one which was the simplest and most elementary booklet with childlike drawings and easy instructions. It was: *The ABC of Meditation* by Kailash Beyer. As I had already tried meditation and not really succeeded, I wanted to really start from the beginning, again telling my mind to stop interfering. I wanted to really go deep and do the right thing by feeling it. I knew I had to fight the ego, which of course wanted to buy more complicated and sophisticated books. Adesh bought *The Inner Promise*, so this was a good combination.

When we took the tamboura from the corner and played it, it was already completely in tune with the song being played in the store at that time. I looked at Guru's picture and thought: "But this miracle is not necessary, I want to come anyway."

Gunthita answered so many questions of ours. But there was one thing that caught my eye: She had one front tooth that was black and this made me think: "Wow, this is a real sannyasin, an Indian renunciate. She does not in the least seem preoccupied by her appearance." Gunthita was so natural, friendly and open and really impressed me deeply.

I was determined to give my photo. But would my mind later tell me it was only because Adesh also did the same? I wanted to wait two days and see whether my deep inner feeling would still persist. After these few days I then happily sent my application. I never had any doubts. Ever since the short time we spent in the shop, I felt that I belonged to Guru.

ANANDASHRU
Auckland, New Zealand

Long ago, when I was a young farmer's wife with two very small children, there was a time when I found myself in an awful 'black hole' of depression. I had never been particularly unhappy in my life before then, rarely saw a doctor, and thought one would just say, "Grow up, you have responsibilities now." For many weeks I had been listening to the 15-minute programme, *A Faith for Today*, on the radio every morning. Weeping copious tears, I would pray and pray to really believe in the existence of God and Jesus Christ and not remain indifferent any longer.

One morning after the broadcast was over I was washing up the breakfast dishes and crying into the sink as usual, when my view through the window and across the valley was silently rent down the middle with a slight zigzag shift, and the world changed. The view was the same, yet all looked subtly different, slightly shimmering. It seemed as though the trees along the distant horizon had joined hands and were dancing, for one thing – but my real understanding was *inner*. I saw, somehow, or rather understood, how everything IS. I saw how all things are connected and that love is the key, and I was swept along and upward in a joyous unfolding vision of how this could blossom into Heaven on earth one day, with love for one another spreading across the land and around the world until it encompassed all nations and all mankind; and all the time I found myself whispering, "Of course, of course!" as if in ecstatic recognition of something long forgotten.

That is the best I can do by way of explanation. At the time, I tried to write down all that I had 'seen' – and could not. It was somehow impossible to express the wonder of it in ordinary words. One of my favourite talks on radio had been on Jesus' teaching, "You are the light of the world..." I knew this parable but always assumed that it applied to His disciples only. Now I knew it meant me, and you, everyone on earth.

I was totally uplifted. I knew the light shone from my eyes, my face was radiant and my heart was overflowing with happiness and love. (This was not just a mood swing! I have never been depressed again in all the years that have passed since.) I had been given far more than I had asked for. Now I did not just believe, I *knew*.

Today I feel that, in answer to my genuine, anguished cries, God's Compassion came down mightily and temporarily lifted the veil of *maya* or illusion, long enough to give me the answer I so desperately sought. Then the veil descended again, inevitably. The high consciousness also descended, slowly, without lots of prayer and meditation to maintain it, and I was left with just the essence of the experience to sustain me. I attended churches of several different faiths but could not find lasting inspiration anywhere and gradually just returned to 'normal', but that knowledge was always there, deep within – God IS.

Years went by, but the search never ceased. I read every book on spirituality and any loosely associated subject that the Hamilton City Library could provide.

The best one started off, "God is Love. God only loves. All God can do is love..." and ended with, "Say yes to God today – yes yes yes yes YES!"

There was a book on meditation that sounded interesting, and just what I needed, but I tried it only once, on my own. One day there was an advertisement in the *Waikato Times*, 'Four meditation classes for $25.00', so off I went. My only recollection is that we sat in a circle on the floor in a darkened room with a lighted candle in the middle. I found it weird, sitting in the dark with shadowy figures all around, and made no progress there.

The following year a small paragraph appeared in the local mid-week paper; a lady called Subarata, from Auckland, would be coming to Hamilton to give free meditation classes. Feeling a bit dubious after the last strange experience, I wanted to give it another try but thought it would be nice to go with a friend, so asked my daughter on the off-chance that she might like to come with me – and she said she would.

During the introductory meditation I concentrated hard on my breathing and the 'little imaginary thread in front of the nose', and soon found myself focused on a space, like a tiny rift between clouds, where it seemed something important was just out of sight, but which could be revealed at any moment. Entranced, I gazed yearningly at that space; time passed, then, as from a distance, I heard a quiet voice saying, "Now bring your attention slowly back to the room..." Oh, no, No, NO! Not yet! But that was it. What else could you do?

I never saw that space again – the doorway to the ever-beckoning Beyond? But my course was now set fair towards it, towards my goal – and my Guru.

Though I did not know it then, again I would be given more than I could ever have dreamed of asking for.

ANTARANGA
Munich, Germany

I remember, as a child, when I lay in bed at night, I sometimes looked at the ceiling and wanted to see God. But I could not see Him.

My belief in God was refreshed when I was around thirteen. Dust rose and white broken stones flew up into the air passing my eyes. I looked straight up into the blue sky. Not so much was aching. Also my orange bicycle seemed alright. I sat on my saddle again and looked down to the pedals. My favourite blue jeans had a big hole! It was clear that my mother would throw them away. This frustrated me unusually deeply and I realized that everything and everybody I love is fleeting. May be Buddha had a similar experience, when he – still a prince – met with an ill, an old and a dead person for the first time and understood that all earthly things are but transitory. I started to ask myself questions, like, "What will remain from me, when I die? Will I see my dear ones in Heaven again?" My questions ended up in reading the Bible and a mental belief in God, the soul and Heaven.

When I was seventeen, my first journey without my parents led me to Morocco. I went there by train with one of my school friends. On a very hot summer day, we explored the city of Meknes in the north of Morocco, and our long walk ended in the slums. Houses there were made of planks crudely hammered together and plastic bags. I was really shocked and sad as I saw that human beings had to live in such poverty. Born in Germany, I had never seen anything like that before.

After my return to Germany, the sympathy I felt for the poor and needy urged me to join a 'Third World' group and Amnesty International. I read a lot about all the hunger in the world, the wars, the torture, the ecological disasters. Such an unjust world, full of suffering! Hundreds are dying daily from hunger and diseases. Why does God tolerate this? I could have had the same fate. Is there an immortal part in human beings? Does retributive justice exist after death? I looked intensely for answers and ways to change the world for the better. God provided me with a clear mind and the ability to understand that power can change situations for a while, but that real and lasting change will start only when human beings feel more sympathy and love in their hearts and start to share. But how could I help to bring about this change?

After I had finished school, I moved with a friend to an old farmhouse where we grew organic vegetables in the garden and I started my civilian service. I did not want to join the army and chose instead to serve disabled children. One day I had to take one of the disabled children to a hospital. After saying goodbye to her and walking back through the corridors of the hospital, I passed by an arrangement of tropic plants. The beauty of the plants attracted my attention and suddenly my consciousness changed. I was full of joy, and everything around me seemed so beautiful. Unfortunately this celestial experience lasted only for a few minutes and then I had to return to my everyday feelings. I was unhappy in those days.

A few weeks later I went to a pottery market where I saw a poster announcing a movie about Zen meditation, which was to start in a few minutes in a tent on the market. I entered the black tent and watched the movie. All of a sudden the whole world around me changed. For a few seconds I had the same celestial experience as in the hospital, while the movie showed a monk practising meditation. I realized that meditation must be the key to this kind of elevating experience. I started to practice Zen meditation.

One day Peter, a participant in the Hatha Yoga class I attended, put a brochure in my hand saying something like, "This is about a real spiritual Master." I was looking for a real Master of meditation who could teach me, because I was unable to get this celestial feeling again through my regular Zen meditation practice. I wanted to see God and experience lasting peace and bliss. Some months earlier I had read in Yogananda's *Autobiography of a Yogi* that this is possible while living on earth. I was also very inspired by the support Yogananda received from his Guru Sri Yukteswar.

A few months later, I met the spiritual Master Sri Chinmoy, whom I had read about in the brochure, which I received in the Hatha Yoga class. While shopping in Munich, I saw a poster that announced a Peace Concert by Sri Chinmoy. I drove there with three members of our flat-sharing community at the old farmhouse.

Sri Chinmoy played many instruments at the Circus Krone in Munich, but I did not have any inner experience. For some reason, I decided to sign up for a meditation class given by Sri Chinmoy's students in Munich.

Nine months later, I moved to Munich to study homeopathy, acupuncture and a few other alternative healing methods. I attended the meditation class and learned a lot, but the celestial feeling did not come back. At the end of the class I was asked if I wanted to become Sri Chinmoy's student. I was not sure because I had had no significant meditation experiences during the class. Therefore I decided to go by train to Florence, where Sri Chinmoy would offer another Peace Concert in a few days.

The moment I arrived in Florence, I was very happy, even though I was quite tired because I had not been able to sleep well in the coach section of the night train. I was asked to give a photograph and a completed questionnaire to Nivedak, one of Sri Chinmoy's students, in case I wanted to become a student. I gave Nivedak both even before I had listened to Sri Chinmoy's performance! I felt that Nivedak's big heart and my happiness inspired me to act immediately. I decided to stay a few days longer in Florence to enjoy the springtime, because I was so happy there. But the next day, my happiness had disappeared. I realised that the reason for my happiness had been Sri Chinmoy's inner and outer presence and not the springtime.

A few days later, while sitting in a car on the way to Oslo, Sri Chinmoy accepted me as his student. I meditated very regularly, and my general mood moved in a positive direction after meditation from the day on which Sri Chinmoy accepted me as his student, but I did not have my celestial experience again. Was my choice wrong? In April 1989, a year later, I stood beside the entrance to a hall with many tropical plants in the Hilton Hotel in Munich. Sri Chinmoy was there to meet and honour a Nobel Laureate in Physics.

Suddenly Sri Chinmoy approached me as he went to welcome the Nobel Laureate, who was standing quite close to me. Sri Chinmoy looked briefly into my eyes. My consciousness changed. I felt deep inner peace and everything around me looked beautiful. A similar celestial feeling I had experienced first in the hospital when I looked at some tropical plants was there again! This time it lasted for a long time. From that day on, I was sure I had found the right person to lead me to enlightenment.

But what about the answer to my question, 'how to change the world for the better?' I still like shopping in health food stores, I like fair trade, giving a signature for a better world, and I am involved in the humanitarian service of the Sri Chinmoy Centres and the Peace Run. The difference to the time before I accepted Sri Chinmoy as my spiritual teacher is: I am happy, I feel that by bettering myself I am getting happier and I inspire other people to become better and happier citizens of the world. Or in other words: I feel after improving my consciousness and becoming a better person, this consciousness enters into others according to their receptivity and they improve. A better consciousness is contagious. It is like that; if you are sitting beside a calm person, you get calmer yourself. My inner experiences and the teachings of Sri Chinmoy provided me with the optimistic feeling that each human being will become good at God's chosen hour, and there will be a happy ending for this world.

At the time I became a student of Sri Chinmoy, living in Germany it was considered pretty unusual to have a Guru. In India and other parts of Asia it is absolutely normal. Guru is a Sanskrit word which means 'he who illumines'. I must say to accept the support of a Guru was the best decision and the greatest blessing of my life.

From the first day on which Sri Chinmoy accepted me as his student or disciple I could feel a very positive energy entering into me during every meditation. I did not feel this when I did my Zen meditation for half a year without being accepted by a true spiritual Master. Later on I read in one of Sri Chinmoy's books that every day he meditates on his disciples, and often he projects his consciousness into their physical consciousness.

I used to say my Guru created a tube connecting me with God's energy, which he himself was bringing down. That is what all true Gurus do.

I had read a few interesting things about Hatha Yoga and realised by the knowledge conveyed that my breathing wave was too flat, and I had many tensed muscles. In the first year, during meditation my body started sometimes trembling and bending backwards. I could see how the tensions in my breathing muscles disappeared through the trembling step by step. Finally I had a healthy breathing wave like a baby, and felt relaxed.

Through meditation my capacities in every field of life increased, and my fears and other bad qualities decreased. I had been by nature very nervous. Nowadays I feel most of the time a certain poise, confidence and courage. When my computer is hanging and data gets lost, it hardly affects me anymore.

What I love is that through meditation I developed more and more detached oneness with other people I come across. I can feel what they feel. I feel their needs and I try to be of service to them, according to my capacity and what my inner voice is telling me. At the same time, if somebody is depressed or angry it does not drag me down, or in most of the cases I can get rid of a bad feeling quickly.

Imagine a hot summer day. You have finished your work. Your body wants to go swimming at a lake. Another feeling tells you it would be nice to go shopping and your mind is telling you should meditate at 6.30 p.m. What to do? For sure, there are much more important decisions to make in life, but all decisions are about either having joy and peace, or not. Reading spiritual philosophy, I became aware of the fact that I have voices within from different parts of my being. One thing which made my life very simple and peaceful, is that before I do something I ask my inner voice. Of this inner voice I became aware through my regular meditation practice. Sri Chinmoy taught us to listen to our inner voice, because then you are acting in accordance with God's will, which provides you with peace. Feeling an urge to do something, I concentrate on my heart and ask if I should do that or not. When I feel a calm joy or peace in connection with a question, I act. Otherwise I do not act, because we all have a few voices within from different parts of our being which lead to actions ending in frustration. Nobody is perfect. Even nowadays I discover myself sometimes lying on the shore of lake without having joy. I forgot to ask my inner voice and followed the urge of my mind, which told me: last time you could relax so well and had so much joy at the lake. But your soul gives you new instructions every day and it is worth following them to have continuous happiness.

After meditating for 27 years, observing the improvements in my behaviour and my consciousness, I am sure something I came across in Sri Chinmoy's writings is true:

Most of the sincere, dedicated disciples have already

made such progress in the spiritual life that they have eliminated the need for quite a few incarnations.... All spiritual Masters have said that when spiritual figures descend, it is like an oceanliner that can carry many people very fast.

– **Sri Chinmoy**

I remember in 1992 sitting in a large room of a Public School in New York, just two or three meters away from Sri Chinmoy. Peace emanated from him and I could feel how this deep inner peace was entering into me. You want to stay in this mood forever, but after a few minutes or hours it usually disappears. It takes many years of spiritual discipline until inner peace becomes your permanent state of consciousness. Over the years I had many uplifting inner experiences like this with Sri Chinmoy's spiritual support. They are like beautiful flowers inspiring you to enter the evergreen garden of enlightenment forever.

ARANYANI
New York,
United States of America

In 1973 Sri Chinmoy gave a lecture series on Kundalini Yoga at New York University which I attended as a seeker. (These talks were later published as the book, *Kundalini: the Mother-Power.*) These talks were well attended and I was never able to get a seat up front. I always wound up sitting at the back of the very long and narrow room. Though I attended the entire lecture series I did not feel any special connection to Guru.

At the end of the final talk Guru offered us prasad – but in an unusual way. We did not take the prasad from him. Instead, sari-clad girls appeared with trays of samosas and Indian sweets. They walked along the sides of the room and passed the 'food' out. This created a lot of commotion because everyone wanted to make sure that they got one of each. Suddenly the quiet room became quite noisy. In the midst of all this I looked up at Guru. He seemed almost forgotten as everyone had turned their attention to the 'food'. Guru was looking out at us and he was smiling the biggest smile I had ever seen. It was so big I felt that his face had to stretch to accommodate it – it was more than 'ear-to-ear'. From deep within I heard myself say, "That is the most beautiful smile I have ever seen. I will do whatever I can in this life to make him smile."

* * *

I became a disciple in 1973 when Guru formed the Manhattan Centre. Our Centre meetings were held on Saturday night. Guru would come to our Centre meeting and afterwards was the public portion of the program.

During one of our Centre meetings we were given fortune cookies that contained Guru's aphorisms. Guru asked for each of us to read our aphorism to him and he would expound upon it. My aphorism was, "When I meditate God loves me." Well, I was having a lot of trouble getting up in the morning and meditating. I was sure I was going to be exposed and that Guru was going to say that those who did not meditate were unworthy of God's love. When it was my turn I was so scared. I read the aphorism out in a timid voice. Even before I finished reading the aphorism Guru said, "Dush! Who has done this? Who has misunderstood my philosophy? God loves me no matter what I do but when I meditate I feel God's Love more." I was so grateful! God loves me even though I am so imperfect!

ASHRITA
New York,
United States of America

My search started when I was 15 years old. It all happened very quickly. I just kind of decided that there must be a deeper meaning to life and I didn't want to follow in the footsteps of the rest of the world and my parents. So I started searching for a deeper truth. I was going to go into the woods and realise God. I started doing Hatha Yoga and meditating, and I carried this book around in my pocket called *How to Survive in the Woods*.

I grew up in Queens and I went to Jamaica High School. One day I had just gone to a party, and I was so disillusioned with the world. I was walking down Hillside Avenue when I saw a poster with a picture of Guru. I thought, "Wow!" I was looking for a teacher. The poster had a phone number on it, but I had no pen with me. So I took out my book *How to Survive in the Woods* and scratched in the phone number with my key.

The next day I called this number and got Dulal on the phone. He was a prominent disciple of Guru's who took care of this kind of thing. I told him that I had just turned 16 a week earlier. He said, "Then you probably have long hair?" I said, "No." Then he said, "You probably take drugs?" And I said, "No." So then he said, "All right, you can come on Thursday." I was deeply grateful and mentioned that I had read, "When the seeker is ready, the Master will appear." He replied, "Let us see."

Things were a little different in those days (1970). The meditations were in Guru's house. For some reason I thought I should wear white, because I was wearing white. I actually got to Guru's house early. The door to the front porch was open. I walked in and Guru was sitting there on his couch. I didn't know what to do. I was just a kid! I remember I was actually standing in front of Guru, kind of flapping my arms. I got very nervous and Guru asked me who I was, I answered, "Dulal invited me to come." Guru said, "Oh, very good. Please come back in 15 minutes."

So I came back and I remember waiting outside Guru's house with some of the disciples. I was very shy so I didn't say anything, but I was amazed how pure everyone looked. When we got inside, Guru had a meditation. It was in the main room of Guru's house. Guru asked all the disciples to come up and meditate. There were only about 30 people. As soon as I saw Guru, I saw a holy light around him, and I knew Guru was my Master.

People were getting up and I actually thought I was a disciple. So I started getting up. I was standing, but it was too late – everybody else was already up there meditating. Then everybody came back to their seats. Guru saw me standing there and said, "Now new people come up and meditate." So I went up and meditated and that was it. I just knew from the moment I saw Guru that he was my teacher. I certainly wasn't ready but, out of his infinite compassion and grace, my divine Guru had appeared.

BHASHINI
London, England

Your mind has
A flood of questions.
There is but one teacher
Who can answer them.
Who is the teacher?
Your silence-loving heart.

– Sri Chinmoy

This was the dream:

It's the early hours of the morning.

The sound of the doorbell ringing wakes me from my alcohol-induced stupor.

I get out of bed, still in my clothes from the night before, make-up smeared on my face.

Over the full ashtrays and piles of dirty clothes, I step, past the fallout from a late night, drunken game of indoor cricket, played with an empty wine bottle and a tennis ball. Broken things litter the floor.

I open the front door.

The instructor from my meditation classes is standing there. He gives a polite Japanese bow.

He speaks softly and reverentially, "I'd like to introduce you to Sri Chinmoy."

He gestures towards a tall, athletic-looking Indian man in shining blue robes.

Before I can say anything, the tall man strides past me into the flat.

Purposeful. A man on a mission.

"He's come to clear up," I think.

I turn round and look at the mess behind me.

He's got his work cut out.

***

I got off the train in Berlin. No plans, no direction, nowhere to sleep that night. All I had was a *Lonely Planet Guide* and the firm conviction that it was time for my life to change.

As part of my degree course in Modern European Languages, I'd spent the previous eight months in the south of France with two of my fellow students. With very few assignments to do and the French government paying most of our rent, we'd had more money in our pockets and more time on our hands than we were used to. The wine was far too cheap. Although I'd spent some of the time productively – learning to ski, giving up smoking, volunteering for a homeless charity – the rest was a hazy blur and those things I did remember I was now trying to forget.

A friend had lent me Herman Hesse's *Siddhartha*, recommending it as a "good book." In the retelling of the Buddha's journey from Prince to Enlightened One, I came across the concept of reincarnation for the first time – being born again and again in different bodies, each lifetime taking us closer to the ultimate goal of spiritual realisation. For me it was more than a good book. It was a call to action, a call to start searching for life's deeper meaning, to strive for something higher and more fulfilling than the 'normal' life had to offer. Why hadn't this book had the same effect on my friends? Was I weird?

Soon enough I'd found accommodation and a part-time job in the kitchen of an Irish pub. At the market I bought a book about meditation and a cassette of Tibetan singing bowls. Back home, I lay on the floor and listened to the cassette. An hour later I woke up unsure whether I'd had a deep meditation or just an afternoon nap.

In the museum at Checkpoint Charlie I'd seen a display of some of Gandhi's writings. In one he said that if you don't know what to do with your life, try fasting for a day. This will take you inwards to a clearer mental state and help you find direction.

I decided to try it once a week. My kitchen shift finished with a pint of Guinness – it was free. Who says no to free Guinness? After that, I'd fast for 24 hours. There's an island nature reserve called *Pfaueninsel* (Peacock Island), a short ferry ride from Berlin. I used to go there on my fast days to walk slowly and commune with nature.

If I had to define what I was looking for, I thought, I'd call it a sense of oneness with all around me, a feeling of connectedness with all of nature and humanity.

One day, walking to work, my head full of my new spiritual ideas, I spotted a poster. It was stuck to a wall, slightly set back from the road. It showed an Indian man in purple robes, with his eyes closed, playing a stringed instrument I didn't recognize. There were trees in the background. He looked as if he were in a kind of a trance. My immediate thought was, "He has what I'm looking for." Somehow I could tell he'd achieved the elusive state of oneness with everything around him, of connectedness with all of nature and humanity that I myself had wished to attain. There was a timelessness about him, as if he belonged to the distant past, yet he was wearing a digital wristwatch. I was struck by this incongruity: he seemed so ancient, yet here he was, obviously living in the modern day world.

I gazed, mesmerised for a few minutes, and then

looked at what was written underneath the picture. This man was giving a Peace Concert in Berlin. The only trouble was the Concert was in May 1992. It was now June 1993.

And I was late for work.

* * *

I returned to Edinburgh in September to complete my final year of university. For the past three years I'd done the minimum amount of study, devoting myself instead to alcohol, nightclubs and amateur dramatics. If I wanted to get my degree I'd have to work hard this year. At the same time I was beginning to see the limitations of the intellectual world. I sat in the university library – six floors packed with shelves and shelves of books – the collected knowledge of humanity. Was there even one book in this whole place that could show me what I was looking for? I'd spent most of my life developing my mind. Was I happy? Was I fulfilled? Books could only take me so far. If I wanted to go beyond the mind, I'd have to learn to meditate properly and that meant finding a class.

The first class I went to didn't quite do it for me. Led by two women, we practised different techniques: walking round the room in silence, chanting, speaking in tongues, lying on the floor to release our primal screams. Somehow I knew this wasn't what I was looking for. A final objection was the cost. Five pounds per class was a lot for a penniless student.

The next day in the lunch queue I was telling my flatmate I'd been to a meditation class. "Oh, did you go to that place next to Greyfriars Bobby?" (Our landmarks in those days were all pubs.) "You should try that one, it's free. I think it's called the Sri Chinmoy Centre."

Later that week I saw a poster stuck to the noticeboard of the German Department. It showed a big square maze with a figure at the centre of it, seated in meditation. It was advertising a class given by the Sri Chinmoy Centre. I made a mental note of the time and location and duly showed up, only to find I'd gone to the wrong place. The class was being held at George IVth Bridge Library and I'd gone to George Square Library.

The enormous wave of disappointment which overcame me took me by surprise. On the face of it, this was just another class like all the other classes I attended on a daily basis. Why was this one so important to me? Fortunately, it seemed the Sri Chinmoy Centre was quite active, and I soon found another class I could go to.

About twelve of us sat on the floor round the edge of a blue-carpeted room, listening to a young man talk. He spoke about our existence as being like a huge mansion with many rooms. Most of the time we stay only in our mind-room. Meditation was a way of getting out of our mind-room and exploring all the other rooms we had inside us. This struck a deep chord with me, but by now I was impatient. I was already convinced of the benefits of meditation; I just wanted someone to show me how to do it.

After some relaxation, breathing and concentration exercises, the instructor asked us to look at a large framed black-and-white photograph that was hanging on the wall. He explained that this was a photograph of Sri Chinmoy's face, and that it was taken when Sri Chinmoy had entered into a very high meditation. As such it represented an elevated state of consciousness in which the human personality was dissolved. It was called the Transcendental Picture. By meditating on it we could identify with that state and achieve a high meditation ourselves. This sounded like an unlikely story to me, but I was aware that I knew next to nothing about meditation, so I resolved not to rule anything out. I'd give it a try.

I relaxed and focused my eyes on the photograph. Almost immediately, extraordinary things started happening. As I looked at the face, the features began changing rapidly. I would see a baby, then the features would quickly change into those of an old man, then a young woman, then a small boy. The images came one after another. It was as if I were seeing a thousand different faces inside this one photograph – male, female, all ages, all the different races of the world, all of humanity in one simple photograph. Throughout this experience, my mind was telling me that what I was seeing was impossible, but in my heart I was feeling so much joy. Here was oneness. Here was connectedness. Here was what I'd been looking for, for such a long time.

The class was early in the evening, so there was time to go for a swim afterwards. Every time I closed my eyes to go underwater I could see the Transcendental Picture as if imprinted on my eyelids. Rather than scaring me, this reassured me. Here, I felt, was someone who was on my side, who'd be a very dear friend to me for as long as I wanted him to be.

That should have been the end, a happy ever after, but as it was my mind needed a lot more convincing. Was this the right path for me? Was it safe even? Everyone knew groups like these only wanted to take your money and force you to join a harem. My friends urged me to be wary.

After one of the meditation classes another attendee

voiced similar doubts. "You have to listen to your heart," replied the instructor. "If this kind of meditation gives you joy and a sense of peace, it's probably right for you. If it doesn't, you should look for another meditation practice." Instantly this put my fears to rest. Surely, if they wanted to exploit me, they wouldn't be telling me to listen to my heart! Right now my heart was shouting with joy and I ran all the way home.

The instructor told us that it was easier to meditate in a group than alone, because together we created a certain kind of spiritual energy which helped us. It definitely felt to me like this was true. My scientist friends disagreed. "That's nonsense. You can't create energy through meditation."

I sat on the bus trying to puzzle it out. "Do you know how electricity works?" asked a voice inside me. "Do you need to know how it works to use it and get benefits from it? Do you know how this bus works? Do you need to know how the bus works to ride it and let it take you home?"

This was the first time I clearly saw the difference between big me and little me. Big me was my heart and soul, my deeper self, which wanted to love and embrace the world, the part of myself I'd been ignoring up till now. Little me was my limiting mind, which wanted to categorize and put things in boxes. It didn't want to expand. It was all too easy to listen to little me when what big me was saying was challenging and uncomfortable. The instructor was advocating getting up at six o'clock in the morning to meditate, running to keep the body fit and giving up alcohol altogether. Big me was ready and willing. Little me was having a tantrum and wanted to give up.

In spite of this conflict, I always felt an underlying certainty which I couldn't ignore. It was there when I woke up in the morning and when I went to bed at night. "If you give up now, you'll spend the rest of your life regretting it." It seemed if I stuck with it, I'd have a shot at happiness, peace, purpose and complete, total fulfilment. If I quit, I'd live a half-life, always wondering what could have been, what I could have become.

I imagined living the rest of my life in one small room, never having explored all the other rooms in my mansion. I started dreaming that I saw doors in my house that I'd not noticed before. They opened onto vast rooms, sometimes whole wings. They were dusty and unused, sometimes filled with outdated or broken furniture, but, as estate agents put it, they had potential.

In one of the classes the instructor told us that Sri Chinmoy had just completed one million bird drawings. "What a waste of time, drawing one million of the same thing!" said left-brained, little me, fresh out of the debating room. But as I walked out of the front door, my heart exploded with joy. "He's drawn ONE MILLION BIRDS!" I shouted with delight at no one in particular and once again ran all the way home.

My exams were getting closer. Every Tuesday I would sit in the library and think to myself, "I'm not going to meditation tonight. I have to study." As eight o'clock approached, I would tell myself again, "I'm really not going to meditation tonight. I really do have to study." At five to eight I would throw my pen down and run down the stairs, out of the library and across the university grounds. I'd arrive at the class late and out of breath but with joy in my heart.

The instructor told me that ideally I would meet

Sri Chinmoy in person at this stage of my involvement, but as that wasn't possible – he lived in New York – I could send Sri Chinmoy a photo of myself and he would meditate on it and connect with my soul. The instructor was leaving for New York in a few days' time, and if I dropped off my photo at the Sri Chinmoy Centre before then, he could take it with him.

More nonsense. I definitely wasn't going to do that. Nonetheless, on the day the instructor was due to leave, I found myself running to the photo booth in the student union, cutting a photo of a panting, slightly surprised girl with messy hair off from a strip of four, putting it in an envelope and posting it through the Centre letterbox. As I walked home I looked at the three remaining photos. I could barely recognise myself. I was smiling.

Two weeks later, my flatmates and I had a party. Around two in the morning we were playing cricket in the hallway with an empty wine bottle and a tennis ball. I fell asleep in my clothes. That night I had a dream....

* * *

Alcohol was a big hurdle for me. University social life revolved around beer. I'd seen too many brilliant people destroy themselves with drink though, and secretly, I'd wanted to stop for a long time. Now I was determined to give it a try. I wrote on a piece of paper: 'Wendy Neve has given up alcohol 2/8/94' and stuck it on my mirror.

I tried.

"Why are you drinking water? Just have a half. Go on, just have a half," my friends chorused.

"Why are you drinking halves? Have a pint, what's wrong with you?" Soon the piece of paper looked like this:

Wendy Neve has given up alcohol ~~2/8/94~~

~~3/8/94~~
~~4/8/94~~
~~5/8/94~~
6/8/94

Eventually, there were no more crossings out. I took the piece of paper down. I didn't drink anymore.

Running was the next hurdle. I'd never been athletic. Shorter and weedier than my classmates, I'd always been picked last for teams and had spent much of my school-life devising ingenious ways to get out of Games. Still, I could see the sense in it. Meditation was keeping the inner me healthy; running would do the same for the outer me. So I put on my clubbing trainers and headed for Edinburgh's Peace Mile. Twice I sprinted round it at breakneck speed, collapsing at the end in a nauseous heap, my muscles on fire.

It hadn't occurred to me I could just jog.

By now I was meditating when I woke up every morning. Six o'clock was still far too early for me, and I only managed it when I'd just got home from a long night out. My mind was becoming clearer and my heart lighter. In the meditation classes, we practised singing some of the thousands of songs Sri Chinmoy had composed. Some were slow and soulful; others light and joyful – they made me smile; still others were dynamic and energising. I sang a few of them at home every morning after I meditated. They brightened my day. It didn't bother me so much when my flatmates drank all the milk and left me none for my morning cup of tea.

One day as I was walking home from the shops, a woman smiled at me; a little further along another woman smiled at me, then an old man, then a teenager, then some children. At first I enjoyed it but as it continued it started to unsettle me. This wasn't normal. Was there something wrong with me? Had I put my clothes on back to front? Was there something stuck to my face? Maybe they were all laughing at me. By the time I got home I was completely freaked out. Dropping my shopping in the hallway, I slumped against the wall. On the wall opposite, at head height, was a mirror. I caught sight of my reflection – I was smiling the biggest ear-to-ear grin I'd ever seen on myself. That explained it, I supposed.

Later, I was hanging out my laundry.

"What's that?" asked my flatmate.

"It's a sari. We wear them for meditation. Sri Chinmoy says it helps to wear something specific you don't wear for anything else."

"Not a very nice one is it?" He was right. It was bright orange with big pink, yellow and green flowers printed all over it. It looked like a pair of curtains from the seventies.

Why did I like it so much?

Sri Chinmoy had several requirements for his students. I'd been a vegetarian since I was sixteen and I'd quit smoking the previous year. Alcohol was now taken care of, and I hadn't even wanted to do drugs for quite a few months. Now it turned out that relationships were also on the banned list. If you were single he expected you to stay that way. No more boyfriends.

"OK, well here's the perfect excuse to give up," I thought. "It's ridiculous to expect people to live like monks in today's world. Besides, it's impossible, surely." I'd quit this meditation lark straightaway and find something else to do with my life. They'd pushed me too far with this one. As I walked home, I expected to feel relieved, as if a weight had been lifted off my shoulders. Instead I was hit by another enormous wave of disappointment. I'd got so much out of this. I'd cleaned up my life and I was happier and healthier than I'd ever been. Was I really ready to abandon it now? Why did I get the impression I'd be throwing away something precious, irreplaceable even?

If I were honest with myself, wasn't I a bit fed up with the whole relationship game anyway? It had always felt a bit like acting. I felt like I was playing the role of so-and-so's girlfriend: lines to be learned and recited at the appropriate moments, particular behaviours to be adopted in particular situations, codes of conduct to be adhered to. I'd seen so many of my friends morph into their boyfriends' counterparts – taking on his likes and dislikes, his turns of phrase, even his mannerisms sometimes. Wouldn't it be nice to live just for myself for a while? To find out who I really was? Did I really like Jimi Hendrix's music? Iain Banks' novels? Mexican food?

I'd finished my degree by now. Most of my university friends had moved away, which had made adjusting to my new lifestyle a little easier. I was working temporarily in a vegetarian restaurant and planning to travel to Egypt in the autumn to study to become an English teacher (the Cairo teaching course was half the price of the UK one and the qualification was the same). I'd already had the inoculations I needed and arranged to stay with a friend of a friend who had a flat there. Maybe I could postpone it for a year? I could give the spiritual life a try. Just for a year. If it worked out, well and good. If not, I'd just pick up where I left off, but with a deeper sense of who I really was. I made my decision.

It was now that I felt relieved, as if a heavy weight had finally been lifted from my shoulders.

***

In October 1994 I heard that Sri Chinmoy would be going to Rome to meet with Mother Teresa. I would finally be able to see him in the flesh. A group of his students decided to hire a bus to drive us there. We met at Kings Cross Station – a disparate bunch: male, female, young, old, different races. One young woman, about my age, greeted me with, "Welcome to your first nightmare disciple trip." The route took us across the Channel and through France and Germany. There was plenty of time for singing, meditation, joking and telling stories about life with Sri Chinmoy, stories which filled me with wonder and anticipation. They seemed to me like an alien race; they spoke a different language. They didn't say they didn't like someone, they said they didn't "feel much oneness" with them; they were never in a bad mood, instead they were in a "low consciousness." Nonetheless I couldn't help feeling at home with them, comfortable and safe.

When we arrived at the campsite in Rome where we were to stay for the night, I had a St. Peter moment. As I watched the others play frisbee, one of the campsite workers, who happened to be English, came up to me. He inquired, "Are you with that bunch of weirdos?"

"Not really," I replied. "I just came along for the ride." Later, as one of the girls helped me put on a sari before the function with Sri Chinmoy, my conscience pricked. This bunch of weirdos had been kind to me. I saw sincerity in them. They were genuinely trying to improve themselves and make the world a better place.

I was far from relaxed about seeing Sri Chinmoy for the first time. My questioning mind was resisting with all its might, shouting louder than ever, making me confused and nervous. When we arrived at the function hall where we were to meet with Sri Chinmoy that evening, I saw him standing on the stage, meditating with folded hands. I tried to feel my heart, but it was as if it were totally blocked, drowned out by the commotion going on in my head. Around me were several hundred women in saris and men in white. They all seemed to know each other. I felt completely out of place, a square peg in a round hole. Sri Chinmoy was talking now and I tried to listen but I couldn't hear anything. All I could feel was the pain in my head.

I gave up and picked up a book someone had left on the chair next to me. It was a book of talks Sri Chinmoy had given to seekers. I opened it at a random page, where Sri Chinmoy was saying that if any of them wanted to become his disciples they could send him an application. If he was the right teacher for them, he would accept them. If not, he would tell them to look elsewhere. My chaotic mind snatched this information and turned it on its head: I'd never applied to be a disciple. Sure, I'd sent him a photo six months ago but that was something different – something to do with contacting my soul. If I'd never applied then I'd never been accepted. If I'd never been accepted then I'd been rejected. If I'd been rejected then I wasn't good enough, I was useless, unworthy, unlovable. All my insecurities came to the fore and I spiralled downwards. I slumped in my chair and let the dark cloud of self-created misery envelop me.

All of a sudden I heard Sri Chinmoy's voice. "I have accepted you," he said in loud, clear tones! Those were the first words I'd understood all night. "I have accepted you and you have accepted me," he continued. "Now we must prove ourselves to each other, prove that we are worthy of our mutual acceptance."

Instantly the cloud of misery dispersed.

* * *

I stood on the ferry's deck and gazed at the sunlight reflected on the water below, my heart lit with hope. Silently I spoke to Sri Chinmoy. I thanked him for accepting me and promised to do my best to prove myself worthy of him. As England's shores came into view I knew that this time it was a new me coming home.

At Dover we compared passport photos on the bus. Mine had been taken a year previously. "It doesn't look like you," said one of the others. "Now you've got a disciple consciousness."

* * *

I ended the year in Cambridge with a group of Sri Chinmoy's disciples who'd got together to meditate for the New Year. The meditation room was decorated with paper snowflakes. Orange-blossom incense filled the air. We sang Sri Chinmoy's song, 'Vishnu Debata' – O my beloved Lord Vishnu. In the Hindu trinity, Vishnu is the preserver, the one who sustains us. My heart was full of gratitude, my happiness complete. Tears fell.

As I left the meditation room I saw a poster on the wall that I hadn't noticed before. It showed an Indian man in purple robes, playing a stringed instrument with his eyes closed. There were trees in the background.

A memory stirred.

More tears.

DATABIR
New York,
United States of America

When I graduated from Wesleyan University in the summer of 1971, my dad asked me what I wanted for a graduation gift, and I told him that I wanted to hitch-hike around the world. He agreed and gave me a $1,500 bank certificate. I flew to Ireland in September and started my journey through Europe, to Israel, Yugoslavia, Turkey, Iran, Afghanistan, Pakistan, India, Malaga, Singapore and Australia – and finally I was en route from Sydney to the Panama Canal. For two years I had travelled, experiencing the oneness-heart of the world. Those people who had much less wealth than I did, had taken me into their hearts and homes and forever changed me. I will always have real gratitude to everyone who helped and loved me.

Anyway, I left Sydney Harbour on a Russian passenger ship bound for Southampton, England. My plan was to get off at Panama and hitchhike up through Central America back to the United States and finally to my home in Connecticut.

One night aboard the ship, I went into the chess room and saw a young man playing chess alone. I asked him if I could play with him and he said, "Yes." We got to talking, and it turned out that he had a Guru in Thailand, who had instructed him to return to England to find another Guru who could take him further on his spiritual journey. He told me that the goal of life was self-realisation and that you achieve it by meditating.

I had meditated maybe twice before, but this time all his words made perfect sense. It was 2 o'clock in the morning when we finished talking, and I decided to start meditating on a small upper deck of the ship. I went to the deck and no one was there. All I really knew about meditating was that you sat cross legged. As I began to sit down, the physical world around me disappeared and the Supreme came and embraced me like a mother who had found her lost child after millennia of searching. I cried and cried with gratitude-tears. It is impossible to express how much love there was in the Supreme's embrace, but I can only say that it lasted for about two hours and I was not aware of my external surroundings. I was only crying in gratitude. I promised the Supreme that I would always offer my gratitude-tears to Him, if He allowed me. And He promised that He would always protect me. I pray that I will fulfil my promise. I know the Supreme will keep His promise.

Needless to say, I changed a lot after this experience. I became a vegetarian. I didn't talk for one month. I cut my hair short. I stopped taking drugs and alcohol. And I meditated every day.

I jumped ship at the Panama Canal, as I had planned, and hitch-hiked up through Central America back to my home in Connecticut.

One day I was reading our local newspaper, where I saw an article about the spiritual groups in our town. The only one that I was not familiar with was the Sri Chinmoy Centre in Norwalk, Connecticut. I decided to go on the first Saturday to Akuti's meeting for seekers. I bought and read Madhuri's book about Guru and learned that Guru was a God-realised Master.

I wanted to make sure that Guru was the same as my

experience on the boat, so I asked Guru inwardly to show me. One day at Tapovan, Guru's sacred grove in upstate New York, I was all alone reading Guru's poetry book *The Dance of Life*, when suddenly one poem triggered the same experience. Again I cried and cried and cried.

Guru is the same as my sweetest embrace on the boat and a trillion times more. By Guru's grace we can become a portion of what he is and offer it to the world with utmost gratitude.

DEVAKI
Montreal, Canada

My story is a little unusual in that I had actually met Guru when I was 12 years old in 1967, but at that time he was to me just a friend of my Aunt Esther's. She was my mother's sister and had met this man named Chinmoy in India. In fact, she had helped to bring him to America to share his spiritual wealth with Western seekers.

At that first meeting, my whole family: mother, father and three younger brothers, was on its way to Israel via New York and London. In our hotel, we met with my lovely aunt whom I really didn't know that well and this quiet Indian man with whom I didn't exchange one word! He gave us chocolate bars and other gifts, which impressed my younger brothers very much! As my youngest brother, who eventually joined the Centre, commented: "He gave me *two* chocolate bars, which no one had ever done before."

I was in my own teenage world then and not very aware of spiritual matters. After returning to Canada in 1969, I continued to lead a typical teenage life and decided to pursue a career in acting. Theatre became my passion, and I got involved in summer stock, one of only three students in my high school drama class chosen to go. We learned about all aspects of the theatre, and I was fortunate enough to be in one professional production with well-known Canadian actors. Then I got the lead part in my high school play. I was dreaming of Broadway! I began auditioning in theatres all over Toronto, where we lived. One day, my Aunt Esther paid us a surprise visit. We had a nice discussion about my life and my goals. She must have conveyed all this to Chinmoy, for some time later she announced that he didn't think that life was right for me.

I thought to myself, "What does *he* know and where does he get off telling *me* what to do with *my* life?" The weird thing was I was starting to feel that maybe I should pursue other things. I had always had this subtle inner awareness that there must be more to life, but I couldn't put my finger on it. When my aunt was visiting, I had asked her about her meditation with Chinmoy, who by then was called Sri Chinmoy. But I wasn't really ready to get into meditation at that point.

Ironically, it was one of my aunt's best friends who did explain meditation to me when I was 18 years old. She had been meditating most of her life and had a poise I had never seen or felt in anyone before. I said to myself, "Whatever she has, I want it!" I asked her to explain it, and so she took me up to my room, found a little crate and put a cloth over it to serve as a meditation shrine. At that time, Sri Chinmoy had not published any books, but my mother, who was also beginning to be interested in the spiritual life, had a few pamphlets that he had written. My aunt's friend took the picture of Sri Chinmoy that was printed on the back of the pamphlet and placed it on my new shrine. She told me to sit at the shrine in the morning and in the evening and look at the photograph, which would give me inner guidance on how to meditate. Normally, I would have been very sceptical about such instructions. However, coming from her, it seemed to make perfect sense! I trusted her for some reason.

My first experience meditating was very strange because I was sure I saw that photograph smiling at me! Then, I felt this inner smile as if my heart had a face with a big smile on it. I felt really happy. I am not sure if that was meditation, but I liked it. When I saw the picture 'smiling', at first I thought it was a hallucination and rubbed my eyes. But it kept on smiling. I ran downstairs to tell my mother what had happened and she said, "You must be a saint!"

At that time, my parents had split up and were going their different ways. My father headed back to Israel, and my mother, on the advice of Sri Chinmoy, moved to Ottawa, where my aunt's two university friends were running the Sri Chinmoy Centre.

Coming from the big city of Toronto, the prospect of moving to a boring little city like Ottawa was not very inviting, so I had opted to go to Israel for some new adventures. However, when I started to meditate, everything changed. I announced to my mother that I would now move to Ottawa with her and also wanted to join the Centre. My youngest brother also moved to Ottawa, while my two other brothers decided to stay in Toronto.

Mukti, one of my aunt's friends, had set up the Ottawa Centre in the living room of her apartment. I wrote a letter to Sri Chinmoy asking to become his official disciple, and he sent a message asking me to *call* him! I didn't think I could do that, but my mother said, "Don't worry; he'll do all the talking. You just listen." With shaking hands, I dialled the number and shyly told the person who answered that I had been told to call. Suddenly Guru, as we had begun to call him, came on the line. My heart felt like bursting, partially from nervousness but mostly from joy. He told me that he had received my letter and that I was now aspiring, so I should come to New York to see him as soon as possible.

On September 23rd, 1972, I arrived in New York (in my blue jeans!) and was taken immediately to someone's house where a birthday party was in progress. Guru so kindly welcomed me, as did all his students who were there. The women looked so lovely in their saris, and I felt as if I had entered some ethereal world. They were singing beautiful songs and showed a sweetness and self-giving attitude that I had never experienced before.

The next day, I was dressed in a sari to attend a morning meditation. After the meditation, Guru called my name and asked me to sit in front of him. I was nervous and kind of embarrassed, as this was all very new to me. He placed his hands on my head and told me that he was initiating me as his true disciple and that he would make me a divine soldier in the inner worlds who would always aspire for and fight for Truth. He also said that there was nothing here on earth or there in Heaven that he would not do for me. With those words, I was now officially his disciple! Once again, I was in a dreamlike state for days, feeling as if I were floating on clouds of peace, hardly aware of my outer surroundings. I went back to Ottawa with two new saris to start my spiritual journey there. Four years later my husband and I moved to Montreal to become Centre leaders.

I have now been on this path for 42 years, and in spite of our dearest Guru's parting to the other world, his words to me on the day of my initiation have always proven true. There is nothing on earth or in Heaven that he has not done for me. I feel his presence in my meditation and know that he is with me at every moment, helping and guiding me to do my best as a spiritually aspiring person. I still feel his smile in my heart and try to the best of my ability to share that smile with others, be it my Centre members, co-workers or university students. Everyone needs a smile. One of Sri Chinmoy's simplest yet most profound aphorisms states:

> *Every day*
> *There is only one thing to learn:*
> *How to be honestly happy.*
> **– Sri Chinmoy**

I am truly grateful every day of my life for the awareness of my spiritual self and the determination to aspire for inner Truth and Perfection.

DEVAVIRA
Toronto, Canada

It is *often* said that when the seeker is ready the Master will come. In the sixties I was caught up like many others in the transformation from rigid social structures to a new flowing freedom of expression. Rejecting the dogmatic ties of the Church and my strict Italian upbringing, I put away my Catholic school uniform and joined the throngs of young people looking for meaning through our so-called liberation.

Before long my interest in behavior and psychology led me to friends who were dabbling in consciousness altering and Eastern spirituality. I first read *Autobiography of a Yogi* by Swami Yogananda in 1966 and was drawn to the world of spiritual possibilities. I remembered that when I was about 15 years old I had brought home a book from the library which fascinated me with the pictures of Indian yogis in strange postures and the possibilities of mind and body control.

So I slowly found my home becoming a meeting place for a small group of friends who were also traveling the road of the seeker. A few of us joined a Tibetan Buddhist centre and eventually I took part in the 'empowerment ceremony'. This took place over a period of six or seven weeks and involved receiving a mantra and taking the Buddhist vows. The ceremony ended on an astrologically chosen date on which the 'Bikkhu' blessed you by chanting mantras and was completed by him extinguishing a lit candle on your third eye. I was happy to be trying to follow the rules of right living but there was not really too much change in our daily habits.

We took advantage of the many teachers who were then visiting Toronto. Swami Vishnudevanda, whom I met through a friend of his Toronto centre leaders, convinced me of the validity of the vegetarian lifestyle.

In 1971 I first read *The Three Pillars of Zen* and was thrilled to discover that Roshi Kapleau was going to give an all-day meditation session. The idea of silencing the mind to arrive at the Truth was very appealing to me and I found great stillness and charm in the Zen poems and stories. After our all-day session I practiced Zazen faithfully, early in the morning after my Hatha Yoga. However, I somehow still felt the longing for deeper connection.

Months later I heard from one of my friends who had accompanied me to Roshi Kapleau's meeting. He had gone to live at the Toronto Zen Centre and for some time we had lost touch. He wrote to me saying he had moved to Ottawa and joined the Sri Chinmoy Centre. He wanted me to meet a very special woman, a disciple of Sri Chinmoy, who also happened to be the wife of Roshi Kapleau. She would be visiting the Zen Centre in Toronto for a day or two and would tell me more about Sri Chinmoy. He enclosed a small book, *My Rose Petals*, which had a picture of Sri Chinmoy on the cover. I remember feeling a great beauty and purity emanating from the picture and felt a kind of thrill in my being.

The night before we were to meet I had a dream. I was going to meet the captain of a boat who would take me across a river. I was wandering through a forest to meet him but was hesitating because I was waiting for a friend. I was becoming anxious that I would miss the captain so I decided to leave my friend behind. I went on alone to meet a very old bearded man and just caught a glimpse of the river in the distance. The next morning I relayed the dream to my friend as we made our way to the Zen Centre. He was very excited about the symbolism but at the time I did not really understand it.

At the Zen Centre I was invited to a room, and it was here that I first saw Maitreyi. I remember being struck by her uniqueness and spiritual culture and feeling, "Wow, if she is Sri Chinmoy's disciple, he must really be a great teacher."

She encouraged me to read the little book *My Yogi Friends, My Avatar Friends* and told me to concentrate on the picture that she called 'the Transcendental'.

On my way home I was thrilled at this meeting and felt a deep sincerity and purity surrounding Sri Chinmoy. However, I decided I could not join the Centre until I had really given up my lingering bad habits, including my heavy cigarette smoking.

That afternoon when I was sitting on my bed reading the book and looking at the picture, I must have fallen asleep sitting up against the wall. When I opened my eyes, I saw the cigarettes beside me and said, "I am never going to smoke again." I never did smoke again.

Now of course I realize it was all Guru's blessings.

So for a few months we started to have a few friends meditate at our house. I was living with my brother at the time. We were the unofficial first Sri Chinmoy Centre in Toronto.

It was not long before we heard that Guru was going to Ottawa for the inauguration of the Ananda Niketan restaurant and we were invited to join the celebration.

During the morning function, Guru asked the people from Toronto who wanted to join his path to come up.

Three of my friends went up to Guru but I hesitated, still unsure if I could keep the high standards. I felt such strength, peace and purity from Guru and I wanted to be sure that I came to the Centre with full sincerity and could be faithful to the Master in every way.

It was in Ottawa that I first met Shivaram. He told us that Guru had come to Toronto in October 1970 and had asked him to meditate with seekers there. Guru asked Shivaram to meditate with us.

Later we learned there was also a young disciple from London, England, living in Toronto so we started to meet at his house, with Shivaram leading the meditation. When Maitreyi came to visit, she was shocked by the casual attitude and unsuitable environment. We were all sitting on the young boy's bed with the Transcendental Picture propped up near the headboard.

At Christmas in 1972 I decided to throw a last party for my friends before going to New York to ask Guru to become his disciple. This was a formal goodbye to my past. I was now ready to faithfully commit to Guru.

A few days later, Shivaram, Devakripa and I drove to New York and entered into a new world. Guru graciously accepted us – Pasqua (Devavira) and Pamela (Devakripa) – as his disciples on New Year's Eve at 1:00 a.m. in his house in Queens.

Later that night the inner atmosphere was charged with a new energy; there was no need for sleep. The next day Guru asked Shivaram to cook an Indian meal for about fifty disciples in honour of someone's birthday, and Devakripa and I were to assist him. That was my first experience cooking an Indian meal. Almost 40 years have passed and we are still fulfilling Guru's first request – cooking Indian food.

DHANU
**New York,
United States of America**

Recalling the inscrutable events that led me to Sri Chinmoy forty years ago fills me with joy and gratitude. It is another thing for me to write about it. I don't have the writer's touch; my story randomly goes forward and backward in time, awkwardly incorporating vignettes and arcane details. Regardless, I've decided to keep it a rough read and not hand it over to an editor.

Let's start at the beginning. I first heard of Sri Chinmoy in 1972 when I was 15 and living in Williamsville, a village in Western New York, seven hours' drive from New York City. The Sri Chinmoy Centre was eight years old and Sri Chinmoy had probably five hundred disciples worldwide, but he had no Centre near me.

Here's what happened. On January 29th 1972 I went to a concert at the University of Buffalo, about five miles from my house. Jerry Garcia, a musician from San Francisco who I had been following for the past year, was performing with a few of his friends. He was a unique, deep, natural, articulate musician, devoid of superfluity. He had a charming way of juxtaposing elemental simplicity with fathomless complexity, as a leaf or a drop of water does in nature. He liked chaos. Infinity was always inferred, even when he played a common folk song, not unlike Woody Guthrie a generation before him. He has an enormous following; in fact I'm still his admirer, although he passed away years ago. He led a band called the Grateful Dead. From 1965 to 1995 they played an average of one concert every four days. The surviving band members played a big concert in 2015 to celebrate their 50th anniversary, and 70,000 people came. In 1973 I saw them in Watkins Glen and 600,000 people came. It's easy to not like this band, especially if you don't appreciate the 1960s hippie subculture. One thing I love is the way their fans devotedly documented each of the band's thousands of concerts.

This wasn't a Grateful Dead concert, but it was my first chance to see Garcia. Another band was also performing that evening, before Garcia's band, and they were called the Mahavishnu Orchestra. Both bands had released new albums a few weeks before and, although they made very different music, they were giving concerts together in six East Coast cities. I had never heard of the Mahavishnu Orchestra.

The leader of the Mahavishnu Orchestra was a spectacular English jazz guitarist and composer named John McLaughlin. He was a disciple of Sri Chinmoy, who had given him the spiritual name 'Mahavishnu'. He moved to New York in 1969 and performed there with jazz greats Tony Williams and Miles Davis. The following year he organized some of Sri Chinmoy's very first European activities, and in 1971 he opened Annam Brahma Restaurant in New York, which is still run by disciples and doing great.

Although Mahavishnu is no longer in the Centre, from time to time disciples see him and he speaks highly of Sri Chinmoy. He came to visit Sri Chinmoy a couple of times after he left. Now 73, he still plays a lot of concerts. In recent years his band has included mainly Indian musicians. Around the year 2000 Sri Chinmoy told me that Mahavishnu's soul came to him inwardly for blessings on a regular basis. In 2006 at a disciple function Sri Chinmoy sold about a hundred copies of Walter Kolosky's new book on the Mahavishnu Orchestra, *Power, Passion and Beauty*. Sri Chinmoy is mentioned in this book. It also tells how, during the 1972 tour, Garcia watched Mahavishnu perform from backstage, "totally amazed." That year the Grateful Dead went on to play some of their finest concerts; there's a wacky movie of one iconic concert from that year called *Sunshine Daydream*.

Mahavishnu almost never described or explained Sri Chinmoy. But inside his powerful music was the unmistakable fragrance and lion-roar of Sri Chinmoy's spiritual path of love, devotion and surrender. The music itself had Sri Chinmoy's fingerprints on it. Inside some of his albums you would get a profound photograph of Sri Chinmoy and a profound bit of his writings, and after you heard the music and saw pictures of Mahavishnu you got a sense of who Sri Chinmoy was and what he was doing.

Pretty soon, people would see Mahavishnu, and they would think of Sri Chinmoy. And vice versa. In 1979 Sri Chinmoy was training to run a marathon, and one day in the street a passing motorist shouted, "Hi, John McLaughlin! I love you!" In 1995 a young man who came to Sri Chinmoy's book-signing at a Borders Books in Virginia asked him to sign his copy of the Mahavishnu/Santana album *Love Devotion Surrender*. In 2005 the manager of a Sbarro Pizza on Long Island said he recognized Sri Chinmoy from pictures on Mahavishnu's record albums and asked to have a picture taken with him. Sri Chinmoy framed the picture and personally brought it to him a few days later. Like this, thousands and thousands of people carry with them a sentient impression of Sri Chinmoy that they got decades ago from Mahavishnu. The enormity of this manifestation-achievement cannot be overstated.

On October 4th 2007, a week before Sri Chinmoy's passing, I was repairing Sri Chinmoy's CD player in his house; he said he wanted to listen to recordings of his own singing and instrumental performances. Out of the blue he asked me, "What is Mahavishnu doing?" I had no Mahavishnu news, but it left me wondering why he asked me. It was the kind of question he would ask a disciple who was keeping in touch with a former disciple, but he knew I wasn't in touch with Mahavishnu.

I went to the concert with my friend Steve. The Mahavishnu Orchestra was a brand new, unknown band; they played a bold new kind of music that people called jazz-rock fusion. It had lots of instrumental and compositional virtuosity, intuitive improvisation, and was scary loud. No lyrics or regular time signatures. Occasional Indian effects. Big surprises around every corner. A really intense sound over-all. Combine Jimi Hendrix, Ravi Shankar, the Beatles, Stravinsky and maybe Palestrina. And also John Coltrane, Led Zeppelin and a 1920s Mississippi Delta blues singer. And turn up the volume.

In pictures I took from my balcony seat you see five rather dissimilar musicians surrounded by huge loudspeakers on a small black stage lit by bright spotlights. A dazzling Panamanian drummer, a violinist from Kansas with hair as long as mine, an energetic keyboard player from Czechoslovakia and an Irish bassist. Mahavishnu himself looked like he just stepped off a spaceship, dressed all in white, with unfashionably short hair. He looked overly peaceful and happy. He played a big double-necked Gibson guitar with astonishing intensity and speed, and his Marshall amplifiers were just meltingly loud. In those days we loved fast, and loud. Sometimes while he was playing he looked like he was in some higher world, and I liked that. My little sister was 12 and stayed home that day but she listened to the concert being simulcast live over the university radio station.

During the concert Mahavishnu spoke a couple of times to thank the audience, his band members and the concert organizers. His manner made us giggle; he spoke formally, as though the concert was some of kind sacred ceremony, like the priest in our church in Williamsville.

My friends and I loved many different kinds of music, old and new, and we were constantly buying records and music magazines and going to concerts and listening to the radio. FM radio had good programming in the 1970s – I listened to a couple of Buffalo stations and one from Toronto for several hours a day, and late into the night. As much as I loved music and grew up with music in the house, I didn't show that talent myself. After I saw the Beatles on *The Ed Sullivan Show* on February 9th 1964 I bought a guitar for $6, took two guitar lessons and started to grow my hair long. That's as far as I got but my sisters eventually became successful music teachers. I tape recorded the Beatles on the *The Ed Sullivan Show* directly from the TV speaker terminals, and we listened to that tape for years; we knew every Beatles song by heart and covered the walls of our rooms with their pictures.

A few days after the concert Steve bought the Mahavishnu Orchestra's album *The Inner Mounting Flame* at Record Runner on Main Street across from UB. He encouraged me to listen to it, "Man you gotta hear the drums man, I really like the drums." Vinyl LP record albums were big and heavy, and the medium itself was steeped with cultural and technological history. There was a natural, tactile 'record album experience'. You could tell by looking at the surface of the record if a particular song was going to be long or short or even loud or soft. The records even smelled a particular way. The big record covers were important. This album had pictures of Mahavishnu looking pretty amazing, as though his life depended on the music. There was a round pin on his shirt with Sri Chinmoy's picture. Song titles like 'Meeting of the Spirits' and 'Awakening'. In fine print, the name of his publishing company, 'Chinmoy Music'.

Hours were spent examining the record cover, trying to figure the whole thing out. Inside the album you got an 8x10 inch color poster with Sri Chinmoy's essay 'Aspiration' and a 5x7 inch copy of Sri Chinmoy's Transcendental Picture, both of which went up on the wall of my room right away: these were sacred objects. After a few days I began to really like this album. It was like a journey to an absolutely new, faraway place that was hauntingly familiar but also desperately important. This music was fierce, uncompromised, unrelenting, and it was touching something high and deep inside me. The album was like a faithful guide – it would take me where I wanted to go. The music just grabbed you and picked you up and pushed you into another realm. Of course, music had been doing that for centuries, but somehow this was much more intimate.

My time in school was split between being a photographer on our very professional yearbook staff, and working on the school's stage crew, where I did sound, lights and stage-set construction for some very professional productions, like *West Side Story*. One of the stage crew guys, Mark, got a key to the backstage door, and four or five of us would sneak back there between classes and talk about Tolkien and Dostoyevsky, and how to hot-patch a phase angle SCR dimmer under full-load conditions without blowing the main breaker. In my senior year I had a key to the projection booth, and that was really fun – after school we would play favorite records over the auditorium's powerful sound system, like 'Dark Star', 'Pharaoh's Dance' and 'Toccata and Fugue in D minor'. Such a thrill to shake the walls of a big room with the sublime sounds.

Around this same time I became eligible for the military draft. That means that I could have been chosen to go fight in the Vietnam War. This disturbed me to the extreme. The draft circumstances changed at the last minute and boy was I relieved, but the implications of going to war reverberated in me for years.

I was working long hours in the school's darkroom, three or four days a week, and I think this is where I had my first real, intense silent meditation experiences. Previously, any spiritual experiences I had were associated with music or nature or people or hard labor or other non-silent things, and I never tried silent meditation until after I became a disciple. There was no way I was going to sit down and just be still and do nothing at all and try to meditate. But: the photographic darkroom was the perfect ecosystem for meditation. It was an exercise in total immersion. At the time I just thought I was working in the darkroom. I'm not saying this is for everybody, but it sure was the perfect thing for me at that time.

When you enter the darkroom, you have a very

specific task, say, to print five pictures from last night's football game. Nothing else is in your mind; you leave your whole other life outside the door. People know not to bother you until you emerge. It is silent in there. You can only see a few essential things under the dim, amber safelight. There is the familiar smell of the processing chemicals. Your whole being is concentrated on a few critical things. For example, temperatures and timings require real accuracy, if you expect to produce a fine photo. The negative you are printing must be immaculately clean, without a speck of dust. All this prepares you for: the moment the exposed paper is slid into the tray of Dektol developer. Here it remains for two minutes with a little agitation, and the image slowly and magically is born. You stand there absolutely still, free of movement and sound and thought. It is even more magical than a television image, because here you're making the image yourself. An enforced two minutes is the perfect time for a restless American teenager to go deep within, and I used to feel, and crave, that raging silence. But it was natural, and I never thought of it as a spiritual experience until years later.

My regular student life was pretty miserable. I never wanted to be a regular student. In class I would fill the pages of my notebook with Sri Chinmoy's name and gaze out the window. I loved some of my classes like American history and Latin and English literature but instead of doing my schoolwork, I listened to music and went to concerts with my friends, probably fifty concerts during my high school years: the Mahavishnu Orchestra with the Buffalo Symphony Orchestra; the Santana Band with Mahavishnu in Toronto; the Yes *Relayer*-tour concert, with their towering quadraphonic sound system; Keith Jarrett solo piano; an 18-hour rendition of Eric Satie's 'Vexations' in Baird Hall; the McCoy Tyner Trio; the Nuts and Volts Convention of electronic and experimental music; jazz guitar legends Herb Ellis and Joe Pass; minimalists Philip Glass and Brian Eno; big-band drummer Buddy Rich; and even the Firesign Theatre, undisputed masters of esoteric, erudite humor, performing on a makeshift stage in Norton Union.

I was listening to records ten or twelve hours a day. Really intensely: background music was for elevators and shopping malls. JS Bach organ, Weather Report, Bartok, Van Morrison, the *Woodstock* album, Stockhausen, John Cage, Hot Tuna, Mahler, Holst, Pink Floyd, Debussy. Playing a record was serious business – you stopped everything that you were doing. Things like eating and schoolwork were done later if you had time. The thunk of the needle on the record was the Zen gong signaling meditation time. We thought this music was perfect, and worthy of our undivided attention and worship, and for us it seemed way higher than religion. And we were building audiophile sound systems to make the recordings sound like live concerts when we listened at home. The quest was on to build a high damping factor, high slew rate power amplifier. Often I would switch off the stereo after sunrise, and getting to school at 8:20 in the morning was really hard.

As the months went by I wanted to know what made Mahavishnu tick. His music was getting world recognition and winning awards, and in interviews he would always say things like, "I am just trying to become an instrument of the Supreme," and explain that Sri Chinmoy was responsible for the success he was having. His attitude intrigued me. I cut my hair for the first time in eight years and became vegetarian. I wore white clothes to school. Only a couple of Sri Chinmoy's books were available at that time but I read them constantly, over and over. *The Inner Promise* was like a huge museum full of treasures, and I used to carry it around with me in school. I read it during intermediate algebra class. I had every word memorized, including the copyright page and back cover.

We went to all the Mahavishnu Orchestra concerts that were within a few hours' driving radius, six or seven of them. They became pinnacle holy days on our calendar. You were aware that anything could happen to you there; you could expect complete transformation, and we had a lot of jokes about that. Once after a concert Mahavishnu and disciple-drummer band member Narada signed my only book by Sri Chinmoy at the time, *Commentary on the Bhagavad Gita*. I picked up junk from the stage floor after concerts and displayed it on my wall at home. A few months before I moved to New York I talked with disciple-musician band member Premik backstage after a 1975 concert, and he was bubbling over with news from New York, "...and we had a big celebration for Guru's 200th book..." I wanted so much to be there.

After one concert I told Mahavishnu that I was interested in becoming Sri Chinmoy's disciple, and he said, "Write to me and I'll send you Guru's books." I wrote and told him I'd also like to help him with his sound equipment. He sent me *Beyond Within*, *A Sri Chinmoy Primer* and the very first issue of *Anahata Nada*. I still remember unpacking the books, it was a major dream come true. The books smelled like incense; they were absolutely incredible. I started receiving *Anahata Nada* every month and would bring it and show my friends at school the things that Sri Chinmoy was doing. They were respectfully amused by my change of style, and although some of them liked Sri Chinmoy, they didn't end up becoming disciples.

In my senior year there was a boy a couple of years younger than me who had some incurable disease. He was exceptionally kind and cheerful, and very smart. We all knew he was sick, you could just see the chain around his neck, the darkness, but he was always trying to outrun it or outsmart it, and he was desperately trying to fit in with the other kids. One day he came up to me and said, "I heard you know an Indian Guru, can you tell me about him? Does he say anything about illness?" I think he knew that the Guru's teachings were of a lofty nature but he asked anyway. At one point his mother also asked me to give him some of Sri Chinmoy's books. People knew that I was studying a Guru. Sri Chinmoy's books weren't readily available, but I made some photocopies and the boy was very, very happy to get them, and later again he stopped me in the hall and told me how much he liked the Guru's writings. By the end of the year we heard that he was gone.

The few books by Sri Chinmoy that I eventually got were absolutely like gold in my hands. It was as though the top of the mountain was being handed to you. Each word was living, flowing light. There was such a huge obvious difference between Sri Chinmoy's books and any other spiritual books I had seen. One time I methodically tore up a couple of spiritual books by other authors because I was sure only Sri Chinmoy's books were genuinely spiritual and I didn't want anyone to be misled by these false ones in case they found them in the trash.

I wanted to become a disciple but there was no Centre

where I lived, and I wanted to move to New York but there was a rule in Erie County that required students to complete high school. When I turned 16 I was old enough to take driving lessons during the summer, and I decided to also take a typing class because I had read that Sri Chinmoy was encouraging his disciples to work at the United Nations, "even in menial positions." I had read that Sri Chinmoy went to watch a disciple run the Boston Marathon and gave him a trophy, so I went to our school track but couldn't run more than a lap or two.

I remained at home another year after finishing high school. I took two weeks of night classes in thermodynamics and architectural acoustics at the university, but I didn't fit in there. I had a persistent, almost ancient peer-pressure desire to be educated, probably because my friends and family had all been good students.

Magazines were very important: New issues of *Stereo Review*, *Audio* magazine, *Popular Photography* and *DownBeat* were eagerly awaited every month. *Life* magazine and *Scientific American* had articles about drugs that managed to scare me away from using them. The latest *Radio-Electronics* showed how to build a simple brainwave monitor. The article told how some yogis in the mountains would test their disciples' concentration by draping a wet blanket on their backs in freezing weather, which would immediately turn to ice. They passed the master's test if they could melt the frozen blanket using only their mind. The magazine claimed this electronic device could train your mind to perform similar feats. I immediately understood this; the back hallway of our house wasn't heated in the winter and to get upstairs to our rooms you had to walk through it, and it could be well below freezing there. When I was five or six I figured out how to concentrate in a certain way to ignore the hallway's chill. I didn't build the device but I got the idea that I might have some spiritual talent, and in a small way this encouraged me to follow a serious spiritual path.

Around this time our family went to visit one of my sisters at Boston University and I couldn't believe it, I found three of Sri Chinmoy's books in the university bookshop. On June 9th I took the Amtrack train to New York with my friend Dave. He wasn't specifically interested in Sri Chinmoy but he inspired me in a million ways and he saw that I needed help moving to New York. He knew Charles Silver, a nervous, chain-smoking businessman who ran the small, struggling Longsilver Recording Studios on the third floor of 142 East 32nd Street in Manhattan. He allowed us to stay a few nights for free in a back room of the studio. I eventually stayed there for three months and significantly ran up their phone bill before a talented Cuban-American musician-disciple invited me to stay in his apartment located two minutes' walk from Sri Chinmoy's house in Jamaica, Queens.

We had to spend the first two nights in Dave's hippie-friend's dirty Manhattan apartment, and one night in a $14 midtown hotel. What an adventure. The apartment was overrun by cats and marijuana incense, and in the hotel we were robbed while we slept; Dave's wallet with $35 and his Amtrack ticket were gone, but my father's antique Leica camera was still there on the kitchen table. Dave said, "Wow, you see, Sri Chinmoy protected your camera." My sister still uses this camera.

We went two hours by subway on a pilgrimage to a famous electronics supply store in the Bronx that sold only resistors and potentiometers. We visited Seymour's Exakta on West 31st Street, distributors of those quirky East German cameras. A scientologist with a pen and clipboard ran up to me on Lexington Avenue and tried to get me to sign up with his religion and pay $15. I said no thanks. Dave and I went to see the audacious jazz pioneers Cecil Taylor, at the Five Spot on St. Marks Place, and Sun Ra, at the Bottom Line on West 4th Street. Phenomenal concerts.

Then I took the subway from Manhattan to the Jamaica, Queens neighborhood where Sri Chinmoy and his disciples had lived since 1968. I wasn't sure of the way but sitting across from me on the F train was someone covered with dust and paint, wearing a torn Sri Chinmoy Centre T-shirt. There was considerable paint on his wristwatch. This was Pulak, going home after doing construction work at Rijuta's new bakery, Nectar-Bliss, at 713 Second Avenue, four blocks from the United Nations. He was happy to show me Parsons Blvd., and I visited the enterprises that I had read about in *Anahata Nada*.

At Guru Stationery I asked Ashrita for his business card. I examined the items in the shop. Even the pencils were exciting – these were things being sold by actual disciples of Sri Chinmoy. I bought a big Mahavishnu poster for $3 and stationery to write home on. I saw the other shops. There were disciples all over the place, these people that Sri Chinmoy had transformed. It was so amazing. After a day or two we headed back home and I made plans to move to New York. I phoned 212-523-3471 and Ashrita told me that Sri Chinmoy would be having a public meditation soon. A few days later I was back at Longsilver with a cardboard box stuffed with clothes and a blanket. My parents sent me $40 every few weeks for food – I ate provolone cheese on rye sandwiches, bananas and orange juice almost exclusively for the next three months.

For a few days I worked on wiring the outdoor sign lights at Nectar-Bliss, and scouring their giant second-hand pizza ovens with steel wool and a caustic gel that contained sulfuric acid. And meeting lots of disciples. One day Rijuta took me up a Midtown skyscraper to meet Mahavishnu at his manager Nat Weiss's office, but he wasn't there.

My first opportunity to see Sri Chinmoy was at the Wednesday night public meditation on June 18th in the big, beautiful St. Francis Xavier Church on West 16th Street in Manhattan. I got there early and sat off to the side. Incense was burning. Three hundred people were perfectly still and silent, waiting for Sri Chinmoy. In the distance I heard a flute playing. A simple, familiar, melody; now I realize that this would have been Sri Chinmoy backstage. The sense of anticipation was enormous. For the first time I was surrounded by disciples and by people who were meditating. You can't imagine how intense that was; I had never before seen anyone meditating, anywhere.

Sri Chinmoy appeared on the stage and somehow I knew what to do. I had a very profound experience which continued for several days. It was like having Niagara Falls flowing inside my whole body, even in my fingers and toes. That night in a dream I saw Sri Chinmoy smiling at me, close up and vivid, the same smiling image that was on the public meditation poster I had on the wall at Longsilver Studios, and which was on the back cover of *The Inner Promise*. For the next day or two if I concentrated a little I could see that smile inside my chest, like a living hologram. It seemed very natural, but as soon as I thought about it, it would go away. I remember smiling a lot for the next few days, somewhat irritating the people around me; one guy at Longsilver couldn't take it and in a quiet rage he grabbed my copy of *The Inner Promise* and threw it out the window.

The next Wednesday public meditation I was sitting closer to the front and Rijuta had given Sri Chinmoy a note that said, "Sitting next to me is the 18-year-old boy that I told you about. He said he wants to become your disciple." Sri Chinmoy smiled at me very directly and I felt a little self-conscious. Outside afterward from his car he told her that he had accepted me as his disciple.

DODULA
Zurich, Switzerland

What prompted me to leave the convent and to become a disciple of Sri Chinmoy?

I was a happy nun at the Baldegg convent. I had friends and was successful in my job. The institution where I worked and lived was situated by the lake with a view of the mountains. I felt like I was at the zenith of my life. Even today, after 20 years, I recall with gratitude the time I spent there. No outer circumstances could have made me leave the convent.

In 1988, the children's home in Mariazell required a therapy station for children displaying particularly strong behavioural problems. I was suggested as a candidate. I agreed on the condition that I would be able to first take an advanced training course at the University of Zurich. I was hoping it would help me to serve these young people better. I was looking for teachers whose theories reflected life, but with the majority of the professors I did not see any correlation. One evening, after the lectures, I was on my way out when I saw a poster in the foyer that said 'Introduction to Meditation'. I thought to myself: when I studied at this university in my younger years, this topic was unknown. But the Bible says: "Try all and keep the best." Therefore, I turned around.

The lecture was given by AK Beyer (Kailash), a psychologist. In his case I felt that word and deed went together. After the lecture I registered for an upcoming meditation seminar. After about 5 weeks, I received an invitation. In the classes I learned to meditate, and I also bought a book about happiness and another about meditation by Sri Chinmoy. While reading I recognised the same message as the one Jesus had offered mankind 2,000 years earlier. Sri Chinmoy's philosophy even helped me to understand the Bible better and to love it more.

In the fall I opened up the therapy station and taught 5th and 6th grades. I always had the gift of teaching and was able to direct a class without too much difficulty, but after I started meditating in accordance with Sri Chinmoy's method, any burden whatsoever left me. Even the most difficult students seemed to sense something that was giving them the strength to behave well and to learn better. For me it was like a miracle that these seriously afflicted young people were making so much progress. I often thought that, if we adults had been able to change so quickly, we would have become saints long ago.

As I read more of Sri Chinmoy's books, a new

spiritual horizon opened up for me. Meditation filled me with joy and greater love of God. His disciples told me that Sri Chinmoy had been to the Vatican several times. Pope Paul VI told him during a private audience: "Your message and my message are the same. When we both leave this world, you and I, we will meet together." Sri Chinmoy also met several times with Pope John Paul II.

The fact that a human being could have such oneness with the divine made a deep impression on me, and I subsequently had several spiritual experiences.

In 1989, Sri Chinmoy expressed the wish to visit a convent in Switzerland. He gratefully accepted the invitation of the prioress of the convent in Cham. Upon arrival, he first went to the chapel, where he prayed, meditated and sang. After he answered various questions from the nuns, we were offered a light meal. Then Sri Chinmoy came to my table and invited me to come to New York in August. I said: "How is this possible?" He replied: "Through God's Grace." After his return to New York, I did not think about this invitation anymore because I did not see any possibility of going to New York.

Shortly after, I was accused of being in a sect. I knew it was not true, but out of obedience I broke off all contact with Sri Chinmoy and his disciples. I even put aside his books. I wanted to test myself to see if my experiences were authentic and would persist independent of outer aids. I tried to be a totally normal nun, but my inner connection with Sri Chinmoy remained. My heart's wish was to be a disciple of Sri Chinmoy and to remain a happy nun at Baldegg.

When I went to the religious services for Easter, I had

an inner call: "Are you ready to leave everything?" This question was clear and required a straightforward answer. Since I loved my sister-nuns and the kids so much, I was sad and cried. Then there came to my mind the story of Abraham, who was supposed to sacrifice his son. So I thought that if I said "yes", God would be satisfied with my readiness. But my "yes" was not unconditional, and therefore I heard the call: "Stop, Abraham (Sister Elda) – no!"

After the religious exercises, I returned to the children's home. One evening I prayed with all my heart that Jesus would reveal his will to me. To my greatest surprise, I received a phone call from Gunthita in Zurich. She said Sri Chinmoy had called her and asked her to give me the following message: "Yes, it is God's Will for you to leave everything and become my disciple." It was hard to believe that I could meditate intensely in my attic in Mariazell in order to know God's Will and the answer would come from New York. Later I experienced several times that an authentic God-realised spiritual Master is one with God's Consciousness and can therefore know God's Will – not only for himself, but also for his disciples.

But I still did not have the courage to take the necessary step. I was doubting, like Thomas at the time of Jesus. The ties to the convent were too strong.

I received a third sign. I had a dream that was more real than life. I saw a health food store and went in. Gunthita was at the counter selling a big crystal for a good price. A lady was sitting in front of a pillar. I looked at her and realised that she knew everything about the present, past and future. I thought of asking her if I should stay in the convent or not. She got up and went to the door. I followed her and said: "May I ask you something?" She looked at me and replied: "Yes." So I asked her: "Should I leave or stay?" She answered: "For you it is better to leave." I wanted to know why. Her clear reply was: "They do not understand you, and they are preventing you from living according to your inner destiny." I wanted to know: "When should I leave?" The answer that followed stabbed my heart like a sword: "Better today than tomorrow."

In this way I received the answers through my embodied soul itself. Later Sri Chinmoy said that Jesus himself had brought me to him, and this I can confirm. After I took the necessary step, all my doubts vanished and my heart became calm and happy.

I could tell many other things that happened, but, with love and gratitude, I think I have answered the question about what made me leave the convent and become Sri Chinmoy's disciple.

ESHANA
Novi Sad, Serbia

I will be eternally grateful to my mother Biljana, who was the divine instrument to bring me to Guru.

While still a student, my mother was taking an interest in Eastern philosophy and yoga. After some years, she joined the group that followed the teachings of Sri Ramana Maharshi. They had a very beautiful centre in our little town, Zrenjanin – an old house all arranged in Indian style. I was still a kid then, and, as far as I knew, my mother was just going to yoga three times a week. I remember telling her, as I looked at the photo of Ramana Maharshi that was hanging on the wall in her room, that one could really see that man was truly good.

At the age of 13 or 14, I was passing through a difficult period. I started noticing a change in my school friends, and something within me was really in pain as I saw them starting smoking, drinking, becoming arrogant adults. Typically, at that age, you try to do everything so that others will accept you, but I found everything so unnatural and unpleasant that I started thinking that something had to be wrong with me. I must have been born at the wrong place and at the wrong time, I thought.

In October 1993 the first lecture on meditation and the teachings of Sri Chinmoy took place in our town. It was divided into three evenings. At that time I was in my first year of high school. My mother asked me if I would come. I said, "OK, why not?" – although not with a great interest. I came to the second evening. The room was totally filled up with people. I remember the pleasant smell of incense and the predominant blue colour. I found the lecture quite interesting and came the third evening as well. Then, Tyagananda, the lecturer, gave us a sheet of music – two songs by Sri Chinmoy. First he played them on the tape recorder and then we sang them. When I heard the first notes of the song 'Usha Bala Elo' in a recording by the group Akasha, I was completely amazed; how could something so beautiful exist on earth? Guru's music enchanted me.

Soon after, we had to decide whether we would join Sri Chinmoy's path. It was not easy for my mom, as she really loved Ramana Maharshi. But on the other hand, she was in need of a living Master and she really felt something in Sri Chinmoy. Eventually she decided to become Sri Chinmoy's disciple. I gladly joined her. I will never forget these first days at our Meditation Centre. Finally I felt at home. With such joy I attended every meeting; I would run from school after classes to the Centre to be ready for meditation. And how much delight I was getting from Guru's songs! That delight remains the same even now.

I realised that actually I was born in the right place, at the right time – a blessing unparalleled! My infinite, infinite gratitude to Guru.

ISHANI
New York,
United States of America

In November of 1969, I had been meditating for fifteen years with another spiritual group in Manhattan, but felt that I was not making much progress, so I started actively searching for a living spiritual teacher.

One day, I walked into a new health food store only about five miles from my home in Westchester. I wanted to tell them how happy I was that they were opening in my community, because in those early days the next closest health food shop was at least an hour's drive away. As I entered, ready to introduce myself, I noticed a tiny Transcendental Picture of Guru on a book displayed on a shelf in the far corner of the shop. Its light drew me like a magnet; as I came closer to the photo, I asked, "Who is this?"

The shop owner replied, "That's Sri Chinmoy."

I heard the intensity in my own voice as I responded, "Is he alive?"

"Yes," the owner replied. "He is going to give a talk about meditation at my home in Larchmont in a few weeks. Would you like to come?"

My heart started to pound. "Oh yes. I'll get a baby sitter for my children and I will be there."

He gave me the directions to his apartment and, on January 13th, 1970, I drove from my home in the worst snowstorm the New York area had seen in fifty years. As I passed many accidents on the road, a part of me wanted to turn back, but the need to see this man kept me going. The journey, which should have taken only twenty minutes, lasted almost two hours.

As I rang the apartment bell I thought, "I am so late that Sri Chinmoy has probably finished and is on his way home." But when the door was opened, I saw Guru sitting at the other end of a large room. After removing my coat and boots, as I sat down behind the other seekers, Guru looked up at me. Suddenly, all the problems I was facing at that time seemed to wash away; I experienced pure bliss.

My eyes filled with tears of gratitude to Guru for allowing me to walk this earth with him. I never dreamed he would accept me as his disciple, but he did! And that was the beginning of a new, remarkable and fulfilling life for me.

JAITRA
Auckland, New Zealand

One book that held a special place in my heart was a picture Bible, given as a present on my seventh birthday. Simplified to the very essentials, drawn in the fashion of a contemporary comic, here were adventures of a different sort, and they struck a deep chord in a way that my occasional, very much forced, obligatory attendance of church didn't. Church, for me of the Anglican variety, consisted of an, "It's so boring, do I have to go?" mother-baiting pre-ritual, counting the minutes slowly pass on a brand new digital wristwatch during, and afterwards wonder as to how an hour and a half "could take soooo long?"

Quite unlike dreary Church proper, here in the picture Bible however were adventures of bravery and faith that I hoped one day I might be able to emulate. I marvelled at the story of Paul, a disciple of Jesus who heroically sacrificed his life for his faith, awe filled at such courage and bravery. Likewise the stories of Christians and lions, Abraham offering his son as sacrifice, and priests who stepped into an open furnace, remaining untouched. I actually had no idea how one could be so brave or strong, in faith or otherwise. A child afraid of visits to the doctor, such courage was beyond my comprehension. Yet I dreamed that one day it might not be. Imagine those adventures!

Children will always find a way to subvert adult activities to their own joy-necessity, and adventure could be going to Church as well. Dragged against will by weekly God faring mothers, a group of adventure-possessed delinquents dressed in Sunday-best staged epic dirt-clod wars behind hall and steeple, where adults gathered in the Spirit.

On occasion my mother succumbed to her own peace of mind rather than Peace of God, leaving son behind to watch television's *Big League Soccer*, a highlights programme from very distant English soccer leagues. The adventure continued at programme's close, ball kicked against wall outside, over and over and over, mind lost in sights and sounds of games and heroes just watched, calls inside for lunch obliviously ignored.

* * *

While adventures up until this point in my life were mostly of the sort typical to any young boy – adventures of activity and imagination pursued with all breath and vigour at my command, here and there were a few notes hinting of another tune, a distant, somehow familiar but without context melody of other worlds, dimly heard on occasional pause or reflection but never retained, a hidden meaning and direction to life that I had yet to attain.

At the age of twelve such a moment occurred, a dream from nowhere of spiritual portent, portent which I could neither place or comprehend, even feel was deserved. I had just spent a month in England in a Christian community, headquarters of an international missionary organisation my mother spent the previous year working for, I living with father in Canada. One of the happiest times of my life, I returned home to New Zealand with the firm, heart-felt conviction to do something for the world, although what that would be I had no idea. Alongside still distant dreams of an adventurous adulthood as perhaps lawyer, sportsman, artist or musician, a spiritual longing and aspiration for adventure of a different sort was taking birth.

The dream was of a most beautiful girl, in her teens or later, with whom I travelled to a house where there was a gathering of people, a meeting perhaps. Seemingly invisible in the way only possible in a dream, the girl pointed to a small speck of white light in or above each, saying over and over, "This is the soul."

The girl? Although never a Catholic, with an overwhelming sense of love that I could not explain, I knew her to be the Mother Mary.

I mentioned the dream to my mother, but dubious reaction combined with my own puzzlement and confusion saw it filed under mystery, quickly forgotten. On reflection, it was a harbinger of a great adventure still a few years distant, the discovery of meditation in my late teens.

* * *

Adventure changed its meaning with the onset of young adulthood, much lamented death of childhood. I deeply resented the transition, understanding not its necessity, or how to relate to the chaotic teenaged world now within. The terms upon which I had long learned to meet the world – oft-cultivated, sometimes practised sincerity, kindness and truthfulness, as ingrained by mother and Bible story and felt intuitively by heart, now mattered nought, and I was at a loss to fathom the new terms – at best sophistication and confidence, worst aggression, arrogance and haughtiness – upon which adventure was now defined.

Adventure was still sought in games, in Saturday

sporting contests keenly anticipated all week, yet joy was no longer simple on football field or cricket pitch – even here you were peer reviewed by shoes or jacket, haircut or boasted off-field exploits, rather than simple God-given talent or on-field success.

Seemingly out of my depth in this impending adult adventure, I pined with nostalgia for happy days only a few years previous, seeking without success to somehow expedite their return.

It was meditation that returned adventure to my life, and long craved inner peace, certainty and meaning. Mentioned in the pages of a book – meditation as the sure and certain path to union with God, life's so-called ultimate meaning – I pursued it immediately with vigour and determination. Here was adventure in my life again, adventure in terms infinite and immortal, and it imbued all I did with new found purpose and inspiration.

Almost immediately after beginning meditation's practise, the long ago dreamed bright dot of white light returned, a brilliant pin-prick in centre of vision when meditating, accompanying sudden thoughts of inspiration as well. Avidly reading every book on spirituality that could be found, I deduced it to be a glimpse of the soul – ultimate tiny speck of light inside each of us, and form of grace affirming the treading my life's true path. Here in meditation at last lay life's long sought ultimate adventure – the adventure of self-discovery.

My best meditation experience to date came in these early days, a glimpse of the sunlit road ahead, now walked every day. Without a doubt the most powerful spiritual experience of my life, it was a glimpse of my own soul – albeit only for a fraction of a second.

Meditating more powerfully than I have ever before

or since, I felt myself ascending upwards as though borne upon an infinite wave, rising visibly through layers of mind, layers which became levels of consciousness and then worlds. The higher I rose the calmer and more peaceful I became, in fact profoundly, indescribably so, and all sense of physical life, of body and society disappeared – sense of self drawn upward and inward as consciousness rose.

The experience lasted about the length of the song I was listening to, a nine minute masterpiece from the early nineties with repeated chorus: "I can see the blue light..." The pinnacle was literally that: entering into a light in the very centre of my being – the very same speck revealed in dream years before. Veil lifted for just a second, I encountered a light beautiful beyond description, and was sure in the knowledge that you could want nothing on heaven or earth more than this, need more than this. It was the soul, my own soul.

The discovery of meditation began the greatest adventure of my life, an adventure that continues to this very day. At a time when it seemed life no longer held adventure, nothing to look forward to, explore or discover, meditation appeared, and with it a new, infinitely seductive world of profound peace, power and joy – adventure too!

Meditation is the key to self-knowledge and thus self-mastery, a sure pathway to a self ultimately infinite in capacity, beauty and power – the Self universal. Travelling into space via rocket or farthest corner of our globe via plane is a pale imitation to the adventure of travelling silently in infinite space and time, breath stilled, mind focused to a single point.

I practise meditation today as a member of the

Sri Chinmoy Centre, Sri Chinmoy as teacher and guide to inner worlds of unfathomable adventure. I follow the small streak of light still.

JANA
Prague, Czech Republic

"Let's learn how to meditate!" This was a text message I got from my friend late at night in spring 2008. And it was one of those things that straight away touch your heart. Yes, this is it. This must be a solution for my current feeling of emptiness, loneliness, the lack of joy and happiness in my life. Okay, I wasn't in the state of the hopeless despair (yet), but I felt I needed to change something in my life. But what was I actually looking for?

As a student in the final year at the Law School of the Charles University in Prague, Czech Republic, my life looked like it was heading towards a successful career and a prosperous life. But without actually experiencing it I already felt it was all just an emptiness in disguise. I strongly felt that no outer success or prosperity would guarantee happiness in my life. It took me 26 years to realise that my life was missing something higher or deeper.

Despite the intense two-month studies for my final examinations in law, I failed. As I already had my full-time job in an international law company at that time, passing the final exams should have been just a 'formality' I needed to fulfill in order to become a proper lawyer, in order to immerse myself in the serious lawyers' world that was already awaiting me. However, the Yiddish proverb says: "A man thinks and God laughs." And the fact that I didn't pass the final examinations at the first attempt was a big turnaround in my life. On the day I failed, apart from being shocked and upset, my inner voice was telling me that there had to be a 'higher purpose' behind that. At that time I just couldn't uncover what exactly it was. Only much later I realised that this failure was actually a great boon.

To be able to focus on finishing my studies, I decided to take a longer break from my work. You see, this was when my boon started to germinate. Postponing my adult work responsibilities gave me some extra time to start searching for that higher purpose in my life. And soon I set off on a journey of my self-discovery.

I'd attended several various 'new age' seminars and therapies, but none of them had really helped me to find what I was looking for. The night I got the text from my friend, I immediately started to search the Internet to find free meditation classes in Prague. On the website of the classes that I liked the most, I filled in an application form and sent it out to learn about the dates available. In the form I didn't forget to share my enthusiasm about meditation, and asked to be contacted back, but I somehow completely forgot to put down my contact details. And the form wasn't sent via email either. So the Sri Chinmoy Centre in Prague who was organising these classes didn't actually have the opportunity to get back to me. But apparently this wasn't needed, as the inner world is based on completely different principles. This wish of mine was heard and was being taken care of, although in a different way than I had expected at that time.

***

There is a saying: "When the student is ready, the teacher appears." And it seems like I was ready in the beginning of May 2008, when I saw a poster about the Festival of Mediation in Prague, organised by the Sri Chinmoy Centre. I was still on my break from work, focused on completing my studies, so it was perfect timing for me to attend the whole week of meditation workshops. And I was very eager to do so.

Thanks to my mother and grandmother I have believed in God since my childhood. But I had really no idea about the existence of spiritual Masters, let alone wished for having one. Coming to the meditation workshop I was 'only' hoping to find more happiness and the higher purpose of my life. In fact, I was completely blown away by seeing so much joy and happiness in the eyes and faces of Sri Chinmoy's disciples, who organised the meditation workshops. No matter how cheesy it may sound now, I have to say that I had never ever seen such pure joy and happiness before. It wasn't anything superficial or pretended; the happiness and joy were very contagious and coming apparently from a source that was unknown to me at that time. No doubts, I wanted to discover the secret that allowed those people to look like they were living on a completely different planet to mine. The meditation exercise we did that evening only increased my eagerness to learn the art of meditation. For a few fleeting moments I managed to enter into an inner reality of peace, where the outer world felt very unreal and unimportant. I wished I could have stayed there longer.

The follow-up meditation classes that took place twice a week were an absolute delight for me. I still remember how happy and uplifted I felt coming back home from the classes. And this sweet joyful feeling also usually stayed with me during the next day. A few years previously I had attended meditation workshops organised by different groups, but what I found so unique about the classes organised by the Sri Chinmoy Centre was the special atmosphere filled with true purity, peace and joy. Soon I noticed that the regular meditation practice was more than a hobby for me, it became an inseparable part of my life. It was like a new world opening in front of me and I was happy to adjust my lifestyle to it, in order to take my meditation experience to the next level.

In the beginning, I didn't really pay too much attention to Sri Chinmoy. But I guess it was only my mind that found it a bit difficult to connect with someone whom I didn't know and who didn't know me. (This was, at least, what I thought). But I loved many things that were coming directly from Sri Chinmoy – his songs, his books, his flute music. And the special atmosphere or energy I felt in the Centre and in the disciples was drawing me to come back to the classes again and again.

I had been attending the classes for about two months without knowing where it was all heading, until something special happened. It was during my holidays at my grandparents' house, where I was enjoying the peace and beauty of the Czech countryside. As I continued with my regular meditation practice twice a day, one night I was inspired to have my evening meditation outside in the garden. It was a warm summer night and with the gorgeous starlit sky above me I was sitting on a bench and meditating. My mind had completely quietened down and I was feeling infinite peace within and without, when suddenly Sri Chinmoy appeared in front of me. Clothed in his light-blue dhoti, he was beaming with peace and light. With his soulful smile he said to me lovingly: "I want you to become my disciple."

This was the experience that completely changed my life. But I can't say it came out of the blue. For the last few weeks I'd been praying to God to show me what my path was and if I was meant to have a spiritual Master. Once I heard somewhere that we should be careful what we wish for, as it might just happen... and this was exactly my case. God had certainly fulfilled my prayer and now it was up to me to prove my faith in Him, to prove faith in my meditation, to prove faith in my Master. He had already accepted me, now it was my turn to accept him.

Meeting Sri Chinmoy in my meditation was a cornerstone of our connection, of our inner relationship. Gradually I started to feel Sri Chinmoy's presence not only during my meditations, but sometimes even during the day. Occasionally, I even saw his face again – when I was walking or running. The mind of the lawyer in me was still, of course, quite doubtful and suspicious, trying to avoid anything new and unknown – which discipleship certainly was for me. Although I had always been listening to the dictates of my mind, I thought that for once in my life I should also give opportunity to my heart, I should listen to the guidance of my soul, the guidance of God. So in September 2008 I joined the Sri Chinmoy Centre. And only six days after joining the Centre I passed my final examinations as a lawyer. In fact, for my second attempt I was studying less than for the first one. But apparently, there was no more reason for me to have extra time for finding the right direction in my life, so the circle was closed.

To be absolutely honest with you, I still quite don't understand how it all came about that I became a disciple of such a great Avatar as Sri Chinmoy. But I am most grateful that it happened. And I am also extremely grateful to all the meditation class givers who have been such a tremendous inspiration for me. I'm sure without them I wouldn't have been able to make this significant step in my life, without them I wouldn't be even able to recognise or appreciate Sri Chinmoy's light and value the experience I had with him.

It is said that a spiritual Master knows in advance who is destined to become his disciple, but in most of the cases he cannot tell the person, until the time is ripe. It's quite amazing for me to look back and see that Sri Chinmoy had been a part of my life much earlier than I actually discovered him, or (to be more accurate) than he gave me the satisfaction of my own discovery.

Only since becoming a disciple I've found out that on several occasions Sri Chinmoy was already trying to enter my life, long before I even took up the meditation classes. However, at that time my view was probably still covered by the veil of ignorance, so I wasn't able to recognise him. After I joined the path I was really surprised to find out we already had Sri Chinmoy's book on meditation at home. This was a Christmas present from my sister to my father in 2003. I remember seeing the book at home, but didn't get the inspiration to read it, until I actually became a disciple. The other missed opportunity of meeting Sri Chinmoy and his path earlier was about a year before I joined, when I was invited by my yoga teacher to a workshop about the Peace Run, the world's longest torch relay, that was organised by her son, a disciple of Sri Chinmoy. I was very excited to go to the workshop, but then I got flu, so in the end I wasn't able to make it. And finally, I would like to mention once again my unsuccessful attempt to sign up for the Sri Chinmoy Centre meditation classes online, when I failed to put down my contact details. I must say that looking back to all those 'coincidences', I'm still quite fascinated to see how hard Sri Chinmoy and my soul must have been trying to help me to overcome the veil of ignorance and to bring the rest of my being to the spiritual life.

* * *

Despite having such a unique meditation experience with Sri Chinmoy to start with, it still took me a while to strengthen the connection with my Guru. For my mind it had sometimes been difficult to comprehend the fact that my spiritual Master is someone I have never seen in real life.

But Guru has always been very kind, and continued to feed my inner flame of aspiration by giving me his special attention, either in mediations or in my dreams. A few times Guru came into my dream, either to bless me, smile at me or give me some important messages. At these times I had no doubts it was him, for my dreams with Guru have always been extremely powerful, like no other dreams before. And after having these dreams, I have felt completely flooded with peace and love for the next few days. Apart from my direct experiences with my Master, another great way for me to get know Guru was through disciples. In the very beginning of my path I was looking up to the innocent joy, happiness and love they embodied. And later on I was more touched by seeing their purity, love and devotion to Guru.

Since becoming a disciple, my life has been transformed significantly. Not that I was told by someone from outside what exactly to do. It's been a gradual process of inner awakening and transformation, in accordance with the dictates of my soul and my Guru's loving guidance, that resulted in the outer change of myself and my life in general.

In the past I used to really struggle when having to make decisions, not to mention any important life decisions. I used to ask all my family and friends their opinions. And then I was usually so puzzled and stressed that I wasn't able to decide anyway. It's because when you listen to your mind, one day you will get this answer, and the very next day you can get the very opposite. It was only on Sri Chinmoy's path I learnt how to firstly hear my soul's command (or you can call it the inner voice) and secondly how to obey it. A few years ago I went through a very interesting life-lesson that helped me to understand the importance of the soul's messages in my life.

After finishing my studies, I started to work as a lawyer. I had been practising law for about three years, but my work wasn't really bringing me joy anymore. (I'm not sure if it ever was.) Anyway, it was at that time when I heard a very subtle inner voice telling me to quit my job. I didn't want to pay any attention to it, as I was really proud of my new position as a candidate attorney. At that time it somehow happened that I lost my ID card. It was quite a hassle having to arrange a new one, but well, what can you do. The time went on and I heard the same voice again, this time a bit louder, telling me to quit my job, as it wasn't making my soul happy. I pulled up shortly, however, this inner message wasn't obeyed either. My ego loved the prestige of the law profession, so I didn't really want to change it. And I tried to ignore the fact I didn't actually feel happy doing what I was doing.

Now, I had a beautiful accordion, a musical

instrument, I used to play in the Centre. One evening I left my accordion in the Centre to pick it up the next day. What a terrible surprise awaited me the next morning when I came back. Someone had broken into the Centre and stolen my dear accordion. I was really upset and started to wonder why I had such bad luck recently. But I couldn't figure out any cogent reason. And the inner voice had been coming back to me more often and with bigger intensity, but I still didn't want to hear it. I had studied law for eight years and practised for three years, so I really didn't feel in position to suddenly quit and lose all these years of studies and preparation just because of some 'silly inner voice'. Of course, this was my mind's grumbling. I let it grumble for a few more weeks, and kept ignoring my soul's message, until my soul said: "Enough is enough!"

One day I had to visit the local authorities on behalf of one of our biggest clients. I had to take lots of documents with me, so I put them into a suitcase. The only trouble was, that I didn't realize that the zip on the suitcase was broken. So when I was running with these important documents down the hill, you can imagine what happened. At the bottom of the hill when I checked my suitcase, I was horrified to see that the zip had opened up and at least half of the documents were gone. I cancelled my meeting and went to search for the documents. But they were nowhere to be found. As many of the lost documents were actually very important originals related to the power plant construction, I felt like I was in a bad dream only waiting to finally wake up. And my awakening was coming: however, not the outer one, but the inner one. I was walking the streets in the hope I would find the documents, but instead I found something else.... Why, why, why? Why did this happen to me and why have I been losing things recently? Inwardly I was calling Guru to help me out in this awkward situation, but outwardly I stayed surprisingly calm, as I had faith in Guru and knew he would help me out, as he always does. Moreover, I felt there was a higher purpose behind this experience....

Guru's help came to me in the form of my inner realisation (not God-realisation yet). Finally, I came to realise that there was a single cause of all the three losses I had experienced in the last few months (my ID card, an accordion, the client's documentation), and this was my disobedience to my inner voice, disobedience to my soul. In my meditation later on that evening, the inner voice was more powerful then ever: "If you continue ignoring your soul, you will lose much more...." Oh no, this is not what I want. I was determined I had to put things right. Despite not having any other alternative job, I promised my soul that evening that I would quit my job. The very next day after making this decision, things were starting to get solved. It actually looked like someone had been taking care of them.... In response to the leaflets I put up in our neighbourhood, I received a phone call from a lucky finder. He was not only lucky, but also quite calculating, as he took advantage of the reward offered for the documentation and even started to blackmail me to get more. I told my boss I would pay the reward, as it was my fault, but he was incredibly compassionate with me and insisted on paying the reward himself.

As promised to my soul, soon after that incident I quit my job and set off for another life-adventure, not really knowing what I was going to do, but having a strong faith in my Guru that he already had a plan for me. And soon I realised what the plan was: I was meant to work in a running store, Run and Become. Having already learnt my lesson, this time I was determined not to mess up, as I found out that true happiness comes when we act in accordance with our soul.

So here I am, seven years after becoming Sri Chinmoy's disciple, I have completely changed my profession: coming from the lawyers' world in the Czech Republic into the UK running world, as Run and Become is based in London. You can tell that Guru has saved me from doing the job that I wasn't really inwardly happy with, and gives me courage to carry out changes in my life that I would never dare even to think of. I started to run marathons and ultra-marathons, took up a new musical instrument – harmonium – and now give meditation classes in London. I am very grateful to Guru for coming into my meditation that summer night to show me that my life can be truly rich, colourful and fulfilling, if I only dare to try and have faith....

Thank you, Guru.

JOGYATA
Auckland, New Zealand

If time is a river – that old metaphor – then 1979 was a high-speed, white-knuckle boat ride, a wild and turbulent watershed year whose great currents of change swept us along like balsa on a swollen mountain stream. In New Zealand Subarata and I had been dabbling in the Chinese Book of Change, the *I Ching*, and had abandoned ourselves to its mysterious suggestions and its now exciting advice that "it will further you to cross the great waters...."

So we flew across the great waters of the Tasman ocean to Australia, landed in Sydney with our future as unknown and empty of intent as a wide blank canvas, hired a rental car, tossed a coin – heads, north; tails, west – across the remote stretches to Perth or Adelaide. The Book of Change turned us towards the setting sun. I had glandular fever, lay groaning and pale in the rear of a station wagon while Subarata sped west across endless plains of eucalyptus and the growing darkness of a strange land punctuated by clumps of farmhouse lights. How long were we travelling? I can't remember.

But one day inside that year we moved from the remoteness of Western Australia across to Adelaide in South Australia via circuitous ways and innumerable adventures, eventually settling out near Port Adelaide and the beginnings of another kind of odyssey. For it was here we found the Centre.

Travelling east from Perth you can cross the endless Nullarbor Plain by road along the Eyre Highway – a 2,700 km epic – or in leisurely fashion on the Indian Pacific railway, gazing out for two days at the vast, unpopulated desert, which features the longest dead straight stretch of rail in the world – 478 km! So flat you can see the slow curve of the earth's rim. But we caught a ride by car on the edge of that red expanse, shared the journey with two strangers who ended up being firm friends and who gave us four months of work in their outback motel on the edge of another wilderness, the Flinders Ranges. Subarata became the new waitress to the tour bus arrivals, I a charlatan wine waiter and handyman, and we lived in a caravan parked up in the dusty backyard of the motel.

Sometimes our new friends towed our caravan-home 200 miles north and left us for a few days at road's end in the empty, endless hills, their rust-orange escarpments and valleys of pale eucalyptus spread out in all directions. Wandering under extravagantly beautiful sunsets and dawn skies filled with flocks of wheeling birds, their wings turning grey, then pink, then silver as they turned in unison in the first sunlight, aerial speculars high up against the blue, exulting in the new day's gift of life.

One day we moved to Adelaide, and all at once, our first encounters with Guru. Crossing a city street for a cooling drink, there he was smiling down at us from a photo on a café wall; beneath his photo an aphorism reminding us that "peace that comes from the inner awakening is the peace everlasting." He kept turning up, unfamiliar yet vaguely remembered in some other plane of knowing, a long-lost friend from some other time or life. Looking at his picture I felt a whisper of recognition, a stirring of the soul, something faint and faraway and as easily forgotten as a dream.

Then in a newspaper, that 'learn to meditate' advert, an enquiring phone call or two and Sipra inviting us around, not to a class as there were none then running but to her flat for some starting tuition. And there he was again in a photo on her shrine! He kept finding us, beckoning us in some beautiful tryst with Destiny. Sipra has a great sense of humour and will forgive me recounting this next incident. We were shown into a small room where we saw for the very first time a large Transcendental Picture. We were invited to sit on the carpet, to look at Guru's third eye and to breath in peace. Then she said, "I have to go shopping for a while, I'll be back soon," and thereupon left us, returning over half an hour later clutching her shopping bags. That was the only lesson in meditation we ever had. A short time later Sipra invited us to become disciples and our photos went to New York for our new Guru's consideration.

Looking back you can see the quiet perfection of everything, the inevitability of it all, your life river finding its way to the sea, everything a preparation and a readying for what lies waiting next. We thought we had made our choices, but we had simply 'chosen' what had already been chosen for us and those inner currents determined where we would go – free will and the currents of determinism collaborating nicely.

MAGDALENA
Vienna, Austria

In spite of a pretty turbulent start with many obstacles, I am very happy to be on this path. I simply have more joy in life. My name is Magdalena. I am 45 years old and have been meditating with the Sri Chinmoy Centre in Vienna for three years. I would like to tell a little about my own experiences with Sri Chinmoy and the Vienna Centre.

I work as a nurse in a public hospital. From the beginning, one of my colleagues attracted my attention because of his unusual purity and gentleness. After a while I noticed that my consciousness was higher in his presence and I always had the feeling that he was somehow guiding me towards a spiritual path. I never spoke to him about it, though. After some time he quit working at the hospital and we lost contact.

At that time I was practising Hatha Yoga according to the teachings of *Yoga in Daily Life* by Paramahansa Swami Maheshwarananda. I was looking for a meditation class, since meditation was my weak point. I chose a meditation class offered by students of Sri Chinmoy. How surprised I was when I opened the door of the Sri Chinmoy Centre the night of the first class and my former colleague warmly welcomed me! At that moment it was clear to me that I had not come here by mere chance, but had been guided for sure. In retrospect I realised that it was not my colleague who had guided me. Already back then it was my Master who had prepared the road for me and pulled me towards him. My colleague had played the role of a perfect instrument.

After having attended the meditation class several times I was very surprised that the highest spiritual discipline could harmonise perfectly with a Western lifestyle, with a job and everything that involves – and not just in theory. When I got to know several disciples of Sri Chinmoy, I realised that they lived true spirituality in this place, Vienna's inner city! I was very impressed.

In the beginning of my spiritual life I unfortunately met with strong resistance on the part of my family and my children. The fact that I had an Indian Master, whom we usually call Guru (a Sanskrit word that simply means the one who leads from darkness to light), was too much for them. It is actually very understandable that doubts and fears arise, because everywhere you hear wild stories about exploitative sects and false teachers. After my whole family besieged me with their doubts and fears, I started doubting as well. At least I was sure that this was a true

Guru and a sincere and direct path, but how would I know if it was my path?

"Is this path really meant for me?" That was my big question initially. I loved the philosophy, the Guru and the disciples, but the rules, hmm.... Even though I was a vegetarian, did not drink alcohol or smoke and did not have a partner – and was actually very happy living that way – my mind vehemently rejected the idea that it had to be like that from now on. Looking back, I can only laugh about it. I knew that there were also rules for the closer disciples at the Maheshwarananda Ashram and that a certain amount of spiritual discipline is required for every authentic path (for example, to meditate every morning). Still, it took me some time to be able to accept this fact. Only after a while did I understand why Sri Chinmoy wants us to adopt this kind of lifestyle and to 'renounce' certain things. It makes sense that if we want to have higher spiritual experiences, we cannot numb ourselves with alcohol. After all, we want to wake up and realise the truth and not descend into the unconscious.

In the same way other problematic topics started making sense to me after I read quite a bit about those topics and started dealing with them. I realised that Sri Chinmoy simply wanted to create a path for those ready to run very fast, without detours and distractions, towards their highest goal. Sri Chinmoy's disciples are grateful for every small clue as well as the discipline that enables them to reach their goal as soon as possible.

There will always be people who will not like the guidelines of a spiritual group and will therefore leave after a while. Of course, everyone is free to decide if he or she wants to lead such a one-pointed life or to give it up at any moment to return to the old lifestyle. For me, this question does not arise anymore. I know how much I am gaining from my spiritual life and I would not want to miss it for anything.

In a certain way my life has become simpler, because I feel strongly guided and have faith that the right thing will happen at the right moment. I have broadened my thinking and overcome some mental barriers, and now I do not consider anything to be impossible. We can achieve much more than we think we can. In particular, when problems arise, I face them in a different way than before. For me, problems are nothing but experiences that offer me the possibility to grow. They are necessary for my development and will eventually lead me towards my destination.

I have become more conscious of many inner changes that are taking place and I realise how much work is still ahead of me. With a clearer point of view I am also able to empathise more with other people – like my children, for example. Through my meditation I have developed more understanding and compassion toward them, and I can deal better with a lot of situations. I am able to perceive and treasure the small and truly beautiful things that life offers. The blossoms of a tree or the beauty of the world, for example, evoke in me true feelings of happiness. I simply enjoy life much more than before, and this has a lot to do with my changed perception.

My health has become much more important to me. I try to eat healthful food and practise sports regularly. My lifestyle has surely improved a lot since I started meditating.

In my eyes, Sri Chinmoy has become my spiritual father, who guides me inwardly, takes care of me, looks after my needs and concerns himself with my progress. I feel safe, loved and protected under his guidance. Even though not everything that happens in life is to my liking, I know that everything is for the best.

The warm family atmosphere and the feeling of oneness among Sri Chinmoy's disciples attracted me from the beginning. They are no saints, of course – they are people like others, with their shortcomings and weaknesses – but they try to act from their hearts, and you can feel it. It is wonderful to exchange ideas with like-minded people – the inspiration is always mutual. The group meditations help to concentrate and increase everybody's strength and make it easier to reach a higher consciousness.

MEDHYATA
Toledo,
United States of America

My first steps on Sri Chinmoy's beautiful sunlit path began with me falling to my knees, crying out to God for help. I was begging God to send me guidance. I was praying that although I knew about Jesus I wanted someone here and now to direct me.

Sri Chinmoy has said that in order to enter any spiritual path a seeker must cry. Sincerity is necessary, along with readiness. So here I was, sincere and evidentially ready.

The following events led me to this heartfelt cry. In 1982 my 23-year-old son, Brian, died of aplastic anemia, a bone marrow disorder. This event started my spiritual search to find some meaning in life. I pondered about where Brian had gone, thinking that he could not simply have just vanished. In the aftermath of this I attended an Elisabeth Kubler-Ross workshop. Kubler-Ross told us that she was 99% certain that there was life after death. Later I attended a Ram Dass seminar. Ram Dass (formerly Richard Alpert), had traveled to India to find his Guru. He was given the spiritual name Ram Dass, which means God's servant. Thus I became acquainted with spiritual Masters and the importance of being with a Master. I read many spiritual books and continued gathering information.

Later in the early 1990s we discovered that our youngest son, John, was involved in drugs. I became depressed and overwhelmed. I was not able to contemplate losing another son. This is what brought me to my knees, desperately praying to God. Soon after this episode I saw a notice for meditation classes. The classes were offered in Toledo, because Sukantika from Chicago had traveled to Toledo to offer them. Soon a Sri Chinmoy Centre formed and offered classes. I devoured Sri Chinmoy's books and was uplifted to discover that a spiritual Master was close by and available.

In 1994 our Toledo group traveled to Jamaica, New York, to see our Guru in person. Almost immediately at the tennis court I felt a peace descend upon me. The following day, Guru called the Toledo group to come in front of him. He meditated on all of us. I began to feel my depression lift and found myself sobbing. It felt as if a burden was taken from me. When I returned home my husband immediately noticed a change in my demeanor. I recall that as I started to repeat old negative thought patterns, I told myself I will not think this way again, and I never did! Those thoughts never recurred and I have never been depressed since that time.

Still, I wanted my son to recover from his addiction. This was to take some time. During that time Guru came to me in a dream saying, "Your son will be alright." Eventually John entered a Christian rehabilitation program, recovered and turned his life around. He married, then spent two years on a mission trip in Romania. There he worked with drug addicted street people. Presently he is leading a productive life and has three beautiful children. In addition John studied and obtained a master's degree in counseling. He recently opened his own practice and is counseling couples, single people, and children. He enjoys his work and is at peace with himself.

It is comforting to recall days spent at the tennis court, being enveloped in silence and peace, with the Supreme's Love and Grace descending on this space. Now I know that the Supreme is always beside me and my faith is unshakable, not with 99% certainty, but with 110% certainty. Each day I offer heartfelt gratitude to Guru: for finding me, for accepting me, for healing me, and for providing guidance on his sunlit path.

MRIDULA
New York,
United States of America

With deepest humility offered to my beloved Guru, Sri Chinmoy, I have written the following account of my spiritual birth.

Even during the lovely period of childhood, I remember that I was always conscious of something nagging me in the back of my mind and that I was forever trying to identify this something. I felt it was something I should have been focusing on that I was not. I innately knew that it was something of the greatest importance that I would ultimately have to deal with and that it had to do with my very being. I gradually came to identify this something as Truth-Reality. The awareness of the need for finding and dealing with Truth, dim as it became at times during my life, has been the overriding idea-thread of my entire existence.

During childhood I was not very interested in doing anything unless it made sense to me, and to me making sense was anything that would help me find this Truth-Reality, spiritual values or God. I examined my friends' reasons for their actions and found that they either did not have a need for reasons or that their reasons did not satisfy me. I would search the eyes of Christian ministers for clues to their hopeful closeness to God, but I found nothing impressive. I read all the spiritual books in the library but never discovered the yogic books, perhaps because my public library did not have them. Inspirational literature and poetry studied in school gave me temporary joy and an even deeper spiritual thirst.

When I was a young teenager, I had very strong spiritual urgings and aspirations to find God. I also had a very strong urge to surrender myself to and to serve some worthy being exclusively. Frequently sweetest joy welled up within my heart, and this joy was the most important thing in my life at that time. However, the joy alternated with unbearably sharp psychic pain in the heart area due to an emptiness, a lack of God's Love and Presence.

When I was still a young teenager, I took a momentous train trip alone to Philadelphia to innocently ask a psychiatrist at the University of Pennsylvania to tell me how to fill this unbearably painful void in my heart. I guess I was one of his oddest clients. He looked at me in disbelief, told me there was nothing missing in me, did not charge me a fee and sent me home.

My heartache continued and a part of me also continued to tell me that Truth, the all-encompassing knowledge of the universe, did exist, and my strong desire to contact this Reality persisted. This strong inner craving never left me.

One day while still in my teens, when I was as usual sitting in a chair in my bedroom meditating and trying to find this Truth, I silently chanted, "Truth is, Truth is," etc. After an unaccountable lapse of time, the next thing I knew I was lying on my bed. What I then experienced was the most marvelous memory of what transpired during the lapse of time.

Without knowing how I got there, I suddenly found myself in a higher plane of consciousness. I found myself in a limitless area of darkness and emptiness, yet there was the most indescribably beautiful light in the immediate area, very bright and yet so soft. All was peaceful and quiet. Joy permeated the area. Surrounding me was the most beneficent formless Being whom I simply knew to be God. There was no question about it, and He was showering me with the most warm, friendly, heart-fulfilling and satisfying Love. In front of me in a vast tract of space was deeply impressed in the ether a most beautiful, loving and divine Smile smiling down upon me with all Sweetness and Goodness. I felt complete acceptance and understanding. All was perfect Perfection. I remained motionless and gazed fixedly in delight and absolute satisfaction at the smiling Being. The ambience of delight, serenity and sublimity was a totally new experience for me and had no earthly counterpart. No words were spoken but ideas were deeply imbedded into my mind by silent words such as "Everything is all right" and "The only thing that matters is finding God."

On that plane there was no earthly time and the experience could have been long or short; I could not tell. I was very deeply impressed with the fact that this experience was much more real than life on the earth-plane. Earth life held no attraction for me afterwards, and I had an insatiable desire to return to the higher plane, of which I felt I was a part.

To this day I feel inexpressible gratitude for the experience, which gave me the certitude without a doubt that the Truth I had been seeking was real and did exist. By God's good Grace alone I had this affirmation. I told no one about this most marvelous event because it was so extremely intimate, and no one would have believed me anyhow. Also, I did not want to invite the hostile forces to enter into the experience and exploit it.

For a long time after this event I had boundless energy and my body felt as though it were levitating. Food had no attraction for me, and I was actually repulsed by it for a time. Everyone and everything appeared more beautiful and more alive to me. Most importantly, I smiled with the joy of the certitude that Truth is the sole Reality, that God exists and is all Goodness, Love and Compassion. By sheer Grace alone I experienced the inexhaustible and omnipresent well of divine Love.

The above was the most important event of my life until my Guru, Sri Chinmoy, found me – at which time that became my most important experience. I tell you the sole and only reason for my relating the above spiritual happening: it was none other than my Guru, Sri Chinmoy, who gave me this most valuable and meaningful experience! After my Guru found me years later in the outer world, I recognised and realised that it was he who appeared to me, smiled at me and communicated with me! I feel deepest, deepest gratitude to my Guru for this Grace. Only after Guru found me did the experience begin to lose its vividness and clarity which had lasted so long.

Even though I was most fortunate to have had this profound experience giving me the verification of the existence of Truth, it did not end the ache in my heart, and for a long period of time afterwards I suffered because I became lost in outer world values and could not find my way back to the spiritual path.

During my adult life my contacts were with persons who were satisfied with their lives on the material plane. I questioned their motives for actions and was left unsatisfied with their empty, pleasure-seeking motivations. If actions were not going to help me to find God, I was still not interested in them. I could not communicate with anyone about my feelings because occasionally, when I would start to do so, I would meet with rebuff and incredulity.

No lasting satisfactions were obtained from relationships. Whereas I observed that my acquaintances functioned on the basis of their self-constructed egos, I needed a basis in God for my life and my living. I knew my ego was no ultimate authority and would not gain salvation for me. I prayed for the good fortune to be raised above the miasma of our human pettiness and self-centredness. I prayed for the good fortune to be associated with extraordinary persons. Nevertheless I drifted on from day to day, just carried along by life, and followed a certain plan of existence because I could not find high spiritual alternatives at that time. At times I experienced hopelessness. My thirst for Truth continued to remain unfulfilled and my pining for Reality continued.

Never did I receive satisfaction from anything on the material plane, not to mention joy, except for the memory of my high experience which could not be taken from me. No matter what plans I followed through on, the inevitable thoughts came: why, what for, will that help me find Truth? I could not find that outer world actions would help me meet my goal. This longing for God was always with me and I found no peace. I felt that people knew nothing. The most absurd situation existed: no one knew who we were or knew the purpose of life. The persons I knew took the marvelous design of the human body for granted as well as the entire universe. I could not accept these attitudes and I needed a spiritual authority from God to help me find the sense of life.

For a period of time I was extremely happy raising my children, whom I knew were miracles sent to me from God, but when that joyful responsibility was over, my discontent and languishing reappeared. My subsequent involvement in social welfare work gave my surface mind temporary relief but not my crying heart. Nothing ever satisfied me permanently: not schooling, not marriage, not friendships, not joining the Quakers, not social life, not social work, not traveling, not material possessions. Always I was seeking for someone who would represent for me spiritual authority and direction. I simply could not settle for anything else, but it seemed the solution would elude me forever. I resigned myself to enduring the heartache forever.

Then one day my son Philip, a Columbia University student, showed me the picture of the spiritual Master Sri Chinmoy, and he urged me to go to New York to see him. Philip had been attending the Master's public meditations at Columbia's St. Paul's Chapel, and he was a member of the Columbia Sri Chinmoy meditation group. I was smitten with the very absorbing and engrossing photograph of the Guru, and I decided to see him as soon as possible. A few days later I went to New York, met Philip and went with him to a meditation that Sri Chinmoy was leading at the United Nations. It was January 11th, 1972.

Sri Chinmoy went onto the platform, and I began to meditate with closed eyes as I was used to doing at home and in Quaker meetings. Suddenly I felt a powerful tugging at my heart. Some part of me in my heart area was being pulled right out of my body to Sri Chinmoy. Being stunned at this new and unusual experience, I quickly opened my eyes and saw that the Master was looking at me and giving me this experience.

As I continued to look at the Master, I felt a mighty sweep of spiritual strength and power coming from him.

An overwhelming attraction to him surged up within me. During the remainder of the meditation, warm, friendly sensations of Sri Chinmoy's divine love and goodness penetrated into me and enveloped me. I realised that at last I was finding in Sri Chinmoy's eyes and in his entire being what I had been seeking: the identity of a genuine spiritual power who was in touch with Truth and Reality and who would communicate this Truth to me! Gradually all the events of my prior life culminated in these moments, and I knew definitely that my life would now at last start out on the final path to Reality. I put my life into the hands of Sri Chinmoy that day.

The episode of meeting my Master is of such extreme importance in my life that I am unable to convey it in writing or speech. From that day onward the quality of my life began to improve and improve and to get better and better up to the present day, thanks to Guru's loving care.

Sri Chinmoy brings down the Light divine into us, uprooting and replacing our ignorance. This most miraculous of all happenings he brings about through his selfless love and his compassion for us. In my opinion this is the greatest boon and blessing one can have on this earth.

I attended as many of the Master's meditations as I could and I read all of his beautiful and enlightening books. I knew I had limited time at my age of fifty-three years. But, feeling relief, I knew that I was at last on the final and spiritual path after what seemed like a lifetime of sorrow. Making the start was a very big step, and at last this was accomplished by Sri Chinmoy's finding me. I shall ever be grateful to my son Philip for being the instrument whereby Guru found me.

As a disciple of Sri Chinmoy, I am experiencing for the first time true love, real love, ideal love, selfless love and also wondrous joy, all from him. My values are now all of the inner, lasting, spiritual level and my thinking is no more limited by the natural laws of the material world. After being a disciple for nine years I feel as if I have returned home after a bad experience of being lost. I realise that I am just beginning to wake up to the existence of Reality, but at least I have made the start on the final and spiritual path, thanks to Guru's finding me. Facing Reality takes tremendous will and effort, but Guru gives one tremendous support and, in fact, when one has faith in him, he takes total responsibility for one. I have the conviction that Guru has already done everything for me and that I must just become receptive to him and his light. It is just a matter of time.

As yet I am not able to maintain a high consciousness at all times, nor am I able to remain unimpassioned and steady in the face of difficulties, and at times I still experience inner upheavals. However, when I look back and see the extraordinary improvement that Guru has wrought in my present life as compared to my past life, I know absolutely and without a doubt that he will continue to purify and perfect me! Gradually the inner chaos, confusion and obscurity are diminishing, and I am losing my reliance on past wrong convictions. Although I do not see my way clear from where I am to my goal of God-realisation, I know that my Guru sees the way and will take me to the goal. I do have an awareness that life is real, is sacred, is not to be wasted on finite pursuits and has a divine goal.

We disciples need to become purified and perfected so that we can receive more and more of the limitless, infinite divine light and love which Guru pours down upon us – the most marvelous of happenings. By receiving Guru's light and love our outer and inner natures become perfect vessels for containing and manifesting divine light and for progressing onward towards God-realisation. Obedience to our Guru will greatly speed up our progress.

I feel Guru's light surrounding me in an aura which is a lively vibrating force and is very exhilarating and encouraging and gives me strength, satisfaction and reinforcement. During meditation periods the force becomes stronger. Sometimes the joy in my heart is very delicate, exquisite and beyond description, for which I am extremely grateful to Guru. Disciples aspire while meditating so we can go beyond the boundaries of the finite world. Our Guru promises to take us to the supreme goal of God-realisation. And I know this is true because I feel it to be so in my heart and soul and because Guru has already produced miracles in my outer and inner lives. He gives our souls inner messages which are needed to transform our natures.

When our Guru goes into the highest consciousness with the Supreme, he channels down onto us the powerful Light divine and becomes a beautiful, golden, glowing being, who is all perfect perfection, all goodness, all sweetness, all love and all compassion. He has no equal. Being in Guru's presence is being at the most sublime spot on earth.

I feel that our Master is here amongst us by sheer divine Grace. He, indisputably, has nothing to gain, being a perfected being, and in fact his life is all sacrifice. He is giving of himself as an instrument to elevate the consciousness of humanity. Unfortunately we do not have the capacity to understand his mission clearly. Nevertheless every day I pray for my Guru's mission to be a worldwide success.

I see the Lord Supreme in my beautiful Master, in his eyes, his rounded cheeks, his nose, the curve of his mouth and lips, his head, his hands, his feet, his entire body. So sweet and precious is my Guru's beautiful and perfect body! One must see him to realise he is real!

I am now aware that it was Sri Chinmoy for whom I carried so fervent a desire throughout my life – to surrender to and to serve; and when I become totally liberated from ignorance, I will have the capacity to execute this. I deeply love my Guru. He is all goodness, love, sweetness incarnate. He is my last hope, he is my only hope, he comes first in my life, he is my ALL! Guru is an absolutely trustworthy being. I need nothing but oneness-love with my Guru. I feel such deep, profound gratitude to my Guru for so selflessly taking me from a life of despair to a life of the sweetest communion with him.

Never in Eternity will I be able to express or manifest adequate gratitude to my Guru for finding me, accepting me, loving me, purifying me and leading me on the yogic path to Reality. I cannot speak for others, but I can truthfully say that I was totally lost in the material world, where I suffered continuously before Guru found me. I could find nothing of value, and I craved the knowledge of Truth only. In my own limited way I shall thank my Guru forever and forever for finding me and for saving me from the death of the finite life.

It is due to Guru's pure grace and compassion that he gives me his divine love, for I have not earned it. Even though I cannot really realise my good fortune, I do consider myself the luckiest person in the whole world that Guru has taken me into his heart and into his boat. Now, at least, I am safe forever, thanks to my sweetest Guru.

PANKAJA
Zurich, Switzerland

How does one find a meditation Master? This question is justified, since not even one in a thousand has a spiritual Master to provide him with inspiration and support in his inner and outer life. First of all, there has to be an inner hunger and then we start seeking. Somewhere on the way we find our Master. How it happens is a mystery, a mystery as multifaceted and individual as the children of this earth.

When I was about nine years old, one day I was lying by the pool looking at a blade of grass. I asked myself if what I was seeing was really everything. I had a strong feeling that there was more to it than I was able to see. When I was 13, one day I was riding uphill for some time while thinking about God. It had always been clear to me that God was beyond any institution, but I asked myself which form of God I would be able to believe in. I came to the conclusion that, for me, God was above all ascertainable as happiness. From age 15 to age 40 I stopped watching television and therefore had lots of time to read. Some years of conscious search for the meaning of life began. It was like a puzzle that was taking shape more and more as a real picture. Domains such as philosophy, psychology, parapsychology, mysticism and the esoteric were my teachers on the road. I was particularly attracted by occultism. I stayed the longest with Theosophy, which also deals with occult knowledge. Theosophical books report that humanity is guided by Masters. Certain Masters dictated parts of these books by telepathy.

At the age of 16 I started meditating – irregularly at first, then with increasing regularity. Only at the age of 22 did I start practising meditation seriously. In March 1978, a new health food store called Madal Bal opened up about 500 metres from my place. I went there quite frequently. In this health food store there were photos of Sri Chinmoy, and I also bought my first book by Sri Chinmoy, *Samadhi and Siddhi*, which I liked a lot. I knew that Sri Chinmoy was a spiritual Master, but I thought that I could meditate and make progress all by myself. A whole seven years passed before I had an experience which made me realise that I should definitely call on the help of a true spiritual Master. Sri Chinmoy then accepted me as his disciple and I accepted him as my Master.

My experience with Sri Chinmoy has only been a positive one. Untiringly he offered inspiration to his disciples and all those who came in contact with him. He always tried to bring to the fore the best in every human being and taught us first to ignore our weaknesses but then to work towards transforming them. I have known Sri Chinmoy as an active and wise man who worked selflessly on all levels and worldwide to promote a harmonious coexistence and oneness. He cared for us, his disciples, like a loving father. He gave me the right thing at the right moment, be it silence or words, concerts or songs, paintings or other creative works, challenges in daily life or in the field of sports, and much more. In every way he was an absolutely reputable person, and at the same time he had a childlike purity and cheerfulness that would often truly surprise me. Through his example he demonstrated how to live a divine life here on our planet. Also, he never gave up if he did not succeed on the first attempt. He lived and practised his philosophy of self-transcendence in an impressive manner. In every way he was a role model for me. He encouraged everyone to transcend their own limitations and to go beyond themselves through divine love, devotion and surrender.

To describe a spiritual Master from an outer point of view can only show a faint reflection of his inner existence. Almost everything happens on the inner planes, and that is where one finds the relationship between Master and disciple and between God and the Master. There lies the true treasure of the heart and soul. There lies the unfathomable kindness and loving care that I and many others received.

In the course of my life as a disciple of Sri Chinmoy, I experienced that gratitude can grow. I am grateful for a lot of things, specially when I see gratitude growing within and around me. We can be grateful for an unlimited number of things, but are we really? My personal experience is this: if we succeed in being grateful, we help ourselves and all the people around us. We always have the opportunity to be grateful and thus to elevate our consciousness. I am grateful that I started to believe in God and to search for Him. I am grateful for the certitude that God-realisation is possible. I am grateful for the insight that there are people among us who have reached this goal. But I am most grateful that my Master Sri Chinmoy guided me towards him, enabled me to accept him, allowed me to follow his path and continues to lead me to ever-increasing gratitude.

PIERRE
Montpellier, France

Everything started in Havana. I had been studying in Costa Rica for about six months and I was enjoying my summer holidays visiting Cuba. I had always wanted to see this island and these people, and was specially interested in their spirituality.

As in many other places in Latin America, the meeting of African, Catholic and indigenous beliefs in Cuba has given birth to a unique form of spirituality, La Santería. Every Catholic saint also encompasses the figure of an African deity and is worshipped as such, with rum, tobacco and animal sacrifices. Although it was quite primitive in some respects, I was surprised to see that every Cuban house had a shrine dedicated to the family deity and that worship of the deity was part of the daily routine of every Cuban.

On Wednesday, January 19th, 2005 (I still don't know why I remember this date so precisely), I decided to take a walk and visit the National Cemetery, resting place of some of the most important historical figures of the island, including poets, artists and politicians. And what does one do when he visits a cemetery? One often reads the names on people's graves and tries to imagine what their life was like, who they could have been, what the island was like when they lived....

I stopped, stunned, in front of the grave of someone named Pedro Ponte Blanco. The reason I was so surprised is simple. In the Spanish culture, one has two surnames. In the case of this person, the given name and the two surnames composed a sentence which in English could be correctly translated as, "Pierre, you have to dress in white." I say "Pierre" because that is my name, the equivalent of Pedro in Spanish or Peter in English.

So here I was in front of this grave telling me to dress in white. I had no idea how to interpret this sign. I smiled, tried for twenty seconds to make my mind blank, and returned to my tourist activities.

Later on in the same day I was invited to a special celebration. There is a very intense spiritual process through which most of the Cubans go. For a whole year one must not drink alcohol, nor smoke, nor dance, nor eat meat; one must dress in white; and there are probably many more things that people did not want to tell me. The apartment in old Havana was packed with children running everywhere, buffets of sweets, shrines to different deities, people playing congas and other kinds of drums, a thick cloud of tobacco smoke and laughter. It felt altogether very cheerful. I sat with an old man musing about what Cuba was and how it would be after Fidel left. An hour might have passed.

Suddenly something happened – something in the atmosphere changed. An old lady I had been chatting with was shaking, and her eyes were bulging. Children had disappeared, the sweets were gone, the rum was finished, the drums were playing much faster. In her trance the old lady could not speak, but she was making signs that everyone but me could understand. I felt awkward. A friend came to me and said, "Pierre, you are not Cuban, you don't know our saints, you should not be here. But because all the doors are closed, the room is sanctified and we cannot let you go. Just stand by the door and make sure this lady does not leave!"

I felt better now that someone was giving me some instructions. I really had no idea what I was meant to do. I was the only white, the only non-Cuban, the only one who had no clue what was happening. But in my mind I thought, "If that old lady really wants to exit, I don't feel very confident to stop her." People in those states are extremely strong and determined... I was not sure I felt like actually impeding her.

During what seemed to be twenty minutes but was probably much less, she stood in front of different people and made signs to which people would respond. I could not understand what was expressed, but as the audience would cheer and react to any of her moves, I understood that a saint was acting through her and that people were seeking his blessings.

After a while she stood in front of me. I think I raised my arms as if to say, "You are not going anywhere," but my shaking legs were probably saying, "Just do as you wish!" She started gesticulating in front of me. I was petrified. I had no idea what she was trying to say, but she was obviously expecting me to answer.

A friend came to my rescue and told me the first thing she had said with her gestures: "Pierre, you have to dress in white!"

I hoped his assistance would make me feel better, but I actually felt even stranger. Twice in one day I had been told, in two mysterious ways, to dress in white.

As the old lady kept on gesticulating, my friend

translated: I had to be very careful with an area of my stomach, to which she clearly pointed. As I answered that I had been operated on one year earlier in this precise spot, a wave of comments exploded in the audience. I felt, if possible, even more helpless. I had in front of me someone who was obviously trying to tell me something that would change my life, but I had no clue how to interpret it. As she said a few more things which I cannot repeat here, my friends got me to bow down to her and make a few more signs that I have completely forgotten now.

Ten minutes later she was smiling again, having some cake and chatting with the owner of the apartment. But I felt so lost, so defenceless, so traumatised. I just had no idea what would happen to me after that.

In the following weeks the old lady took me through a few ceremonies of purification in the Cuban way. I used to call her 'mi madrina', my godmother.

I left Cuba, finished my studies in Costa Rica and finally came back to France. Coming back to your country after a long journey is never an easy thing to do. I had changed so radically after such a long time abroad that the discrepancy between Paris and what I had become was difficult to face. I wished I could protect all the inner richness I had acquired from so many experiences, but I was aware that I also had to accept the unavoidable challenge of my return to the old continent.

Yoga, tai chi, painting, theatre: I think I was just looking for any activity that would allow me a sense of interiority. One day I saw a poster for free meditation classes twenty metres from the place I was born and raised. I thought, "It's free! I am poor in money but rich in time... why not!"

I really enjoyed the class Ashcharjya gave. On the second night we were told all the guidelines Guru had established for his disciples. While I felt that I completely understood what this path was about, I also completely negated the possibility of following such a pattern myself. But in my heart something attracted me. In fact, I was telling God inwardly that if He ever thought about sending me a sign, that would be a good moment!

The last class finished and I was ready to say, "Well, thank you very much, what you are doing is great, I enjoyed it... Ciao!" But many people wanted to speak to Ashcharjya and, as I waited to speak to him, I saw Unnatishil, who is always dressed in white regardless of time and space. So I told him, just to chat, "How interesting! You have dressed in white as the Cubans do in order to purify themselves." And then he explained to me that Sri Chinmoy actually wanted his male disciples to dress in white when meditating.

Always be careful of what you ask for, because you will get it!

I had been longing for a sign, and here it was, crystal clear.

PIPASA
*New York,
United States of America*

My mother was a spiritual person and was a good example to me of what it meant to lead a spiritual life. Her grandfather was a Methodist Minister, but we belonged to a small open-minded Christian church that tried to operate in the world as if Jesus Christ's teachings were being applied to the Twentieth Century. She lived her Christian values: she was cheerful and self-giving. I had the feeling that she really saw the Christ as her Teacher.

My father proposed to my mother by asking her if she wanted to be the wife of a Minister. He was a seeker and a hippie. He did not end up becoming a Minister. He changed his major and ended up being a school counselor. My mother said he could not pin down his faith and present it in a neat little box every week as you would have to do if you delivered a sermon every Sunday. Like my mother's, his family was also strongly Christian-oriented and he was a conscientious objector, because he felt no Christian could in good conscience advocate war.

I came to know of Guru through friends. I was reading spiritual writings and had an experience while trying a visualization exercise. I was just out of high school and had gone to church all my life, but I had never tried to practise prayer much on a daily basis. I tried a visualization for guidance with a place called the 'Live Institute'. The visualization was to imagine walking down a forest path, with brambles covering the trail, then coming across a clearing. In the sunny field you see someone smiling at you with unconditional love. I felt I made a connection there, something was happening inwardly and I felt a sense of joy.

After this experience I started reading more spiritual books and became interested in Eastern philosophy. I read Paramahansa Yogananada's *Autobiography of a Yogi*. I had a friend who was also interested in Eastern writings and he knew a disciple of Guru's. This disciple knew my brother and seemed very kind. This was Ekatma's son. He had only been a disciple for six months and he invited us to come to a meditation at the Sri Chinmoy Centre in Seattle.

I had a strong feeling of peace after meditating on the Transcendental Picture, and I liked the people in the Centre. A month later Guru was coming to Oregon, and my new-found friends at the Centre were going to see him. I was told only disciples could go on the trip. I said I wanted to be a disciple and was accepted on October 16th, 1980, thirteen days after my 18th birthday. I saw Guru for the first time on October 17th. It was the Seattle Centre's anniversary and it also happens to be my brother's birthday.

Guru was meditating at the Garden Center in Eugene, Oregon. He asked all the new disciples to raise their hands. He meditated on each one of us individually and then smiled this incredible smile. I felt that he knew everything about me, and I became a little shy or even embarrassed, and looked at the floor. When I looked up again, Guru was still smiling at me. I could not believe he could smile at me with such unconditional love. My soul was thrilled. Later I read one of Guru's own poems that described the experience perfectly:

My Lord granted me His Compassion-Smile
Long before I even wished to deserve it.
— **Sri Chinmoy**

PRADEEP
The Hague, The Netherlands

When your heart
Has genuine tears,
Your true Master appears.
— **Sri Chinmoy**

Sri Chinmoy came into my life much earlier than I was aware of. Opposite the primary school I attended was an enterprise run by students of Sri Chinmoy. Maybe I have sometimes watched them unload a pallet of maple syrup or Celestial Seasonings tea while I was playing hide and seek in the schoolyard. Later on, my secondary school was around the corner from the Sri Chinmoy Meditation Centre. The Congress Centre where Sri Chinmoy gave a big concert in 1988 was on the other side of the road. For some reason a friend and I sometimes enjoyed sneaking into the building and wandering through the halls in one of the breaks between classes. Then, when I was 17 years old it turned out a new friend who was about ten years older than me had been a student of Sri Chinmoy. He mentioned it once and showed me a picture of Sri Chinmoy, but I didn't look closely enough, the whole concept of having a spiritual Master was completely alien to me. I kept asking though what he exactly did when he was meditating. But since my friend had given up on trying to meditate he wasn't very keen on explaining it, he called it 'staring at a candle'. We went running instead. But always Sri Chinmoy had been there on the sidelines of my life waiting for time to ripen so I could have the joy of discovering him myself.

I hadn't been overly drawn to spirituality as a youth, except for a distant feeling that I would like to spend some time in a monastery one day. I went to church with my parents every now and then and actually enjoyed that. The whole idea of meditation had always struck home with me but only as a university student I started to get interested seriously. I was studying geology at the time and by my own standards rather happy, but somehow the real purpose of life seemed to elude me. I was happy but not satisfied. I was doing well in sports and in my studies, but that didn't seem to provide any real, lasting satisfaction. After studying for two years I decided to take half a year off and travel around by myself in Australia, New Zealand and South East Asia.

In a second hand bookstore in Australia I had an experience beyond the confines of everyday life as I was strangely drawn to a book by the Hare Krishna movement. The book seemed to stick out from the shelf calling for my attention, though I was standing too far off to see a title. The philosophy was intriguingly different from anything I had ever read. Rather bold, but it appealed to me nevertheless. After finishing the book I selected a title from the list of suggestions for future reading in the back of the book and made a mental note to get this book once I would be back home in Holland. Then I put the book down and didn't think of it again. However the 'book-experience' repeated itself in a youth hostel on New Zealand's South Island and exactly the book I had chosen jumped out at me even before I could read the title.

My experiences in New Zealand in many ways had been an awakening to me. I was hiking the various long-distance trails by myself. Spending many days in nature, meeting hardly anybody, was refreshing and satisfying in a new way. Away from the hurries and self-imposed pressures of life in hectic Amsterdam, slowly I started to get a new scope on things. One day I was walking the Abel Tasman track on the northern shore of the South Island, and by the end of the afternoon reached a beautiful beach. There was no one around for miles and I had been walking by myself in silence for almost a day. I was in a serene mood that was nurtured by the sun starting to set, bathing everything in a warm golden light that seemed to intensify the colors of nature. Suddenly there were many small dolphins very close to the shore. They were surfing the waves and enjoying themselves. I threw off my big backpack and jumped in the water. The dolphins swam away though and slightly disappointed I returned to the beach. When I was halfway through drying myself and warming up from the water that was still pretty cold, as summer hadn't really started yet, the dolphins reappeared. I gave it a second chance and got back into the water. This time the dolphins did not swim away. They didn't allow me to touch them but they were all around me, hardly a meter away, singing their high-pitched songs. It struck something in me. Something very deep. I was drunk with joy. I was splashing about like mad, trying to swim alongside the dolphins, a joy surging up in me that completely overwhelmed me. That was the first time in my life I experienced real joy, divine joy. It was beautiful and at the same time it made me more acutely aware that there was much more to life than I was getting out of it at the moment.

I ended up travelling for two more months after that and then returned home. The second day after getting back to Holland I was approached in the street by a girl of the Hare Krishna movement. I talked a little with her and bought the book she was selling. I figured I had to follow the Hare Krishna lead the universe was offering me. I read the book and even wrote a letter to the swami that had written it. I'm afraid the letter was pretty presumptuous. Probably the swami deduced who must have sold the book to me. The girl called me one day and invited me to come with her and some others to one of their big temples in Belgium. We would meet at their temple in Amsterdam and then travel together to the Ardennes in Belgium by car.

I entered their temple in Amsterdam on a cloudy Saturday morning. I saw the girl that had invited me sitting on the floor in the corner of the room threading flowers into a small garland. The love and devotion with which she was doing it left a huge impression on me. As if I was looking into some kind of magic mirror deeper into my own self, beyond the surface view of things. I suddenly strongly felt I also had that kind of love and devotion within me; I just had to find a way to express it. The trip to Belgium was in every way a disaster, though the temple was beautiful and some of the people really inspired me. However I was making one mistake after the other and started to feel more and more uncomfortable. I followed the girl around since she was the only person I knew. At some point I sat down to have lunch with her in one of the dining rooms. I hadn't noticed though that it was 'women only' and I was told in no uncertain terms to get out of there by an older lady. Another time I said loudly, "Enjoy your meal," when everyone just turned silent to meditate on their food. A few more things like that happened and eventually I fled the place to save any further embarrassments and to go home by myself. I was rather sad. I knew I had found what I wanted in life: to lead a spiritual life. However, this path was not meant to be mine.

I decided to study comparative religion in university besides studying geology, in order to keep feeding my hunger for spiritual knowledge. One day I was studying for an exam on Christian and Jewish mysticism, and reading on a particular saintly person who had composed a great many prayers, one for each moment and activity of the day. Suddenly I felt a very deep emotion welling up from inside and I found myself crying. I felt an absolutely intense inner longing, I also wanted to be able to pray and meditate and discover the deeper meaning of life. It was a few weeks after that at the faculty of comparative religion that I saw this absolutely tiny yellow leaflet on a big poster board between hundreds of other flyers of a lecture by the Sri Chinmoy Centre. I went there in the beginning of 1999. A kind young man opened the door for me that evening. Everything was nice, but then I noticed something funny; as we were chanting *Aum* at the beginning of the meditation exercises the others in the room would be able to hold the sound much longer. I figured out pretty fast that all the others in the room, there must have been about 6 or seven, were part of the group somehow. One man in the front row was looking so stern that I thought this was some kind of examination, as the girl who was giving the lecture seemed a little insecure here and there. I didn't mind though, what she said was nice and I felt very much at home. However since it turned out I was right and I had been the only one coming that evening, there would be no meditation course following that evening. I rode my bike home happily with Sri Chinmoy's book *Meditation* and the phone number of the girl in my agenda.

The weeks following the lecture I started cancelling all activities in the evening and would only read the book on meditation. Trying out some of the exercises felt a little odd though. Usually I would give up after half a minute, laughing at myself. For months I kept calling the girl but somehow there was never a new meditation course starting at a time I could make it. Finally there would be a course in Den Haag, the city where I grew up and where my parents still lived. I decided to travel there once a week to follow the course. I showed up well ahead of time, somewhere in the city centre of Den Haag. After waiting for almost an hour I realised that I had gone to the wrong address. At that moment I almost decided to leave the whole matter. I was already on my way home when this tiny little voice in my head said: "Like this you will never get anywhere in life." I had the correct address with me, but I didn't know where it was. So I decided to phone my mother from a telephone booth and ask her to look on a map and explain it to me. I arrived that evening at the meditation course more than one hour late, but it felt like coming home. That feeling basically never left me. Not only did the meditation techniques of Sri Chinmoy provide a definite sense of happiness, my life had finally found its meaning in the pursuit of enlightenment or 'God-realisation' as Sri Chinmoy calls it. Finally all the pieces of my life seemed to fit together. I didn't have a clear picture in mind about the relationship between a meditation Master and his student, but I was absolutely determined not to let go of this new horizon that had opened up before me.

Somehow the first time I gave my application to become a student of Sri Chinmoy the form got stuck in someone's mailbox or something like that and it didn't reach Sri Chinmoy. However, a few days later I had a life-changing experience. I was lying in bed one evening when I suddenly felt a strong presence in my room. It didn't feel bad particularly, but there wasn't supposed to be anyone in my room. I was afraid and stiffened in my bed. Then a presence entered my body and suddenly my world was upside down. Something raced from the bottom of my spinal column into my brain and I had an intuitive vision of a huge book, like a medieval Bible. A page of the book was turned and I was completely overwhelmed by an all-knowing feeling. It lasted only moments, but for those moments I understood everything of life and death. I didn't see the book any longer, I had become the Universe, I had become knowledge itself. Truth filled and fulfilled me to the brim. Then as suddenly as it had come everything vanished and I was back in my bed, still uncertain of what had actually happened.

After this experience my meditations became deeper in sudden jumps and by October 1999 Sri Chinmoy accepted me formally as his student. The day he accepted me I was sitting on a train having by my standards a good meditation, when I saw a double rainbow with predominantly blue colors. I knew then that Sri Chinmoy had accepted me, although outwardly I heard only two days later.

PRAKHARA
United States of America

I wasn't really looking to settle down with one path, because I was enjoying the experience of going to a different spiritual group every night. Also I had a dream to return to India, which I had visited a year or so before.

Then Guru came to give a public meditation in Santa Barbara, California – where I was living. It was very nice, and afterwards I went to Ranganath's art gallery, where Guru and the disciples from Santa Barbara, San Francisco and Los Angeles were meeting. One of the girls asked me if I wanted to become a disciple, and I said that I might be interested. It was a very casual comment and I certainly wasn't seriously considering it.

Guru was also offering a meditation in Los Angeles that same day, so people started to get in their cars to make the two-hour drive down south. Someone invited me to go with them, and I decided I would go along. Guru was in his car, and several disciples were standing on the sidewalk watching him depart. Unbeknownst to me, Aditi, who was in the back seat, told Guru that there was a girl who was interested in becoming his disciple. Guru pointed to me on the sidewalk (I saw him pointing to me) and asked if I was the girl. She said yes, and Guru said that I was already his disciple. Aditi was very excited and wanted to get out of the car and tell me right away, but Guru told her to let me wait.

The meditation in Los Angeles was also very nice, and I was becoming more interested in asking to be a disciple, but there was no invitation to seekers afterwards as there had been in Santa Barbara. After a short function, everyone went out to the street where Guru was in the car, leaving for the airport. I was beginning to feel that maybe it wasn't the right time, when Aditi got out of the car and came up to me. She said, "Guru wants to know if you want to be his disciple." I said, "Sure, OK, why not?" or something to that effect. Basically it was, once again, very casual. She said, "No, you have to be serious. Do you want to be a disciple or not?" So I very emphatically said, "Yes."

Now I was feeling very elated. For one thing, I had been fasting for a week and all the activities of the day had brought on quite a headache. But when I said, "Yes, I want to be a disciple," the headache immediately went away. So I thought it was only proper to go and tell Guru thank you for letting me be his disciple. I went right up to his open car window and offered my gratitude. I wasn't there long, because the boys guarding Guru promptly shuffled me away.

A short time later I realised that it was all meant to be. I remembered that when I first arrived in Santa Barbara, a couple of months before I saw Guru, my friend and I had been looking for a place to stay. We had seen the Sri Chinmoy Centre listed in a book and went to inquire if they took in guests. Of course we were told that was not their policy. It was my birthday, August 22nd, and I was thrilled to notice that the address of the Centre was 822 Orange Avenue.

Although I had been accepted as Guru's disciple, I still wanted to go back to India. It seemed especially appropriate, because I learned that Guru had lived in the Sri Aurobindo Ashram. That had been the exact place I had visited a little over a year before. One month later I was on my way to Pondicherry via New York. The Los Angeles Sri Aurobindo Centre had given me a slide projector to take to the Ashram, so I had a real mission and I was very excited to be going back. I planned to spend a few days in New York before departing. Guru had a meditation at the All Angels Church in Manhattan and a very curious thing happened there. Dulal read from one of Guru's books as part of the programme. It was a question for Guru – "Do you ever miss India?" Dulal read the answer, which was something to this effect: "No, because my home is in my heart. I can be at home wherever I am." At that exact moment I realised that I didn't need to go to India and that I shouldn't go to India! Luckily I was able to cancel my airline reservation and give the slide projector to someone else to take.

A few years later, I had an even more profound confirmation that I had made the right decision to join Guru's path. We were at a function in Connecticut during August Celebrations, and there was a slide show in the evening. A picture of a young man was on the screen and the presenter announced that it was the son of Norman Dowsett. I couldn't believe it, because I had met Norman Dowsett when I was visiting the Sri Aurobindo Ashram. In fact, at the time I thought he was my Guru. He was the first person who ever spoke to me about the spiritual life, and I felt such an affinity with him. One night my friend and I were up until 2 a.m. talking and asking him questions. Norman Dowsett was a very special man. He was Guru's English teacher at the Ashram.

How very, very grateful I am that life led me in the right direction.

PRATUL
Oslo, Norway

I was only 16 years old, walking with my mother and my great-aunt in the centre of Innsbruck. A poster caught my attention, hanging on the wall of a house. It said, 'Masters of Meditation'. "Hmm, that could be interesting," I was thinking while going closer. It showed the portraits of three men – I suppose those Masters of meditation – whose names I had never heard before. Underneath there was an aphorism. I was looking at the pictures, feeling perplexed and, at the same time, deeply moved. How much love, how much peace and light emanated from these faces!

I could not avert my gaze from the faces. Somehow they seemed familiar to me. For an instant, a whiff of otherworldliness touched me lightly and evoked a gladdening and homelike feeling within me. I read the aphorism and dwelled for a short while in this blissful state until my mind turned back on. "Too good for this world," it told me. For comparison, or to come back to reality, I looked at the faces of the 'normal' people rushing by; they seemed lifeless to me now. "But I am in a hurry, too!" – these words came into my mind. "And where is my mother, after all?" I quickly looked at the date on the poster. I would have time to go to the lecture, but a voice within me said, "No; it is too early. The time has not come yet. It is necessary to gather more experiences."

Two years later, everything fell into place. I was not doing anything; I was only the observer. There was a lecture on music and meditation given by a Swiss psychologist – exactly my thing! What he was saying I forgot right away. During the meditation exercise, my mind was as calm and silent as a disco on a Saturday night. Very annoying! What impressed me, though, was the calm and cheerful aura of the lecturer. He told me afterwards that he had been meditating for many years under the guidance of his Master, Sri Chinmoy. He certainly did not fit into my formula of a cave-dwelling yogi: he owned a health food store, propagated a healthy diet, ran marathons and was actively engaged in many other things. He also mentioned that his Master would soon be coming to Cologne to give a big concert, and I could join some other seekers who were going there if I wanted to. By then I had been meditating on my own for three months, with moderate success, and was therefore not averse to trying it with some expert help. But, above all, it was pure curiosity that persuaded me to come along.

What happened at the concert resembles a dream – in the literal sense of the term. As soon as the Master starts playing the first melodies on an indefinable Indian bowed instrument, I fall into a deep, coma-like sleep from which I abruptly awake only at the very end of the concert. "Oh no, I missed everything!" I angrily think, and my consciousness descends into the abyss. Then, however, the unexpected happens: Sri Chinmoy invites all seekers who have travelled from Austria to have a short personal meditation with him. Has my hour struck after all? Yes, this could save the evening! I line up in a semi-circle together with a small group of spiritual seekers, with very mixed emotions.

My head works flat out, at once confused and curious. In my heart, however, nervousness is paired with a feeling of ecstatic joy. What will happen now? Finally the door opens and Sri Chinmoy, dressed in an Indian dhoti, slowly walks towards us. A touch of a smile is on his lips. His fast-moving eyes give me the impression that he is not totally, or at least not exclusively, dwelling in this world. He is of short stature, but his emanation is all the more sublime and majestic. From one end of the semi-circle, Sri Chinmoy starts meditating on all the seekers, one by one. His eyes move fast, and after a short time, it is my turn.

What happens in the seconds that follow is one of the most impressive, lasting and fulfilling experiences of my life. Sri Chinmoy glances at me, but at the same time his glance seems to go through me. Suddenly I become aware of many things within me that were previously masked from me. Some are radiant and luminous, but some horrifyingly dark – so dark that I would normally have wanted to hide myself away in a mouse hole. At the same time I do not feel left alone with all this anymore. I feel a deep connectedness; I feel accepted by the Master, understood, taken by the hand, as if he were sharing the burden with me. Time stands still, my mind is overstrained, but I am unbelievably relieved, happy and grateful. It is as if one has returned home after a long, exhausting journey.

The rest is sheer formality. I decide to tentatively try this thing for six months and give my application, with a photo, to become Sri Chinmoy's disciple.

On the way home from Cologne, we miraculously escape, by a hair's breadth, a serious car accident in our old VW van. In the critical moment I close my eyes and clearly see in front of my mental eye Sri Chinmoy's Transcendental Picture.

Ever since that moment, I have always felt sheltered

and protected in critical or dangerous situations in life. Later, with Sri Chinmoy's advice and guidance, I generally became much more cautious in adventurous undertakings.

What it meant in practical terms to be a disciple was not clear to me at this point in time. My day-to-day life hardly changed, but the quality of my daily meditations truly did, because I received the Transcendental Picture. From then on I knew from within how I was supposed to meditate. It was like a quantum leap. Meditation now gave me much more joy, regardless of outer incidents, as well as a strong foothold in my outer life. This feeling of inner guidance in my meditations as well as in my day-to-day life has never left me since I was accepted by my Master, Sri Chinmoy. It is one of the most precious things in my life, because it is in reality the link to an inner Source, the Source of all existence, the Self, the Divine. It is 'becoming pregnant with God' – I found this most beautiful expression in a Sufi book. With this presence, this feeling in my heart, I have always felt safe, ever since, in my outer and my inner life, and never alone or lonely. I think this is the most beautiful gift that one can receive in life, the only gift that fulfils us everlastingly, the only sure support in this impermanent world. And deep inside I know who gave me this gift.

With eternal gratitude....

PURABI
Bratislava, Slovakia

It is said that when the soul is coming into the world, it knows what role it has to play in the Cosmic Game of the Supreme. According to this the soul chooses the circumstances into which it is born, the country, the family and even the physical body and the mind. Young children know all this. But when they grow up, this knowledge is covered by the veil of ignorance. When the mind is developed, it covers the direct perception of truth by the heart.

I was lucky that my parents were believers, but they never forced me to share their view of life. I remember we prayed before meals. We dedicated one whole day a week to God. Then we did not work, but we sang, prayed and read the Bible. I liked the songs most. Some of them I still remember.

When I grew up a bit and started to create my own opinions of the world, I saw also things that I did not like so much. My parents were Seventh Day Adventists. We were nicknamed Saturday people, because the day we dedicated to God was Saturday. All my friends did it on Sunday. I did not like to be different. But what I disliked most was the opinion that the Adventists were the only ones to be saved and go to Heaven. It seemed to me unfair, especially when I saw that people around me were not perfect either.... But my parents' religion also had a good point: children were not baptised at birth but at the age of eighteen, so they could decide for themselves. And so I decided to remain unbaptised.

My decision was definitely influenced by the era I was growing up in. Religion and spirituality were not supported in Eastern Europe in the 1960s, just the opposite. But now I think it was not just the right time for me; I still had to experience certain things and realise that the world without God is empty.

Luckily, my parents let me go my own way. They used to call me to join them on Saturday, but when they saw it was useless, they did not insist. I am grateful for this today.

And so I started to look for my own life. I studied at the university and almost nothing was impossible. Later I got married and had three children. I was reading a lot at that time. I also read books about yoga, not knowing what it would mean in my life later on.

I was an English teacher at a secondary school. One of my students was also interested in yoga. He found a book by Sri Aurobindo and wrote a letter to the publisher, to the Ashram in Pondicherry. As he was not very confident about his English, he asked me to check his letter. He was a very talented boy. One day he showed me the reply – a letter from Pondicherry. They also sent him some books and he let me read them. In this way I became acquainted with the philosophy of Integral Yoga. I liked it very much, only I did not know how to use it in my life. I became a theoretical yogi.

Nothing in our life happens only by chance. The things, the meaning of which we do not understand, will after some time turn out to be a preparation for something to come later. Ten years later my English student decided to go to India and become a member of the Sri Aurobindo Ashram. And I became a student of Sri Chinmoy, who grew up in the same ashram.

Once at Christmas time my elder daughter gave me a book called *Know Yourself*. I do not remember what it was about, but the name of this book seemed to set the direction of my life. As Sri Chinmoy says:

> *The moment you know*
> *Who you really are,*
> *All secrets of the world*
> *Will be an open book to you.*
>
> **– Sri Chinmoy**

But the last impulse came when my younger daughter, then about fifteen years old, asked me: "Tell me something about God." I have to explain that at that time we did not discuss God at all. My husband was a stark atheist and I was a teacher in the communist regime. I said something like there is a Cosmic Consciousness, but it obviously was not what my daughter wanted to hear. Not being satisfied, she went with the same question to her father. Then she looked for the answer in different Christian youth organisations, but I do not know if she was successful. For her, I was not an expert in this subject anymore.

We used to attend hatha yoga classes together and I liked it a lot. We became vegetarians, but only my daughters and me. My husband and son were sceptical about it. I always cooked two meals: one meat meal and the other one vegetarian. My son recently told me that he always appreciated that I cooked meat for him while being a vegetarian myself.

Soon after that I found a small leaflet at an esoteric festival in Bratislava. It said there would be a concert of meditation music in my home town the following day. The concert was in the afternoon, so I went there straight from school. There was a short introduction before the concert where they explained what meditation is and invited us to meditation classes. The concert was beautiful. It was one of the few concerts by Mountain-Silence in Slovakia. I think most of the time at the concert I cried, although I did not understand why I was just sitting there and shedding tears....

I went to the meditation classes with my daughter. There were some of my colleagues and a few of my English students. After a month Satyaki (who was giving the classes) told us that we could send pictures to his Master Sri Chinmoy and ask him if we could be his students. I did not understand why we needed a Master. I thought that Satyaki was the Master. Besides, I was worried what would happen if his Master does not accept me. But then I picked up my courage. It was my first step into the unknown on the spiritual path, incomprehensible for the mind but inwardly inevitable.

In November 1993 Sri Chinmoy gave a concert of meditation music in Bratislava. Satyaki invited all of us. We went there with our hatha yoga friends who had organized a bus. I remember it was snowing heavily that evening. The bus was about an hour late, because of the weather. I said to myself it is of no use going to Bratislava because the concert will be finished before we get there. But our hatha yoga friends waited patiently for the bus, so we also stayed. We arrived in Bratislava at eight-thirty, long after the concert was supposed to start. There we found out that nothing had started yet! Sri Chinmoy's plane had also been delayed because of the weather. So we arrived at the right time.

There were so many people in the hall, several

thousand. I felt a little bit lost. But Satyaki told us that all who had sent their pictures were accepted by Sri Chinmoy as his disciples. It was a special feeling, waiting for the concert of our Master. And I was happy that he had accepted us.

The concert was different from what I remembered with Mountain-Silence. It was very intense, especially when Sri Chinmoy was playing the gong, but I felt very peaceful. I bought the tape *Flute Music for Meditation*, not knowing at that time that years later I myself would start to play the flute.

After the concert Sri Chinmoy was giving a TV interview. It was quite late, so I went to the hatha yoga leader and said that now, since the concert was over, we could actually go home. He looked at me surprised and said: "Never leave before the Master has left." And Sri Chinmoy was not even his Master, he was a student of another Master.

Later on I was happy that we had stayed. When the interview was over, we could take prasad from Sri Chinmoy (blessed food, as our hatha yoga friends explained to us later). We had a banana and a biscuit. I did not know what to do with the biscuit, because at that time I was eating only healthy food, no sugar at all. Since our hatha yoga friends were speaking about prasad with great respect, finally I ate it.

In the beginning of our spiritual path our hatha yoga friends helped us a lot. They helped us to get to the concert where we saw our Master for the first time, they explained a lot of things to us and even allowed us to meditate in their ashram for some time. Later our paths separated, but I still have good memories of that time.

Nothing in our lives happens only by chance. Each

experience, as well as each person in our life has a deeper meaning, even though at that time it may not seem so. But most of all our life is changed when we meet our own spiritual Master. Then there is nothing more to say, only gratitude.

PURNAHUTI
Guatemala City, Guatemala

I remember once talking amongst the family. Everybody was asked what they want to become. When it was my turn and I was asked if I ever thought I would like to become a priest my immediate answer was, "Yes, yes, I would like to become a priest." Definitely, that was in my thoughts. At that time I was around 10 years old.

From the age of 10 to 20 there were about ten years with several spiritual experiences. I always was searching. I remember when I was about 17 years old I had the opportunity to meet a yoga master who had some occult power. This person who had some spiritual knowledge amazed me. And I said to myself: "Well, when I grow old I want to become like him. I want to be spiritual. I want to be of service," because he was always being of help and service to humanity.

But I only knew him for 6 months and then he passed away. After his passing I started searching and was going to different meditation groups, spiritual groups – but in each group there was something missing or that did not harmonize with me, it just didn't click. One of these groups had nice ideals, but the practice of the ideals was not there! Another group had 'the only way to reach God'! For me God is all love, I could not believe that being God – all love – there would be only one way to love him.

Around that time, I remember one night being in my room and I had just started invoking the presence of this yoga master, so that he could guide me and show me the right path. What I had experienced in the different spiritual groups was not satisfying me and I needed something deeper in life. After some time I started crying, I remember clearly, I was seated next to my bed. The next day I woke up, tired, and with very little interest in the world. I needed something deeper and more fulfilling in life, and the outside world was not giving me the happiness and fulfillment that I was looking for. The next night, again I seated myself next to my bed and I tried to invoke the presence of the master again. After some time, probably an hour, I started crying, and I went to sleep again feeling alone and bleak. That night I had a dream that I will never forget. A vivid dream that changed my life. It gave me faith, strength and a feeling that everything is being taken care of.

In the dream he came to me. We started flying; it felt like how you see that Superman flies. We started flying and went to a place that looked like a Buddhist temple. There we landed, very smoothly with our feet touching gently the ground. He said to me, "Just wait here, I have to take care of something, but feel free to walk around."

The place was very nice, with small squares and trees. The floor was of stone and had a very tranquil feeling. I started walking around, and about 20 meters away there was a monk seated and meditating. The monk was wearing an ochre tunic. I approached him very respectfully, and slowly. I bowed down a little, and then the monk nodded. That was the signal that I could sit down in front of him and could ask questions! Everything was very sublime and I could feel that place was from another realm. So finally some talking and asking questions! This is not an everyday experience, so it was good to be able to speak with someone. So I sat down and asked him questions. I got replies. I don't remember what I asked or what the answers were. There were quite a few questions and it felt that I was there sometime, but could not say how many minutes or hours. It felt like actually there was no time there. After the questions were over he nodded again and I understood that my time was up, and very respectfully I got up, bowed again and started walking in the squares again.

I was walking on this very nicely constructed stone floor, and on my right there was a wall about 3 meters tall, and I kept walking next to this wall. When the wall finished I turned right, and as soon as I turned there was a very tall person dressed in a tunic. This tunic was much more impressive and felt like the tunic of a very special person. His eyes were full of light, he had a dark skin, and very little hair. He was in his late forties. He was very tall. When I turned right I was looking straight to the horizon and I saw this man's chest, and literally moved my head up to see his eyes and I asked him, astonished: "Who are you?"

His reply was, "When the time comes you will know who I am. Follow me."

I just started following him. We started walking and the path of stone turned into a path of rocks. After sometime there were arches on the sides and people in the arches. We keep going, and a voice from a being that I could not see said to me: "It's boring here. Let's go, let's go somewhere else." I started slowing my walking pace, and the distance between me and the Master was increasing. The voice said again to me, "It's boring here. Let's go."

"No, I am happy here, if you want you go."

The being disappeared, and I started walking faster to be next to the Master.

We kept walking on the stones. Between the stones, there was a little water, and as we walked further there was more water and we stopped when the water was up to our knees. I was next to him, and looking at the horizon, I saw a big lake and two volcanoes in the back of the lake. I observed the beauty of the scenery and then without any notice, I started flying again. I could feel that on my left he was flying. And it was like he was guiding and taking care of me. I remember seeing my family's dog in my house while I was flying. He was a few hundred meters in front and down, and I heard his barking ahead. When I passed over, in the direction of my room, I heard the dog's barking coming from behind. It was a really interesting experience.

I went into my body and felt a jump when I entered it. From that moment on I was not worried about finding a path. I knew everything would be taken care of.

* * *

Years later, either 2006 or 2007, on my birthday, there were about 30 disciples at Guru's house. Guru asked, "Do you have any questions?" Everything was absolutely nice and perfect, I had no questions. Guru said again, "Does the birthday boy have any questions?" This story just came to my mind, and I told Guru about it, and said that the person was very tall. Guru said, "Yes many spiritual teachers are very tall in the inner worlds, but in the physical they are short." I knew this was my golden chance and I said to Guru, "Guru I feel it was you!"

And while I was asking Guru the question, he said, "Yes there are many spiritual figures that in the inner worlds are very tall but their physical was not tall at all."

So I asked again when Guru finished, "Guru was it you?"

"Of course it was me. It was me, I was taking care of you long before you came to me."

A few years earlier I had the chance to ask Guru the same question but the words did not come out of my mouth. It was in Bali on the Christmas Trip, I was about to leave in a few hours to go back home. I was in the meeting hall and Guru was there with about 15 disciples, and a brother disciple, Ashok, told Guru about an accident that he had long before he knew about Sri Chinmoy. Ashok gave all the credit to Guru that he was alive and felt that Guru was protecting him. Guru was about to stand from his chair to leave the meeting place, and said: "Yes long before you joined the Centre I was taking care of many of you." All the time that Ashok was telling this story I was thinking about this dream. As Guru was about to stand up, out of respect I stood up while Guru was talking with Ashok. Nobody else stood up, I was the only standing, and Guru just made the move to stand up but actually did not stand up. I was thinking about the dream and Guru looked straight into my eyes and said: "Purnahuti are you going to say something?" I could not talk. My mouth mumbled and I could not get a word out. Guru said while looking at me, "Yes I have been taking care of many of you even before you accepted the path."

From the moment I had the dream I felt that I did not have to worry about myself. Everything was being taken care of. When I saw Guru for the first time in London, I knew he was the Master in my dream. Outwardly I saw a poster in Hamburg, Germany. I went to three classes and then I heard from Satyaki that Guru was coming to England for a concert. I was so desperate to see a Guru. I was supposed to study in Germany, and Guru was going to give two concerts in England. I could not miss this opportunity, so I packed my suitcase and went to England and saw Guru at the Royal Albert Hall concert. It was fantastic to see Guru there and at the concert in Oxford.

I came back after a week, and went to two or three more classes. Then I applied, not really understanding what the path was and went back home to Guatemala. There I received a fax from Satyaki, saying that I was accepted and that for the Christmas Trip Guru was coming to Guatemala, to Lake Atitlan. Guru gave a concert at Lake Atitlan and the backdrop of the concert hall was the volcanoes of Lake Atitlan. Having the dream years earlier and then experiencing it was a very convincing experience.

PURNAKAMA
Winnipeg, Canada

I grew up Catholic. Being Catholic encompassed my life and shaped who I was. I went to Catholic school, attended church once, sometimes twice a week, played in a Catholic youth orchestra, attended a church youth group, and sang in the weekly folk music group at the Saturday night mass.

I even wanted to be a nun when I was 10. I remember our teacher came around to each of us individually as part of a class project and asked us what we wanted to be when we grew up. The answer came so easily; "A nun of course!" I told my teacher brightly. I think I surprised her a little with my quick and confident response.

I had a very good experience in the church. I made many good friends, I enjoyed learning about God and Jesus, and most especially I was moved by the beautiful devotional music that I was privileged to learn and perform. To this day I treasure all of the wonderful things that I learned growing up Catholic; a sense of devotion to God, the message of doing good to others, and compassion through the teachings of Jesus.

So how does a good Catholic girl headed for the convent end up becoming a student of an Indian spiritual Master and believing in reincarnation?

As I moved further into my teens, as most teenagers do, I began to question. I began to question things that I had never really thought about.

As with almost every church of every denomination and faith, our church had a missionary component to it whereby nuns and priests in the diocese would go to third world countries and minister to the poor. I had always just accepted that there were very poor people in the world, or people living in war torn countries, and that we needed to help. But I began to question why. Not why we needed to help, that was obvious; but why was I so lucky to be born in a peaceful country, with enough food, and clothing, and enough support needed to grow and thrive, while others had to suffer in horrific situations? This seemed so unfair and I could not justify it in my mind or heart. I did ask questions, but the nebulous answers that I received about the mysteries of God just could not satisfy me, and so I began a quest, seeking answers to my unanswered questions.

As I entered my twenties and went off to university, I was opened to a whole new world; a world far from my lovely but sheltered Catholic world. I met people of many different faiths, with many different worldviews and I felt a part of me opening. I began seeking answers to my questions, looking for a deeper inner knowledge. I wasn't sure where my search would lead me, but I felt that I would be guided along the way.

I began with books. I suddenly found myself drawn to new-age bookstores and was fascinated by the range of topics, ideas and ideologies that I found there. I could spend hours sitting in a comfy chair reading the back covers of books trying to decide which new treasure I would take home that day. What new bits of wisdom and knowledge would wend their way into my heart and mind?

During that period I read everything from the *Celestine Prophecy* to the *Upanishads*. Through all of the books that I read, there was a common theme that wove its way through my newly created knowledge tapestry, and that was the idea of reincarnation. It seemed to gently call me to listen.

Having been a firm believer in 'You get one shot at life, and then either heaven or hell for eternity', (or purgatory, which I never really understood anyway), this new idea that a part of us, our soul, lives on in another form, learning new lessons, and gaining more and deeper knowledge each time, began to slowly flower within me.

And with the flowering of each petal, these new ideas went from knowledge, to knowing; from the mental facts, to a deep feeling of ancient remembering.

There was no one 'aha' moment, but rather a gentle unfolding of my understanding over time until I could not remember a time when I did not believe in or understand reincarnation.

All of the questions that I had about the unfairness of life seemed to make sense now. I was once that person suffering in the streets of that broken country.

Because of this new understanding, my compassion poured out tenfold for those who were suffering in the world. I felt a oneness with all of humanity.

It was about this time that I met my spiritual teacher, Sri Chinmoy.

Sri Chinmoy taught me about oneness with humanity, and the power of meditation and inner silence to help heal ourselves and others on an inner level, which is where all healing begins, with the healing and liberation of the soul.

I still hurt at seeing the pain that is being felt in the world, but I am also buoyed by the wonderful and beautiful things that are happening in the world as humanity evolves and goes through this cycle of birth and death, moving from ignorance to knowledge.

And my pangs are assuaged in the knowledge that all souls in the end will ultimately reach the goal of liberation of the soul and God-realization.

And now, as I continue along my spiritual journey, I try to think of each new day as a new incarnation. If I have not achieved my spiritual goals today, then today must be forgotten, and tomorrow will appear again full of hope and promise.

> *Exhale the dust*
> *Of the past.*
> *Inhale the fragrance*
> *Of the future.*
> **– Sri Chinmoy**

SARAL
New York,
United States of America

In November 1970 I was a student at Stony Brook University on Long Island. Like many who have since come to Guru, I was extremely unhappy and unfulfilled. I had a longing for peace and happiness within myself, and for a better world, but had no real way to find this peace. I was really lost. In desperation I had been trying to find some glimpse of truth through artificial means (meaning drugs) but this was making my mental state even worse. I was in a very bad state.

However, I never gave up hope. One day I saw an

ad in the school daily newspaper for a class given by a student of Swami Satchidananda, which was to include breathing exercises, hatha yoga and meditation. The ad said to bring a dollar donation and a towel for the yoga exercises. I arrived at the class early, or so I thought. I was surprised to find that the class was already in progress. On entering the room I felt a vibration which was absolutely new and unfamiliar to me, but this unique vibration compelled me to enter. The man giving the class was reading from some spiritual writings and playing a recording of some spiritual music. Amazingly, the entire session, all the writings and music, seemed to have been orchestrated by God just for me! Everything that was read seemed to have been a message sent by Heaven. In the span of an hour of so, all the deepest spiritual questions I had ever had were answered. My despair and doubts suddenly vanished. I was assured that God indeed still loved His creation, and that we would all someday realise Him.

We chanted 'Aum' a few times. Though I had almost no previous experience with meditation, I heard the sound of Aum reverberating inside me, at different pitches and rhythms, after we had stopped chanting. When I opened my eyes I was crying, and the entire room seemed to have been elevated, and was glowing softly and beautifully. After all this had happened, I felt like a long-lost child that had come home.

The class had ended and still I had not used the towel. I had not been asked for the dollar donation. I said to the man who had given the class, "You have given me so much. At least let me give you a dollar."

He replied, "There is no donation, but if you would like there is something called a love offering."

Finally I began to wonder what was happening, as I asked, "Is this the Swami Satchidananda class?"

He replied, "No, this is the Sri Chinmoy meditation group."

With great joy I exclaimed, "I came to the wrong room!"

He replied, "No, you came to the right room."

Since that time I never looked back. Starting from the very next day, I started meditating daily, stopped eating meat, and stopped taking drugs. I began to learn more about Guru's path, and become a disciple less than two months later.

Guru had given me the chance to come to him consciously a few weeks earlier. I had seen a poster on the university campus with his Transcendental Picture (in those days it was permissible to use the Transcendental Picture for postering) with the aphorism:

> *When the power of love replaces the love of power,*
> *man will have a new name: God.*
>
> **– Sri Chinmoy**

I was deeply touched by the poster, but instead of attending the class on Guru's teachings, I kept trying to raise my consciousness by artificial means. So Guru had to reel me in like a divine fisherman!

The song that was played was 'The Golden Flute'. The message of this song perfectly describes my plight before Guru came into my life, and the miraculous Grace that saved me. This was my situation, beyond hope, or so it seemed.

A sea of Peace and Joy and Light
Beyond my reach I know.
In me the storm-tossed weeping night
Finds room to rage and flow.

I cry aloud, but all in vain;
I helpless, the earth unkind
What soul of might can share my pain?
Death-dart alone I find.

A raft am I on the sea of Time,
My oars are washed away.
How can I hope to reach the clime
Of God's eternal Day?

But hark! I hear Thy golden Flute,
Its notes bring the Summit down.
Now safe am I, O Absolute!
Gone death, gone night's stark frown!
– Sri Chinmoy

To my utter surprise and greatest joy, Guru's 'Golden Flute' brought a glimpse of the Summit down for me.

Ironically, many years later I had the chance to see Swami Satchidananda when Guru met and honoured him. I was very fortunate to be invited to that meeting as one of the singers. This was more than 30 years after I had tried to attend Satchidananda's class and had walked into the Sri Chinmoy meditation group at Stony Brook. As they say in India, "When the disciple is ready, the Guru appears." I am supremely fortunate that my Guru appeared on that occasion in November 1970. He has been with me ever since, and will be with me for all Eternity.

SARAMA
New York,
United States of America

By 1967, I was married for the second time and had two children in high school. My husband, a teacher of special education, was starting a small summer camp for 'special' children in Glen Wild, New York.

Inspired by a couple of old books by Yogi Ramacharaka, we took a healthful yoga vacation at Val-Morin in Canada. We returned as vegetarians and I started to teach yoga, moving easily into that new field after 25 years as a teacher of dance. We also integrated Hatha Yoga into our campers' daily schedule.

One summer day in Glen Wild I was visited by an old violist friend, Sol Montlack, whom I hadn't seen in several years. I recalled that the last time I had seen him, he had been with a spiritual group called Subud. A friend had told him of my new interest in yoga. He was no longer with Subud or any of the many other groups he had tried. He said, "I have found a Guru who is everything I have been looking for. His name is Chinmoy." He pronounced Chinmoy so that it sounded Chinese. The thought raced through my mind that I would meet his Guru and that he would be *my* Guru, which surprised me. I was not even sure what a Guru was.

I learned that my old friend Sol was now 'Dulal' meaning 'favourite son', the spiritual name given him by Sri Chinmoy. He also was president of the Aum Centre, as the Sri Chinmoy Centre was known in the early days.

At the end of summer camp, the conversation with

Dulal flashed through my mind and, with a feeling of great urgency, I phoned him and said, "I'd like to meet your Guru." Dulal mentioned that he had shown me Guru's picture at the camp. Although I had no recollection of that, I learned later that when you see a picture of the spiritual Master who is meant for you, the bond may be established then and there. I do believe it was!

I was living in Westchester at the time, but Thursday happened to be the one day of the week that I regularly went into Manhattan for a Spanish dance class. Luckily, it was also the day Guru held meditations for seekers in Manhattan. The following Thursday after my dance lesson I tucked away my castanets and Spanish shoes and, sweaty clothes and all, grabbed a cab and made it crosstown just in time for meditation with Guru.

I climbed four flights of stairs in an old brownstone building on East 84th Street to a small railroad flat apartment. This was the early home of the Aum Centre and its young Guru. Everyone sat in the living room, most of us on chairs, and a few on a sofa against the side wall. The room was filled with the delicious aroma of incense and a small shelf in one corner held a flickering electric candle. The Guru stood with folded hands in front of us. The silence was profound. I had already been meditating for over a year on my own, so I closed my eyes and turned inward to enjoy the peace that I felt in this room.

After a few minutes, my eyes flew open spontaneously to find Sri Chinmoy standing right in front of me with a small flower in his folded hands. He looked at me with a warm otherworldly smile and gently put the flower into my hands. As he placed his hands over mine, I felt a thrilling vibration flow through my whole being.

I watched him as he moved about the room offering a flower to each meditator. I had no idea that this was the beginning of a 45-year blessing for this former atheist!

Guru then sat cross-legged with folded hands and meditated with us some more. When the meditation was over and everyone had gone home, Dulal introduced me to Guru, who bowed humbly. In my naïveté, I asked Guru if I could have an interview with him. He very kindly offered to speak with me on the following Thursday after the meditation. Some time later I learned that I should not even have asked for an interview until I had been attending meditation for several months. But Guru was all kindness to this new ignoramus.

SHARANI
Rhode Island,
United States of America

I came to the path at the age of 25, after taking a weekend session of meditation classes held at Harvard University in 1985. In some respects, no one was more surprised than I to embark on an inner journey as a disciple of Guru. During my youth and early adulthood, I had a secular approach to life – even considering myself an atheist for a brief period of time.

I did seek a sense of greater meaning in life but looked mostly to politics to try to find fulfilment. I participated in numerous social change movements – everything from socialism to radical feminism to serving as a town meeting member in local town government. Social activism meant a lot to me and I played a leadership role with students and faculty during the nascent stages of women's studies at the school where I began college. Then I transferred to a school well-known for various progressive departments and majored in women's studies, which was already well-established in the curriculum. However, the more causes I volunteered for, the more I found myself discouraged that the liberal groups working for change (including me personally) seemed to mirror in a microcosm the very problems in society that we wished to see transformed.

After college, I worked as a typesetter at a weekly newspaper and enjoyed the job until the paper went out of business. This led me to move to Boston. By the time I moved into an apartment with a friend I knew from college, I had switched my main focus to education and career as a possible alternative to find deeper meaning in life. I was attending graduate school part-time to get a master's degree in library science and I was working full-time at a library at the prestigious Massachusetts Institute of Technology. I tried to play the part of the high-powered career woman and found my studies and job fairly challenging and interesting. Yet when I tuned in beneath the surface, I felt this ringing hollow inside as a raison d'être. I was also at a watershed in my personal relationships and did not feel inclined to marry and have children with my now long-distance boyfriend, who had moved to Connecticut to take a job as a union organizer.

It never occurred to me that there might be other places to look in my search for meaning. Spirituality had to land in my lap for me to consider it. That friend from college whom I moved in with had first exposed me to

Guru while we were in college. Whenever we travelled as a group of friends on some adventure to Cape Cod or environs, she always started her day by meditating on a photo of someone (the Transcendental Picture). I found it odd at the time, but we never even discussed spirituality because I had no interest in it. Nevertheless, looking back on it now, this was when I first learned of Guru.

Then she began attending Boston Sri Chinmoy Centre meetings while we lived together and eventually she encouraged me to attend a free meditation intensive being offered at Harvard on a Saturday and Sunday by a visiting lecturer who had come to town. I felt I had too much homework to do and did not plan on going. However, the night before the workshop I had a dream that I was meant to attend the workshop and that the person who was teaching it sat across from me and we had this long and meaningful telepathic conversation. We bonded without saying a word and I felt so appreciated, understood and supported by this person. Without words, we were discussing my background as an organist and how it felt to be a dedicated, accomplished musician. I was kind of fascinated by the dream when I awoke because I am not a musician and have never played the organ.

This dream convinced me to attend at least part of the workshop. To my astonishment, the person teaching the workshop was the exact same person who had appeared in my dream the night before. I often had premonitory dreams, so I took this as a sign that I was really meant to come to the weekend workshop. Despite this experience, I stayed for only a small portion of the day's events. Then, when I went back on Sunday, I missed much of what happened on that day but arrived in time for the introduction of meditation on the Transcendental Picture. I felt something quite powerful inside during that meditation which made me feel I should keep exploring more about this meditation group.

The weekend class at Harvard was in February 1985 and I started attending meetings without yet sending in my photo and application. Through my roommate, I knew details about the lifestyle and felt uncertain about vegetarianism, the whole notion of being on a spiritual path and leading a pure life. I kept coming back to the dream and the way I felt something special while meditating on the Transcendental Picture for the first time, so I agreed to join my roommate and attend a public Peace Concert by Sri Chinmoy offered in New York City during April Celebrations. I often travelled to New York already, so it seemed simple enough to go there for the concert.

My first time seeing Guru continued this theme for me of accidental spirituality. I found the whole atmosphere of the audience and the concert to be too unfamiliar and unusual for my taste but even as I resisted the experience, I realised that there was a part of me that was actually meditating and that I also felt something special and powerful. I prided myself on trying to be open-minded, so I felt that it was important that I not ignore that underneath the turmoil I felt at the concert, something special had also touched me inside.

After returning to Boston, I kept attending Sri Chinmoy Centre meetings, since my roommate belonged, and I mostly just kept focusing my life on school and work. Then the Centre leader, Begabati, announced one evening that Sri Chinmoy requested seekers to formally apply to become students if they wished to attend Centre meetings. I went out for pizza afterwards with another girl who had kept coming since the Harvard meditation workshop in February. We discussed whether or not to apply to become Sri Chinmoy's disciples, and her light-hearted comedian personality served as an antidote to my ultra-serious nature.

With a smile, she said she felt uncertain about joining but that the food was good, so why not give it a try? Begabati had a health food store in Boston and she would often serve delicious vegetarian food at the classes and meetings. The light-hearted approach of this girl from the same workshop made me laugh and I thought to myself that it wasn't so necessary to agonise about knowing if this was IT. Why not just try it out for six months and decide then how it felt to have a Guru?

Well, that six-month experiment turned into 24 years, and I remain profoundly grateful to Guru for showing me that spirituality existed as a source for life's purpose and meaning instead of just politics, job or family. I finished graduate school while a disciple and slowly unfolded into a true appreciation and yearning for God, Truth, Beauty and Guru – all inter-mingled as one and the same in my journey as a disciple of Sri Chinmoy.

SHIRINI
Vienna, Austria

My name is Shirini. I am 73 years old and have been retired for many years. I have been a student of Sri Chinmoy for 14 years. How it happened that I started a new life near the age of 60 and decided to follow a spiritual path, I will tell you now....

I was a bank employee, but when I retired I started looking for a new hobby. I wasn't sure what exactly I was looking for, but I knew that it had to be something fulfilling. The courses at the adult learning centre did not satisfy me, so I kept searching until I saw a poster that attracted me. All of a sudden, it became incredibly important to me to attend this lecture about 'Yoga & Meditation'. Even though I was raised Roman Catholic and felt close to Christ all my life, I went without any prejudice to this lecture. There, I flipped through a book by Sri Chinmoy and thought: "These are words just like from the Bible." I became curious to know more about it, so I attended the follow-up classes as well.

Above all, I was inspired by the music, although I myself am not a musical person. Spiritual music in particular deeply touches my soul. Through the music, I found an approach to Sri Chinmoy and decided after a while to become his student, to accept him as my meditation teacher, my Guru, and was also accepted by him.

The people around me were sceptical at first – one hears quite a bit about sects and so on – but I never doubted for even a second that Sri Chinmoy is a true

Master. It was clear to me. It was the perfect 'hobby' – something I had unknowingly been looking for all my life. Nevertheless it was initially hard to find my place in the Centre, because my mind had a lot of doubts. There were many young people in the Centre and I thought: I don't belong there, I am too old, I don't speak English, and New York, where the Master lived, also seemed quite scary... I was constantly afraid at first, but I tried to overcome my fears because I *felt* 'I belong here' even though my outer existence and my mind were vehemently opposed to it. I also realised that all these problems were my own and not anybody else's.

When the time finally came to fly to New York for the first time to see Sri Chinmoy, I arrived at the airport in New York and felt at home. This feeling I still have today, and all my fears were dissolved little by little.

My whole life I had a strong connection to Christ, and therefore it seemed to me in the beginning that it was a sort of betrayal to all of a sudden accept an Indian Guru. I prayed to Christ: "Please lead me into my Guru's heart." I felt Christ's approval and his guidance on my new path. Christ never disappeared from my life, and today I love Christ the same way as before. Intuitively I felt: Sri Chinmoy is for me the link and the path to God. When I read the Bible now, I feel that I am finding the same messages as in Sri Chinmoy's writings. The words and the ways of expression may be different, but the goal is the same.

Personally, I value this path because Sri Chinmoy's clear, simple and at the same time deep words help me tremendously to be able to live spirituality in today's world. Therefore I am most grateful and blessed to have met such a great living spiritual Master and to have been accepted by him as his student.

I had never meditated before, so it was not easy for me in the beginning. For a long time, I felt that I didn't know what meditation meant altogether, until I became aware, in the physical presence of my Guru, that I was standing in front of effulgent light. I finally realised what meditation is, and Sri Chinmoy inwardly taught me my personal way of meditation.

Every person following a spiritual path undergoes transformation. I changed a lot – to others' advantage! I used to be very impulsive, but with meditation I have become much calmer and more balanced. Quite often there is still an inner battle – it always goes on if you want to change! After all, it is not easy to give up old habits or behaviours, but you receive so much help from Above that your own big problems become smaller and smaller, and finally, insignificant. I have learnt to simply 'hand over' all my problems. Practising meditation on a regular basis gave me strength and tranquillity.

For me, this path is a journey towards myself. Of course, I still have imperfections. We are all trying to be better members of society. Now I am much more concerned to make sure I deal with others in a loving way. My faith has grown immensely and has become infinitely stronger, because I realised inwardly that we have a direct relationship to God if we have a Master.

The first question my son asked me when I chose this path was, "Do you become more tolerant as well?" My husband was quite sceptical at first, but he realised very soon that I was doing something that not only gave me joy but was also useful. He slowly changed. Now he accepts Sri Chinmoy and really likes him. Inwardly he is certainly on the path as well. All other family members actually showed a pretty positive reaction.

I am convinced that Sri Chinmoy has saved my life several times. I have had a heart condition for the past eight years. One day I had acute heart failure and was unconscious for two hours. That I woke up again and was able to live I owe to him, I am absolutely sure. Outwardly he did not know about it, but that was not necessary. I clearly felt that he had helped me. In my Master's love I felt secure.

'Impossible' – this word no longer exists in my vocabulary. My self-confidence has grown immensely; there is nothing that I would consider impossible even if you would think so looking at it from an outer perspective, since I am old and sick. It is mostly a matter of the mind. The mind is the first one to say, "No, you can't do this, you are too old, too weak," or whatever. But I have learnt not to listen to this doubting mind anymore. I push it aside, and that is not even as difficult as you would think.

For example: at the age of 60 I started practising sports intensively. Over a long period of time, I ran every day for one hour – among other reasons, because I realised how important it is to have a healthy body. Here on earth we need the body to live, and I think it is our duty, as much as possible, to keep the body in good shape. For me this includes a vegetarian diet. It is also more pleasant to have a healthy body.

Even today, at the age of 73, I fly to New York by myself, happily and fearlessly. Thirteen years ago this seemed impossible to me, and even the thought of it provoked endless fears. I even flew to New York when I was seriously ill, and had no fear because I inwardly felt strong guidance. This is something you learn on a spiritual path: how to conquer fear. Fear is the biggest problem. I have learnt that it is not the illness that you have to conquer, but the fear. I used to have a lot of fear, like everyone. We all have thousands of fears; sometimes we are afraid of the tiniest ant. With my faith and confidence in the Highest, I simply learned to go beyond fear.

One time when I was in the hospital again I had a very strong heart attack at 3:30 a.m. I intuitively felt that I was in critical condition. I didn't know what to do and I was terribly afraid. The doctor and the nurses came, gave me injections and did everything possible to help me. But suddenly I felt completely calm. Like a mere onlooker I was able to observe the activity that now seemed like a game to me. Sri Chinmoy took away my fear, and the story had a happy ending.

SHIVARAM
Toronto, Canada

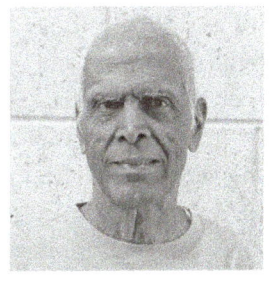

It was so far back, some details have faded from my memory. It was perhaps in May or June 1964. I was working in the Indian Consulate in New York, located on 64th Street near one of the Central Park entrances. My job in the Accounts Department was simple – typing accounts and preparing the salaries once a month. Not being a shy person, I used to go to other departments to meet friends and new recruits.

When I first met Mr. Ghose, he mentioned about Sri Aurobindo Ashram at Pondicherry, which is on the

East coast of South India. I come from the West coast. Although I was not a serious seeker at that time, I had more knowledge and interest than most Indians about the Indian spiritual and religious traditions, especially matters linked to the *Ramayana*, *Mahabharata* and *Srimad Bhagavatham*. These books in some condensed form I had read before I was 15 years old and knew many of the stories and teachings therein.

Although I was familiar with their names, I did not know much about Swami Vivekananda, Sri Ramakrishna or Sri Aurobindo. Coincidentally, when I first left home in 1954 to seek employment, I bought a book at the railway station entitled *Mahayogi – Sri Aurobindo*. This was my introduction to a modern-day yogi.

Mention of Sri Aurobindo's name made a connection between us, for there was no one else in the Consulate I had ever talked with about anything religious or spiritual. Mr. Ghose was quite a shy person. He showed me some of his writings and was interested in having them published in college or university newspapers. I had no acquaintance with anyone outside the Consulate to help with the publication. One of the aphoristic pieces he showed me was from the *Upanishads*, which I did not know at that time. It started with, "Meditation is the bow. Concentration is the arrow. The target is..."

I had a touch of the poet in me and although not very proficient in English, I could appreciate the older-style poems. I was impressed by the aphoristic lines. We used to talk mostly about spiritual things while taking a walk in Central Park during the lunch break. I knew about meditation only vaguely, having read the stories of many sages (*rishis*) who sat in meditation (*tapas*), it is said, for years, hundreds of years. Before leaving home during evening prayers in front of the altar, sometimes I used to sit with closed eyes imagining I was doing *tapas* like the *rishis*.

One day during lunchtime when we were walking together inside the office building, I asked Mr. Ghose, "What exactly is God?"

Immediately he responded, "Is it not pure consciousness?"

His answer without any hesitation stunned me. I stopped and taking a breath asked, "Really?"

I felt the simplicity of that profound response, which deeply touched me, although my understanding was on the surface. Until that time, I associated the word 'God' with the traditional forms of the Hindu gods. The word *Parabrahman* (Supreme beyond form), although familiar, was a very ambiguous concept for me. This incident brought a greater sense of reality to the concept of God.

Another day, at the suggestion of Mr. Ghose, we decided to sit and meditate. First we chose a spot in the basement where there was a table, a few chairs and a coin-operated coffee machine. Here there was too much disturbance from people coming in and out and casually also addressing us. Then we went upstairs to the main floor where there was a big ballroom with a high ceiling, which was used for meetings and receptions and which also had Indian newspapers and a library. Along the wall there were comfortable benches. We chose a quiet corner, sat and meditated. That was my first meditation with Mr. Ghose, who later became my spiritual preceptor or Guru.

In the weeks following we must have meditated two or three times more – sometimes sitting in silence in Central Park. In August 1964 I gave up the Consulate job and moved to Canada. But the contact between Mr. Ghose and myself remained: occasionally by phone, in person in New York, or via the *AUM* Magazine, which Mr. Ghose regularly mailed to me.

Seven years later, Mr. Ghose, whom I now addressed as Guru, came to Toronto to give two university lectures. He also conducted a meditation in my apartment at 3 Drexel Road. I was driving Guru to his hotel when he said to me, "Now I would like you to run our meditation centre in Toronto."

I seriously protested, pleading my ignorance and expressing my unwillingness to become any kind of leader.

Guru said, "You are most qualified... etc."

In a formal sense this is when I considered I became a disciple – on October 7th, 1970.

By that time I was very active as the Secretary in the Sri Ramakrishna Vivekananda group (Vedanta Society of Toronto) and had extensively read Sri Ramakrishna's life and teachings. God, God-realisation and the spiritual life were no longer vague concepts. I had more or less decided not to go and work for a corporation but to be self-employed.

SIPRA
Adelaide, Australia

I first heard my Guru's name on a beach off the east coast of Sri Lanka in 1973. I recall I giggled when I heard the name Sri Chinmoy. This was a most unusual response as I had been seriously exploring various Masters and their writings for a year or so previously. I heard the name, Sri Chinmoy, from an American boy from California who had come into contact with my Guru while visiting the London Sri Chinmoy Centre. He explained that this particular Master especially called to him musicians – Carlos Santana and Mahvishnu John McLaughlin were at that stage devotees of the Master.

During the previous decade I had led quite an exciting and varied life. This included living in Canada for two years, travelling around the USA, living in London for a year and exploring Europe, as well as living and working in several Australian capital cities. Immediately prior to finding myself in Sri Lanka, I had set off to sail around the world on a yacht with three other friends. As the boat was to be put into dry dock for the cyclone season I decided to leave the group and spend time exploring Indonesia, Malaysia and Thailand.

I was 30 years old.

In a Thai monastery I had my first experience of meditation. I spent two weeks in a very austere atmosphere and learned the Buddhist way of meditating. I felt after three or four days that this was something that I needed to master and incorporate into my life; however on leaving the monastic atmosphere I found it very difficult to sit quietly and bring the mind to rest.

I travelled on to Nepal and trekked the Himalayas before beginning my pilgrimage of Mother India. From Calcutta I travelled by train through Orissa state, where I purchased my first sari, and visited many famous temples and places of pilgrimage. My goal was to spend some time in the Sri Aurobindo Ashram which had been recommended by many fellow travelers.

During my two week stay at the Ashram, where my Master spent twenty years of his life, I experienced a most peaceful and powerful meditation at the 'playground'. I visited many other venues and activities that Guru would speak about in later years and found a sweet and sacred atmosphere around Sri Aurobindo's Samadhi.

It was one month after I left the Ashram that I heard of my Guru's name for the first time.

Early in 1974 I left Asia to return to Australia. During a brief stay in Singapore, enroute to my home town of Perth, Australia, I came across an album by John McLaughlin and Carlos Santana entitled *Love, Devotion and Surrender*. Sri Chinmoy was standing between the two musicians and inside printed copies of some of his poems, including *Love, Devotion and Surrender*, could be found. I copied this poem into my notebook and thought little more of it until I was visiting a friend from my university days in Perth a few weeks later.

When I mentioned I had been exploring Eastern philosophy and meditation she let me know that her brother had an Indian Guru. She could not remember the name but she said her brother was a musician. The "musicians' Guru," I guessed, so when I mentioned Sri Chinmoy's name she said that was the one. Her brother was delighted someone had heard of his

Guru. He and his wife had been corresponding with Sri Chinmoy for three years, but had never met him. They were thrilled that I had a poem of their Guru's in my notebook and asked me if I would like to have my photo taken and sent to their Guru for his blessings. I agreed, "Why not," I said, "I can always do with a blessing from a holy man!"

Little did I know that this was the process through which a seeker makes application to become the Guru's disciple!

Soon after, I left to work several thousand kilometers north of Perth, only to feel that my inner life was as dry and empty as some of the landscape around me. Luckily I had the address of my friend's brother, so I wrote and requested he and his wife send some spiritual books. I was particularly interested in reading in more depth about Sri Aurobindo. They posted me a small book written by the Mother from the Ashram and several of Sri Chinmoy's books.

I did not understand that I was looking for a Guru; however a phrase I had read quite often kept coming into my mind, "When the student is ready, the Master appears." Maybe Sri Chinmoy is my Guru, I pondered.

The letterhead on the cover letter my friends had sent me had a photo of Sri Chinmoy and an aphorism that read: "I shall not fail you if you can dare to think that I care for you." My mind wondered about this unusual statement. Maybe, I thought, this is my Guru, but I must challenge this unusual declaration. So inwardly I said to Sri Chinmoy, "Show me you care!"

In the next month or so I was shown both inwardly and outwardly beyond a shadow of a doubt that Guru was caring for me on many levels and guiding my life.

SUJANTRA
San Diego,
United States of America

When I was ten (1972), I was playing with one of my best friends, Peter, down the street from our house at a big parking lot that was behind a row of commercial buildings. The parking lot had a 40-foot-tall concrete wall on one end that we used to throw the ball at. I remember one day looking up at the wall and seeing a huge image of the Transcendental Picture of Sri Chinmoy. Of course at that time I had no idea what it was that had appeared before my mind's eye. It was only years later when I saw the Transcendental Picture that I remembered that incident from childhood.

When the student is ready...

I remember being on the plane flying from San Francisco to San Diego to begin my university life. I was 18 years old and reading a book by Ram Dass entitled *Journey of Awakening*. I was on the chapter where he talks about how, when the student is ready, the teacher will appear. I remember reading that and not believing it. I did not think that the world was that interconnected. I had been reading the books by Carlos Castaneda and wanted to have a living teacher who could initiate me into the mysteries of the spiritual path. I figured that I would need to go to the deserts of Mexico to find a teacher.

...the teacher appears.

I walked into the dormitory room at the university I was going to attend, and there on the desk of one of my roommates was the Transcendental Picture. I started reading the book on the desk: *Yoga and the Spiritual Life*, by Guru.

I then signed up for a free meditation workshop at the university (not knowing it was being sponsored by the local Sri Chinmoy Centre). Prior to that I had been to three or four other meditation/spiritual programmes that never felt quite right. The programme the Centre was offering was a three-part series, I think an hour each Tuesday afternoon. By the second class I knew I had found a meditation path that resonated with me.

I remember walking out of the room that second day and feeling the sensation of my spiritual heart being open. It was a feeling in the centre of my chest that was both new and familiar: new in that I had never experienced such a thrilling and mystical sense of self before, yet familiar in that it was somehow an extension of the innocent joy that I knew from childhood. I had a profound sense that this new level of awareness was exactly what I had been searching for all these years. I walked around the university campus for the next few days with my sense of self, the core of my identity, rooted in my spiritual heart, instead of inside my head, inside my mind.

I remember being concerned that Sri Chinmoy lived so far away. I had hoped to live in the same city as my Master. Soon that concern was put to rest as a deep experience during meditation on the Transcendental Picture showed me that time and space are no limit when it comes to spirituality.

SUMANGALI
York, England

Despite its intensity, nobody remembers being born. Everyone uses their first breath to cry. Raw sound, cold, movement, pain, exhaustion, separation from the source, are too much to bear at once. There is no strength of one's own to call upon, and nothing certain or familiar on which to depend. Abraham Lincoln, Queen Victoria, Albert Einstein; however mighty they became, each arrived naked and alone, and they cried.

My primal bewilderment stayed with me longer than theirs, and perhaps longer than most. The cry silenced, but was always there. Life was a fast road and the human vehicle seemed so fragile on it. I saw pain in others and felt it as my own. I grew no armour in my thoughts or senses.

I was a morbid child – my first dream in colour was of death. I lay awake in fear of everything, craving the release of sleep, but dreading my own dreams more than waking life.

"Empty your mind," said my mother, "think beautiful things or have no thought at all."

So I made my first tiny flame of peace inside. It lit my world a little in that strange perpetual night; spilled into the darkness so at odds with my safe and gentle circumstances.

I worried about life and the end of it, about the world and myself in it, about being small and about growing up. I worried that God had forgotten me on earth. That's perhaps the strangest thing. I was raised an atheist but always secretly believed in God: that there was more to life than earth, that death was not the end of it. Thank God for that.

It was a vague belief though, like a church bell ebbing and gathering on a faraway breeze, or a photograph faded almost to obscurity. There was nobody to sharpen the image for me. To admit to another that I believed in God, and needed to feel closer to Him, would have seemed weak. Delusional even. Like admitting that I couldn't handle myself.

But nobody knew anyway. Nobody knew where we are, or even how far the universe goes. Nobody knew for sure what happens after death. Nobody knew where God is. It didn't seem to bother anyone, and that bothered me most of all.

I blundered through my teens as well as anybody can, still haunted by fears I couldn't name, increasingly sensible to the vulnerability of a world I didn't understand. As I grew, so did the dark. I was trapped in it, a slave to my own fear. The faint memory of God was swallowed in it too, and I was terribly alone.

Luck has a habit of following me, especially when I need it most. A lady where I lived had taught herself to meditate, and gave me some books so I could do the same. She talked about God naturally, like a friend. The picture grew in clarity again, in brief glimmers.

Through each attempt, I collected strength beyond my own ability, harvesting happiness from an orchard much more bountiful than my own – an orchard of sweet fruits that went on forever, where it was always summer. I dared remember that my life is not a solo voyage, but is piloted by Someone bigger. At last I could breathe, as if for the first time.

One day I turned against fear, and it dissolved, like a serpent made of smoke. God had not forgotten me; I had been forgetting Him.

I was a fair-weather friend to God though. Meditation was difficult. Although I practised every day, my efforts lacked vigour, unless I was desperate or in trouble. I reached an agreement – a sort of dual tenancy – with the serpent of smoke. It was always there, but it would keep to its own quarters. God lived somewhere upstairs, and I was often too idle to climb there – perhaps calling a perfunctory hello from the second step each morning.

Courage came then from more comfortable sources: the sort you can buy in a bottle or a pill, that you can win through fickle friendships and small outer victories. It was a cheap happiness, and like most imitations, it fell apart after a few years. I chased it all over the world, but arrived back where I started, and that time with nothing.

I suppose it was a new birth, a blessing in the form of annihilation. There was an accident which nearly took my life. Soon after that I had no money, no job, no family near me, no friends, no home, barely any belongings, and not a shred of hope or self-esteem. I was helpless as an infant, and I cried a good deal.

I knew I had to learn to meditate properly. I had to find someone who knew how to do it and could show me. I dug out the books the lady had given me and tried a new exercise: 'The Spiritual Guide'. It started with imagination, as all visualisations do. I waited on a beach in my heart for someone to come and teach me, and eventually he did.

He was a beautiful Indian man, all softness and sweetness, but with the strength of a galaxy contained in a human form. He loved me, as if he had known me always. He listened and understood, without judgment or harshness. He encouraged me – sincerely, not indulgently, and not in words, but in silence, releasing wisdom and peace like fragrances. I had only to breathe them in.

Here was someone who knew. He knew God. Anything I did not understand, he already knew. He did not need to tell me; the fact that he knew was enough for me, to see it and feel it in him. He contained all opposites, extremes of all I had longed for: subtlety and certainty, beauty and practicality, and most of all, immaculate poise.

He did not answer me or solve anything directly, but having sat with him, I knew what to do in life, and felt the strength to carry it out. Over the span of a year I gained a good job, a car, and a beautiful home. I was safe and healthy, challenged by the world but no longer terrified by it.

I wanted to learn more, to meet with others who knew meditation's secrets. I wanted to practise with them, find new techniques, exchange experiences. The Sri Chinmoy Centre was the first and only place I found.

I thought it had been my own imagination. How could such a man exist on earth as the one who had sat with me every day that year? There he was, in photographs and videos. He had come to life. He had been there all along. I could read his words and sing his songs. Eventually I could sit in his outer presence, as I had done so many times in my heart.

I cannot account for my good fortune. I am small and full of imperfection, but divine love touches all creation like the fingers of the sun. Luckily we need not wait to deserve it.

In Sri Chinmoy I found answers to questions I had not yet formed. In his brief life of 76 years he gave to all equally and abundantly: not what was deserved but what was needed. In poetry, in songs, in physical demonstration and silent meditation, he made maps for us: maps of immediate inner lands, and others we will not reach for a very long time.

Sometimes I miss him. I had ten years to become attached to the luxury of his living presence. But I know he has really given me much more than I need, and much more than all the world can give me. When I miss him, I know I need only sit in my heart and he will come to me.

SUSHUMNA
London, England

Be affectionate and compassionate.
Remember only one thing:
Like you everybody
Is desperately fighting
Against Ignorance-Night
In the battlefield of life.

– Sri Chinmoy

The above aphorism is one of my very favourites, as I feel that it embodies much of the Master's teaching.

It gives me great joy to be writing this. Joy, Sri Chinmoy tells us, comes from the soul, and this kind of joy one can feel even at times of sorrow. Happiness, also a divine gift, usually comes from other parts of our being – the mind or the emotions – but when sadness comes, happiness leaves. Real joy from the soul can be all-pervading.

I first met Sri Chinmoy in 1971, through my daughter, who in turn met him through her Hatha Yoga teacher in New York. I went to New York on a trip and found myself, to my surprise – indeed, astonishment – amongst a small group of spiritual seekers in the house of Sri Chinmoy, my daughter beside me. She had given me little tips along the way. "We only speak if he speaks to us. Sometimes he asks for questions; then you can ask. He asks us to take our shoes off and leave them in the hall. This is not to preserve the carpet, but to leave the 'consciousness' of the street behind when we enter the room to pray and meditate. Also, to remove one's shoes is a mark of respect."

Having removed my shoes, I entered what was normally a large sitting room, tastefully decorated, mainly in pale blue and white. There were some rows of white folding chairs at one end and a small raised platform with cushions covered in a gold material at the other. This was where Sri Chinmoy was to sit, facing us.

I looked around and suddenly I saw him, at that point sitting on the floor talking to a young man. They seemed to be discussing the layout of a book. Instantly I felt a joy such as I had never known before, and I heard myself whisper, "He's real." I'll never forget that feeling, and can recall it at will to this day.

I will not go into further details about that particular day (it could be of limited interest to others), but I will mention one or two facts that I feel are spiritually important. The things that struck me instantly about Sri Chinmoy were total purity, humility and gentleness, light and power, in that order.

During that first visit I learned the basic approach to

meditation according to Sri Chinmoy's teaching, relaxing the body, breathing gently, concentrating on the heart, and – most difficult of all – quieting the mind.

I stayed in America about three weeks, and during that period I was fortunate to have several private conversations with the Master, during the course of which he asked me if I would like to start a Centre for his teaching and meditation when I returned to England. I said I would, and again that feeling of joy filled me. Then I felt panic. I thought: "I don't know anything. How can I?" As if knowing my thoughts, Sri Chinmoy said, "It is already set up – done for you. Just go forward." So I did!

About six months later we were to meet again, in England this time. Sri Chinmoy arrived with two or three students who had come with him, and I had gathered together a few potential students who had come to meditate weekly at my tiny house in London. I can't describe the joy and sweetness of that first meeting when we all joined together with our Teacher – the wisdom, the compassion and the delightful sweet sense of humour. One of the first things I noticed about Sri Chinmoy, the person, was that there was never any criticism, when at times it seemed to me it could have been quite justified. This was explained: all creation is God's unfinished works of art. We, too, until we have reached our highest, are unfinished works of art. An unfinished work of art can look very odd at times, and nothing like it will be when finished. That is not to say that we should accept limitation, but we should work tirelessly to hasten the divine manifestation on earth, through meditation and prayer and our daily work, whatever it might be.

Most of the new seekers in those early days were young. It was 'The Hippie Era' and some had been into that way of life. We saw then Sri Chinmoy's firmness and discipline. No drugs, no drink, no smoking. Young people in good health must get jobs and lead an orderly life. The Master said, in essence, "If you want to follow my path and have a higher, happier life, I can help you. Inwardly I can guide you, but you have to want it. You have to use your will-power, too."

Many of them did and it was astonishing to see those young people change, gently, over a period of time, giving up drugs, seemingly without aid, and entering a new life. I don't want to imply it was easy, 'a piece of cake' for those people. It wasn't. It was a struggle for most of them, but they knew that victory was certain if they had the will and aspiration.

Sri Chinmoy says his only fee is aspiration and sincerity – aspiration and a pure motive to reach the highest realisation. On this path there is never any charge for teaching. Of course common sense decrees that, if we need some material thing, it has to be paid for. When the group grew too big for my small house, a hall had to be rented. "Ask who would be willing to help," I was told. If there is unwillingness or resentment, that is not good. I have to say there was willingness and many gave a little. That is good, because everyone then feels the Centre belongs to them. It is a family – Chinmoy Family, as it was called in those early years.

The need to give selflessly without looking for reward of any kind is very much part of the Master's teaching, the message of which is embodied in something he once said to us many years ago:

My spiritual children,
If I have Love, if I have Compassion,
if I have Light,
If I have Power, if I have Peace,
if I have Delight,
Then it is all for you, all for you, all for you.
O my sweet children,
It is with you, for you and in you that I exist
here on earth.

— **Sri Chinmoy**

SUTUSHTI
New York,
United States of America

In the college newspaper at the University of Connecticut, there was a tiny ad: 'Sri Chinmoy Meditation Group: All sincere seekers invited'. In the aphorism that followed, I found a deep Truth. When an announcement appeared for an Introduction to Meditation, I went. The speaker talked about the spiritual heart, and I was enthralled. He requested anyone who wanted to see his Master to stay after the talk. I was astonished that out of twelve seekers, I was the only one who stayed. I thought it was an excellent, magnetic talk.

Sri Chinmoy was coming to Yale University to give a lecture on December 8th, 1971. The disciples gave me a ride and we entered the auditorium. The plush seats, the rug and curtains, all the details seem etched into my memory. At the front of the auditorium was a small man in Indian dress. I did not understand a word he said, except for the word 'Boatman'. The singers sang a song and it seemed bland and a little uninteresting, compared to the music I was used to. I was surprised when, after the program, people asked me if I had a good meditation. Since I thought I was the doer, I just said yes. After this lecture, I went with the disciples to the New Year's Meditation at Columbia University. But then school was out for Christmas vacation. My usual wordly life took over and I forgot about these events.

A year passed by and I suffered inwardly. It was agonizing, but I had no idea of the cause of my misery. I finally said to myself, "If the door of Truth be open, I will enter." I developed a firm, rock-hard determination from these experiences.

In January, 1973, my roommate told me there was a credit course being offered on the philosophy of Sri Chinmoy. I said, "Oh, I remember those boys, the ones with the short hair." I needed a credit, so I signed up for the course along with about twenty others. The teacher had a PhD from Harvard. When he asked us why we chose the class, I said I wanted to learn about Indian philosophy.

There were about four philosophical books by Guru which were required reading, including the *Commentary on the Bhagavad Gita* and *Eastern Light for the Western Mind*. I loved reading these, but the logic was not linear. We could not memorize facts as in other classes, and test questions were difficult to answer.

When it came time for the final exam, the professor announced that Sri Chinmoy would come to the last class and ask the students questions. We were frozen with fear.

How could we answer questions from the author himself? At the next class, the professor changed his mind. He said we would have a final term paper and Sri Chinmoy would visit, but we would ask him questions. We were so relieved! Guru came and answered questions and offered each of us a beautiful rose.

During the classes, the professor had announced a new group forming in Norwalk on Saturdays where Sri Chinmoy would come to meditate. I went to the second meeting in March, 1973.

In the basement of the home where the meetings were held, we sat in chairs waiting for the Master to arrive. He entered the upstairs first and we could hear him climbing the stairs to the second floor. As he descended, something happened inside my heart. I knew nothing of the soul, but it was like a delighted child doing an acrobatic flip. The Master came into the room and sat on his throne in silence. No one had taught me how to meditate, but I knew profoundly that he could help me in my life.

I also knew that I would keep coming each week. The deep silence in the room was a sanctuary, in which you could feel completely removed from the outer world. Peace was tangible and thrilling. We came to feel the thrill of anticipation of his entering the room. He spoke very few words, softly and lovingly, almost in a whisper. He seemed too ethereal for this earth. I could not understand his trance when his eyes went up, but when he spoke I saw a fiery, intense beauty in those eyes. I saw an otherwordly perfection in his countenance. His motions were from another realm: his hands, a soft, dark gold mystical experience as they touched the keyboard.

Previously, I did not know that anyone could uplift my inner life. I sat at the meetings transfixed. I would look at his strong shoulders and I knew I could depend upon him. I would look at his heart centre and I knew there was such love that he would take care of me inside his heart.

After the meeting, our consciousness was transformed. We would walk from the basement up to the living room. Often he would be there, relaxing, and he would watch us as we walked to the second floor. We were floating in bliss as we purchased books and candles. Infinity and Eternity had become real to us.

I came for about a month and was told that the requirements to be a disciple were aspiration and regularity. We were to write to Sri Chinmoy the reasons we wanted to be his student and include a photo. I could not think of why, so I just wrote, "I want to be a disciple of Sri Chinmoy because I want to follow his path and become a dedicated member of the Centre." This paper was returned to me with a handwritten note, "Blessings and Love, accepted with joy – Guru."

Shortly thereafter, someone announced the first US Joy Day at the Old Mill Farm in Westchester, NY. I was told that the Master had the capacity to be in his highest Consciousness even as he was doing other things. I was amazed. I could not wait to see this! And I could not believe that a day had been designated by him as a day of joy! That would mean that the air, the sky, the people all would be made of joy! As I got out of the car and my foot touched the ground, I could feel joy radiating from the pavement.

Across the field were booths. I searched eagerly and saw the Master standing there. I looked at his eyes to see if it was true that he was in a Universal Consciousness. He later played ping pong and we played Red Rover.

What a fantastic day flooded with joy!

The next year, we were told that Guru had started creating artwork. How could this great Yogi of the samadhi trance pick up a paintbrush and create a painting? How could the Supreme enter into an activity?

I went to the first Jharna-Kala exhibit in Hollis, Queens, in December, 1974. There he was, golden-hued, sitting at a table painting. I was profoundly moved by the focus, the Yogic concentration, that produced these radiating paintings.

At later galleries there were thousands of paintings displayed. There was always the smell of fresh paint as the disciples rushed to renovate the warehouse spaces. You would sense the magical presence of the Jharna-Kala world. And you would see the Master himself, as he continued his artwork, day and night. As Guru said at the Gallery in Grand Central Station, "The small finite realities will become vehicles for the Infinite Realities." For me, this was the start of the Manifestation of the Supreme.

TEJVAN
Oxford, England

My childhood was mostly happy, if uneventful. I often preferred my own company to that of other people, but I had little awareness of religion or spirituality.

After school, I studied Politics, Philosophy and Economics at Lady Margaret Hall, Oxford University. I enjoyed studying and visiting the different libraries and colleges within the beautiful city of Oxford. University life also gave an unprecedented amount of social opportunities, but, after two years, the attractions of parties and a hectic social life diminished. At the same time, the lure of earning a lot of money in the city also dissipated. It seemed all the attractions and comforts of the world were as nothing if you weren't inwardly happy. I began seeking something different, something deeper.

After a particularly difficult episode, I drifted into a spiritual bookshop – the kind of place I would never have considered a few months earlier. I picked up a few spiritual books and became fascinated with this whole new approach to life. It gave an insight into another world where there was a promise of real peace and delight. At the same time, things that used to give me joy now appeared quite lacklustre.

Out of habit, you can cling to certain things, especially when that is the most prevalent choice of society; but I found an inner change pushing my life in a certain direction. I just no longer felt any kind of enthusiasm for the passing pleasures of life.

At that time, quite a few books made a deep impression on me. One book was by an Englishman, Paul Brunton, who travelled through India meeting sages, fakirs and fortune tellers, before meeting his own Guru – the great Ramana Maharshi – at Arunachala in South India. It was in Arunachala that he experienced a particularly powerful meditation. Somehow his description of meditation touched a chord. That was it – I, too, wanted to experience that meditation.

I made a few tentative efforts, but I soon realised that meditation was much more difficult than I first hoped, especially when it feels that the world is running in the opposite direction. I did a little meditation, but most of my time was spent reading spiritual books, following a range of different paths and teachers. I thought the more wisdom I read, the better it would be. But, the variety of paths became a bit confusing, leaving a mild feeling of indigestion.

It was at this time that I became fascinated with the *I Ching* – tossing coins to answer questions about life. The *I Ching* is a great book of spiritual wisdom, but I wasn't using it in the right way. I become too dependent on the toss of coins for every decision. It was during this time in my last year at university that I became very ill and was forced to take a year off university.

The physical illness also co-incided with a period of mental depression. I was very confused, and despaired of ever seeing a way out of the void I had fallen into. I remember hopelessly crying to God, but there seemed no response. You could say it was a dark night of the soul. It certainly was a very painful period, though now it feels like a different lifetime.

But, as quickly as I got ill, I also got better, and within nine months had returned to Oxford with a much greater sense of mental balance and equanimity. It felt like being given a second chance. Away from the desperate clutches of depression, my outlook changed, with a sense of great newness and possibilities. Despite going through much difficulty, the aspiration for a spiritual life was, if anything, intensified.

It was back in Oxford, in 1999, that I saw posters for meditation classes offered by the Sri Chinmoy Centre. It wasn't the first time I had seen their posters. I remember seeing some posters for a Peace Concert given by

Sri Chinmoy a few years previously. I remember being struck by the picture of Sri Chinmoy and really wanting to go and see it. But, a friend somehow persuaded me that a few pints in a jazz club would be more fun, so it was not to be. But, that was three years ago; now the pull of meditation was far greater than anything else.

The meditations were encouraging, though I found that to still the mind seemed more difficult in practice than in theory. I think in the beginning I was impatient to experience some grand trance, which never materialised. But, the simple and clear philosophy of Sri Chinmoy appealed to me and I felt I was making real progress, even if it was not quite how I had anticipated. I also got a very good impression from those students of Sri Chinmoy giving the class. They seemed quite humble and cheerful. You could tell they were getting a lot from what they were practising. There was no sense of duty, just a cheerful offering; the classes were also given free, which I thought very kind. Despite how much they obviously valued their experiences of meditation, there was never any pressure or expectation that I would actually join. They were just very happy to talk of Sri Chinmoy's path and how much they had got from it.

During the meditation classes, some young musicians came up from another Sri Chinmoy Centre and played the most delightful, heavenly music. The music composed by Sri Chinmoy was something that I had never heard before; it was very uplifting.

The other thing that really struck me were the photos of Sri Chinmoy. The image of Sri Chinmoy in meditation was very arresting, other-worldly. I somehow felt that this was someone who really had attained the highest consciousness. It was quite exciting, as I had always expected I would have to travel to India to find a real Guru, but here was a real yogi living in the West. When I read Sri Chinmoy's writings, it appeared in great harmony with all the other spiritual teachings I had been reading, but with an added directness and simplicity. There was no mental speculation. Sri Chinmoy wrote with the authority and confidence of someone who had experienced exactly what he had written about. Yet, though there was great authority, you didn't feel any distance. Sri Chinmoy had this capacity to write and at the same time identify with the seeker. At times you felt you had written what Sri Chinmoy wrote. It may sound strange, but this is how it felt.

Sri Chinmoy only accepts students ready to give his path a certain commitment. He asks his disciples to refrain from drugs, alcohol, and adopt a vegetarian diet. On his path, if they are already single, he also asks people to remain single and not look for partners. After reading *Autobiography of a Yogi* by Paramahansa Yogananda and other books, this is what I expected from a spiritual Master. From one perspective, it was a challenge to adopt such a celibate lifestyle, but deep down, I knew this was what I wanted. I knew I wouldn't ever be happy following a more conventional lifestyle. I felt no attraction to getting the best-paying job and settling down to family life. I really wanted the full freedom to see what meditation could offer.

The funny thing is that, at the last moment before applying, I felt I wasn't good enough to have such a great spiritual Master. My meditation felt quite weak and I was far from perfect. I thought I ought to go away and meditate for a few years on my own so I would be worthy of such a great spiritual Master. Looking back, that all sounds absurd now. Though Sri Chinmoy does make certain requirements, he is also willing to accept students at all levels of development – so long as the sincere aspiration is there. In fact, Sri Chinmoy says the only fee he asks of a seeker is the fee of their sincere aspiration.

I applied to be his student and had a photograph taken. I was later told that Sri Chinmoy briefly meditated on my photo and accepted me as a student of his. When Sri Chinmoy meditates on a photo, he concentrates on the seeker's soul. If the soul is meant for his path then he will give the soul his blessing and accept the student. This is like a moment of initiation. To Sri Chinmoy, an outer initiation is unnecessary because the connection is made on an inner, spiritual level. Sri Chinmoy says that when he accepts a student, he makes a promise to the Supreme to lead that seeker to God – no matter how long and how many incarnations it may take. In everyday life, we are apt to make promises lightly, but even from the beginning I felt it was a very sacred moment. Occasionally, people would apply who were meant for another path. In that case, Sri Chinmoy would not accept them but inwardly guide them to another path or Master. When I heard I was accepted, 31st March 1999, I was really happy – probably relieved, as I feared I may not be good enough to be accepted.

Since I had been very ill just a year ago, I thought it best not to tell my parents the full implications of the new chapter in my life. I worried they might not understand what it meant to me, especially after being recently very ill. Anyway, they were already used to my vegetarianism and giving up alcohol, so outwardly, there wasn't a huge change. However, becoming a disciple and living a spiritual life does lead to profound changes in both your outer and inner life. You may not notice them yourself, because it is very much a gradual process – and never in a straight line. Over time, my parents could see I was unmistakably happy with the lifestyle I had chosen. My mother later went to see Sri Chinmoy in concert at the Royal Albert Hall in London. She also came to a meditation class I was giving, and was very surprised that I had learnt to sing. Apparently, as a child I was a very poor singer, but sometimes meditation can help develop unexpected capacities.

After being accepted as a disciple of Sri Chinmoy, I felt a lot of mental anxieties and worries dissipate. I used to struggle to make decisions, worrying about the best thing to do. I would get annoyed if I felt I had made the wrong decision, but the thing I learnt on Sri Chinmoy's path is that it is not so much what we do, but how we do it. If we can be inwardly happy, sincerely happy, then the circumstances we face are of less importance. But, more than anything, I felt like I had returned home. I had found the path that I had been looking for, consciously and unconsciously, for many years.

At certain times of meditation, unsought tears spontaneously came to my eyes. These were not the tears of sorrow, but the sweetest feeling of re-finding what was once lost, and gratitude for finally remembering the real purpose of life. It is a sweet moment; when you feel you have, at least temporarily, completely abandoned your ego and allowed your soul to come to the fore.

TIRTHA
Munich, Germany

It was in 1980 that my parents and we three children became disciples. From the perspective of a child it looked like this: I remember that my parents were going to different spiritual groups and they often took me along to these meetings. I was always very impressed by the atmosphere, the light-coloured clothing and the many nice people. Nevertheless, I sometimes started crying without any apparent reason. Something didn't quite seem right, I guess....

We became vegetarians and went once a week to one of the small and, at the time, few health food stores in our town. One day, my father was magnetically drawn to a book entitled *Meditation* that was displayed in the window of a bookstore. My parents were so thrilled by the simplicity and truth of this book that they mailed the postcard (inserted in the book) to the indicated address. We were informed that there was a couple with a child in Augsburg whom we could contact. This was the beginning of countless meetings, sometimes in Augsburg, sometimes in Munich. I was 7 years old at the time. I will never forget counting on my fingers how many times I had been to Augsburg already. My heart was jumping with joy every time we met. And I loved this family: Projjwal, Karali and Aruna. Most of the time I was playing with Aruna while the others meditated or were absorbed in obviously deep conversations.

But when Projjwal and Karali came to our place (and we children really should have been in bed by then), I listened to the conversations, sitting on the bottom of the stairs. I had no idea what they were talking about, but I loved it. I loved the people, I loved the vibrations, I loved the conversations, I simply loved everything... and I was always filled with deepest joy.

Some time later, our family picture was sent to New York, and soon after my father travelled there for the first time. He brought back my first 'real' sari. (Before that, we were only wearing curtain fabric!) I will never forget the indescribable joy – almost delight – I experienced!

A few months later, our Master visited Switzerland. That was the first time I saw Guru. He walked by me and smiled. I was a little surprised because his skin colour was unfamiliar, but his smile immediately won me over. Then Guru gave prasad to the children: a plastic heart. This heart is still my little treasure....

When I stood right in front of Guru, he brushed my hair to the side and looked at my name tag. He asked me all kinds of things. I did not understand a word, but Projjwal, who stood behind Guru, answered Guru's questions. I did not want to ever leave Guru's presence.

I had a happy childhood, and this happiness continuously grew thanks to the incredible grace that allowed me to come to Guru in my childhood years.

At that time, Guru showered us children with outer attention and gifts. The teenage years were not always easy, but I knew: "Guru comes first in my life – always." And this truth protected me during all my school years – and still does today!

In my almost 30 years as a disciple I have had so many inner and outer, challenging and happy experiences. My life is rich, inwardly rich. And I am infinitely, infinitely grateful to Guru that he brought me to him.

UPASEVANA & MAHANIDHI
Milan, Italy

In 2001, we joined the Sri Chinmoy Centre. It was April, but we had actually been accepted in March, while we were in India trying to find our true Master.

Everything started in 2000. We were searching for something different but we didn't know exactly what. We thought about moving to New Zealand, but when we looked into it, we found out that moving there required some skills that we didn't actually have.

Next we tried Spain, taking a holiday there to get to know the country better. When we went there, we knew it was not the right place for us, so we came back home.

Mahanidhi had secretly been thinking about starting meditation. For me, beginning to meditate was like a 'brick falling on my head'. From morning to night, nothing around me had any importance.

Something had happened inside of us, but we didn't know what we should do.

At that time I worked near a spiritual/esoteric bookshop, and every day I brought home two or three books. We spent hours and hours greedily reading them. In the meantime we were going to free meditation sessions in the same bookshop. It was nice but quite static, boring. It didn't take us anywhere.

Our dissatisfaction was growing. We wanted a real Master, a living top-class Master. I used to cry every day because I was not born in the era of the Buddha, a real Master. Instead I was living in a period that was empty of living great Masters. Our life was bitter and it seemed hard to keep going.

We decided to move and change our life. We tried to find a spiritual community under the inner guidance of an ancient Master and work for our spiritual improvement. We were ready to sell our home and give everything we had to such a community.

Every weekend we went here and there, but no spiritual community really touched our hearts. We visited all the most inspiring spiritual places in Italy, from north to south.

We were very tired and discouraged, but finally felt that our only possibilities were Auroville in India and a nice community in Scotland. We chose India because we felt some hope that we could find a living Master there. If we found a Master, we would remain there at his feet and serve him all our life. If this was impossible, we could decide to remain in Auroville, as Sri Aurobindo had been such a great Master.

In the meantime, we found a free meditation class by a student of Sri Chinmoy. The teacher in charge spoke about Guru, but we didn't understand well who he really was. We thought he was a simple yogi. Plus, he was living in New York – so far away and such an unspiritual place!

So we didn't give much importance to that class; India was in our minds, as our real Master was surely there!

We had given our photographs to be Sri Chinmoy's disciples, but in our hearts we were thinking we would definitely move to India.

The teacher told us that Sri Chinmoy would probably be in Pondicherry during that period. His home, at the Sri Aurobindo Ashram, was very close to Auroville. We thought it could be nice to meet him there. I left my job and Mahanidhi took two months' holiday.

In Auroville we found many nice seekers, but no one who could advise us about a 'real Master'.

We decided to go to the Sri Aurobindo Ashram. Sri Chinmoy would surely be there.

When we asked the man who checked our shoes in the garden of the Ashram about Sri Chinmoy, he was very happy to know that Sri Chinmoy was coming.

He said: "I am a friend of Sri Chinmoy," and insisted on sending us to the office, where a man would could give us the address of Sri Chinmoy's brother. Sri Chinmoy could be at his brother's home.

We didn't want to disturb anyone but this man insisted. So Mahanidhi stayed in the garden, and I entered the Ashram office and asked for the person in charge. I found him and told him that Sri Chinmoy was coming. He was happy and wrote down the telephone number of Mantu, Sri Chinmoy's brother.

I didn't want to telephone and disturb him, but he insisted and insisted many times. He also explained how to reach Mantu's house. So I thanked him and left.

When we reached Auroville, we didn't call Guru's home for two days. After that we decided to ask if Sri Chinmoy was there or not. Mahanidhi called. Mantu answered.

"Hello. I took a Sri Chinmoy meditation class in Italy. I know that Sri Chinmoy might be there. Can we come there?"

"Come, Come!"

"But... is Sri Chinmoy there?"

"Come, Come!"

Mantu would not tell us that Guru was not there; he wanted just to receive us. "But when?"

"Whenever you want!"

We waited two more days before deciding to go. Two other Italian seekers we came to know in Auroville wanted to join us, as well as the boy who connects Italy to Auroville. He was very enthusiastic.

He told us: "Sri Chinmoy? Oh, he is an Avatar! Such good fortune to meet him!"

'Chinmoy' was written clearly on the wall next to the entrance door. Mahanidhi looked inside. From the door he could see Mantu seated at the end of the hallway. Mantu looked at him and beckoned to him to come in.

We went in and met him. He was very happy and radiant. He started to speak about Guru, showing us pictures everywhere and talking rapidly in good English. His enthusiasm was like a little child speaking about his great father. He was Guru's best admirer. He was very happy to speak about Guru with a pride that never diminished. He told us that Guru was not there because he was actually with President Gorbachev. We listened to many things about Guru's past and present, but our English was not very good, so we did not understand everything.

A kind woman served us with food and drinks. After showing us all the rooms, Mantu asked us to meditate in the meditation room on the first floor, but we were ashamed to disturb such a sacred place. He insisted and insisted, so we finally agreed.

We meditated in a small nice room. There were images of Sri Aurobindo and the Mother on the shrine, which was full of flowers. We received prasad, and then we thanked Mantu and gratefully left. Mantu and the woman who served us were incredibly kind.

Still we couldn't clearly understand who Guru really was. We didn't realise that opportunity was knocking at our door in our city at that very moment.

We decided to find our Indian living Master outside Auroville. For the last two weeks of our trip, we visited several ashrams, but nothing grew in our hearts. Plus, we were quite frustrated because the time for returning home was fast approaching, and we had not found our Master!

We had been accepted on Guru's path two weeks earlier, but we did not know while we were in India.

On the last day of our journey, I was very sad because we had to go back to Italy without a Master. Mahanidhi tried to console me. That day, we had a final darshan in the last ashram.

Then, something strange happened: flowing inside me, I felt quite a strong desire to return to Italy. The day of our departure happening to be April 13th, but we didn't yet know anything about this special day, when Guru came to the West from India.

Just as we set our luggage on the floor of our home in Milan, the telephone rang. We were informed that our first real meeting as Guru's disciples would be that very evening.

VAJRA
New York,
United States of America

At an early age, I can remember saying something unpleasant about someone whom I call today My Dearest Lord Supreme but back then I knew Him only as God. I can remember standing in my crib shouting altercations directed to God and the next moment on my back crying with my mother sitting on a chair in front of me in tears asking God to forgive me for I did not know what I was saying. This was my first experience with anything spiritual that I can remember. I am now in my late sixties and realize I must not have been more than 2 or 3 when I heard the words come out of my mouth, "God I can beat you up whenever I please," words that today still shock me to my core at my own brazen disrespect whenever I think of it.

Fortunately, as the years progressed, my so-called brazen disrespect turned into a real love for God. At 8, 9 years of age to my early teens, such thoughts as "God, should I lose my mind or go insane, do not allow me to forget you," were constant prayers for me during the ensuing years. I still remember scenes of exalting God before my friends at school. My parish minister finally had to admit out of sheer exasperation from all my ceaseless questions on life and death, said, "I too am a seeker and do not have the answers to your questions." At 18 something happened. I lost my cry for God. I lived an ordinary life, but when it came to spirituality, it was a barren desert. It continued that way until I became age

28. I came home one day and happened to turn on the TV. What I saw was a story about a farmer who during the rainy season was very successful with his crops. He and his family had amassed a small fortune and were doing quite well. The next year produced less rain, and the following year, no rain at all. This condition continued for a number of years and all financial, economical and other problems became quite serious. In desperation, the farmer looking up, threw up his hands and fell to his knees, saying, "Oh Lord, have I been so arrogant during those years of plenty that I have forgotten to thank you? Now that I have come to such bad times, will you not forgive my family and I for our lack of humility and our failure to remember you with thanks in our hearts?"

Like a clap of thunder, I had become the farmer. The inner yearning to know God had suddenly returned to my heart. From that moment on, I was like a man possessed. I searched and read whatever I thought could give me answers to knowing God face to face. Amazingly, the more intense the search the more people and circumstances would appear to satisfy my God queries. One day my father left me at home at 6 a.m. seated perfectly still only to return from work 6 p.m. to find me seated in the same unmoved position. I was practicing a newfound word, MEDITATION, which I read from a Zen book. My father must have thought me to be a mad man. Perhaps he was right. A friend of mine, for no known reason, came up to me and presented me with a book and said, "I think you will be interested in this." It was a copy of *Autobiography of a Yogi* by Paramahansa Yogananda. After reading that book, my intensity doubled. A day after I finished the book, my friend again returns and gives me another book, *The Bhagavad Gita*. I finish this book and I am now filled with ecstasy.

Simultaneously, I am attending NYU University struggling to finish my bachelors in civil engineering when I see a poster, Sri Chinmoy lecturing on the *Bhagavad Gita*. I attend the lecture and for the first time I see my Guru. September 1970, Guru appears as a thin, slim athlete who speaks with a high-pitched voice and a heavy Indian accent. The lecture is over and I am not impressed. In fact, if I were to be told that this man is my Guru, I would have said, "NO WAY NO WAY NO WAY." I left the lecture hall not knowing that it would be 7 months before I would see Guru again. In the meantime, I became a follower of Yogananda's Self-Realization Fellowship. I ordered pictures of the six Gurus for that Order and subscribed to their correspondence course and proceeded to study it religiously. During that period, I became a vegetarian and something told me to shave my head. Though I was diligently practicing the lessons, I was beginning to feel a growing impatience with the speed of my inner world experiences and an increased dissatisfaction with the world's global picture.

I came home one day disgusted, dissatisfied and depressed and I could only think of one thing: the dream I had the night before. I stood at the edge of an active volcano ready to dive in. Looking down, I could see a red river of molten lava. I dived in when my descent suddenly stopped and I began to ascend in a seated lotus posture with folded hands. Before awakening from the dream, I saw the figure of someone standing in a cave way concentrating very powerfully on me. I sat down on my bed in a lotus position with tears in my eyes, determined to have a serious inner conversation with all six Gurus over the state of my suicidal condition. I addressed each Guru expressing the desire to exit on life if I did not get some satisfactory experience in answer to my God quest. I have never been one to ever think of giving up on life at the slightest life challenge. I am one who faces the problem and perseveres till some satisfactory achievement occurs. But this was an adamantine will, which refused any other alternative save death itself, if God did not come into the picture of my life. I turned to the last Guru whose picture frame hung with the rest on my wall and finished pouring out my heart when all of a sudden, I felt something heavy hit me in the center of my chest. A wave of peace flooded me from head to foot and a voice from within said, "In a few days time, something very nice is going to happen to you." I dried my tears and thought no more about it. Two days later, I am in the City College Library and I see a poster, 'Sri Chinmoy Lecture and Meditation to be given at Columbia University'. From all the spiritual books I have read, I became convinced that all men are brothers. I felt that if I am to have a Master and for me to recognize him, he must say: all men are brothers.

I enter the classroom where the meditation is to be given. I sit in the last row and first column of seats. My consciousness is out of this world. I don't hear anything Guru is saying for the entire lecture. My eyes are closed and I am enjoying the bliss of it all when I hear a voice tell me to open my eyes. My consciousness descends to normal for a moment just in time for me to hear the final words to Guru's lecture: "all men are brothers." I am inebriated by a consciousness I have never felt or known before that prevents me from reacting to the words I looked forward to hearing. I am again lost in trance when I hear another voice say: open your eyes, fold your hands, and bow. I open my eyes and Guru is standing no more than 2 feet from me. I fold my hands and bow and proceed to go back into trance. Guru then comes behind my seat and proceeds to place his right hand on my right shoulder and his left hand on my left shoulder. Guru sends one of the disciples to speak with me and two weeks later, I am invited to meditate at Guru's house on Thursday evening.

I arrived at Guru's house and found it packed with disciples. It is too crowded to enter the living room so I remain on the veranda with others like Sanatan and Chidananda whom I see for the first time. Guru finishes the meditation and from the mirror facing me, I can see Guru leaning forward to see who is on the veranda. He steps from his throne and comes straight towards me and begins to meditate on me. He finishes the meditation and tells me that I can come with him anywhere he goes. A year and half later, Guru says at the Norwalk Connecticut Centre that he is limitedly pleased with these two disciples and calls up the now Rupantar and myself to get our spiritual names together. A week later, Sanatan takes a pin with the picture of the double *vajra* on it and centers a Transcendental Picture of Guru on it. Guru calls me up to bless me with it and says I am a true disciple and if I had 13 more like you, my mission would be made. That night I left the Centre meeting feeling like I had a minor awakening; the God I so vaguely new as a child, the God I was rapidly growing to know as a disciple and the God I would someday realize as an advanced seeker was none other than my eternal Guru. This was something that he would later confirm with me on two separate occasions.

The first he said, "Vajra, for you, I am your Supreme." The second he said, "Vajra, when you realize me, you will realize the Absolute Supreme."

VENU
San Francisco,
United States of America

I was born in Illinois, but I don't remember much about it, because before I was five years old, my parents moved to Los Gatos, California, about 60 miles south of San Francisco. That's where I grew up and went to school all the way through high school.

I was a horrible student. I wasn't interested in school at all. But at the beginning of my sophomore year of high school, something happened that changed everything – I got into a bad motorcycle accident.

I was in the hospital for a whole month, and I had to be tutored so I wouldn't fall behind in my classes. So even though the accident was unfortunate, it changed the rest of high school for me, because I learned to make schoolwork as easy as possible after that.

The only problem was, I couldn't wrestle anymore. I had wrestled in junior high school and was pretty good at it, so I kept going. But once I got hurt in the motorcycle accident, I had to find another outlet for my energy. I had tons of energy. But when you're young you don't think of it like that – all I knew was that I loved sports.

With wrestling off the list, my favorite sport definitely became surfing. I wasn't that good at it, but I enjoyed it,

I did it a lot, and it was pretty much how I got through high school from my sophomore year on. I feel that for me, for some reason, surfing was just meant to happen.

* * *

I always felt like I should go to college, but because I was never really into the academic side of things, I knew that the only way I could go would be to take the classes I wanted to. So I took fencing, weightlifting, gymnastics, and physical fitness. That's all – those were the only things I could stand doing.

I was still surfing quite a bit during the week, too. Plus, I'd also started running. Around this time I had decided that I wanted to get really, really healthy, and I worked very hard at it.

On top of that, I also had a little stand at the San Jose flea market, where I worked on the weekends selling tools. So I was a pretty busy guy.

After I'd been in college for maybe a few months, I decided I just wanted to surf, so I moved to Aptos, California (which is very close to Santa Cruz) with a couple of my friends. To be honest, though, they took school more seriously than I did. Even though I officially attended college there, I never actually went to class – I just spent my time surfing.

Surfing... and meditating. That was something I'd started around December of 1972, when my mother gave me a little book on Hatha Yoga. It was the simplest little book, with only a single paragraph about meditation, but something about it struck me, and I tried meditating on my own. I didn't know anything about meditation, and I didn't know anyone else who did it. But after only two or three days of trying it, I felt like I'd really found something.

"They only do this kind of thing in India," I thought at the time. That was about all I knew about meditation and yoga at that point, so I started buying books: Paramahansa Yogananda, other books about yoga, meditation, spirituality... I soaked it all up.

Right off the bat, a strange thing happened. After I started reading those books, I immediately became a vegetarian. Just like that! Vegetarianism hadn't been in that first little Hatha Yoga book from my mother, but it must have been in the others, because just like that, I was inspired to stop eating meat.

The odd thing was, it felt like I was giving up nothing at all. And I ate a lot of meat then! It wasn't that I didn't like meat. But for some reason, it was very easy to give it up immediately and become a vegetarian. I'm sure my parents were worried.

* * *

I was also very much into music at the time. At a certain point I saw Mahavishnu's (John McLaughlin's) album *My Goal's Beyond*, which had some poems of Guru's in it and Guru's Transcendental Picture. John McLaughlin himself was shown holding his guitar in a very soulful consciousness.

So that was when I heard about Guru for the first time. There was no explanation on the album, but you could look at it and figure out that this person, John McLaughlin, was a follower.

At the time I was receiving meditation instruction from the Yogananda group in the mail about once a month. But something about those classes seemed a little distant to me. And here's the funny thing about that –

I did not know there was actually a Yogananda place a half mile from my house! I lived up in the hills above Los Gatos, and nearby there was this big sign that said 'SRF'. All you saw was the sign and a little road that went to nowhere, because it was private property. I didn't know what SRF stood for, so I never even knew it was a Yogananda place. Can you believe that? It means I was not meant to be a disciple of Yogananda.

So there I was meditating, but you have to know that there were two sides of me. One had so much energy, and the other was trying to meditate. It was a rough combination! That all started around December of 1972, and things went on like that for about a year or so.

Then around January of 1974, I found out about some classes being given by disciples of Sri Chinmoy. I must have seen a poster in Santa Cruz. I knew John McLaughlin was a disciple of Guru, and I'd been meditating, so I went to the first class. Afterwards the disciples asked me if I had any questions, and I said no. They must have really wondered about that! But I really just didn't have questions.

I went to the class again the next week and probably the week after that, and then I missed a week. And I really felt it when I missed that week. So I made sure I didn't miss any more!

By then I had stopped going to college classes. I just wasn't interested, so I let it go. I was back in Los Gatos living with my parents, I think – surfing, meditating, and spending a lot of time in my room by myself. My parents were probably concerned about me because all of a sudden I had become a deep thinker!

After the classes, one of the disciples drove me up to San Francisco and tried to make it so I could go into the

Centre there. He must have assumed I would become a disciple, but I could feel that a lot of people resented how I was coming to the Centre when I wasn't one. Fortunately, that was about to change.

* * *

Interestingly enough, just a few months after I went to those meditation classes, Guru himself came to Stanford on April 18th, 1974 to give a talk! (This is the date I remember, although one of the books in our Centre library says it was April 19th.) I went, and afterwards I saw Guru walk out of the room down the middle of the main aisle. I looked at him and thought to myself, "Here is a real spiritual person." I could just tell – after reading so much about spirituality and meditation, here was the first spiritual person I'd ever really seen.

Guru was meditating while he was walking out, and I could feel something so special. I thought, "You never see something like this. When in our lives do we see a truly spiritual person?" Guru meditating and walking is a pretty spiritual thing!

I did not become a disciple then, but I do remember asking about it. They might have announced after the talk that those who wanted to become disciples could come; I'm not sure, because I wasn't quite ready. Once I'd seen Guru in person, though, it didn't take very long. Less than three weeks later, I asked to become a disciple.

That was in May of 1974. I drove up to the San Francisco Centre once a week in the beginning, because I had to work on Saturdays and Sundays.

* * *

My very first Celebrations came in August of 1974.

Someone had bought an old used bus, and the disciples were going to drive it to New York. This was the famous bus trip of August 1974, and I went with them. I was very quiet and nervous and meditating a lot, and it was all really quite something.

I'd never been with a disciple for more than two hours at a time, and here I was going to be with them for three weeks straight. Trust me, I was scared! And I was on a real finicky diet at the time, not eating any sugar, being very careful with salt, so that made it even more interesting.

There were four or five guys who were the designated drivers, and it took us eight days to make it across the country, if I remember right. Things were different back then – we had boys and girls on the bus together. But we didn't sleep on it. We would drive during the day and stay overnight someplace… I can't remember exactly where, maybe in some kind of park or something like that. People were reciting poems and trying to do spiritual things on the bus, and I'm telling you, people did a good job. It would never happen like that again.

We got to New York, and Guru himself met us outside of Annam Brahma. People were crying, so of course I had to join them and cry, too. (Okay, I would have cried anyway.) We all got in a line and Guru gave each one of us a rose. I actually used my brain properly for once in my life! I kept it, and I still have that rose today.

PART II

EXPERIENCES WITH SRI CHINMOY

CHAPTER 2

IN THE MASTER'S PRESENCE

Once you have established
A solid inner link
With your spiritual Master,
Yesterday's Master, today's Master
And tomorrow's Master
Will all become one in your life.

– ***Sri Chinmoy***

SUSHUMNA
London, England

I would like to record a few little stories about life in England with Sri Chinmoy in the very early days. Almost everyone could see something special about the Master.

On one occasion Guru took a little group of us to an Indian restaurant in West London. It was a lovely meal and the owners spoke Bengali, Sri Chinmoy's own language, so everyone was very happy. I went back several days later to return a plate that we had borrowed for some reason. They told me how very beautifully Sri Chinmoy spoke Bengali – it was a joy to listen to.

About a year later, a couple who had been in our party went back there for a meal and the proprietor said he still had the tip Sri Chinmoy had given him in his top pocket. He considered it more than a tip – a blessing.

* * *

Another little story comes to mind, one of my favourites, which I often tell new people who come to the group I look after these days.

Sri Chinmoy says everything has a soul. During these early visits to England, I often did the cooking. On this occasion I had bought a particularly fine-looking cauliflower which I left on the kitchen table thinking I would make a cauliflower-cheese dish for lunch. Then our Guru announced that he would take us all out to lunch. We would then drive to another town – I don't remember which, but Guru was going to give a talk there.

We had our lunch and were driving along when Sri Chinmoy said suddenly, "Oh, my cauliflower! Oh, poor cauliflower is so sad I am not going to eat it."

I was in the back seat of the car with a friend. We looked at each other in astonishment. Then I called: "Everything has a soul; everything is evolving." And we sat in silent wonder.

When I got home, I found myself apologising to the cauliflower as I put it in the refrigerator. Next day it would be eaten by me and whoever happened to be around – so disappointing!

I smiled. So many people would still think we were all crazy.

* * *

One of my most joyful memories of those early days was when Guru came to the launderette with me. That such a great being, a spiritual Master, should take part in such a commonplace event has brought home to me always the amazing quality of humility.

I lived in a very little cottage or terraced house (two up and two down!) in those days. Not everyone had a washing machine as they do now, and I was no exception in having to go to the launderette.

As I prepared to set off there, Sri Chinmoy said he would like to go to the local shops. He walked with me to the little parade, which included a shop run by an elderly Indian lady where there were saris, shawls and lengths of material. There was a sweet shop, I remember, and the launderette. I left my Guru approaching the sari shop and I went into the launderette. After a while Guru appeared, all smiles. He had bought surprise gifts for everyone to give that evening. Guru just loves to give gifts. He had also bought me a bar of chocolate.

I was so surprised and delighted, I hardly knew what to do! Guru sat beside me and we watched the washing going round. I felt so honoured to be in this unique situation.

Shops did not lock their doors in those days, but the Indian lady did, and Guru told me at first she did not want to let him in!

Sri Chinmoy is now world-famous, with thousands of students, so looking back to those early days when it was all so simple and there were so few of us brings a special joy that nothing can take away.

ANIMESH
Brisbane, Australia

In the recesses of my desk, there is a piece of paper I have kept for almost thirty-five years. It is a portion of a disposable serviette, the kind which usually has a life expectancy measured in minutes. However, this particular item has been imbued with a certain touch of immortality. Despite the relentless march of time and many moves on my part between continents, countries, states and cities, it has remained with me.

The year it came into my hands was 1976.

In the summer of that year, Sri Chinmoy visited Europe to offer a series of free talks on various aspects of the spiritual life. First stop in his busy itinerary was the northern English city of York, famous for its grand gothic cathedral – the largest in Northern Europe – York

Minster. The venue for Sri Chinmoy's lecture however, was the much smaller Friends Meeting House in Friargate.

On the morning of his talk, Sri Chinmoy visited a nearby café – Riverside Cafeteria. And while waiting for his food to arrive, he began doodling on a serviette.

What he drew were clusters of birds and other tiny beings. Some were on branches, some in free flight; some stared with apprehension, others were confident in their cheerful play; some were feathered, as if insulated from the harsh realities of the world; and some were composed of the clean, swift strokes of a master draughtsman revealing with a few unfaltering lines, the essence of the soul in motion.

This was not the first time Sri Chinmoy had drawn these types of images. He would often do a quick sketch of a bird when signing his name or writing a message. They were not considered part of his formal artwork. Perhaps it was for this reason that he walked away from the table at the end of the meal leaving the serviette behind. Fortunately, Sushumna Mary Plumbly, leader of Sri Chinmoy's London meditation centre at the time, picked it up, carefully folded it and put it away for safekeeping.

A few days later at her home in London, she revealed the treasured memento of Sri Chinmoy's visit. The excitement welled in her eyes as she opened the folds of the precious artwork and displayed it in its entirety upon the table. Interestingly, the ink did not cross the fold marks, enabling it to be carefully torn into four equal portions without destroying the artwork. She kept one portion and presented three of us who were there on that occasion with a quarter. And so it was that the one became four – like the four points of a compass.

Holding my portion of the serviette in my hands now, it feels as light as a feather. The tissue itself has hardly any substance to it – time has dried and weathered its body and it now seems only to be held together by the lines of art upon its surface. It is so delicate in fact, that I can almost imagine the tiny birds taking wing, transporting this vignette of physical reality back to a celestial abode. To me, this tiny tableau of birds on a 6 x 6-inch square of tissue holds impressions of the past as well as a vision of the future; it is a point in time and space where memory and destiny are able to spread out across the vast canvas of time.

Vivid memories of that day in York seem to be woven into the very texture of this small fragment of art: the modern sights and sounds of an ancient city; the age-long vision and meditative silence of a contemporary spiritual Master.

In the late afternoon, we drove to Leeds and from there we began our journey back to London. I remember stopping at an Indian restaurant for dinner and then driving down the M1. It was a balmy summer's evening and Sri Chinmoy was in a relaxed mood. He started to sing one song after another – 'Ore Mor Kheya', 'Ekbar Shudhu Balo'....

The songs were in Bengali, a language so beautifully suited to the appointment of melody that translation is barely needed to appreciate the depth of feeling the songs convey. However, one song from that journey, 'Hiya Pakhi', illustrates how he identifies with the image of the bird as a symbol of spiritual freedom. Here is his own English translation:

> *O bird of my heart,*
> *Fly on, fly on.*
> *Look not behind.*
> *Whatever the world gives*
> *Is meaningless, useless*
> *And utterly false.*
>
> **– Sri Chinmoy**

For an hour or more Sri Chinmoy sang, lost in the enchanted world of the soul's melody. The lights from the motorway added an ethereal dimension as their colours played upon the car windscreen. My hands were on the steering wheel; my eyes, on the road ahead; but my heart was absorbed in song. I remember thinking at the time that it seemed like heaven – I could not have imagined any better place to be. Now, decades later, those memories have lost none of their original delight. Perhaps even then those tiny birds were already winging towards the future, carrying a small portion of divinity with them.

Surely no one could have predicted that simple sketches like the ones Sri Chinmoy drew in York, would one day be transformed into an entirely new art form, one that would amaze and enchant art-lovers around the globe. In 1991, Sri Chinmoy began in earnest, drawing birds at a phenomenal rate. He never missed an opportunity to bring into creation the tiny soul-birds he loved so much and, in the decades that followed, he would draw more than 16 million of them. They have been exhibited in prestigious galleries the world over and have been accorded acclaim by all who view them.

Sri Chinmoy's soulful bird drawings have proven their ability to transcend time and place. The inspiration they carry will continue to expand far into the future. I therefore place this delicate page of sketches back into the book of history, evidence that even in those early days the pen of the artist was never still; it was always ready to capture the beauty of inspiration, wherever he happened to be, using whatever resources he had to hand.

CHIDANANDA
New York,
United States of America

[This article was written several years ago after seeing Sri Chinmoy's exhibition of one million bird drawings in Ottawa.]

It's like a giant aviary. Hundreds of thousands of birds have found a temporary home here – hovering by the windowsills, clinging to the walls, nesting in the archways and vestibules. Everywhere there's movement – birds sweeping through the air in huge parabolas... tumbling from the ceiling like giant waterfalls... exploding through the halls like shards of light. What was once an empty four-story Heritage building in downtown Ottawa has been converted into one of the most astonishing art galleries ever built.

This exhibition of one million bird drawings by Indian artist Sri Chinmoy is unique in many ways. For one thing, according to the artist, they're not birds at all, but depictions of the human soul in the form of birds. Each bird, in effect, is an impression of immortality, a fragment of divinity that he has snagged with his paint brush and brought down from heaven. But that's not too surprising since Sri Chinmoy is not only an artist but a well-known spiritual teacher and mystic. The million soul-birds are inner visions that have risen up from the depths of his meditation, and with pen and brush he has given them form.

"Each of these birds is a prayer of my heart," he declares. "These prayers I am offering to the highest Absolute Lord Supreme." With a million prayers all converging in one spot, the gallery has become a veritable temple of worship. But there's nothing solemn about these bird-prayers. They literally vibrate with energy. A sense of joy infuses the curve of their wings, every thrust of their beaks, every hesitant kick of their newly discovered legs. If these birds are prayers, what the artist is worshipping is the dynamism and diversity of life itself.

The birds, ranging in size from less than a quarter-inch to three or four feet high, have been drawn with colored pens, acrylic paint, crayon and even magic marker on paper, note pads, rice paper, cloth and foam core. They appear singly and in groups, as notes on sheets of music, as messages on postcards, as vistas inside computer-generated circles. Many of the birds, especially the larger ones, have their own quirks and personalities. Some peer out boldly from their frames, staring at the world with eager curiosity. Some are puffed up like divas or shy and graceful as dancers. Some look puzzled, even bewildered, or joyful, vain, proud, quizzical. Some gaze at the viewer with sadness or compassion; others are self-absorbed, oblivious to the outside world. Some look absolutely dumb; others shimmer with intelligence.

In many of these creatures there's a whimsy or playfulness that is quite delightful. Their tiny eyes seem to be looking in all directions – over their shoulders, around corners, up into the air. Their round bodies are engaged in every imaginable activity – soaring off into the sky, plunging to earth, stretching their legs, smelling the fragrance of a flower, poking their heads into the ground.

Some of the birds are like soul mates, eternally paired; others fly side by side in giant columns – like an entire genealogy of families. Sometimes we'll see a large mother-bird surrounded by hundreds of offspring, as though the nestlings were continuations of the larger one's consciousness – like an explanation or footnote. A single painting will contain different species, as when hundreds of small pen-and-ink birds are zooming around a stationary bird drawn with a magic marker. And some of the larger bird souls are actually made up of thousands of smaller ones, which form its beak and the outline of its body.

Perhaps the most striking works are what one might call the godhead paintings – composed of tens of thousands of tiny, multi-colored birds. The birds themselves are almost too small to be distinguished; there's just an impression of movement, a density of consciousness pulsing from the canvas. From afar, the birds resemble a series of furrowed fields viewed from a great height – countless rows of microscopic souls intersecting and parting over the face of the canvas. Each 'field' or section of birds has its own shape, its own color, its own movement. And within each section are other sections – tiny red birds flying their own formation amid the larger pattern of green birds, for example, like different planes of consciousness moving through one another. It's just too complex, too vast, for the human mind to comprehend. There's something transcendental, almost unhuman about it – like the face of God.

Sri Chinmoy has somehow managed to create a body of work as awesome as the monoliths of Stonehenge – a universe as mysterious and sacred as anything any artist has ever done.

Gazing at this universe of souls with its infinite variety of shapes, colors and moods gives an almost religious experience. It's as though the artist has somehow managed to evoke in these paintings the beauty, the wonder, even the holiness of the soul's world. This universe of soul-birds, despite its unbelievable complexity, is very simple, highly ordered and extremely beautiful. There's something uplifting about it – a power, a calmness and, above all, a sense of absolute joy that leaves one deeply moved.

This exhibit of one million birds, and particularly these more unusual paintings, are like some orchestral performance from another world. As we listen to the strange, celestial melodies played by countless instruments, the notes blur into a single resonance, so that it seems more like silence than sound. In the depths of this silence, the mind no longer tries to understand; it surrenders to the heart, and the heart – fully awakened – becomes vast and still as the sky. When viewed in this kind of meditative state, the meaning and significance of Sri Chinmoy's soul-birds becomes most apparent.

The artist has entitled his exhibit 'One Million Dream-Freedom Peace-Birds' and dedicated them to his mother for her birth centennial. "These birds," he says, "are a new creation – the creation that will sing the song of Immortality in the life of mortality. If we can identify with them as they fly in the sky of boundless freedom and peace, it will remind us that our own soul is also flying in the vast freedom-sky carrying the Message of our Lord

Beloved Supreme here, there and everywhere." If we close our eyes, we can almost see these immortal soul-birds, necks outstretched, wings motionless, gliding through our own heart-sky – leaving a trail of hope, beauty and joy that we can forever cherish.

PRACHAR
Canberra, Australia

Towering high above the stage in a shell-like concrete chamber 50 feet high, 43 feet wide and 27 feet deep, the ten thousand pipes of the Grand Organ dominate the magnificent interior of the Concert Hall, the largest of the Sydney Opera House's famous white shells.

Like the building it inhabits, the Grand Organ is regarded with a mixture of apprehension and awe.

Apprehension – because ten years' labour and over 3 million dollars for a musical instrument seemed a bit extravagant to taxpayers who had seen the construction expenses of the Opera House balloon to such an extent in the late sixties that the State Government had to institute a special Opera House lottery to raise the funds.

And awe – because this 37-tonne colossus is the largest mechanical-action organ in the world and, certainly, the most intricate. While most organs fall into a particular category (one hears of the 'German Baroque organ' or a 'late French Romantic organ'), the Opera House organ covers all likely options, simply by containing a lot of all the different sorts of pipes, and some amazing ways of combining the various sounds. It also has a generous complement of ancillary stops – bronze hand bells, two types of bird-call (cuckoo and nightingale), and even an eerie drum-roll reminiscent of distant thunder.

It is an instrument designed to cater to every conceivable musical demand, concealing within its endless combinations and permutations myriad marvellous possibilities.

For Sydney organ-builder, Ronald Sharp, the Grand Organ was the fulfilment of a life's dream: his darling child. When the organ was not ready for the opening of the Opera House in 1973, he continued his painstaking perfectionist work under mounting pressure and criticism for six further years, until the organ was finally inaugurated in 1979. Even a decade later, it was difficult to separate him from his instrument; he was often to be found making minute adjustments to tiny pipes and, indeed, he was doing just that at 6:30 p.m. on Monday, November 30th, 1987, when Sri Chinmoy arrived....

* * *

When first smitten with the idea of Sri Chinmoy playing on this great instrument, we had commenced by approaching organists who were familiar with the Grand Organ to see if they would endorse an application for Sri Chinmoy to be allowed to perform on it. As a general policy, the organ is only made available to organists of considerable renown, and an application from someone with only six months' playing experience would not normally be considered!

Our strongest supporter was the Chairman of the Department of Organ and Sacred Music at the most prominent music conservatorium in Sydney, David

Rumsey. He was also organist with the Sydney Symphony Orchestra and a touring organist of distinction. Having heard recordings of Sri Chinmoy's earlier organ performances, he even informed all his students that they could not afford to miss such an important performance. At this time, Opera House administrators were saying that only three people, including Sri Chinmoy, would be admitted to hear the performance. David Rumsey had readily and eagerly agreed to be the one to introduce the organ and its many particular features to Sri Chinmoy, so he would certainly be one of the three. Yet he was determined to find a way around these restrictions, so that his students and others could be there!

Once the authorities had confirmed that permission was granted for Sri Chinmoy to have a 'private rehearsal' with two other people in attendance, it began to seem very sad that such a momentous occasion would only reverberate through the vast emptiness of the Concert Hall. This was something the whole of Australia, and eventually the world should hear!

We once again consulted with David Rumsey, who gave us the name of the Head of the Music Department of the ABC, Australia's (then) only national FM broadcaster. This lady immediately expressed interest in the idea of recording Sri Chinmoy's performance and began to formulate the concept of building an entire program around Sri Chinmoy, which would include an interview. As an afterthought, she mentioned that she knew of someone who would do an excellent interview, if only he were available... she mentioned the name of David Rumsey! The intricate threads of destiny were being unravelled.

After some weeks of discussion, the ABC proposal

became definite, the Opera House agreed to this new arrangement and granted official recording rights, thereby enabling a much larger crowd to attend.

* * *

David Rumsey, the organist who was to show Sri Chinmoy the mechanisms of this famous instrument led the way up the stairs. Sri Chinmoy, resplendent in red dhoti, followed – quietly, purposely, serenely. Through each door, there would be more stairs, spiral stairs and straight stairs. Each trodden stair heightened the anticipation in the air, the sense that our destination was far more than an organ loft.... It seemed word had already gone out in the higher worlds that Sri Chinmoy was to give a momentous performance. Sri Chinmoy's expression was inward, absorbed – mystical moments.

We had arrived at the loft and passed through to the organ itself. The vast, silent auditorium was dotted with the upturned faces of expectant souls. Sri Chinmoy eased onto the seat and watched attentively as the various stops were pointed out to him. He took particular note of the bell stops and the 'full organ' button.

Then the moment for which Time itself had been preparing – Sri Chinmoy began to meditate.

On tiptoe, we departed the console. Clearly there would not be time to descend all those stairs and be in the auditorium in time for the performance. As the only way for us to depart the organ console was back through the organ itself, and not wanting to be moving around at this juncture, I found myself sitting cross-legged on a kind of wooden platform.

In the silence of Sri Chinmoy's meditation, I became aware of my surroundings. There were pipes to the right, pipes to the left, pipes above and all around, neat row upon row of pipes, tiny flute pipes, larger reed pipes, hooded brass pipes, metal pipes, wooden pipes, massive pedal chorus pipes. It was as though this legion of pipes were themselves silently meditating, inwardly preparing for this moment of destiny, each pipe wholly responsible for only one note, which would be executed wholeheartedly and perfectly.

The first chord voiced forth from somewhere just above and to the right, plunging me into a breathtaking sound-adventure of three-dimensional ecstasy.

Sri Chinmoy's directions to his pipe-army were being relayed via a bewildering network of levers and tracker rods, which were being subjected to a breathless workout keeping up with his rapid-fire fingers. An incessant storm of clucking, bumping, clicking, clumping and thumping, each moving part operating in perfect co-ordination with every other at speeds faster than the eye could follow, was witness to a superlative effort of precision machinery stretched to its capacity in the task of bodying forth the sounds of Sri Chinmoy's transcendental vision.

Just by my left elbow was a huge bellows that only got called into service when the larger pipes sounded. To get sufficient air rushing through a 32-foot pipe takes tremendous lung capacity and, when Sri Chinmoy would suddenly call all the big pipes into action, these bellows would hurtle into a tremendous flap of intense exertion.

Sri Chinmoy seemed to be surcharging the instrument with his own force, the whole living organ bent on transcending its physical capacity in a supreme effort to render Sri Chinmoy's phenomenal fingerwork with utmost clarity and, at the same time, convey the unprecedented power of the loud sections – it was a nonstop blur of exhilarating activity.

When Sri Chinmoy would toy with the delicate flute pipes, or weave subtle counterpoint against the cuckoo or the bells, the bulk of the levers and the bellows would lie dormant, getting their breath back for the next explosion of power. During these quiet passages, one melody might sound from a distant upper corner of the loft, answered by another reverberating right in front of me, at eye level.

The teeming multitude of sounds streaming forth from this ordered mass of metal and wood, sounding above, below, all around and, seemingly, within – this all-encompassing flood of power, joy, beauty, surprise, delicacy, wonderment and awe – was at once a source of deep mystery and elation.

Invisible behind it all was Sri Chinmoy, in trance like Lord Shiva, but at the same time, ordering and instigating every tiniest twitch of each little lever – the omniscient, omnipotent creator embodying and igniting his vision-creation. For thirty-six timeless minutes, this organ became the universe itself, while the supreme musician revealed his cosmic music through ten thousand thrilled voices.

* * *

Retracing the interminable stairs that led back down to the earth-plane, Sri Chinmoy spoke about his performance. These are not his exact words, but a recollection:

"So much was happening... one moment Indian melody, then this world, that world – the beings from different worlds would come and invite me to their world, and the music would come from that world... then other beings would be there. Like this, all the time going from one world to another, to all the seven worlds."

The following morning, back at his hotel in Melbourne, after listening through headphones to several minutes of the performance, Sri Chinmoy exclaimed: "There are forty people playing!"

BIPIN
*New York,
United States of America*

The early 80s in New York was the height of Guru's running heyday. Many of the cute and illumining stories in his book series *Run and Become* were taken from experiences that took place during this time. Guru was running daily, both long and short distances. During the summer, especially while training, he ran anywhere from 100 meters up to a marathon. But as always the speed of track times Guru ran at the ashram in his youth were a haunting reminder and benchmark for what he expected of himself in his present running. With bright eyes he eagerly told us stories of those ashram races in India, recounting inner experiences and challenges he faced with illumining depth.

Humility, intense inner awareness, outer speed and accuracy of distance were the focal points of Guru's present day training programs here in New York, and the building blocks of his success in athletics. In the end surrender to the result was the starting point for the next day.

Guru always said that one must prove one's inner

dedication and meditation through action. Those of us involved in Guru's daily outer activities made ourselves available to help or silently stand and observe, immersing our hearts and minds in the glow and oneness of his fast consciousness. A small percentage of the local community felt strongly that this unprecedented opportunity of being around Guru was priceless, and we therefore wanted eagerly to unconditionally spend every waking minute at his feet in service. Little did we know the personal test of capacity our enthusiasm soon would bring.

What illumining blessings the Supreme had in store for us in the years to come. Guru of course was kind enough to include a handful of boys in helping with his daily running routine, offering a way for us to join in the heart's play. We were more than eager to play a role! Of course, none of us had a clue as to the massive amount of physical activities, nor the rewarding spiritual gifts, we were about to experience! With very different levels of success, our pride and enthusiasm were soon to be exposed, expanded and tested, for it is the Guru's very nature to illumine.

The experience I am about to relay took place in the summer of 1983 in New York. It involves but a sliver of Guru's daily activities, not to mention his running routines. Speed training was a significant part of Guru's approach to running, and the stride length in particular was a major concern – indeed many of the fastest middle and long distant runners have long strides. Guru was very aware of this fact and for years made maximizing his stride a high priority in training.

Guru would often practice longer stride running in front of his home on 149th Street where he lived. Each day in the early morning and late afternoon he would be there for as much as half an hour, running fast in one direction along the 150 meter length we marked with white paint. Then he would walk and slowly jog back to the start and repeat this.

In New York in the 70s and early 80s the public streets in lower tax bracket communities like Jamaica, Queens were poorly maintained, resulting in rough, pothole strewn roads. This made running and training on those roads a hazard, and 149th Street was no exception. Keep in mind also that when Guru ran he was often in a meditative state, and so he entrusted us with maintaining the standard of the road. Depending on Guru's wish we painted stride marks on the pavements of varying lengths, and it was often those marks he concentrated upon. Ideally, sticks, leaves and puddles all should be cleared away from his favoured routes, with some courses totalling 20 miles in length.

The poor condition of the pavement on 148th Street came up one day in our casual conversation with Guru, and he asked if there was not something we could do to improve the quality of the surface. Previously we had placed asphalt in the trouble spots, but over time this really just created a patchwork of very inconsistent road quality, and each season brought more repairs.

So the idea came up – why not repave the street ourselves? Brilliant! But none of us really knew what that involved. Up to this point we had purchased cold patch asphalt, which is sold in 50-lb bags. You simply open the bag then spread the asphalt, but this only covers about two square feet of the road surface – not nearly enough!

Guru loved the idea of a potentially fresh smooth street surface to practice on and said, "Please do it." Then he asked sweetly how much money we would need.

We had no idea how to do it, let alone the cost, but not wanting to disappoint Guru we threw out some blind number we hoped might cover the job and now we were on our way to begin the project. For those who know Guru his next query was no surprise. After all, how many times had Guru reminded us that this is the path of the heart and the fastest route to God. "When will it be ready?" Guru questioned! We said four days, and Guru responded: "Please try to do it in two days." When your Master offers guidance and suggestions on a project, rest assured it is already done. If the mind, heart and body cheerfully surrender to his wish, success is assured. But now the pressure was on.

We frantically inquired about the correct procedure for resurfacing a street. How is a city road paved? Quickly that question was answered. It became obvious that the road surface we needed could not be achieved by simply pouring hot asphalt and spreading it with rake and shovels. The only way to do this in the time requested was to hire a truck to deliver hot asphalt, than a large sit-on roller to compact the asphalt once it was spread on the street surface. And so we went for it.

By the following day we had secured both the delivery of asphalt and the large industrial roller needed to compact the entire street curb to curb. We decided to simply pave two strips at a time the length of the street, with both strips measuring about a meter wide. Guru gave his approval and away we went. Of course, it did not really occur to us that the public or city might object to what we were doing. We simply pushed ahead with the project, faithfully eager to succeed and blind to anything but pleasing our Guru.

There we were with a large 10-yard hot asphalt truck

on Guru's street, our obviously unskilled clumsy disciples operating a huge asphalt roller and laughing hysterically, and grinning from ear to ear as we fumbled about trying to discover the process of achieving the result we wanted.

Inevitably, it wasn't long before a city inspector arrived, calling the project to an abrupt halt. We had completed only a quarter of our task before finding ourselves explaining what on earth we thought we were doing. "The street is in such a horrible condition," we pleaded, "and we are trying to make the surface suitable for our Guru to train on without injury." I think the inspector was a bit taken aback by how naive we were, for our explanation disarmed him, that and the fact the project was already partly done. He said they had received a complaint from someone living on this block that their street was being repaved by rough contractors making a quick buck. He pointed out in no uncertain terms that it was not legal to receive money to do what we were doing, and we swiftly pointed out that this was not at all the case here.

Call it grace or our obviously goofy good intentions – the inspector turned a blind eye and simply drove away. By the next morning Guru was practicing his running routine in front of his house on two freshly paved tracks of smooth asphalt. Mission accomplished! We were all so happy, and Guru was too!

The second part of this story now jumps ahead to later in that same year. As a result of succeeding with the new surface (though exceeding the original budget as usual), Guru gave me and another boy the opportunity to daily maintain the freshly paved track. He requested that every other day I sweep the surface clean before 9 a.m. The second boy would do the alternate day in my absence. It went without saying the responsibility was a wonderful, unspoken blessing. Any responsibility bestowed on the disciple by his Master is not only outwardly a blessing but also a sacred opportunity for discipline and progress – two lessons soon to become painfully obvious to me.

Approximately two months passed. As requested, every alternate day I would come to Guru's street before 9 a.m., in the first weeks with both the eager soulfulness and willingness I felt expected of me. A couple more weeks passed – my silent soulfulness and gratitude were slowly slipping into a secret anticipation of perhaps Guru seeing me devotedly fulfilling my duty. Either that or perhaps the hope of catching a passing glimpse of Guru at home on his porch. It never happened.

Each day my routine beyond my appointed task consisted of long hours working, then the late night function plus a list of things to do longer than there were hours in the day. My morning road-sweeping task became more and more difficult to complete on schedule, in hindsight partly due to lethargy, a feeling of its unimportance plus my mind convincing my heart it was alright to be late.

Then some weeks later I completely ignored my duty. I did not make the effort to perform the job my Guru requested of me. The days went by and Guru said nothing, and I felt reassured in the illusion of how busy I was. Then one morning it happened. I turned the corner on the 149th Street 20 minutes late to clean the running paths. There was Guru walking towards me on his way out to exercise. I was caught!

Those who have been in this position will understand immediately what it is I am about to say. For those of you that never met Guru I will try to express what happened.

Upon meeting your Guru in person when failing him, there is at first a 'deer in the headlights', response, that sweeps over you. One of surrender, but equally a feeling of failure and humiliation. Guru is all love, yet he has the responsibility of carrying us to the goal, and thus his discipline and strictness. Immediately I knew Guru saw every thought, fear, doubt, good intent inside me. In that moment I knew he saw right through me and I felt both his love and disappointment. It was the summation of all those missed or late days gathered into one face-to-face moment.

About halfway down the street we crossed paths. Without breaking stride Guru looked over at me as he walked past then said, "How do you ever expect to realise God if you cannot even sweep the street as I have requested?" I was both devastated and catapulted into heaven all in the same moment. I felt gratitude and the worst kind of failure together.

The opportunity of street sweeping continued for a few weeks to follow before cold weather arrived. Guru said it was not necessary to continue and never requested I restart the journey.

PULAK
*New York,
United States of America*

One of my most memorable Christmas Trips was when we went to Tobago in 1980-81. At this time Tobago, located in the Southern Caribbean, was an unspoiled tropical island with lush rainforests and exotic wildlife. The people mostly led simple lives as farmers or fishermen. Upon leaving the plane I was thrilled to find myself in this earthly paradise.

During the bus ride from the airport, it became clear that all was not well in this paradise: we felt the bus lurching from side to side as the driver sought to avoid the almost endless series of potholes. Some were like large craters in the asphalt. Along the sides of the road I also noticed many mounds of gravel about eight feet high, carefully placed near the craters in groups of three: one coarse grade (1"-2"); one medium grade (¼"-¾") and one fine grade. Something was in the works.

Since there were nearly 200 disciples on this trip, and there was no single hotel big enough to house us all, we were divided into five different places. There was the main hotel where Guru stayed along with many close disciples and other selected ones. Then just down the road there was a nice hotel where the remaining girls stayed and a third hotel about a mile away where many boys stayed. Finally there was the Cocrico Motel and next to it the Cocrico Annex. The Cocrico was a typical motel, and it housed quite a few boys; the Cocrico Annex was actually a converted barn.

I was fortunate enough to be staying in the Cocrico Annex along with about five other boys. We had no air-conditioning – we did not even have true windows. Each room had two full length wooden flaps without any screens – you could either open them all the way or close them. There was a lone light bulb hanging from the ceiling and I believe each room had a small fan.

Another fascinating feature was that we were situated in the midst of a small rural village, and were surrounded by chickens, goats and other domestic animals, and the people who cared for the chickens and goats were our neighbors. Everyone was very friendly and down to earth. Living there was endlessly refreshing and lots of fun.

Around 100 meters from the Annex was the entrance to the national rain forest. I was at the peak of my long-distance running condition at that time and it was an incredible boon to be so close to a beautiful tropical forest with well-maintained trails. It was a true runner's heaven. Also, being nine miles away from Guru's hotel gave me an opportunity to get in some cross-country running. Some days I would run in the forest and other days I would take a backpack with my gear, run to Guru's hotel for the functions, and then catch a ride home afterwards. Since the Cocrico was nine miles away, we were assigned cars with five boys in each one. This proved to be very convenient.

The Centre was at the peak of the running boom then, and not only I, but almost everybody else also, was a runner. Of course Guru was the inspiration behind everything and he literally led every step of the way. His enthusiasm for running was boundless. With iron-willed intensity, he increased his mileage beyond what most of us cared even to imagine. Through running he was a perfect model of his own philosophy of self-transcendence. In New York, his 'road crew' of about a dozen boys worked day and night tirelessly maintaining and measuring his many running routes. I was not a member in New York, but did occasionally assist.

Guru used to love to run very early, even before dawn, when everything else was silent and the air was fresh. So Guru went out the first morning in Tobago with Savyasachi following in a car, but the potholes stole away all his inspiration. Later that day, after the function, Guru said to me, "Sal (my name was not yet Pulak), the potholes make running impossible. Can you not fix them?" He specified the roadway between his hotel and the boys' hotel about one mile away. With confidence I said I would do it, and instantly all those conveniently placed gravel mounds flashed before my mind's eye.

So first thing the next morning I broke the news to the guys in my car group that I would need our assigned car for the day to fill the potholes for Guru. Surprisingly, they took it rather well, only grumbling a little. Somehow they managed to get around. There were a few other cars for the boys at the Cocrico Motel. I found some boxes and placed them in the trunk of the car and headed out to the potholes and gravel piles near Guru's hotel.

I began by shoveling a different grade of gravel into each box and then filled each pothole with first the coarse gravel, along with some fine, then the medium and finally topping it off with more of the fine grade gravel. Every few yards there was a pothole, some as large as four or five feet in diameter, but since there was no shortage of gravel piles, the operation went rather smoothly and I finished before the end of the day and sent a message to Guru.

The next day Guru told me he was very pleased with

the new, improved course. He then asked me if I could fill in the potholes along another section of the road. Savyasachi gave me the directions for this new course, which was a bit longer.

The next morning I borrowed the car again, loaded the boxes with gravel and began filling potholes. While working, I noticed a local man watching me as I was filling a large pothole at the foot of his driveway. It was a very hot day and he started walking towards me with a drink in his hand. At first I thought he was going to reprimand me, but instead he offered me a drink of water, and said, "Thank you for filling these potholes. For years the government has promised to fill them. It just doesn't care." Then he asked me why I was doing it, where I was from and if there was anything else he could do for me. He was very, very happy. We spoke for a while and then I moved on to finish the course.

One of the many interesting features of living at the Cocrico Annex was that at the break of dawn the roosters from all over the village started crowing. Occasionally one would jump through the open flap into my room to give me a personal performance and to inspect my room. I was almost always awake for morning meditation. Gradually the other animals would join in to create a sonorous backdrop for my 'silent' meditation. They all seemed to enjoy having us around and made us feel like we were part of the village.

Soon Guru had a new course for me to fill. He asked me to connect his existing course with the 1-mile course where we would hold our 3-mile, 5-mile and 7-mile races, as well as filling in the race course. The race course was partially sandwiched between the sea and the airport, and I discovered a large quarry of rocks there, which would prove to be useful later.

Filling the potholes was becoming an enjoyable routine for me and a somewhat peaceful meditative experience. I was free to be outside and active all day in the fresh air and lush tropical surroundings, being occasionally greeted and encouraged by sweet-natured locals. At the same time I was continually improving my technique, finding better ways of integrating the three grades of gravel to achieve a more solid and enduring finish. All this digging, lifting of gravel and at times large rocks was also very good training for my running, especially for developing strength in the core muscles. As a result my times in the races were all PRs – around a 6-minute/mile pace – and kept improving. That was a very nice side effect. I can't say if it was one that Guru anticipated, although I wouldn't hesitate to suggest that he did.

Around the third week of our stay, arrangements were made for our group to go by ferry to Trinidad and to stay a couple of days, but before the trip I received a message from Guru that he would like me to fill the potholes between the airport and Scarborough (the capital of Tobago), about a 10-mile stretch. Going to Trinidad was clearly no longer an option – which was OK with me. This was my now my life's calling.

So while everyone else was heading for the ferry, I began hitting those government gravel piles. I had only two or three days to complete this massive new task. As I was beginning the job, I thought, "This is a long way. Maybe I could get the government to give me some asphalt to make the repairs more durable." So I drove to the Scarborough offices for the Department of Public Works for Tobago, and asked to speak with the supervisor. Somehow I was led to his office and I explained to him that I was in Tobago with a large group for our Christmas vacation, and that we had many runners and were organizing races. "So I have been filling the potholes, but now I would like to make the repairs longer-lasting by using asphalt. So I was wondering if you could supply me with some asphalt." He did not know what to say at first, taking it all in, I guess. Then he said, "Well, we will have to discuss the matter." Then he kindly dismissed me without a definite answer.

I returned to filling the potholes, throughout that day and into the next. Eventually, after a few hours, I came to this gigantic one about 8 feet long and 4 feet wide and a foot deep. I decided to go to the beach to get some larger rocks to lie across the bottom of this pothole. I also needed several loads of gravel and I even brought some sand to spread across the top. After working for over an hour I finished it, and it looked great!

As I was moving on to the next one, I saw down the road what looked like a government truck. I could also see that there were workers on the road who seemed to be filling potholes. I went up to them and asked them what they were doing. One of them said they were filling the potholes from Scarborough to the airport. I told them that I had just finished filling the potholes from the airport to this point. Miraculously my job was complete, far faster and better than I had ever imagined.

There was one very interesting aftermath. The next day a small article appeared on about page 11 of the local newspaper. The headline read, "Tourists Fill Island's Potholes." The article explained that for years the roads of Tobago had been plagued by potholes. Because of the negligence of the government of Trinidad (Trinidad houses the central government for both Trinidad and Tobago), the tourists were spending their vacation filling the potholes. Upon his return from the Trinidad side trip, needless to say Guru was both pleased and amused by the turn of events. I wish I could remember exactly what he said at that time. I'm sure it was very illumining and amusing.

Who would have thought that Guru's simple request could possibly culminate in instigating the government to initiate a long-neglected program for filling the potholes of Tobago? For me, this was an opportunity to serve Guru and to directly play a small role in his cosmic play. I may have missed some of the recreational activities of the trip, but in a very down-to-earth way I was never far from Guru's inner presence, and for that I shall always be grateful.

UNMILAN
Brisbane, Australia

Who knows when this story began... and who knows when it will end? Like all adventures Sri Chinmoy embarks upon, the open invitation is always there for us to join him on his journey to the limits of human transcendence and beyond. This is a chronicle of a small part of one such continuing adventure – into the realm of Sri Chinmoy's weightlifting achievements.

To say that this story began with Sri Chinmoy lifting 40 lb above his head with one hand on 26th June, 1985 is in fact only part of the truth. Sri Chinmoy has always stressed the importance of physical fitness and strength in our pursuit of spiritual progress. Ever since his days in the Sri Aurobindo Ashram, Sri Chinmoy has proved that he is not just a spiritual giant, but a force to be reckoned with in athletic endeavours, as well, a modern-day 'Pandava' in every sense.

Sri Chinmoy's success as an athlete is an inspiration to his spiritual sons and daughters, and, true to his nature, he is now breaking ground in the world of weightlifting, where no man has gone before.

In August 1983, Sri Chinmoy asked for 50 exercise machines to be made. All his disciples who were inspired tried to make their machines and then present them to him for approval – or otherwise. Mostly it was otherwise. Kishore Cunningham had an idea for a machine and suggested that together we could make it. When the machine was finished, we presented it to Sri Chinmoy. He sat in it and within minutes had completely wrecked it. "Useless, totally useless!" was his comment.

A few days later, he approached us again, laughing while saying, "That machine of yours was totally useless." It was a challenge we could not refuse.

Instead of trying to find out what would inspire Sri Chinmoy, we asked a friend of ours to ask him what he specifically needed a machine to do. At that time, Sri Chinmoy was concentrating on his sprinting, and so "anything to improve leg strength" was the direction. We visited a couple of gyms, made quick sketches and then work began in earnest. Everyone we knew was caught up in Sri Chinmoy's exercise machine inspiration, so it was no problem to find tools and a workshop (a subterranean store room in the basement of Agni Press). In those few weeks the business of making exercise machines began.

Little did I realise where it would eventually take me.

The first we knew of Sri Chinmoy's serious weightlifting was when he rang his Australian meditation centres in late July, 1985. We were all gathered in Melbourne to help with two concerts which some of the good musicians among our group were performing there. Sri Chinmoy told us on the phone that he had entered into the exercise machine world with great enthusiasm and that when we came to New York the following month, there would be plenty of exercise machines to make. Just how much he was getting into weights and exercise machines was a surprise that was in store for Kishore and me.

On 7th July, just eleven days after he began this new adventure, Sri Chinmoy had progressed to lifting 50 lb, with 60 lb coming shortly after, on 16th July, only nine days later. Before our arrival in New York, Sri Chinmoy was still making progress. He lifted 70 lb above his head on 30th July. The lift was called the 'One-Hand Military Press'. On our arrival in New York, Sri Chinmoy quickly set us to work building machines, which always had to meet his requirements of being "cute, small, strong and yet look professional but not too complicated."

So the 'Sri Chinmoy exercise machine manufacturing headquarters' was set up once again in the small room in the basement of Agni Press. This little room was to become home for the next six months. The 'dungeon', as it was affectionately known – since it was a room about eight feet square with a seven foot ceiling, no natural light and dripping water – was to become a hive of constant activity, producing machines with borrowed tools and resources, kindly lent by bewildered disciples. It was a world of its own, secure and friendly, where machines that were built had to be small, otherwise they wouldn't fit through the narrow door and up the stairs!

Before lifting heavy weights, Sri Chinmoy always warmed up first by lifting smaller weights or by working out on machines. The intensity with which he trained and wanted new machines was such that Kishore and I were only seen at the 1985 August Celebrations on four separate days. At one point, Sri Chinmoy said to us, "It is your job to make me strong. Making exercise machines will be your meditation."

During Celebrations, he would often have competitions with the disciples to see who could lift the heaviest weight, or else to see how many times he or the disciples could push a particular weight up and down. This gave him great joy and enthusiasm to continue his own rigorous training programme.

Sri Chinmoy was progressing steadily. On 13th August he lifted an 80-lb dumbbell with one arm, followed by 85 lb on 6th September. His joy spilled over into the music world, and he composed several weightlifting songs for us to sing, and share in his achievements.

Sri Chinmoy liked to go to gymnasiums or sports stores to try out new machines which might develop his muscles. Some of these machines would have cost many thousands of dollars, so he would ask me, "Can you make?" Out would come the pencil and paper and a few quick sketches and rough measurements were taken. He would also shop for novelty exercisers or just something new which would give him joy and a change from all the regular weights. He would go everywhere without the least bit of concern, which I have to admit was not exactly how I felt going into these places. Some of the gyms in those days were pretty rough. It's no wonder Sri Chinmoy said many people would prefer to train at home on their own exercise equipment, if they could.

Eventually a video machine was set up in Sri Chinmoy's home gym so that he could record his workouts and see his progress. Sometimes he would show his disciples some of his best lifts, especially his new personal records. In this way, he was able to teach us the meaning of true determination (as well as frustration), and what concentration could do for us in our own self-transcendence. He often said that his mind does not believe what he has done, but his heart knows that it is true.

Sri Chinmoy would always meditate before attempting his lifts and he would always offer his gratitude prayer to the Supreme after his success or failure. It is all divine Grace, he used to say.

Because of Sri Chinmoy's injured knee and bad back, it was difficult for him to lift weights from the ground. He wanted to know if there was any way that he could either repair or strengthen these weak points in his body.

Agraha found a place that tested leg muscles and knee joints and then showed how they could be strengthened. The tests revealed that Sri Chinmoy was weaker in his right leg and that his overall strength in his legs was such that an ordinary person in this condition would be getting around in a wheelchair or classified as a cripple! They gave Sri Chinmoy some exercises to do using very light weights strapped to his ankles or using weight shoes. (He had already been doing these exercises, but without the weights.) They stressed to him not to use heavy weights but to use very light weights and few repetitions for a short time, and to slowly increase the repetitions over a month or so and gradually increase the weight by five pounds as he got stronger. It sounded as though the process would take a very long time. Sri Chinmoy felt that if the muscles around his knee could become stronger, they would support him better so that he could lift heavier weights without feeling unstable.

We felt sorry for Guru. But, in return, he showed us how to overcome even the biggest obstacles. He asked Himangshu to make him extra heavy weight shoes, and another exercise machine had to be built to perform these same exercises. Sri Chinmoy was soon using 100 lb on the machine and doing lots of repetitions. His persistence once again defied scientific diagnosis and examination. They were inevitably defeated by heart-power and determination.

Because Sri Chinmoy was training so much, it was important to keep new machines coming so that he would not get bored or frustrated with his training. He always got inspiration as well as fresh enthusiasm and joy from new exercise machines.

Sometimes we would try hard to get another machine finished – only to be met by frustration and delays.

When Sri Chinmoy received a new machine, it instantly became a part of him and if we had to take the machine back for alteration, it would be like taking a child's favourite toy away from him. It became a game to see if we could get the alterations done on the same day and deliver it back before he retired for the night. It gave us such joy to see our Guru happily experimenting with his new machine.

It was the job of Databir Waters to keep Sri Chinmoy supplied with metal weights and also to keep a lookout for any new exercise machines that he could find. Soon Databir noticed that in many cases the plates did not, in fact, weigh what they were supposed to, so he would weigh each one before buying them. How disappointing it would have been if Sri Chinmoy had lifted 100 lb only to find that it weighed 95 lb! That is why some of Sri Chinmoy's lifts have the odd one pound or half a pound weight added to them.

He was starting to lift such heavy weights now that it was becoming hard for us to help him by manually handing him the dumbbells. Apart from it being dangerous, especially if we lost our concentration for even just a second, he wanted to be able to lift weights whenever he wanted to, and not just when we were available to help him. One day he asked if a machine could be made to replace us, and so was born 'The Cage'.

If ordinary human beings lift a really heavy weight, we would usually be satisfied with lifting it once, but not so with Guru. His goal for Christmas 1985 was to lift 50 lb forty times. But he took everyone by surprise and became stronger so quickly that he was able to accomplish this goal on 6th October, two and a half months ahead of schedule.

So when one goal is reached, you set another. That is his philosophy. Now it was to be 50 lb lifted 50 times and 100 lb lifted from the ground above his head, both by Christmas.

September had departed and October was disappearing fast. It seemed that nothing could stop Sri Chinmoy, not even time itself. Disciples were kept busy trying to contact professional weightlifters and bodybuilders to find out their training tips to help Guru get stronger. He tried a number of their suggestions, even their eating habits, and slowly he began to formulate his own diet and training schedule. And, indeed, something was working, for he was losing weight and yet getting stronger. The spiritual and the physical were working in unison.

On 8th October 1985, Sri Chinmoy lifted 96½ lb 15 times, followed by a further 6 times and then another 20 times. Joy was in the air and he now felt confident that because he was able to lift this weight so many times, he could easily lift 100 lb at least once, if not more.

Sometimes he would play tricks on his mind, like using wrist weights while he lifted the big dumbbells and then telling himself that all he was lifting was a 90-lb dumbbell instead of 91, 92 or 93 lb.

Sri Chinmoy was always stressing that in anything we undertake, it is important to set a goal. When we reach that goal, we get such joy and enthusiasm that it will carry us to our next goal. But we should be careful not to set our goals too high and out of reach. We should have intermediate goals to reach our major goal. Otherwise, if we can't reach our major goal, we will get frustrated and we might give up altogether.

Sometimes, while he was practising weights or doing some other thing, he would just stop and suddenly he would be in another world. You just knew that he had important inner business to attend to.

It was strikingly noticeable when some disciples were attempting to swim the English Channel that year. I could consciously feel Sri Chinmoy taking away their pain and fear so that they could accomplish their enormous task. I know Guru does this for all of us all the time, but it seemed so noticeable to me on that occasion. His concern knows no bounds.

Sri Chinmoy would train at all hours of the day and night. He wanted machines built to fit into his bedroom so that if inspiration struck at an odd hour (is there such a thing for a spiritual Master?) he would be able to work out without going downstairs.

Some professional weightlifters were commenting that his muscles were not growing in size because they were muscle-bound from too much exercise and not enough rest. But Sri Chinmoy kept up his intense training programme. He might not have had the muscle size of some of these body builders and weightlifters, but his strength was still rapidly increasing – to a point where he would soon overtake most of them in strength.

Sri Chinmoy would train early in the morning, while we were all asleep, and again at about 8:00 a.m., not forgetting to go out for his regular walk and also to practise his musical instruments in between the two workouts. Later in the day, he would work out around 3:00 or 4:00 p.m. in the afternoon, and finally sometimes between 9:00 p.m. and midnight, when time and his busy schedule permitted. No other weightlifter, not even a super-athlete, could keep this intensity of training, six days out of seven, for months on end, with only two hours' sleep a day to re-energise the body.

Sometimes it would happen that I was putting a machine together or altering one in Guru's house and he would go upstairs to rest. I don't know how much rest he would take, because soon the sound of weights could be heard going up and coming down with a gentle thud on the floor upstairs.

At Aspiration-Ground tennis court on 9th October 1985, he lifted 106¼ lb above his head with one hand, and then did several repetitions. This became the famous poster which many gymnasiums requested copies of. They felt it would inspire people to transcend their own efforts when they saw someone of Sri Chinmoy's age lifting such a massive weight.

At this stage – and not knowing anything about weightlifting records – I was starting to wonder if he had nearly reached the goal he was aiming for. Besides, the exercise room in his house was now about as full as it could ever be with exercise machines and weights. But I still had a lot to learn about Guru's determination. It was really only the beginning.

Until now Sri Chinmoy was still playing tennis and having evening meditations at Aspiration-Ground because the weather was quite mild. His tennis improved as he became stronger, especially his serve, and he was able to move around the court with an agility we had not seen for quite a while, not since the days when he was sprint training. But the vigorous games sapped his precious energy, energy much needed for his weightlifting, and so he cut back on tennis playing in order to use the energy for his weight training.

During Sri Chinmoy's busy day – which included meetings, meditations, solving his disciples' inner and outer problems and weight training – he still managed to find time to practise his music for upcoming Peace Concerts in the United Kingdom and Europe. And, even while he was on tour, he found time to train, using a leg exerciser at interval time and after a concert.

Bipin was particularly good at packing weights and dumbbells for travelling into little innocent-looking red tool boxes. One of these might weigh 50 lb or more, depending on the size of the dumbbell! And while Sri Chinmoy was away, machines were being converted from round weights to rectangular pin weights, so that he wouldn't have to lift them on and off a machine to alter the poundage.

One day, shortly after Sri Chinmoy's return from his European tour, he was sitting on the couch on his front porch, gazing out the window. It was a beautiful day outside and a jogger ran by. He turned and said, "There is nothing quite like running. When you run everything is inspiring you to run. The wind in your hair, the birds, the trees, flowers, grass... even the footpaths and houses are all urging you to run. But here I am lifting inconscient weight, something that I used to avoid doing in my Ashram days."

He went on to say that the leg exercise machine was helping his lower back as well as his legs and he felt that one day soon he would be able to run again. Of all the machines we have made for Guru, I thank the Supreme for this one.

I couldn't contain the joy of knowing that he might run again, and told several of my friends what he had said. They were overjoyed also, and at the first opportunity asked him if it was true. Guru's answer was, "How do these rumours get started? Some disciples I can tell things and they don't believe, but other disciples take everything I say as being true." At first I felt embarrassed, but then I was filled with gratitude.

After Sri Chinmoy had successfully lifted the 106¼ lb above his head the first time, he continued using this weight to practise with. He asked me if it was possible to lower the weight cage so that the 106¼-lb dumbbell would hang one inch closer to the floor, giving him a better starting position. All I could think of doing was to cut one inch out of each of the legs and re-weld them back together. But this would mean taking the cage away and bringing it back at a later time. Other things had to be done first, so I went away trying to think of an easier way to lower the cage.

Later in the day, Sri Chinmoy said, "Unmilan, we are both brainless! It is so easy to lower the weight. We just place a one-inch sheet of plywood on the floor for me to stand on." He was laughing and then he said, "It is like when the dog barks. We run and run and run instead of climbing up the tree!"

Sri Chinmoy worked and worked with his weights until his muscles became too sore to work any more, and he would then take rest. During this rest period he used to practise his musical instruments. He would play four or five instruments and then work out again, take another rest and practise again. None of his other activities suffered while he kept pushing forward with his weightlifting manifestation. Things like music were just placed into another time slot.

Early one morning, I woke up feeling sad and depressed without knowing why. Later in the morning I found out that Guru had been working out on the hyper-extension machine (the roman chair) doing stomach and back exercises, when the machine lost balance and fell on top of him. The Supreme saved Guru from a nasty accident but Guru had hurt his calf muscles, and the next few days found him limping everywhere, just when it seemed that he would be running well again.

The injury eventually healed with the help of massage and he was soon walking and running again in the mornings. Guru maintained his exercise programme, minus the leg exercises, for a few days. The intense training on upper body muscles was continuing unabated, with Guru still practising instruments for the coming concerts, as well as writing new songs, poems and reading all his mail. It never stopped!

By October 29th, Sri Chinmoy was able to one-arm press 106¼ lb 12 times, followed by 28 times and 12 times. Then he had a significant inner experience. His soul told him that more repetitions were needed. So he set a programme to do seven reps seven times with the 106¼-lb dumbbell.

Whenever he was about to lift his heaviest weight, or go for a 'PR', every noise in the house had to be stopped, and pin-drop silence maintained. These 'transcendence lifts' required every ounce of Guru's powerful concentration. He says that he tells the weights to become as light as a feather so that he can easily lift them.

On November 1st, he successfully transcended his own record again by lifting 117 lb. This was to become the starting point of his next goal, which was to one-arm press 150 lb while having a personal bodyweight of 150 lb.

"Is there no limit to what Guru can do?" my mind asked.

Sri Chinmoy would occasionally have weightlifting competitions. He did it for the joy it gave to us all, and to see us struggling with weights that he had far transcended months ago. But he stressed that we should not try lifting these weights without him being there, unless we were already lifting weights seriously, since we could cause ourselves injury. He said that men should not lift more than 50 lb and women not more than 20 lb.

In one of these competitions, Shephali defeated all the boys by lifting the heaviest weight in the calf-muscle machine. Then Sri Chinmoy got us to see who could lift a 120-lb dumbbell from the floor to waist height. He himself could not perform this lift, but those of us that tried could. He felt embarrassed, but our success was only because our lower backs were stronger than his. "Sometimes embarrassment is good," said Guru, "because it makes us try harder." And so this became another goal he set for himself – to lift 100 lb from the floor to above his head.

The machines that were made for Sri Chinmoy all had weights in them that were well above his strength at that time. It seemed that he was having a competition with the machines to see how fast he could transcend their limits. As he got stronger and stronger, there was not one machine that did not require extra weights to be added to the weight stack. With some machines, it took Guru a matter of weeks to use up all the weights, some took only days, and one took only two hours for him to conquer!

Sri Chinmoy could now do a pull-over from behind his head with 120 lb, and in the seated bench press machine he could press 140 lb, 10 times. On November 3rd, he lifted 131½ lb in military press fashion, 22 times. This was only two days after lifting 117 lb. When he completed the lift, he very soulfully spoke these words:

"The Compassion-Light of my Beloved Supreme has made me lift up 131½ lb, 22 times. For everything in my life, I entirely, entirely depend and depend on the Grace of my Beloved Supreme, and this is what I would like all my disciples to do. For everything they should and they must entirely depend on the boundless and unconditional Grace of our Beloved Supreme."

He went on to say that he never dreamed that one day he might be strong enough to be able to lift his own bodyweight with one hand – his Indian bodyweight was always around 131 lb from the ages of thirteen to thirty-one. Guru said, "I am so happy. Let my happiness enter into all my spiritual children, the same happiness. I would be grateful if they could transcend my happiness. First, they have to embody my happiness, and then they have to transcend it. Transcendence is our only goal."

One day Sri Chinmoy was inspired to do a typical bodybuilder pose. Savyasachi took a photograph. The picture was blown up and then auctioned to the highest bidder. At a function to celebrate Sri Chinmoy's 131½-lb lift, Madal Bal bid the highest for this powerful, yet sweet and beautiful portrait.

In the course of time, every room in Sri Chinmoy's home became an exercise room. If he wanted to exercise while talking with disciples, he would exercise on the porch using either exercise machines or free weights (dumbbells). If he wanted to do a serious workout, he would use the main exercise room. In the meditation room there sat a 100-lb chromed dumbbell for lifts from the ground. And upstairs the second bedroom was also transformed into a small exercise room where he could work out. Even his main bedroom had an exercise machine in it.

He would tell us, "If you are inspired then you are energised and you do not need to sleep for so long. Your mind says to go to sleep and it will wake you up... but it never does. Instead, it tells you that you need more sleep."

Sri Chinmoy only takes sleep for two hours each day and in this way he can accomplish the many things he has to do. He advises us to always play tricks on the mind and do what inspires you and not what the mind wants you to do. If you are tired, take a shower or wash your face, especially the ears and eyes, put on the TV in the background to create a noise, sing loudly and out of key – do anything to stay awake.

When Sri Chinmoy wakes up, he meditates before anything else. Then he warms up in preparation for lifting weights. His arms move from side to side, up and down, to loosen the muscles and get the circulation going. Then he takes his position underneath the dumbbell that is suspended in the cage. He simply holds the weight for a minute or two, concentrating and mentally preparing himself in pin-drop silence. Suddenly the concentration, determination and sheer strain all burst into action and a powerful groan signals the start of the upward journey of the weight. For a very brief moment, it is held up, at the top of his straightened arm. His shoulders are square, back perfectly straight and left arm stretched parallel to the floor. Then the weight comes down, only to be halted and then made to move upwards, again and again and again. Suddenly the surge is over and the weight comes back down for the last time into its cradle, crashing like thunder.

The strain is over and the look of pain on Sri Chinmoy's face quickly changes to a smile and laughter. The power in the room is tangible. Then, prayerfully, he offers his gratitude to God.

This was the scenario on November 12th, 1985. He had just lifted 140 lb. We had the feeling now that he was strong enough to lift anything he wanted.

On November 15th, Madal Bal flew me to Germany and Switzerland for a week to prepare me for the job ahead – manufacturing exercise machines in Australia and exporting them to Madal Bal for sale in Europe. Before I left, Guru said he would wait until my return before he lifted his next goal: 155 lb.

On November 18th, he telephoned me in Switzerland to tell me that he had lifted 155 lb 10 times and then another 14 times. He said, by way of explanation, "My determination could not wait for your return and so with your soul's permission I lifted it early." I was deeply touched and overjoyed.

Sri Chinmoy's determination was such that he would keep trying for days and days to lift a weight, even if at first he could not budge it, and put full effort into trying until the capacity was there to do it.

After the 155-lb lift, just like after the 106¼-lb lift, the phones went wild with comments from all over the world. Weightlifters, bodybuilders, athletes, musicians, politicians, doctors and ministers were all eager to offer him praise and encouragement. Some were so overcome that they were lost for words. All this helped Sri Chinmoy to persevere and set new goals, especially comments like: "I see no limit to what this man can do because of his connection with God," or, "He can easily go on to even larger weights with his power of concentration and determination." For some, Sri Chinmoy's spiritual height was forgotten or perhaps unseen, and the achievement was seen only in superhuman terms. But others knew and felt that it was his indomitable spiritual qualities that enabled him to perform such tremendous feats of power and strength. In Sri Chinmoy's life, everything flowed from the inner to the outer.

In just under five months, he had progressed from 40 lb to 155 lb. Meanwhile, his bodyweight had decreased through strict dieting to 155 lbs, and he was now poised to lift, with one arm, more than his body weight – a feat that all weightlifters agreed was bordering on the unbelievable. His goal was now to lift 170 lb. With such heavy weights being used, a second cage was built to enable him to practise for the 170 lb by warming up with the 155-lb weight first. It was hard for me to comprehend that 155 lb was once his goal, and now it was being used merely as a warm-up lift!

The remaining days of 1985 were very busy for Sri Chinmoy... on the anniversary of his paintings, he painted 150 small and 70 large new pieces; he continued to hold UN meditations and special meditations in Washington DC; he met with a number of important people and composed songs to honour them; he held a seven-hour meditation and concert where he played on 21 musical instruments; on Wednesday nights he held public meditations, and there were many more daily activities happening in the ten days after he lifted 155 lb. It was Thanksgiving Day and he still had the 5-day ultra-race to direct and many concerts to perform before Christmas, but the intensity never for a moment caused him to pause in going for his 170-lb goal. Quite the contrary, he thrived on the pace and the challenges ahead. "You have no idea how many times I have tried and how many times I have failed," he said, "but I do not give up."

By November 30th, twelve days after lifting 155 lb, he had succeeded in lifting 170 lb with two hands four times, but he had not been successful in then changing to one hand to do repetitions. He commented, "My biceps are so weak, while my triceps are so strong. We try to hide our weaknesses but our weaknesses come forward so that we can strengthen them."

Until now he had always lifted the weights with two hands. Then he would change to one hand at the top of the lift and begin to one-arm press. But on December 1st, using only one arm from start to finish, he lifted 101¼ lb, 127 lb and 132 lb – all within an hour. This was a major breakthrough and a very special day for Sri Chinmoy. Three days later, he lifted 145 lb in the same way, using only one hand. At a function that evening, he showed a video of himself doing all these lifts and explained, "Today I have tried something new. Without taking any help from my left hand, I only used my right hand on the lift. Meditate. Identify with me. My aspiration and my Beloved Lord Supreme's Compassion – how they go together."

A book was made detailing all these lifts. Some of the pictures clearly show the pain and strain his physical body was going through.

The next day he was determined to lift 120 lb from the floor to his waist, while an audience looked on. He said, "So what if I am embarrassed, it helps us to become strong to fail now and again." Sri Chinmoy did not have to feel embarrassed on this occasion. He made the lift and another goal had been reached.

Still I kept making machines, all day and sometimes all night. For me, nothing else mattered. Guru said to me, "Your devoted service and my determination have enabled me to lift these weights. Without these machines, there would be no joy."

We are all divinely special and unique. While I was making machines for Guru, some disciples felt miserable that they couldn't please him to the extent that I was at that time. But what they did not know was how envious I was of them, seeing how much they were spreading the news of Guru's achievements across the world, while all I was doing was making machines. Such is our fate when we live in our minds, instead of our oneness-hearts!

In Sri Chinmoy's home, he now had 170 lb in one cage, and 127 lb in the other. Three times he would practise pushing the heavier weight upwards, using two hands. Then he would go to the 127 lb and pump it for five repetitions with one hand. Then back to the 170 lb, this time trying to move it using only one hand. Bit by bit, it moved one inch, then four inches, then it finally surrendered.

Sometimes I would ask myself what I was doing half way around the world making exercise machines, sometimes working fifteen to twenty hours a day. Why was I doing it? The answer was simple... for a smile, a very special smile. To me, there was no smile on earth like this one. It was like the smile of the Beyond, filled with divine love and joy. In the ordinary life we work for money but we are never satisfied, and we soon want more money. When we get more, we are still not happy. But Guru's smile was completely satisfying. There was nothing in the outer life that could give me that same reward, that indescribable feeling of oneness and gratitude.

Sri Chinmoy used to say that when we work for him it must be with a feeling of unconditional self-giving. And sometimes we work for a while with this attitude, until the mind consciously or unconsciously begins to demand something for our work, even if it is for him to smile at us. But if he smiles at us when we want him to, we may drown in our pride. He knows what we need to make the fastest progress, and he will supply us with that need at the right moment. In the battle of life we can embody the negative forces or the positive forces, whichever we choose.

The year was fast drawing to a close and it seemed that things were happening at a much faster pace. Boxes had to be made to take Sri Chinmoy's weights to Japan, and he himself was extra busy preparing for the trip and practising for the concerts scheduled there.

On December 10th, Sri Chinmoy officially named his one-arm lift 'The Body, Heart and Soul One-Arm Press'. He established a set of rules and guidelines that were printed along with some pictures illustrating the newly-founded lift, which is similar to the traditional one-arm military press. The main points of Sri Chinmoy's lift are:

The dumbbell must be pressed overhead in a continuous motion to a full-arm extension, where it is held for three seconds. During this manoeuvre, the spine must be erect and the torso may not rotate. The knees may bend slightly, but not more than two inches from a vertical, straight leg position. If a power rack (cage) is used, the dumbbell must be free of contact with the rack at full arm extension.

On this same day, he changed his routine to cook a 13-course meal for a group of disciples who had been trying to guess when he would lift the 155-lb weight. Guru was in a joyful and playful mood, and at one stage he was mixing and patting a very large pot of food with his hands, saying, "Food is God and so I am playing with God!"

There were two special dishes, one extremely hot and spicy dish for the boys, which he said would purify our minds and illumine our hearts, and an extremely bitter dish for the girls to take away their insecurity and jealousy.

It was time for Sri Chinmoy's trip to Japan. His luggage may have not looked big but it was weighty. Besides the ordinary luggage, which included a number of musical instruments and three entire exercise machines, there were seven small boxes and six small tool boxes, each weighing from 40 to 70 lb, depending on the size of the dumbbell inside. So everyone got plenty of exercise when it came to moving Guru's luggage, especially the baggage handlers at the airport!

On the plane trip, Sri Chinmoy did not rest. He did 700 push-ups in the aisle and also used several hand exercisers that he carried with him. In each location we stayed at, he had a separate exercise room to do his workouts, and a set of weights and exercise machines were set up in the hall where we gathered for functions.

When we first arrived in Japan we had to load everything onto buses. But Japanese buses don't have luggage compartments and so the luggage had to fit around the seats of the passengers! Barely a space was left. The driver of the bus was laughing at the never-ending stream of luggage. Then along came the small tool boxes. He still laughed, but you could see the shock on his face as he helped to lift them, wondering how such a small box could weigh so much.

While he was in Japan, Sri Chinmoy did not get as much exercise as he might have at home in New York. But a combination of different types of exercises and the enforced rest probably did his body a lot of good. It did mean, though, that he couldn't lift 170 lb while in Japan because there was no cage to protect him. Without the really big weights, we had no idea whether his strength was increasing or decreasing. But he did find several new exercise machines in Japan and a few of the ones we had left in New York soon appeared with the late arrivals.

Sri Chinmoy competed against himself on the new machines: using an exerciser that measures the amount of pressure it takes to squeeze the hand together, he went from 30 kg to 42 kg (approximately 70 lb to 95 lb). On another machine, he would stand and bend over, grabbing a handle which he pulled upwards. It measured the amount of weight he could pull up from the floor. He started on 60 kg (130 lb) and in thirteen days was able to lift 90 kg (close to 200 lb). Sri Chinmoy used to complain from time to time that he was losing strength because he could not work out in his gym, but I could see that he was definitely getting stronger in other muscles.

In all, he performed nine concerts in Japan, and was constantly active, meeting people, writing new songs, travelling, practising musical instruments, running and walking, and still finding time to fit in weightlifting. Moving from city to city, travelling on buses and trains did not stop this 'divine dynamo' from transcending. He had been practising lifting 86 lb from the floor to shoulder height for about ten days, and then for about five days lifting 91 lb to shoulder height. On January 5th, he lifted 91 lb from the ground to above head height and then one-arm pressed it five times.

On January 7th, Sri Chinmoy surprised us all by doing 2,230 push-ups in 59 minutes 34 seconds. I was one of three counters for this feat. While he was doing the push-ups, he asked some singers to sing fast spiritual songs. The whole audience remained in a soulful and prayerful consciousness. This was to be Sri Chinmoy's first teeming surprise for 1986.

Sri Chinmoy arrived back in New York on January 13th. On January 14th, he attempted to lift the 170-lb dumbbell – but it did not move. Guru said that he had used only 60 to 70 per cent of his strength. The next day he tried again. The weight started going up so fast we all felt that he would succeed, but it was as if the Supreme did not want it done on this day and so it never reached the top. On this day, Guru said that he used 90 per cent strength. He was smiling, as if to say, "It is only a matter of time." The very next day the weight surrendered to him on his fifth attempt.

Sri Chinmoy said, "Prayer-power can do this. In any walk of life, concentration and determination have to be brought forward. Do not be satisfied with failure." And, again, he often said, "How many people would just give up!"

All the fears he had about losing strength in Japan were swept away with this lift. But still his bicep muscles never increased their size of 14 inches when flexed. He longed for 15-inch biceps, but the growth of the muscles seemed elusive. There seemed to be no outer increase in size to match the increase in strength and power. Guru would do every exercise he could think of to increase their size. Then he would measure them again. Poor Guru would look at us and shake his head in disbelief.

Even mathematics did not apply to Guru. We tried unsuccessfully to predict when he might lift a weight, projecting a date from his past progress. But Guru being Guru, sometimes he would be weeks or even months ahead of schedule.

His muscles may have not measured any bigger, but they sure looked bigger. When he rolled up his sleeve to play esraj or cello, you could not help noticing his powerful arms. And when he was playing tennis, his legs looked just as strong and developed.

In all that Sri Chinmoy accomplished with weights, he never went backwards. In running you can go up and go down, losing fitness through injury or losing your edge, but with weights he went from strength to strength. He always warmed up first on lighter weights before he tackled the heavier ones, and this might be one of the reasons why he never suffered an injury while lifting. He knew intuitively what to do, and this was undoubtedly the best protection of all – the Supreme's inner guidance.

"I do weightlifting and all that, but I have to be frank, compared to my inner power it is a drop," Guru told us.

On January 20th, Sri Chinmoy had the 170-lb and 200-lb dumbbells placed in the cages so that he could 'warm up' on the 170 and begin pushing on the 200. The next challenge was on again. When he first started lifting weights, who would have thought his goal would be as high as 200 lb? Only the Supreme knows where it will end.

I left New York for Australia after seeing Guru lift the 200-lb weight up one inch. I felt that this 200 pounds of inconscient weight was on the move to meet its destiny with Guru's goal. And then, six days into the miracle month of March, Guru transcended his own personal record yet again with a lift that surpassed all others – he lifted the 200-lb dumbbell in the true style of the Body, Heart and Soul One-Arm Press.

CHIDANANDA
New York,
United States of America

For years they had stood at the entrance to the temple, two 1,000-pound stone lions, eyes blank, like sentinels of heaven. Passing between them, one could almost feel their power. With their massive physical presence and forceful inner presence, they seemed to straddle two worlds – half-alive and half not-alive.

Then one day in 2004 they appeared at a great indoor arena, the auditorium of York College in Queens, where Sri Chinmoy planned his November 13th weightlifting demonstration. That day, the auditorium would become the scene of heroic contests and deeds, where the denseness of matter would confront the openness of spirit.

By all accounts it promised to be an unforgettable event....

On one side lay thousands of pounds of metal weight. On the other, stood the lone figure of the man hoping to tame them. The metal plates were cold, dark, stubborn in their unwillingness to budge. The man was determined, implacable in his will to move them.

Using the muscles in his arms, his shoulders and his legs, 73-year-old Sri Chinmoy planned to lift 20 tons that evening. It was his 19th weightlifting anniversary, and he wanted to commemorate the occasion by breaking all previous records. Over the course of the night, he raised off the ground everything from automobiles to books to metal weights – using various kinds of lifts.

Many Olympic gold medalists and other world class athletes came to watch the performance... and be part of it. They filed onto the stage in a great procession, and one by one this weightlifting maestro also raised them into the air.

The whole evening was a vivid demonstration of the philosophy of spirit he has been expressing through his writings, paintings, music and lectures over the past forty years. It's a philosophy that strives to bring forward the inner life, awaken the divinity buried inside each object and person.

It's a philosophy that finds its most dramatic symbol

in the physical act of lifting. When he lifts, Sri Chinmoy says he does not try to conquer the weights; rather, using the power of concentration and meditation, he strives to lighten them, to transform their dense, heavy physicality into the lightness of spirituality.

Nothing captured the essence of the evening so strikingly, and profoundly, as his lift of the two lions. Though made of stone, they exuded a presence, an aliveness, so they seemed to exist halfway between matter and spirit. One could say they represented matter on the edge of spirit, stone inconscience on the borderline of consciousness.

In lifting them with his calf-raise machine, Sri Chinmoy was striving to cross that line, not just to bring light into darkness but to perform a far greater alchemy – transforming inert matter into the substance of life. The muscular effort he exerted, though absolutely real in its own realm, was also a metaphor for the infinitely more difficult spiritual struggle.

For a moment he stood by the lifting apparatus, his body hunched under the padded bars. Then suddenly he straightened, pushing against the bar with his shoulders – calves straining as he sought to raise the two half-ton lions into the air. At first nothing happened. The lions did not budge; he might as well have been trying to lift a building off the sidewalk.

But he continued pushing, pushing, until all sense of time vanished, all points of reference disappeared, and nothing in the universe seemed to exist except that enormous mountain of weight and the terrible, implacable urge to raise it.

The tension became almost palpable, as though the resistance of the stone lions and the strain of trying to raise them were both reaching the breaking point. Something had to give – either the straining muscles and the spirit they cloaked, or those eyeless creatures of stone, yearning for life, for consciousness.

Then, miraculously, the lions started to tremble. The master weightlifter was not exerting more effort; he had long ago reached his maximum. But inwardly he had crossed some line, broken through some barrier so that, somehow, his physical body had merged with the force within.

Now it was not muscle straining against stone, but spirit reaching out to spirit, prepared to go on indefinitely – for hours, for days, for centuries, if need be, until the stone itself disintegrated to dust.

And, finally, when matter could no longer bear the relentless pressure, when the physical universe could no longer tolerate this implacable tension, the weight suddenly gave and the lions began to rise off their supports. From inconscience he had brought forward the essence of life, from matter he had invoked spirit.

There were other lifts that night, but none seemed as memorable as those two stone-faced lions, which he raised across the threshold of consciousness.

* * *

The Mongolian steppes stretch as far as the eye can see – right to the edge of the sky: hard-packed dirt and shale punctuated by small shrubs and feathergrass. Here and there, a lone ger – the round nomadic tent – with dung smoke rising through its roof hole toward a pale sun!

Just a few weeks earlier, frozen stallions galloped across the white plains and giant snowflakes, like pounding hooves, tumbled from the sky. But now it was early spring, just before the rains, when rivers still ran dry and half-starved animals wandered the dusty plains. Caught in the gap between seasons, lost between the emptiness of the land and the bright, unchanging stillness of the sky, life in the steppes seemed to hang suspended – trembling with readiness.

And then that fateful call was heard – carried by the fierce winds blowing in from the Gobi desert – that a high monk had come to their land, a great Buddha-like soul who had descended from Heaven to raise the 'horse spirit' of the nation. From the far-off mountains and distant valleys, they collected their white stallions and drove them to gathering points beneath the blue of the sky.

And for two days the great spiritual figure, who had crossed oceans and continents to reach these tiny spots, lifted the horses into the air – using a modified calf-raise machine to raise a wooden platform, on which the animals stood. When all was done, Indian spiritual Master Sri Chinmoy had lifted 58 white horses, symbolizing what the nomadic people believed was the 'wind horse' of their country – its inner strength or spiritual essence.

One of the nomadic riders presented Sri Chinmoy with a white racing stallion – a most precious and sacred gift from a Mongolian nomad – as well as a white mare. Sri Chinmoy immediately composed a song about it, called 'O King of the Horses', which his students sang on the empty steppes, their voices lost in the wind.

The 75-year-old spiritual Master also lifted with one arm some of the youngest and oldest souls in the country – little children as well as centenarians over 100 years of age. Jargal Dolgor, wearing her finest rubber boots and del, the traditional robe-like dress, said afterwards, "Sri Chinmoy is not an ordinary man. He is a monk. I am feeling very good, very happy inside now." The 104-year-old woman received the 'Lifting up the World with a Oneness-Heart' medallion but was too frail to mount the stairs to the overhead lifting platform to be lifted. She said Sri Chinmoy's students from America and Europe – who had accompanied their teacher to Mongolia – were the first Westerners she had ever seen in her lifetime.

Sri Chinmoy came to this central Asian country, he said, to serve the heart and the life of the Mongolian people, and their President, Nambaryn Enkhbayar, presented him with his nation's 'Medal of Friendship'. Sri Chinmoy came as a brother and a friend, but he swept through the land like a warrior, a 21st century Chingiss Khaan. In 10 short days – from May 14th-24th – he conquered the minds and hearts of an entire people.

Mongolians encountered on the street said they regarded him as their own teacher. The Director of the Choijin Lama Temple Museum, where the 75-year-old spiritual leader meditated before the statues of Mother Kali and Lord Buddha, called Sri Chinmoy "the teacher of my heart." The host of *Morning Guest*, after interviewing him for national TV, asked Sri Chinmoy to consider himself and his crew "your followers and keep us in your heart."

The people of Mongolia were like the wild ponies ranging over the steppes – ribs protruding, half-starved from the long winter. They were spiritually famished, and this Indian teacher was like the spring rain that sent sweet grass shooting up from the dusty plains and brought new hope and light to a people still recovering from the cold winter of Communism. Sri Chinmoy came to this country with nothing but his inner simplicity, his spiritual depth and his meditative grandeur. For this parched land, it was like a great rainstorm, and wherever the drops fell, the dry Mongolian desert blossomed with flowers and trees – with art, music and spirituality.

Great flocks of birds filled the meditation hall in his Ulaan Baatar hotel from the hundreds of bird drawings he completed each day. His luminous Jharna-Kala paintings gave the city's 'Art' Gallery a subtle, ethereal beauty not previously seen in this rough land. The Vice Chairman of the Union of Mongolian Artists, which sponsored the Master's art exhibit, presented him with the Union's highest award – the first time ever to a foreigner. "Many artists have come up to me and thanked me for bringing your art to Mongolia," he told the spiritual leader. "This gallery will always be open for you."

Music seemed to fill the air wherever Sri Chinmoy walked. He composed more than 50 Bengali and several English songs in Mongolia, and his World Harmony Concert at the Ulaan Bataar Palace brought a soaring musical consciousness to a country where music is as integral to life as the wind and sun. The famous Mongolian composer N Jantsannorov introduced the concert.

In the tradition of the great Buddha figures of the past, the spiritual leader delivered two major talks during his stay. His poetry lecture at the Government Palace was introduced by MP Gandhi Tugusjargal, who described the experience as "one of the most precious moments in my life." Afterwards, Dr. G. Mend-Ooyo, President of the Mongolian Academy of Culture and Poetry, presented Sri Chinmoy with the Academy's 'Pegasus' Award. "May your... genius soar like the legendary winged horse in the eternal sky covering the four corners of the globe," the award proclaimed. At a later meeting, the Mongolian poet presented the spiritual teacher with a copy of his newly published *Nomadic Lyrics*, "dedicated to my dear friend and brother Sri Chinmoy."

Sri Chinmoy's lecture on art at the State Academic Theatre of Drama was opened by the Rector of the Mongolian University of Culture and Arts, who presented the Master with his University's cap and mantle, along with an Honorary Doctorate Degree "for his great contribution to the development of human peace and enlightenment."

The spiritual leader also made several presentations of his own. He offered the U Thant Peace Award, plus an original painting, to President Enkhbayar when he came to visit the Master's art exhibit. He also presented the 'Lifting up the World with a Oneness-Heart' medallion to several cultural and political luminaries.

Even the brightest of times must come to an end, and Sri Chinmoy left Mongolia shortly after midnight on May 25th. When his plane flew off into the cold night, vanishing among the stars, this Indian spiritual teacher left behind a special brilliance that shall forever light up the vast Mongolian steppes. "I shall never forget my visit to your country and the boundless love and compassion that you and your people have showered upon me," he told President Enkhbayar just before leaving. Mongolia, too, will always remember this Indian Master whose love and simplicity found an eternal home in the Mongolian heart.

JOGYATA
Auckland, New Zealand

New Zealand in December, 2002. Guru stands in a field surrounded by last spring's lambs, all around him rolling landscapes of green hill country, clumps of forest, above him a deep blue sky with high-up skeins of wind-brushed cirrus. In this arcadian setting an extraordinary event is unfolding, one that will capture the imagination of the whole country for weeks to come.

Guru has set himself the goal of lifting 1,000 lambs during his stay in Hamilton and Taupo – on a number of central North Island farms over the next several days, musterers will bring their flocks of sheep in from the hills, draft the lambs into holding pens in readiness.

In spiritual literature the lamb is often seen to embody the qualities of innocence, helplessness and purity, qualities Guru saw as foundational in our reliance and dependence on God. Iconic symbols of New Zealand's pastoral heritage, lambs presented Guru with a completely novel opportunity in a weightlifting career filled with wonderful innovations.

Two or three lambs were placed in each of two large bamboo and aluminium cages – and each cage was placed above Guru on his 'Lifting Up The World With A Oneness-Heart' apparatus, one cage positioned independently above each arm. Guru would meditate briefly, summoning his inner reserves, then simultaneously lift each cage of lambs together, holding them briefly aloft before lowering them gently back onto the platform.

With each filled cage weighing up to as much as 265 pounds, the combined lifts often exceeded 500 pounds. These heavy lifts were repeated until 100, 200 or more lambs had been lifted in each session, a feat of both remarkable strength and sustained endurance.

Media interest was considerable and this colourful and imaginative tribute to New Zealand and to the symbolism of the lamb received a great deal of television and newspaper coverage. Guru the musician also rose to the occasion – several lamb songs were composed and sung by the group accompanying him, a vocal performance marrying the extraordinary with the charming. Under a wide summer sky an unforgettable blend of athleticism, joyful tribute songs, a delighted crowd of onlookers and a memorable message of inspiration.

Guru commented: "Why am I doing this? I have a deep love for lambs. The Saviour Christ had a very special affection, love and fondness for lambs and I also have a very special inner feeling for lambs. We all need to be God's lamb-children."

"My goal is to inspire people – by lifting up one thousand lambs I feel God has given me a golden opportunity to be of service to Him and to inspire others to fulfill their own goals."

Of New Zealand I have many lovely, random memories. Guru was so happy lifting the 1,000 lambs and 100 hundred cows! Who would have imagined him wandering so contentedly about in the muddy yards with the animals, leaning familiarly on the old farm fences and gates, relaxed as can be. When the boys pushing the reluctant cows up the chute onto the lift platform became thoroughly besmeared from head to toe in dung, Guru laughed and laughed in delight. Guru called Shardul over and said, "Shardul, you will win the world beauty contest!" In the interviews taken at these times, Guru is in his usual transcendent mood but looking more than usually satisfied, gratified, content.

* * *

Guru was very inventive and very practical in training us. In response to the common lament that it is hard to be meditative and spiritual in the 'ordinariness' of daily life, he once conducted the following exercise. He would tell a joke, at which we would all smile and laugh – then he asked us to immediately go up into our highest meditative consciousness. After some minutes, he again told another joke, and again we were all invited to laugh, to 'come down'. Following this second joke we were instructed to once more 'go into our highest'! And then another joke, back down into the mind, the world, the commonplace, followed by another effort to soar up into the soul, the silence, the eternal.

This happened a number of times – Guru's jokes and then his lofty meditations, up, down, up, down.... We were learning to go from laughter and the everyday up into the sacred, the God-conscious, to quickly reconnect with heart and spirit – and being shown that these two worlds are only one world, a thin veil apart. We were running up and down the ladder of consciousness, from mind to soul to mind to soul, being shown that inner peace, stillness, soulfulness are quickly accessible through practice and intent, that meditation can be found and practiced anywhere. All of our life is our spiritual life and through proper understanding and practice we can consciously part the veil, bring mindfulness and spirit to each passing moment, stay close to the Self while living in this challenging and changing world.

* * *

After a lifetime of travel and lifelong encounters with many great human beings – our path took us to so many places, to encounters with so many people – it is a truism for me to say that Guru was, by a very great distance, the greatest person I have ever met. Even after my own 30 years of examining him he was always far over the horizons of my comprehension – and what I could comprehend was always wonderful and breathtaking.

I often marvelled at those hundreds of times that Guru walked alone on to a concert stage before audiences of up to 18,000 people, folded his hands together over his heart and simply by standing there, through the force of his love, the power of his meditation, his abandonment to God, bring a hushed, pin-drop silence to the entire auditorium. His tranquillity and absolute poise and the great achievement of his realization were felt by everyone. Then I would marvel at how he would sit in front of an unfamiliar piano or pipe organ with absolutely no idea of what he would play, no sheet music, no keyboard training, no mind or anxiety, entirely trusting in the higher worlds of music to pass through his fingers, the same surrender to God.

Guru's personal example in this area of his life – and which he demonstrated in everything, everywhere – taught us much. He wanted us to understand our own capacity to uplift and serve the world, to live cocooned in God-trust, our confidence and power resulting from our growing oneness with him and God.

Once I was very touched by a small incident that occurred prior to a Peace Concert in Auckland. I went to Guru's dressing room backstage to let Guru know the hall was full and all was ready – there were 3,000 people waiting expectantly in the auditorium. I imagined Guru would have at least a little of our human apprehension or pre-concert nerves, but instead he was looking at me with an absolute attentiveness, so calmly and so lovingly, and then asked me how I was! "Are you alright, Jogyata?" he asked, and looked deeply at me, wanting me to tell him of anything troubling me. He was about to walk out in front of a packed concert hall and play for two hours, but his only concern was in my welfare. I was amazed and tears came to my eyes.

* * *

While many of Guru's teachings take years to penetrate the stubborn shell of our ignorance, others are learned very quickly – sometimes painfully – and were often learned through Guru's personal intervention.

I was once on a lengthy stay in New York, and on one particular day had been working hard on a Centre project. That evening at Aspiration-Ground a troupe of Indian magicians was to perform and I rushed home from my day of manual labor, showered, then dashed back to the evening function.

Hurrying down the driveway of Aspiration-Ground, I passed Sanatan, who asked me if I would help him get prasad – I mumbled some excuse about needing to be somewhere and began moving on. He kindly said, "No harm, I can get someone else." I felt a little guilty at my response, then came a redeeming wave of self-righteousness – after all, had I not been laboring all that day? Inside Aspiration-Ground the show was about to start and I sat near Guru, able to see the magicians and

Guru both. Then Guru suddenly turned to me, and said, "Oi, Jogyata, Sanatan did not ask you to help him?"

Naturally I felt smitten with guilt. Guru was positively beaming at me, a huge all-knowing smile. Rather evasively, I replied that Sanatan had now found someone else to help him – but Guru was unrelenting! "But did he not ask you?" Guru responded, then turned deliberately away to watch the show. I felt absolutely mortified, and after a few moments left the court and went in search of Sanatan. When I returned some time later, chastened and contrite, Guru turned and beamed at me again – my lesson well and truly learnt.

Looking back, I really cherish these difficult life lessons so much, and how Guru with a glance or a few words could shift our ingrained stubbornness and illumine us. These tiny moments were powerfully catalytic and brought about great change, and later I came to see and understand how self-offering engenders a heart-widening oneness with others – along with humility, self-effacement, kindness – and is one of the great secrets of a high-velocity-ride back to God. And from a similar teaching about self-giving and God-dependence on another occasion Guru's words still linger, hinting at the same inner treasures and attainments... "You will see in the future how you will be most surprisingly rewarded."

* * *

When I first saw Guru at an evening meditation in New York in early 1981, I remember seeing white light all around him and how something far away stirred in my memory – a pleasing feeling of recollection and of coming home. I stood afterwards in the school corridor down which he walked on the way to his car and in those few moments I think something quite significant happened. Guru looked at me and smiled very beautifully – his eyes flickered up and down and he was looking at my heart centre. I could feel something happening there, a block removed, a small explosion of feeling. After that I never worried about how to meditate anymore – I felt it had all been taken care of, an initiation of some kind, and that meditation was really a gift or an act of grace. I just had to be willing to keep trying and be available.

I remember at one of our celebrations in those early years presenting 800 chocolate-covered marshmallow 'fish' from New Zealand, a prasad or 'blessed food' item. Guru had one, then another. He liked them. There were 300 left over so I stored them in their boxes under my bed, savouring the prospect of a second popular 'fish' prasad. At night I would often reach down and take a chocolate fish as a late night nibble – finally a sense of mounting guilt and declining health resulted in my again presenting the fish for prasad.

But this time Guru glanced at the chocolate fish and made a face. "Are these fresh?" he asked.

"Reasonably fresh," I answered evasively.

"How fresh?" Guru asked, smiling and unrelenting.

"They don't really go stale," I replied, "they are in sealed boxes."

"How fresh are they?" Guru asked again.

"Well, I've had them for three weeks," I replied, a final admission.

Guru poked them with his foot. "Dead fish," he said and made a face. It was my first lesson in prasad etiquette.

Guru had a quick and wonderful sense of humour. But you would need to when you have oneness with the suffering of the whole world. A tiny example – once during a function we had some delicious ice-cream prasad and we all filed by the tables groaning under the weight of this perennial favourite to help ourselves. Several boxes were left over so Guru called out, "Greedy people come and have more." Nobody moved. So Guru smiled very sweetly and said, "Alright, willing helpers please come and have more." Of course hundreds of 'willing helpers' surged forward and in a short time dispatched the remaining ice cream. Greedy? – no! Obediently willing? – yes!

ADHIRATHA
New York,
United States of America

I was not a disciple for very long at the time of the first Puerto Rico Christmas Trip that many people were going on – maybe 30 people! Guru was asking if there were other people, but I hadn't been a disciple long enough, so I didn't even apply. And then one night I got a call from Sunil. He said, "Do you want to go on the Trip?" "Sure, I'd like to go on the Trip," I said. "Well, Guru was asking if there were any other people because some people who were planning to go can't go." And I said, "But I haven't been long enough," and he said, "Guru's not asking, so why should you? I already told Guru you were a possibility." So that's how I got on the Trip.

What I remember was that it was all so new to us, and also being that close to Guru. They rented buses and we all went on the buses together. I remember we went to some place where there was a very steep hill. I think Ashrita started to climb it and fell down. I thought, that's not the right thing to do. Then I looked over and there was Guru climbing up. So that was a different view that I had of Guru – he was right in there with us. I still had what Guru called 'reverential awe', which he said was better than disrespect, but it wasn't really oneness with him. So that started to break down the feeling that there was a separation.

One of the disciples had a beachfront house. We went there one day to enjoy the beach and to be with Guru. Guru was composing and writing, and all of a sudden he starts drawing pictures for people – and it's their animal incarnations. People kept asking me what mine was, and I wasn't sure, and I didn't want to say.

Then Guru made a point of asking me, and I said I wasn't sure. He just looked at me! Other people have had interpretations of it since then. Guru never said. It's like a big bird sort of thing, and I felt it was maybe an ostrich with its head in the sand, because of certain things that came up later.

I remember a big concert in Ponce, and for us it was a really big thing – we had to be at attention as guards. We had to look very smart. That was the first time we had to do that.

Florida was 1976. What I remember was that we bought three old school buses. Some of us got in the school buses to drive down to Florida. The buses broke down... but eventually we got to Florida on time. And that was where we got to ride with Guru more often, because he'd be on the bus.

I remember there were cold showers; we went to Disney World; miniature golf with Guru – which was really precious – and it rained a lot. But then Guru began to think of games for us. He played ping-pong for hours with everybody, and we saw how good Guru was. Against the best players, Guru could win. Like he did later with tennis, Guru played at your speed to keep the game going especially if you were hopeless. Guru would relax, then all of a sudden he would smash one. He would let you know that he really could win.

Another memorable thing for me personally was the first time I saw plays: Kishore, Prashanta and Sipra were doing a play. The girls were designing it, and they had Kishore come out in this costume that was like some sort of bird. To me it was so embarrassing! I was cringing with embarrassment for Kishore. I didn't know who he was, and part of me was afraid that we were going to have to do the same thing. It was the first play. But then I became Kishore's good friend, partly because I thought, "God! This guy is so surrendered. This is something I could never do."

And it reminds me of Pulak in Tobago. He told us of the great experiences he was having. But, you know, when you get on the plane you think you are having two weeks of sun and fun with Guru, and all of a sudden someone is out there on a road crew filling in potholes! He told us what a great experience he had, but in our minds, it was like, "Oh my God!" It was the same thing when I wore a dhoti for a while to the UN. It ended up being a tremendous experience, because Guru made it that way. Chidananda said to me at the time, "I hope I don't have to wear that to Mobil Oil!" – where he worked.

Guru would choose something that was a challenge for some person, but it was what he or she needed and what they would grow with. We who were watching it didn't understand everything that was going on between Guru and that disciple.

Another thing – we would all cook together, taking turns. We didn't have plays so much, but that was our challenge – then, of course, the boys against the girls, and who could come up with the nicest dessert and things like that. So, whatever the situation was, whatever our finances were, Guru found a way to bring joy to us – and to challenge our ability to work together with people we wouldn't naturally work with.

KODANDA
New York,
United States of America

My fondest memory is one breathless evening in Harrison, NY at the Old Mill Farm, a 17-acre estate, home for about twenty disciples. I lived there in what was for me a Camelot-like Utopia. I felt I had found my true spiritual contemporaries, "All for one and one for all," in a true enduring bond of divine love.

This particular night, however, was the ultimate pinnacle... Guru was arriving to host UN Secretary-General U Thant at a performance of his play, depicting the most compelling scenes from the life of the Buddha. Accompanying them was Dulal, a noble, advanced disciple.

As they arrived I was asked to offer my blanket to cover a muddy area they would be walking across. My blanket was the very one which I had cherished since childhood, a bit like the character of Linus in the cartoon *Peanuts*. For a moment I hesitated... but then again, it's for my Guru, so... yes... sure... OK... by all means, use it.

As I go outside to take a seat on the hill in front of the outdoor stage uniquely built with utmost care by disciples just for this one event, to my surprise I see my blanket, a blue and white comforter, not on the ground, but neatly folded in the center of the stage!

Instantly, to my joy, I knew that Guru would use this to sit and lead the opening meditation. What an inexpressible miracle, for a Master of his height to touch my little blanket. Yet, it had been with me through all my experiences, and I was horrified that its impurities could have some harmful effect on Guru.

As Guru began, he did indeed sit and begin to sing, 'Buddham Saranam Gachhami', the universal invocation to Buddha, playing upon his harmonium, a hand-pumped India organ. As he did, I felt the whole hill being inundated with a rich ochre aura of all-embracing light. This was the colour of Buddhist renunciation, and its effect was beyond nurturing.

Then as U Thant took the stage... Guru placed a garland around his neck from the same place, my blanket still blessedly beneath his feet.

In that moment I knew behind all shadow of doubt that I had truly found my life's destiny. I was to be one of the sacrifices of lesser earthly dreams for the honour of serving the potentiality of man towards the nobility of human peace and dignity among brothers.

PRACHAR
Canberra, Australia

On Saturday, April 10th, 2004, there was a 2-mile race, at which Sri Chinmoy had arrived and given the following prayer:

Each time an unconditionally
God-surrendered seeker
Meets with God,
God tells him,
"My child, you are the beauty
Of My Soul's
Transcendental Dream
And you are the duty
Of My Heart's
Universal Reality."

– Sri Chinmoy

Around 10 past 8 this morning, many were flocked around the food tables, enjoying a post-2-mile race breakfast of muesli, a scrambled tofu concoction and fruits.

I was walking with two friends along the street when a young lady ran past: "Guru has come to the race!"

This news had spread fast, as from literally every direction, tracksuit-clad forms were reconverging, some walking briskly, some running excitedly, back to the race course. In reality, they were converging from a radius of not just a few blocks, they were coming and they have been coming on planes, trains, boats and prayers from every corner of the globe. (Yes, the globe does have corners – and you and I are each one.)

My mind played a little game, asking the rhetorical question: "For what are so many grown men and women so eagerly hurrying and scurrying, as little children to a candy give-away? To catch a glimpse of our Guru? We saw him last night for many hours, and we shall be seeing him again for most of the day, so why the flurry? Why the haste?" The question was noted and filed, as I quickened the pace.

When I and my friends arrived, the morning prayer had already been given and recited, and a walk-past meditation was under way.

The women were filing past our Master first, giving me and my friends time to absorb the scene and prepare ourselves inwardly for the moment....

Even as we joined the slowly moving line approaching our Master, details from the physical-mental-temporal surroundings were evident – trees across the street swaying a very muted and gentle dance, I must do my laundry today, a middle toe reminds me these shoes are a half-size too small, birds' cheerful chirping, remember to inform so-and-so 9 o'clock singing practice is cancelled, a twig cracking underfoot...

then all is gone...

... in a smile.

There are no words for it – you can try 'beatific', 'heavenly', 'sublime', 'exuding compassion', all are good and correct, but none do justice to the interactive reality of this smile.

This is more than a smile representing an exalted state of consciousness – this smile communicates to every level of your being. It thrills the soul, magnifies the heart, silences the mind, surcharges the vital and even lightens the physical body. It transforms you.

First you look at the smile, then it draws you into itself and you find yourself inside it. For this smile is not just an outer smile on a face, it is an inner, all-pervading reality, a state of grace, blessedness and perfect oneness. In a few short minutes, hundreds of people have dived into and are swimming in that smile. It is everywhere, you don't have to see it now, you feel it as you float in its lap.

So that is why the people were hurrying, that is why many, many more would hurry, desperately and breathlessly hurry if they knew....

This smile strikes you dumb, takes your breath away, obliterates your worries, and elevates you instantly into bliss. Nothing else in this world can do that in one instant.

Only later do you wonder – how? For this smile sees no imperfection, no sorrow, no limitation, this smile sees only absolute perfection, absolute bliss, this smile sees and feels only God. This smile can only exist in the presence of God, a God who conquers all through His own Smile.

Yet how can that be? For this smile was at me, right into me.

More than that – this smile is within me.

It is mine. It is I.

That is why I and we each hurriedly ran, to merge into this smile, to sip of this ecstasy, to rediscover the immutable reality that...

I am God. My Guru's smile is the proof.

NAYAK
*Seattle,
United States of America*

In gratitude for the opportunity to share some thoughts, I would like to say some things that are very important to me. These are things that have impressed me about Guru Sri Chinmoy – things that relate to the soul.

When I first met Sri Chinmoy I found it remarkable that he bowed to his students and bowed to so many people. Here I was, meeting a wonderful Avatar, and he was bowing to me. Why? I do not feel that I deserve that, but here is what I have learned. Sri Chinmoy once commented in a talk or informally that when he sees us, he sees a golden glowing soul. His writings on the soul are luminous, and he describes the soul as the personal representative of God within us. It is something that guides us and attempts to carry out the work of the Supreme Lord in and through us. The soul is the only reason that we are here. When the soul departs, it is over. The soul goes to another world and rests to wait for the next cycle. OK, then, you can see how someone who is seeing that glory of a soul will be moved to bow to it. He is not bowing to the silly thoughts, the ego that dances, no. He is bowing to that golden glowing soul. You have it. I have it. Consider this. If you invited a personal representative of the Supreme over to your house for lunch, you can imagine yourself showing some real respect. Wouldn't you?

Lately I have been paying more attention to the meaning of souls' names. I like to call or greet my friends on their birthday, and now I commonly ask what their soul's name means, if they have such a name. This soul's name is not just any old name, like Joe the Dip. This name embodies the reason that you have come to earth in this incarnation; it tells you what to do. When I hear the soul's name of one of my friends, I am truly moved, because I see vast capacity and a high resolve by this very beautiful soul.

I received my soul's name on November 6th, 1977, at Jamaica High School Track. After Guru played tennis in the courts at the southeast corner of the field, he called me over and offered me the name in a very meditative session at 8:40 a.m., lasting 7 minutes. Here is what he said (excerpts).

"With my heart's soulful love and my life's blessingful gratitude I offer you your soul's name. It is a most significant name bringing to the fore all your divine qualities. Not only will it bring your divine qualities to the fore, but it will manifest the divine qualities for the Supreme here, there and elsewhere.

"Nayak is the one who leads, guides, illumines and fulfils the seeker divine, a liberator divine, a transformer divine and a fulfiller divine. Nayak is the one who leads, marshals ignorance-force, leads and illumines the human force and fulfils God the infinite Compassion, liberates man...."

I am quoting this here without bragging or promoting myself, but just to show what lofty things my soul came to do. If you know me, you know that I am just a speck of what is promised here, sincerely, but the value of this lies in knowing that I have a mission and that my beautiful soul wants to do something most magnificent. The short form of my name is 'leader', and in other comments that

Guru has made he also made it clear that he wants me to lead from behind.

I have seen Guru bow to so many people, and sometimes the unkind person in me says, "Why is he bowing to that person? There is nothing worthy there." But Guru sees the soul and he loves and respects that soul. Alas, I do not see that soul. But I do have a growing respect for the human race – that I can say. My growing awareness of the soul and its mission has reminded me countless times that whomever I am talking to contains a spark of the Supreme and a soul that has a purpose. Oh boy! I like that.

Guru once commented during a talk about the soul, in Hawaii, that I, Nayak, believe in the soul. It was a very helpful comment, because, while I was startled for a moment (Huh? Do I believe in the soul? Really?), I realized that I do, indeed, believe in the soul. Guru took an inner feeling of mine and various notions floating in my life, all pointing to a purpose, a meaning, a direction, a vastness, a love (and so on) and he put it all into that word: the soul. Yes, I do believe in the soul. Plus, I was privy to a couple of comments that Guru made at different times about how you can feel the soul. He told me directly once that you can feel the soul like an ant crawling up the back of your chest, the context making it clear that the little ant was crawling inside the back of your chest. A little, nice scratchy feeling. He made a crawling motion with his fingers to illustrate it. Another time I heard him talking with someone else, and he made the same statement – the ant crawling up the inside of your chest in back – I liked that. I do feel that ant crawling from time to time. I can't force it or demand it; the soul just decides to visit my awareness from time to time in that way. Once I feel it, I can meditate on it, and I like that very much. I have great respect for Nayak, which does not mean that I respect my personality, my career, my ego, my jokes, it just means that I have great respect for the soul that dwells within me. I (whatever 'I' means) find it a great honor to have this affiliation.

So, bottom line, you have a soul, you have a mission, and you can discover it. You do not need to have a soul's name to find that mission, you just need to meditate, pray and dive deep within. It is there. That is why it is worth respecting all beings, human and otherwise. They all have souls, as does everything large and small in Creation. That is worth bowing to. If you want to read more about the soul, please read the books by Sri Chinmoy explicitly about the soul. Very informative and inspiring. You feel like you are getting on the cosmic sleigh ride when you read those.

PRIYAVADIN
Salzburg, Austria

It was on one of my first Christmas Trips, maybe 16 years back. I think it was in Mexico. We had a soccer match against a local team. It might have been a team formed by the hotel staff where we stayed. It happened that Guru came as a spectator and watched the whole game. Afterwards he even took time to train us. He showed us a few really fancy tricks and we had a playful dribble competition in front of Guru.

I very sadly failed in the dribble competition.

Interestingly, and to my great disappointment, if nobody watched me I was really good at it. During the whole match I was not happy with my consciousness and playing. I felt a little useless and insecure. According to my own judgment my performance was quite average.

From my very early days, when I started to play soccer in a team from my little home village, at maybe 6 years of age, my father started to tease me for being an unskilled soccer player. He did it in a humorous way, not in a bad way. But nevertheless inwardly it hurt me. He kept doing it over the years, which had a rather strong impact on me. Maybe it increased some insecurity in me or gave me an extra burden in my life to fight with.

Now coming to the point, Guru cleared all my soccer-related inner disharmony with one sentence that he told my dear spiritual brother Ketan on that day. After playing soccer we had our regular evening function, and I felt tired and in a way relieved from the nervousness that came from playing in front of Guru. I felt cozy and at home at the evening function, being back in our meditation hall and enjoying Guru's caring and loving presence. At the end of the function Ketan came to me and gave me Guru's 'bomb'. He told me, "Guru said: this boy knows how to play soccer!" meaning me.

On the outer plane Guru, being my spiritual father, never heard a word about my situation with my physical father teasing me. A few months later, we had a small soccer match in New York, just playing with a few disciples on small goals with small teams. I absolutely had the game of my life. It was all just about having fun. But Guru's compliment made me so unbelievably free and joyful. It gave me such confidence I could nearly do whatever I wanted and it just worked out so well. I scored an unbelievable (nearly ridiculous) amount of goals. My heart of gratitude to the spiritual father and to the human father, as both were needed for that small story.

PRAMODAN
Dortmund, Germany

In November 1994 at a Wednesday night meditation in Munich, Tirtha – my Centre leader – read out a message from Guru: "Who among my German children accepts the challenge to build me a Tote-a-Tune?"

I had no idea what a Tote-a-Tune was, but I immediately knew that I was meant to build one. I asked Tirtha what it was all about, and she told me that a Tote-a-Tune is a small organ that Guru uses to compose his songs. She also told me that it has round buttons instead of keys.

I could hardly wait until the end of my next day's work. I took the train to Munich and started my shopping tour. I ended up in a toy shop where I bought a children's keyboard. I went back home, then on to Turiyakanka's wood workshop where we immediately started building. My simple idea was to just make a new chassis and have buttons which press onto the keys of the toy.

Meanwhile Tirtha informed Guru that we were building a Tote-a-Tune and Guru sent a very nice message encouraging us and telling us how happy he was about it. The message came via Minati who was at that time in New York with Guru. We had almost finished when she measured one of Guru's Tote-a-Tunes and gave us the actual measurements. Oh God! Our Tote-a-Tune was almost double the size of Guru's. What could we do? We tried to shrink it somehow, but instead of getting smaller the electronics broke down and there was no more sound at all. Even my best intentions failed to bring the electronics back to life.

By now it was Friday night and our German Joy Day was on Saturday. My idea was to bring the 'patient' to the Joy Day and to ask Harkara for help. I knew that he was an advanced electronics doctor and that he would definitely be able to bring it back to life. At the Joy Day I went straight to Projjwal's book table but there was no Projjwal! There was only Karali. She told me that Harkara was with Projjwal at home. They were building a Tote-a-Tune and would not come. I was really shocked. How could they miss a Joy Day!

In contrast to myself, they finished the Tote-a-Tune, and Projjwal took it to the Christmas Trip. They had used Karali's Casio keyboard and made it smaller. Guru played it and commented, "Total failure, total failure." Then Projjwal stopped his Tote-a-Tune journey. Now I asked Harkara whether he would like to make a Tote-a-Tune together with me. He would be in charge of the internal organs, that is to say the electronics, and I would make a very nice outer body with very smooth buttons.

We did it, and this Tote-a-Tune finally made it on Guru's 50th UN Anniversary Concert Tour. The absolute highlight was to hear it together with 13,000 seekers at the now legendary Prague Concert in October 1995. But it was just the journey's start.

We knew we could make it a little better. So we built a second one and sent it to Guru. Then we got another idea how to better it and we made the next one and the next one and so on. At one point Guru was so happy with the recent Tote-a-Tune that he asked us if he could have one or two more of the same type. Since he was using them in different places, he would not have to carry the same one with him all the time. Every Tote-a-Tune got better and better and we kept on building these small organs, until ten years later we brought Guru our 20th Tote-a-Tune! It was the 2004 Christmas Trip in China. It had a real harmonium sound and was able to record Guru's singing and playing. But it all started with two total failures: Harkara's first Tote-a-Tune and my first Tote-a-Tune, which had already failed even before Guru could test it.

CHAPTER 3

INNER COMMUNICATION

*Grace carries us
Far beyond
The limits of time and space.*

– Sri Chinmoy

DEVASHISHU
London, England

The first time Sahadeva and I saw Guru was one of those amazing coincidences in life that turn out to be no coincidence at all. It was in Kensington High Street in our hometown of London.

A big transformation had already taken place. It started on the day Bhavani, my mother, first saw Sri Chinmoy at a meeting room near Euston station in London in 1976. At that meeting my mother knew that she had found her spiritual Master. Beautiful Jharna-Kala paintings began to appear on our living room walls and the bookshelves were filled with Sri Chinmoy's poetry and stories. Our father taught us some delightful songs in the Bengali language. The biggest change was in our parents themselves – they radiated happiness.

One day, in the summer of 1977, our paternal grandmother came down from Coventry to stay with us for a week. My grandma was born in India into a British family in the final decades of the British Raj. Shortly after India achieved its Independence in 1947 she brought her two children with her to England. On this particular day we were driving into central London to visit an exhibition at the Royal Academy of Art.

In those days my father owned a Renault 4 van. Kaivalya, my father, was driving and his mother was in the passenger seat. There were no seats in the back so my mother, brother and I were all sitting on the floor. I was eight years old and my brother Sahadeva was six.

My mother was looking out the rear window and

suddenly she saw Guru. He was standing on the pavement in Kensington High Street, all on his own, with what appeared to be some takeaway food in his hands. He was waiting for an opportunity to cross the street. She screamed, "It's Sri Chinmoy, Sri Chinmoy!" My father looked in his side mirror, and perfectly framed in the mirror was the reflection of Guru. My father was a physics schoolmaster and never did anything extreme or dramatic. But without a second thought he made a 180 degree turn in the middle of the road and pulled up metres from where Sri Chinmoy was standing. We were filled with excitement and burst out of the van. As I remember it, Bhavani was running with Sahadeva and I hot on her heels. My father was persuading his mother to join us. She couldn't understand what all the fuss was about.

We all ran up to Guru. Poor Guru seemed a bit taken aback. Bhavani explained, "Oh, Sri Chinmoy, we are your disciples." Guru was very happy and he said a few words to my parents. Then he put one hand on Sahadeva's head and the other on my head and blessed us. It felt like a long time, like time had stood still, but it was probably only a minute. In that minute of silent blessing, of silent meditation, I found my Guru. He smiled in silence and conveyed a universe of love and joy that was abundant and infinite and yet familiar. We were in ecstasy, absolute ecstasy. My brother and I couldn't stop smiling for a whole week.

VIDURA
Montreal, Canada

It was a beautiful sunny August Celebration Games Day. The teams were North America against Europe. A boy's ultimate joy, playing soccer, a game Guru used to play at the Ashram and encouraged his disciples to play to foster dynamism, oneness and good old discipline.

It was an intensive game and I was playing defence. One of our players pierced the defence of our European brothers but the goalie made a beautiful save and the European team made a couple of very fine passes.

Suddenly one European player broke away and was coming towards our goalie. I was running after him as I had gone forward to help on the last play and was caught off guard. I ran with all the speed I could gather up and caught up with my European brother from France. As he was about to kick the ball, I also swung my right foot to block and we both hit our own foot and collapsed on the ground. The game was stopped momentarily. My brother-disciple seems to have gotten the better of it as he was OK, but my foot had inflated in size. I had pulled something, probably a tendon (as confirmed by Pradhan the genius chiropractor from Chicago).

I had to limp off the field and exit from the game and I think the European disciples won that game by one point. Guru was informed of the situation and I was immediately grateful for that. For some reason I felt I should walk on my foot but everyone was giving me advice as to what to do and what not to do, which was not to walk on my foot. I inwardly felt all the time that I should be walking on my foot and it was a very powerful feeling. I felt uncomfortable all afternoon for not listening to that inner voice.

Later that evening I went up for prasad and Guru saw me walking with one foot off the ground and the other taking the whole weight. Guru motioned to me come and see him. I went up to Guru and he told me that he had put a very strong force on me and asked me why was I not walking. I apologized to Guru and went back to my seat walking quite comfortably on both feet. The pain and whatever the problem was had disappeared, and voilà – a truly incredible instant miracle cure had occurred.

From that day on I learned a very precious lesson, and that is to listen to one's inner voice, especially with the calibre of Guru we have. Gratitude to our beloved Guru, who is ever alive within our hearts and entire being.

ARTHADA
Vienna, Austria

I was incredibly lucky to meet Sri Chinmoy, my spiritual Master, twice in person in Europe, only six months after becoming his student. On these two occasions I received special inner experiences beyond time and space. This was very exciting and gave me the crazy idea that God-realisation was in my immediate reach, just around the corner. Today, 19 years later, illumination seems to be much more distant than ever and is persistently eluding me. To tell the truth, I have never again had experiences such as those that were bestowed on me at the very beginning, although I have time and again tried very hard. It seems that my Master understood my need back then for drastic experiences, so as to turn a new page in my life and make me ready to totally surrender myself to the spiritual path. After all, coming from the hippy movement, I was already used to drastic experiences – albeit by using illicit means.

Be that as it may, only six months after becoming a student, I went to New York to see Sri Chinmoy with the goal of taking 'another' huge step towards God-realisation. My determination and aspiration were such that I got an exception – actually, going to New York was reserved for students over one year – and for good reason, as I soon found out.

On my first or second day in New York, I suddenly found myself in an abyss of overwhelming doubt, despite the exceeding enthusiasm that I had felt at first. All of a sudden, everything appeared absolutely ridiculous to me, and my parents' insistent warnings seemed to come true indeed. How could the seekers there, with folded hands and full of devotion, pass by a seated person, who limped away after the meditation like an old and sick man? Everything in an instant appeared to me as the blind worship of an idol. At that time, I just couldn't make the connection between the yogi's human and divine aspects. I only saw the human in the Master.... Today I know very well that we students usually feel joyful and completely carefree after such 'walking meditations'. We give all our inner impurities to the Master, who subsequently has to suffer physically for our mistakes.

Anyway, I was deeply disappointed and decided to take the next plane back to Austria. I had obviously been wrong about this Master. I was ready to go, and I stood alongside the driveway, just at the time that the Master himself was leaving that place. Sri Chinmoy came towards me, and I felt greatly disturbed and desperate: Had all of my experiences been hallucinations? Is he really the wrong Master? Sri Chinmoy passed by me, his eyes almost closed, and did not seem to pay any attention to the students waiting by the roadside; his mind did not seem to be in this world at all. I was gazing at the Master, who was limping away, when I sent my last and most fervent prayer to heaven: "Please, this is the absolutely last chance. Please, please, give me a sign, only a very small sign that you are a real Master!" No sooner had I finished thinking these words than Sri Chinmoy stopped and very slowly turned towards me. Time seemed to pass in slow motion. Our eyes met, his gaze penetrated me as if he really knew all about me.

Guru's face remained completely motionless, but his eyes said everything that needed to be said. Never will I forget this look – I was so embarrassed I wished the ground would open up and swallow me! Though not a single word was spoken, this moment was worth more than a thousand words!

After Sri Chinmoy in his compassion thus replaced my stupid doubt with humility and devotion, I spent two of the happiest weeks of my life in New York.

KANAN
*New York,
United States of America*

Sometimes when I would feel that I was really aspiring, I would slip and find myself at the bottom again. Then the frustration of knowing that I had made myself fall would often leave me in a very sad mood. Such was this day, many years ago.

On that day I went to rake leaves at Guru's house. Guru came out onto the porch, called my name and said "Hello" with a wave of his hand and his divine smile. Usually I would never see him when I went to rake, so this filled me with joy and consolation.

Later that day I was making a garland for Guru to wear that night – he was to give a talk at Barnard College on the Vedas. I had some roses which were fully bloomed, and even though I knew they might drop some of their petals, I decided to use them. I just imagined someone seeing Guru for the first time, and as Guru was walking by, the garland would be shedding petals, and this seeker would pick one up and cherish it forever.

That night at Barnard, before the lecture, Guru was sitting alone in the back reading, but the whole hall was flooded with his light and peace. As I sat down, I felt his force acting within my heart, inspiring me, even though I was not in a good consciousness. I closed my eyes, and soon I felt like I was climbing upwards within a vast light. I was very moved. I had not meditated so well in many months.

In the joy of my meditation, I suddenly felt something

brush by me. I assumed that someone was trying to get past my aisle seat, and their clothes were brushing against me. I opened my eyes to find Guru dropping his coat on my lap to hold it for him during his lecture. His compassion, his love and concern for me, even when I felt I had not been doing well, was very moving. His coat was like a blessing – it tingled with spirit.

After the talk, Guru walked up to me, gave me a beautiful smile and took his coat. While he was turning to leave, a flower fell from his garland and landed at my feet, and I realised that I was the person I had imagined that afternoon.

SUSHUMNA
London, England

In the very early days, most of Sri Chinmoy's students were in Queens (a borough of New York) or in Connecticut, these two points being about an hour's drive apart. Mostly these people were young, with very little money.

On this particular occasion, a group of boys were working on a project in Queens and they needed extra help. A young man who lived in Connecticut (I forget his name, so I will call him Bill) said he would help. When he was about to leave home, he realised that he only had enough money to get there – nothing for the journey back. He knew it was unlikely that the young men he was going to help would have any money themselves.

He said to himself, "Well, I must go. I won't worry

about getting back. I'll think about that later." He worked hard all day and forgot about the problem. When the work was finished, he realised he had to get home. He was walking down the road, wondering what to do, when he saw Guru walking towards him. "Ah, there you are!" said Sri Chinmoy. "I have been looking for you. I wanted to give you this." The young man was handed some money which more than covered all his expenses.

This to me also demonstrates our inner connection – our oneness with our Guru.

TANIMA
New York,
United States of America

In early March 1983, I was at home with a big cast on my leg. I had broken my leg in February. During this recovery time at home, Guru was so kind to occasionally call me and also send prasad to me.

Guru was going to India, and all the disciples had gone to see him off. Sitting at home, I was sad that I couldn't be at the airport. I was picturing what Guru was doing and envisioned him giving prasad to the disciples. Thinking that Guru might remember to send prasad home for me, I said to myself, "I wonder if Guru will think of me."

Within literally five minutes of that thought the phone rang. It was Guru. There was none of the usual small talk ("Oi, good girl, how are you doing?"). He merely said, "I always think of you," and hung up. Guru was not at home where he could just pick up the phone and call. He was at the airport! It is amazing to think that Guru first not only heard my thought, but then immediately had to find a payphone in the airport, get my number, get small change for the payphone, and call me (there were no cell phones in those days!), and all within minutes of my thought! But then again, perhaps Guru did it all from a plane of consciousness where payphones are not necessary. Nevertheless, I was overwhelmed with gratitude for his love and concern for me.

SIPRA
Adelaide, Australia

In each city we visited on the Christmas Trip, Guru would usually offer a Peace Concert for the local people. On occasion these Peace Concerts were quite spontaneous, with only a few days to prepare, promote and make final arrangements.

When we were in Yangon, the capital of Myanmar, I was assigned to try and find a venue for a large Peace Concert to be given in this spiritual Buddhist city. Unfortunately we had no luck with the authorities in waiving red tape and official permits. The only place that was available was outrageously expensive, so Guru decided to hold the Peace Concert in the meeting room of the hotel where quite a few disciples were staying.

Because we did not have official permission from the authorities, we could only advertise it by word of mouth. Disciples invited taxi drivers, people they met in the street and even storekeepers at shops where they had purchased goods. The day of the concert, Sarama approached me and asked if she could invite the owners of the small hotel where she was staying, which was in a different location from the hotel where the concert would be.

I suggested that Sarama approach one of Guru's assistants and ask him to check with Guru. We were standing in the meeting room, which was being rearranged for the concert, and Guru was sitting in the front of the room sketching his Dream-Freedom-Peace-Birds. When Sarama approached Guru's assistant, he considered this not an important enough reason to disturb Guru. Sarama was upset, but I could see that the boy was adamant in not disturbing Guru.

I looked at Guru and inwardly said: "Guru, what can we do in this situation?" He immediately stopped sketching, looked up and said: "You people must bring in more chairs as the disciples staying at the other hotels will want to invite the owners."

ARPAN
New York,
United States of America

This event took place in December of 1974 at the very first gallery of Guru's first thousand Jharna-Kala paintings, at the Unitarian Church in Hollis, Queens. There was a raffle for some prints of different sizes of some of the first thousand paintings. I bought one ticket, number 44. I was standing near Guru when he was picking the numbers from a hat. I was thinking of my number, wishing he would call it so I could get some prints, as I could not afford to buy many.

As he mixed the tickets around in the hat with one hand, Guru was smiling and looking around at us. He glanced at me with one of those wide-eyed, intense and very quick looks. It was only a split second but it was quite evident to me that I was the only one he did this to as he looked around at the audience in front of him. I was a bit surprised and confused as to why he would give just me such an intense yet quick glance. Still smiling almost mischievously, he pulled out the next ticket in the hat, good for three prints, and he announced the number 44. A thrill went through my body as a real sense of playful occult power, an easy task of innocent mind-reading for Guru, just brightened my day. It has lasted strongly within my consciousness, giving me joy every time I think of it even to this day, twenty-eight years later.

Even though Guru does not encourage the development or use of occult power or feel it is truly helpful to our aspiring consciousness, in cases like this when it is done out of playful and harmless fun, it can really create a sense of love and concern, and definitely have a positive effect on those who take the proper attitude toward it. My attitude was, of course, only gratitude, not only for the paintings, but for the first-hand and quite powerful yet innocent experience of Guru's love for us, which can easily transcend human limitations.

APAGA
Graz, Austria

Singing or playing music for oneself can be truly enjoyable. The same activities with others are at times challenging. Performing for a small audience is often thrilling; for a large one possibly scary.

But standing in front of your Master on top of it all could be downright heart-attack inducing! At least in my experience. Not that Guru was likely to criticize a performance. No, not at all, except maybe in the rare case when he tried to get the utmost out of one of the very talented and very established singing groups. But otherwise, he mostly reminded me of a benign grandfather, who lovingly and quite often rather indulgently listened to and tirelessly encouraged the countless groups on our path, coming from all over the globe.

His patience in observing a never-ending stream of musicians and singers, displaying all kinds of musical standards, was unwavering and by far surpassed mine!

Especially when it came to the occasional unfortunate performers, who sometimes did not quite manage to carry a tune, causing even my mostly untrained musical ear to cringe. Guru, however, never seemed to suffer from this kind of torture. Quite on the contrary, actually: instead of just quietly enduring the musical offering and being relieved to see (and hear) it finally end, Guru would sometimes even applaud those kind of performers, talk to them and ask them to sing another song. And another. And another. (Sigh...)

Of course, as a true spiritual Master, who has the blessingful capacity to detach himself completely from the superficial manifestations of the outer life, Guru reacted to the inner realities of those standing before him much more than to the outer result of their endeavors.

Poor me, on the other hand, was not so lucky. Especially not late in the evening, or rather; early in the morning, when I was feeling exhausted, sweaty, hungry and just generally uncomfortable.

Knowing and having experienced all this, you might wonder why I would ever feel anxious when being scheduled to sing in front of Guru?

I guess it was due to the intense spiritual atmosphere surrounding him and the inner awareness that just to be able to stand in front of a Master of his caliber for a few minutes, and to have his undivided attention during that time, was something incredibly precious!

The occasional doubt about the authenticity of my Master always immediately disappeared and melted into complete nothingness, the moment I came into contact with the vibrant energy field surrounding Guru.

How can you possibly deny the existence of the sun, when you're facing it?

In the same way, how could I possibly deny the reality of the true Master before me, when his vibrant consciousness-field simultaneously lifted my own consciousness, opened my heart and – more than once - weakened my knees. (Luckily, it never got to the point that I fell down, but to counteract the effect, I sometimes had to force my legs into a rather rigid stance....)

The reason why I was practically terrified on the evening this incident took place, however, was only partially due to the fact that Tirtha's Group was scheduled to be the first item on the program. I had been a member of this particular group for a few years already and we were well used to singing and performing together. Still, some ongoing problems with my voice and some deep-rooted fear (a long story) had me sweating profusely and trembling slightly, while I was waiting for our turn.

As the first group, we had the privilege of being able to wait for Guru at one of the entrances leading into the big assembly hall in PS 86, where our functions took place in the evenings during Celebrations.

"Guru is coming!"

The information was passed on in hushed voices by the masses of disciples leisurely milling about in the long hallway leading to the big hall. Within only moments, the picture of people slowly – very slowly, due to the sheer number of them – moving back and forth within the narrow confines of the hallway, turned into one resembling a tidal wave: suddenly, everybody was hurriedly trying to get out of the hallway and into the hall as fast as possible as nobody wanted to block our Master on his way to the front.

At the same time, the happy, expectant excitement that had been in the air before increased manifold, and became so intense it was almost palpable.

Only a few people remained in the hallway, standing behind the tables lining the long walls that were laden with miscellaneous goods, such as Guru's books, prints of his paintings or pictures that had been taken of the Master by various photographers.

As I was watching the scene unfold, I realized that this was it: within the next few minutes, I would be standing on the stage together with six other girls, attempting to sing with a voice that was almost completely hoarse. My eyes widened at the thought, my heartbeat was suddenly way up in my throat and the panic within me clenched my stomach. Retreating a bit into the depth of the doorway, I instinctively straightened my posture and folded my hands in front of my chest, mirroring the actions of the other girls around me. I took a few deep breaths to steady my nerves, while noticing that the hallway had fallen completely silent, except for the soft voices of Guru and the various students he was talking to on his way to the frontmost hall entrance.

I cautiously edged to the corner connecting the small door space we were occupying to the hallway, to catch a glimpse of the slowly approaching Master.

I had to peek around three of my friends, who had obviously had the same idea, but had got there first.

From what I managed to see, Guru was busy talking to a girl who was selling photographs that she had taken of him. They were too far away for me to understand what they were saying, but the girl appeared rather pleased with the way the conversation was going. Her hands folded, she was grinning widely, nodding at something Guru said, and pointing at something on the table.

After a few moments, the Master moved on, smiling at some waiting disciples, blessing others and occasionally stopping to talk to somebody.

When he had finally reached the end of the two rows of tables, we quickly ducked back into our doorway out of courtesy to our Master, as we did not want to stare at him, while he was approaching.

I swallowed hard, the panic within me almost causing me to crumble to the floor. (Again, I was nervous because of our impending performance, yes. But the panic within me had other reasons... but to explain its origins would lead too far for this short story.)

When Guru passed us, he did so swiftly and without even glancing our way. "Guru, please take my panic!" I silently called out to him, trying to imagine that I was offering him my chaotic emotions at the same time.

Guru did not bat an eyelid, nor did his steps falter or his head turn towards me. But in spite of the absence of any outer signs, I suddenly had the distinct impression that something was pulling on my emotions. It only took a moment, in which I almost heard something like a slurping sound... and suddenly my panic was gone.

Vanished.

Completely disappeared!

Astonished, I just stood there, amazed at what had just happened. After all, this panic had been my constant companion for several years. A moment later, my conscious awareness was drawn to the overwhelming sensation of lightness and intense bliss that originated in the area around my heart and quickly spread throughout my whole being. My heart had literally opened and I was flooded with joy and gratitude. Or, to be more precise: the cover of heavy emotions blocking my heart had been removed, freeing the inert qualities of my being and thus allowing them to permeate me completely.

My facial muscles, which had been rather tense for quite some time, relaxed and my mouth widened into a broad smile. In bliss, I followed the other girls right to the same entrance the Master had just walked through, as this was also the way to the steps leading up the stage.

"Tirtha's Group!" The MC of the evening called us a few minutes later, and soon we were standing before Guru and several hundred disciples, who were silently watching us sing from their wooden seats.

But – to be honest – the only person I really noticed was my Master, who was sitting on a wide chair in front of the first row, facing the stage.

Before we started to sing, Guru took a brief moment to silently mediate on each one of us girls, while we were facing him and the rest of the audience in a single file, forming a semicircle.

In the meantime, one of the boys swiftly adjusted three microphones on stands, which were necessary to broadcast our soft voices all the way to the very back of the large hall filled with people.

I barely registered the movement, however, as I was completely focused on the dark-skinned Indian man, who had become so dear to my heart over the last few years.

Having finished his wordless blessings, the Master nodded once, indicating for us to start singing.

A short burst of excitement exploded within my chest, only to be replaced by the blissful sensation of the familiar melodies of our songs filling me up to the brim, while floating (suddenly without any obstruction) through my lips to meet with the voices of the other girls to create a finely-tuned sound that connected us as one. At this point, all thoughts – except for the words of our songs – ceased and I simply existed in a realm of vibration and sound.

During our performance, Guru kept his eyes half open, silently watching us with this inimitable, otherworldly gaze of his that can – in all honesty – never be adequately described. It has to be experienced, as it was the outer manifestation of a soul that was fully at peace and perfectly still without thoughts.

As song after song resounded in the hall, my heart

expanded and I felt so incredibly blessed! In that moment, there was no place on earth that I would rather have been than right there, in the blissful presence of my Master.

I realized – not for the first time – that this feeling of contentment, this sense of fulfilment and happiness I was experiencing was all that I needed and would ever need in and from my life. If I could only remain in this state of consciousness forever...!

Of course, meditation, running, singing our spiritual songs and generally just being in the atmosphere of our path, frequently brought those emotions to the fore, but not with the same intensity that I was experiencing at that moment.

Besides, for so long, all these feelings stemming from the heart had always been tainted by the sensation of panic in my body, which had been holding me firmly in its grip for a few years at that point, never wavering. Until that evening.

It felt incredible to be once again free from any kind of fear! I felt so... light and unbelievably happy!

After we had finished and while everybody was clapping, Guru gave us the widest smile.

Had I thought that my heart had been filled to the brim before, I discovered that I had been wrong, as it suddenly expanded even more.

"Very good!" The Master's velvety voice sounded through the hall, causing my heart to finally overflow and me to giggle happily with the rest of the girls around me. Which might sound rather girlish, but what else can you do, when you are bursting with happiness and you are, in fact, a girl...?

Guru then proceeded to talk to us for a few more minutes – just small talk, like asking us how many songs we had sung – but when a Master shines all his heart's love on you, it doesn't matter what he says, really. He could have recited the phone book for all I cared, since I could feel his love pouring over us like a torrential rain through his words.

In bliss, I basically floated down the stairs leading off the stage, after Guru had blessed us one last time by nodding at each one of us.

Later that evening, when my ability – and the urge – to form sentences other than, "I am so fortunate, I am so blessed, I am so happy," returned, I realized that my panic was still gone.

Just like that – in a flash – Guru had taken something from me, which had been torturing me for years!

Some of it did come back after a while, but it was not as strong as it had been before. Looking back at it now, I know that it only did because it was necessary, in order for me to be able to learn more about the workings of the mind and the emotions. But on that evening, I received a huge blessing and the inner assurance that – no matter how difficult my life might seem at times – my Master is always aware and ready to help (and yes the present tense in this sentence is deliberate, as the inner connection between a true spiritual Master and his true spiritual disciple never dissolves. Not even in death!).

After a few more years, I managed to get rid of the fear altogether, again, with the help of my Master, but this is a different story....

BHASHINI
London, England

The highlight of the 2004 Christmas Trip for me was a boat trip we took from Sanya. Guru was inspired to compose songs and he was teaching them to us as we sailed along. One particularly beautiful song started with the words 'E nahe swapan nikhila dharan'. We sang it over and over, happily and soulfully as the sun shone on the water around us.

A couple of days later as I was standing waiting to take prasad, this song came to me again. As I picked up the prasad I started to sing inwardly, "E nahe swapan...." Guru looked straight at me and sang out loud, "nikhila dharan." This cute experience of inner communication gave me so much joy.

SHARANAGATA
Salzburg, Austria

After I had been a disciple for a number of years, I came to know Guru better and better, and developed a deeper and deeper understanding of him. An indescribable happiness grew within me. As time passed, a deep feeling of oneness with the Master developed. I was able to experience in a few instances the extent to which Guru himself experiences this oneness, and knows and feels our thoughts.

Once at a function, I was admiring an exotic flower that was part of a big bouquet next to Guru's little table. All of a sudden he called me up to the stage and gave me this flower.

Another time during a function, I was lost in thought, imagining how it would be if I were allowed to sing a song for Guru. As Guru was leaving the function room, he said to me as he passed by: "Sharanagata, will you sing two songs at the next function?"

At another function I had a strong desire to have Guru write a song with my name in it. Three days later Guru wrote four songs with the word 'Sharanagata', my name.

What Guru does for us in the inner world, we cannot express in words. We cannot fathom these inner blessings; we can only be happy and grateful for having such a lofty Master.

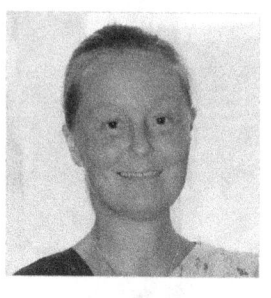

SHILPA
Zurich, Switzerland

When I had been a disciple for about four or five years I wasn't able to go to Christmas Trips. My health was not very good at that time. Instead, I used to go to New York for one week before Guru left for the Trip.

It was my last evening with Guru, before he was leaving for the Trip. In those days we used to have functions at PS 86 (a public school in Jamaica, Queens). The function was over and Guru was about to leave the hall. I thought, "Guru, I am not able to come to the Christmas Trip to see you. I will not see you until April next year. How will I live for such a long time without seeing you?" But then, like a response, I said to myself: "All right. I have to go back home. But even when I am not able to see you, I will take you with me right inside my heart, always, no matter where I have to go."

Right at that moment Guru turned around, and went back onto the stage, and went up to the microphone. Guru said: "Not all of you will be able to come to the Christmas Trip. But I want you to know that I will take you with me inside my heart, just the way you take me with you inside your heart."

SHAIVYA
Warsaw, Poland

I work at a museum in Warsaw, Poland, where I organise art exhibitions. Usually I tolerate my job, but at one time it was too much for me. I lost patience with my co-workers and manager.

Whenever I asked Guru for his advice if I could do something, the reply would come, "Yes, if it will not affect your job." This time I wanted to be really clever. I said to myself: "I will not tell anybody and I will not ask Guru for advice, because most likely he will say no to my sweet little plans. I will just say to my manager that I am immediately resigning my job!"

The next morning when I got up, I was absolutely sure that day I would resign. I felt free and happy. When I came into my office, I sat down at my desk – just to leave my bag and go to my manager. Just then Agraha called and said that Guru wanted me to do something – he explained what it was. At the end he added, quite unexpectedly, "And Guru wants you not to quit your job."

So suddenly my secret and subtle plans had gone with the wind! And again Guru proved to be quicker and more clever than me.

SARAMA
New York,
United States of America

Guru never wasted a minute. While riding, he would write poems or songs or add to his collection of thousands of bird drawings on an ever-present sketch pad.

One day Pulak was driving Guru around while he was drawing birds. From time to time, Pulak would glance over for a glimpse of Guru's drawings. He wondered to himself why Guru was drawing all the birds facing in the same direction. No sooner had the thought crossed his mind, than Guru started drawing birds facing the other way.

Pulak said, "Guru, are you reading my mind?"

Guru smiled and said, "Reading your mind is as easy as drinking water!"

CHAPTER 4

LIFE AND DEATH

*A realised soul
Is a fortress of Eternity
To protect humanity
From the inconscience-blows of death.*

– Sri Chinmoy

AGRAHA
Seattle,
United States of America

One day, I think it was around 5:30 in the morning, Guru called and said, "O my God! What is happening with Nayak?"

I said, "What is happening, Guru?"

He said, "He is in the hospital. Call and find out what is happening. Something very, very serious – he is very seriously ill."

I called Nandita, and she had just brought Nayak to the emergency room. I called Nayak, and he sounded very, very, very weak. He was waiting to be seen. When I told Guru, he asked if I would please go quickly to the hospital. When I saw Nayak, his EKG showed that it was very, very serious; it showed that a very serious myocardial infarction, a heart attack, was actually in progress. The whole left side of his heart was blocked. Nayak looked so ashen – he looked very bad. He was very emotional, and the situation was very, very difficult.

Guru had said to call him as soon as we had any news. So I called and Guru said, "Please tell Nayak I am putting a very, very, VERY strong force on him. And call me in fifteen minutes."

I told Nayak and Nandita, and they were crying. Then the doctors came in. They had drawn blood to see what kind of heart attack it was, and they were looking at the heart tracing on the EKG, but the funny thing is, Nayak started to get better. He started to talk, he was joking, his colour was getting better. The cardiologist was asking the assistants, "Why are you going so slowly?" – but it was because Nayak was doing better. They were sort of joking with him.

The hospital cleared the whole schedule of patients so that Nayak could get a catheterization, a tube so they can visualize the heart. They put the tube through the big vein and they can see the heart. The cardiologist was extremely good; it was at the University of Washington Medical Center Hospital, which is really the best hospital in the whole Northwest. We wanted to stay with Nayak, but they said no, it would be about ten minutes, and then they would do whatever they felt needed to be done.

I had called Guru again after fifteen minutes, and Guru had said again that he was putting a very, very strong force on Nayak, and by that time, Nayak was actually joking with the doctors. He was looking so good, yet apparently there was a major heart attack going on. It was amazing.

After a while, the nurse found us in the waiting room and said, "OK, now you can see the doctor. The procedure is over." When we entered the room, the doctor said, "I want to show you something. These are the films we took of Nayak's heart a year and a half ago. These are the films now. Do you see any difference?" We were looking at the films, and he said, "We did not see any difference. We discussed it. We could not imagine what was going on. We have a mystery here, because here we show signs in the EKG of a major heart attack, and now there is nothing going on inside the heart, and he is doing very well."

I said, "Well, what about the lab tests? Do they show anything?" Because you can see from the tests if there is any damage to the tissue.

He looked at us and said, "The lab tests are normal. Something is going on!" The doctor was absolutely astounded.

So I told him, "We have a meditation teacher. I don't know if you believe in prayer."

He smiled and said, "I very much believe in prayer." We all knew that Guru had saved Nayak's life.

VIDAGDHA
Perth, Australia

In 1981, I was travelling from Melbourne to Canberra with a friend who was the wife of Australia's top marathon runner. It is a distance of 738 kilometres along the Hume Highway, a trip that normally took just over eight hours. But my friend was at the wheel and not even six hours had elapsed before we reached the outskirts of Canberra. She was driving a two-seater sports car and we were almost lying down as we flew along the country roads in the middle of the night. My conversation was minimal, my eyes were frozen on the blackness of the road ahead, and inwardly I chanted Sri Chinmoy's name over and over in rising panic. I hadn't bargained on being caught up in a road race that was beginning to resemble the Indianapolis 500, and she wasn't the kind of driver to whom I could drop gentle hints.

We sped through the outlying suburbs of Canberra at speeds I thought one could only attain in the air – until there came a moment of horror when I glanced out my passenger window and saw another car approaching at high speed from a side street. It was heading directly for us. Sure enough, the driver ran the stop sign and crashed into our car, just behind my passenger door. The collision caused our car to spin 270 degrees and slam into a concrete traffic barrier. The entire front of the sports car was compressed like a concertina. Meanwhile, the most of the back portion of the car had caved in upon impact with the other vehicle.

For a few seconds, my friend and I sat in utter silence in the two front seats, which were virtually all that remained untouched. The car was only fit for scrap metal now, but miraculously neither one of us was hurt. The other driver also emerged from his car wreck unhurt.

Later that night, I telephoned New York to convey a message of deepest gratitude to Sri Chinmoy. I had read that when something serious like this happens in our lives, all our subtle nerves are affected by the shock, and this was certainly true for both of us. Soon afterwards, Sri Chinmoy telephoned and spoke to my friend, her husband and me. He offered us so much love and consolation. Somehow he erased that nightmare memory.

Sri Chinmoy blessed my friend's husband before many of his important races, including his marathon in Japan where he set a new world record. But this experience touched them on a very deep level. They were convinced, as was I, that only Sri Chinmoy's protective force had saved my friend and me from certain death.

ANTARANGA
Munich, Germany

On a beautiful summer day in 1989 I visited a friend from my youth. At that time I had been a meditation student of Sri Chinmoy for about 15 months. I was also studying homeopathy, acupuncture and other subjects at the Josef Angerer School in Munich where I hoped to qualify as a health practitioner. We had a great time chatting about old times while my friend prepared a typically Chinese dinner of vegetables with rice and sour cherry jam. The food was delicious and I had already eaten a little bit too much when I suddenly noticed a devastating sensation in my stomach. The reason for this sensation was not the food that my friend had served, as he felt perfectly well, but was rather the beginning of a life-threatening situation.

But before my life changed its course, I flew to New York in the middle of August to see my spiritual Master Sri Chinmoy for the first time for his birthday celebrations. In the plane, high above the clouds, I was overcome with a deep and beautiful feeling of joy, but unfortunately this joy did not remain when I arrived on the soil of North America. Even though I thoroughly enjoyed Sri Chinmoy's 58th birthday celebration, with all its music, plays and meditations, by the time it was time to return to Germany I was not truly fulfilled – because I had not had any deep meditation experiences in the presence of my Master. I had read in one of Sri Chinmoy's books that it is best not to expect anything so as to avoid any disappointment, and also that it is

God's gift to have a deep meditation and it can happen at any time and at any place. But our human nature has its own needs, and theoretical knowledge versus a true feeling of unconditional surrender are two different things.

As it turned out, I left Frankfurt airport with a few of my fellow Munich meditation students. I was leaning casually against one of the airport pillars while waiting to be picked up by our friends when suddenly my consciousness changed drastically. All of my thoughts stopped, I felt peace and then everything around me became absolutely beautiful. Everything was the same but I felt like I was in paradise. I remembered that as a small child I had had such feelings on a few occasions. One of the Munich meditation students could see the change in me and asked if I had entered into samadhi. This peaceful and delightful consciousness stayed with me during the whole trip from Frankfurt to Munich and continued even during the last part of the journey on the tram. Everything around me was so fulfilling and I simply wished that this feeling would never end. But as soon as I entered my apartment the experience left me. So I had seen and felt the wonderful experience that meditation can bring to the fore. At a later time I interpreted this experience as the descent of God's Grace to inspire me to meditate regularly and to serve humanity, so that in the future I might stay in such a consciousness permanently. I can see now that it was very important that I had had the most fulfilling spiritual experience of my life so far without Sri Chinmoy's physical presence. As it turns out – due to personal health reasons – I was not able to enjoy Sri Chinmoy's presence very often, but I know now that Sri Chinmoy can offer a spiritual seeker experiences at any time and at any place.

A few months later the same devastating feeling in my stomach came back, even after eating just normal food in small quantities. My digestion stopped functioning properly, I started to lose weight and I was losing strength rapidly. A visit to the doctor to check on my jaundiced face and eyes brought no alarming explanation. Ikterus Juvenilis – teenage yellow fever is the translation in the medical dictionary. Nevertheless, I seriously felt that my life was in danger. Homeopathic remedies, which had helped me in the past with digestive issues, did not provide any improvement at this time.

During February 1990 Sri Chinmoy offered a concert tour in Germany on the occasion of the reunification of East and West Germany. Even though I already felt very weak, I decided to participate in the tour. I felt sure that Sri Chinmoy would save my life. Tirtha and her family, all of them Sri Chinmoy's students from Munich, gave me a ride in their large white Citroen and took care of me very lovingly. Right at the beginning of the tour I felt miserable even after very small meals and I asked Tirtha to please tell Sri Chinmoy that I had the feeling that I would die soon. Tirtha suggested that I should tell Sri Chinmoy personally and arranged a meeting with my Master.

Somewhere backstage and close to the elevator that Sri Chinmoy would soon be using, I waited, with Tirtha and her family standing behind me. Sri Chinmoy came towards me, I bowed down spontaneously and Sri Chinmoy bowed too. I bowed again and so did Sri Chinmoy. This happened a third time and then I don't know what happened. I was deeply moved and very happy, without a single word having been uttered. A short time later I saw Sri Chinmoy and his companions entering the elevator. Tirtha understood that it can be an overwhelming experience to stand just a couple of feet away from your spiritual Master for the first time, so she promised to talk to Sri Chinmoy the next day about my situation. I waited excitedly for her answer. "He will definitely not be dying," was Sri Chinmoy's response. I was very relieved and felt confident that this would definitely be the case. During dinner after the concert in Nurnberg I saw Sri Chinmoy concentrating on me a few times. As a result my pain and discomfort diminished.

However, on returning home after the concert tour I felt so weak that I could only walk a few very short steps. This meant that I had to interrupt my studies and move back in with my parents who lived about 100 km east of Munich. Computer tomography of my pancreas, gastroscopy and endoscopy did not reveal any organic disease. Without my approval I was given a sedative by injection, which only made me delirious and had no positive impact on my digestion. Even though my weight had dropped to 44 kg by April 1990, I never for a minute doubted that I would survive. The experiences of deep inner peace that Sri Chinmoy had blessed me with at various times were so positive that I had no doubt concerning the statement Sri Chinmoy had made during the concert tour.

I had to find a diet that did not leave me weak and useless after eating. I found out that some banana, dried dates or figs taken every hour or so did not drain me of too much of my strength and my low periods were shorter and more bearable. Very slowly I regained my strength and was able to study at home for the final examination of the public health department. Passing this exam would permit me to work as a health practitioner. I passed the exam in April 1991 and felt strong enough to look for a job, as I did not believe I had enough strength to start my own practice. The problem was that every 90 minutes I had to eat some of the bland mixture of sweet fruits so as to keep my pain within reason. Eating anything else meant that I was attacked by pain and could not work at all. What company would hire such an employee?

But Grace was with me and Tirtha's brother, Jwalanta, offered me a job in his family business. His family understood my situation and was very compassionate, and as a result let me work at their publishing house.

So for about two and a half years I had to survive on only fruits. Even so, my body still didn't show any sign of recovery. Kailash, one of Sri Chinmoy's first disciples in Switzerland, was so kind that in October 1992 he encouraged me to write a personal letter to Sri Chinmoy and he delivered it personally. I had asked if there was anything special that I could or should do to be able to eat proper food to regain my strength. Sri Chinmoy said that I could start eating a little more regular food and he drew one of his birds on my letter and wrote underneath: 'Blessings, Love, Joy, Gratitude'. I still have this letter and every so often look at it with great joy and gratitude.

During 1993 my health once again took a wrong turn. Immediately after eating a meal, I would feel a burning pain in my stomach. In April Tirtha decided to inform Sri Chinmoy again about my situation as neither homeopathic doctors nor regular physicians seemed to be able to help. Sri Chinmoy's answer was very illumining: I am dealing with major karma but have already made significant progress. It is my good fortune that I am leading a spiritual life as otherwise I would not be among the living anymore. I should continue to meditate and pray regularly, because that is the only thing that can help me. Sri Chinmoy is also praying for me. I need to convince my soul, my heart and my mind that my body will be healed and I should go to one doctor in whom I have complete faith.

This confirmed my feeling of years before that I was standing at death's door and that this was not just a thought, but a reality. And that I should stop looking for better homeopathic practitioners or another method of healing – this was simply my fate. I then went to a doctor who requested a series of hospital tests, but I was basically very, very grateful to God that I was on Sri Chinmoy's spiritual path.

In the middle of 1994 after getting a high dose of a homeopathic medicine from my homeopath, I found that I could eat normally again without any painful side-effects. I had taken the same formula and dose previously, but never with such success. It seems that my food-related karma had been nullified, and so, after 4 years on a diet consisting of fruits I was able to rediscover just how wonderful real food tastes.

The year 1994 did not only bring relief in that way, but rather another karmic wave was waiting for me at the beginning of 1995 that continued to create quite a lot of problems for me.

I had to move back in with my parents, who took care of me with much love and compassion. Towards the end of June a big Joy Day was planned very close to where my parents lived. During Joy Days, students of Sri Chinmoy come together from Germany and the neighbouring countries for a weekend of all kinds of festivities, meditation, music, plays, videos and more. Pramodan called me and invited me to come with him. I was very happy and grateful, but had a little doubt that I would be strong enough.

The night before the Joy Day I had a very strange dream. I dreamed that during the Joy Day I was sitting on a wooden chair in the middle of a large hall with huge glass windows and rows and rows of chairs. I saw a few of Sri Chinmoy's other disciples seated around me. Suddenly Death appeared before me, coming straight towards me. He looked like a skeleton with a black hooded cape and a scythe in his hand, just as you might see him in a movie. He came closer and closer to me and I tried to run away, but he followed me. Suddenly I saw myself inside a room and as I turned around Death was standing right in front of me. There seemed to be no escape. But suddenly Dinesh appeared – the tall and strong brother of Pramodan – pushed Death to the side, threw him against an open cupboard and just kept hitting him very powerfully with a flail till he collapsed. Now at this point a train appeared which moved in a spiral with pictures of party scenes like those of a new youth in a future incarnation. Then I woke up. I had a little trouble breathing, there was some pressure on my heart and as I stood up I felt dizzy. So I lay down again and rested a while until I felt stronger, and ready to drive with Pramodan to the Joy Day.

As I arrived at the Joy Day I immediately saw Dinesh. He and Pramodan told me that Sri Chinmoy had asked his Munich disciples to pray for me, as things were not going that well for me. I asked Dinesh if he really did pray and he confirmed. Then I told them my dream and the role that he himself had played. Never before had I dreamed about death and I have never since done so either. Perhaps that night, with the help of the prayers of my friends I had defeated Death a second time. What a frightful thought but at the same time I was filled with deep gratitude for everybody who had prayed for me.

The result of my illness in 1995 was that I remained very weak and could not work without heavy pain. So I received a disability payment and was not able to travel and visit my spiritual Master in New York for quite a few years.

In January 2001 during the Christmas Trip, a journey which Sri Chinmoy and his students undertook each year between November and February, Tirtha showed Sri Chinmoy photos of the Munich disciples. When he saw my picture, Sri Chinmoy asked: "How is Antaranga doing? I haven't seen him for such a long time. Can't he take a boat to New York?" Tirtha immediately called her mother Tapaswini to tell me what Sri Chinmoy had said. I was deeply touched that Sri Chinmoy wanted to see me but at the same time was irritated since a two-week trip on a ship in my present condition was even more impossible than an 8-hour flight to New York.

The application deadline for the August Celebrations, which take place every year in New York to celebrate Sri Chinmoy's birthday, passed. This year it was Sri Chinmoy's 70th birthday, a very special birthday, but I did not feel strong enough for that trip. However, about 3 weeks prior to the start I suddenly felt stronger and I even put on weight. In my meditations I started feeling so much happiness just thinking of traveling to New York. So I called Ashrita, Sri Chinmoy's secretary, and told him that I felt strong enough to come to New York. He said he would need to ask Sri Chinmoy since, due to my illness, I had not been in New York for 5 years and was still weak. Sri Chinmoy's answer was simple and touching: "Let him come!"

I can still clearly see everything right in front of me – it was August 14th and I stepped into the airport with my blue suitcase, having no idea what might happen. First and foremost, I could usually not even walk for more than 500m without feeling long lasting pain afterwards, and at the same time I needed my surroundings to be at a temperature of around 25 degrees Celsius. If it fell below 23 degrees my lungs would immediately start to burn and I would feel weak and perspire heavily. While walking to the check-in counter and towards the plane, the temperature was definitely not around 25 degrees but I felt no problems. Once in the plane I immediately took the sleeping bag out of my rucksack and stepped into it and took one of the blankets from above and put it over my head. I wanted to survive the 8 hours in the 22 degree temperature without major problems. But after a relatively short time I started to feel too warm, so I took the blanket off my head and soon afterwards took the sleeping bag off as well and put it back into my hand luggage. A little later I even took off my warm ski pants which I was wearing on top of my regular slacks. I normally wore the ski pants throughout the day since my body cooled off so quickly. Well, what I experienced definitely was a miracle. I reached my flat in New York without any damage and was welcomed with a wheelchair to cover the longer distances.

During the birthday celebration the students of Sri Chinmoy had organized a parade – with colourful costumes and floats from a total of 50 different countries. The parade went through the local neighbourhood for a good 3-5 kilometers giving joy to the people living in this area. I had decided to walk to the starting point of the parade without my wheelchair since it was very close to my living quarters. I stood quietly on a corner watching everything with great interest but without much enthusiasm, since I did not see a way for me to be involved – the distance was too great for my condition. Nevertheless, I was handed a costume – a bandana and a piece of colourful material from Bali. It was very nice and I just stood there holding it in my hand when I suddenly saw Sri Chinmoy standing close to me and watching all the activities with great joy. He did not look at me but I could suddenly feel enormous strength coming from Sri Chinmoy and entering into me. Could this really be happening, I wondered.

The excitement grew as the parade started to move and even touched me so that I took the bandana and the Bali cloth and wrapped it around me. I wanted to just walk with them for a little while before my pain returned and the cold air started to affect me. After a while I realized that I had been walking for quite a distance – without any pain or discomfort. A little while later I decided to jump on one of the floats – I didn't want to be too bold. I had joined the float with the Japaka Orchestra and was sitting with the other boys happily waving to the crowds lining the sidewalks. Suddenly I realized that I was not even aware of the rather cold wind and that I was not cooling off. When the parade was over, it became clear to me that once again I was the witness of a miracle – Sri Chinmoy transferred his own power into me so that I too could enjoy the festivities without feeling pain.

On the way back from New York to Munich my friend Pramodan and I met at the airport – we had both booked the same flight by coincidence. My sleeping bag was no longer in my hand luggage because I now knew that Sri Chinmoy's protection worked up close as well as thousands of miles away. This time I didn't even feel the cold air coming from the ceiling, but Pramodan felt it. Due to a broken tube, regulation of the cold air stream was not possible at this place and so Pramodan asked for us to be moved to a different seat.

This afternoon it is cool and the sky is grey. After many weeks of drought it finally rained. The calendar shows Saturday, 3rd December 2011. I am sitting at my desk and I think back over my life. I am now 47 years old. Had I not joined Sri Chinmoy's path, I would have died 21 years ago. My body is still very weak and I cannot work at a regular job, but most of the time I am cheerful and very grateful to still be alive. The morning depression that I suffered with for the first 15 years of my discipleship due to my karma is a thing of the past. If ever I wake up in a bad mood it disappears by the time I finish my morning meditation. I feel a certain inner balance and poise, a feeling of security and a deep trust in God that is now part of my daily life despite my body's limitations. These are the fruits of my 24 years of daily meditation.

Despite all that, my health is still fluctuating – sometimes for the better, sometimes for the worse. It seems that I am still dealing with my karma despite the great length of time. During a Christmas Trip in Sri Lanka Sri Chinmoy told his students that he can take 50-90% of the karma of his disciples. How many times Sri Chinmoy eased my own karma!

This year the old weakness returned to my body. After only simple tasks I could again feel major pain in my liver, to the point that the most I could do was very light work like editing on a computer, broken by frequent periods of rest. And at night I would spend my time lying down in a relaxing chair and resting. If I ever worked a little too hard and my discomfort got out of hand, I would rest and normally I would feel well by the next morning. Once it happened that I did not recover by the next day, on the contrary it got worse. I felt extremely weak, my liver felt raw and I simply felt very unwell, despite taking the homeopathic remedy that would normally always help. I sat down at my meditation shrine and prayed spontaneously like a child for help. After a brief period of time I felt deep inner peace rising through me and a few minutes later all the pain and discomfort had disappeared and I felt very well.

Such an experience I had quite a few times when Sri Chinmoy was still alive – once in April 1989 when Sri Chinmoy was visiting Munich. I had a massive headache while driving to the Hilton Hotel, where Sri Chinmoy was going to honor a Nobel laureate in physics. Suddenly I felt deep inner peace and my headache totally disappeared. After arriving at the hotel, as I stood a few meters away from Sri Chinmoy for the first time in my life and he looked into my eyes, I felt the same inner peace for a few moments.

In October 2007, Sri Chinmoy passed away and his body left this earthly abode. I can from personal experience confirm the following statement of Sri Chinmoy:

> *But if the original Guru made a promise to you, no matter where he lives, after leaving the earth, he has to be within you and with you to help you, even if you stay on earth for another forty or fifty years. In this case, it is just like having two rooms. Here is one room (life) and*

there is another room (death). Ordinary people cannot open the door. So when the Guru opens the door, he sees you, and when he goes back to his own room, he still has free access to this door. So once the Guru has made a promise, he is bound to keep it. He will not leave you until he has given you full realisation and has brought you to God.

–Sri Chinmoy

I will forever be grateful that my Guru has accepted me as a passenger in his boat. I feel it drives me to the shore of lasting peace and joy, despite all these inner and outer battles in life.

LOTIKA
Moscow, Russia

Some years ago, my mother was diagnosed with cancer, and it was very serious. The doctors did not even want to admit her into the hospital because the cancer was so advanced that there was no hope for her to live. Doctor Elena, who recently came to New York, helped us to put her into the hospital. The first day that she was admitted, she was very scared. She had never been in a hospital before, and she asked me for a Transcendental Picture. She was always positive towards Guru, but she never took our philosophy very seriously. She is a very realistic type of person. I gave her a Transcendental Picture, and she wore it on a chain around her neck as long as she could, until they inserted some tubes into her neck. And then she would just hold it in her hand all the time.

When they operated on her, only the lower part of her body was under anaesthesia, because she is allergic to many kinds of medicine, so during the surgery she was actually aware of what was happening to her. As I said before, she's very realistic and she never believed in any kind of spiritual experiences. But later she said that she actually saw Guru's physical presence in the operating room. Two days after the surgery she was released from the intensive care department. She called me on the phone and when I went to see her, she was already walking in the corridor. I was shocked, as the recovery normally takes about a month for this kind of patient, if they recover. Many of them actually die within a few weeks because of the tumour. The tumour that was removed from my mother was 12 centimetres big. But on the second day she was already walking.

The entire hospital staff was totally shocked. They were telling me, "What's wrong with your mother? She is not bedridden or anything. She is walking and she can do everything for herself."

Guru called on my cell phone while I was there, and he wanted to talk to her. I told Guru that she doesn't speak any English; she is just a simple woman. Guru said, "Tell me her name and put her on the phone." My aunt was also there with me in the hospital. My mother got on the phone, and she started crying right away. I could hear through the cell phone Guru repeating my mother's name and saying, "I love you, I love you." She was just crying and saying thank you. That was the only thing she could say in English.

My aunt had never heard about Guru, because I do not

keep in touch with her. After the conversation was over, my mother was just sitting there crying. My aunt asked my mother what was going on, and my mother said, "You don't understand. I just talked to God."

Now my mother is fine. Guru accepted both my mother and father as disciples. Guru teased me by saying that they are far better disciples than I am! He said that the case had been so serious, but that his love for me is very strong, and "when love is strong, it is not so difficult to have some miracle-jugglery."

MRITTYUNJOY
Athens, Greece

Let me first tell you how it all started: I had been Guru's disciple for just four years, and I was a very devoted disciple. I clearly felt that this was my path to self-discovery, so I was determined to offer all my capacities to the goal of making fast progress.

An important part of this progress was the so-called manifestation of spirituality. This meant sharing the inner light which I got from my meditation with other people, right from the beginning.

I always loved giving classes in this field. And I did have opportunities, even in my second year of discipleship, to give occasional lectures and seminars in Switzerland and in all the neighbouring countries. My favourite place was Austria, where I felt more warm-heartedness than in Switzerland or Germany. (This was only my temporary and subjective judgment at that time.)

Also Austria had the advantage that I could still use my mother tongue.

However, while doing this I developed the dream of going to a Southern European country, preferably one where I could start right from the beginning, with no established disciples or centres. (I must admit that I imagined this would be a bit easier than it turned out to be.) So the choice was between Spain and Greece.

For me it was quite obvious that it was more worthwhile to learn an international language such as Spanish, than to start studying Greek, which is used only in one tiny country worldwide. So I immediately started learning Spanish on my own, and I definitely wouldn't miss Guru's Christmas Trip to Spain, in December, 1984.

Everything went smoothly – at least until my second or third day in Barcelona, when I came back from my usual morning jog, and I had to cross the final road right in front of my hotel....

At that time the Supreme guided my destiny in quite a new and surprising way.

It was definitely not me who did it, because I woke up about one month later in a hospital in my hometown, Zurich. Actually even at the time when I woke up I didn't understand too much about what was going on around me, because the disciples who were visiting me at the hospital seemed to me to be boy scouts, and all I remembered was that I had a very beautiful journey with Guru in the inner world. By the way, one of the things that Guru had told me during that inner journey, was that I was destined to have a very serious car accident within the upcoming year, but that this would be only for my own benefit, so I should not worry about it.

But back to the facts which took place in Spain, as I

was told them later by Guru, by my brother and by other disciples. My soul then immediately came to Guru and informed him of my accident, and it told him also that there was no use of returning to this body which had been very seriously damaged. However, Guru asked my soul to return to the body, which he would personally take care of, a command which my soul followed with great delight. Guru at that time was inspired to compose the 'He Param Pita' (O Lord Supreme) songs, which are now my favourite songs.

On the same evening that Guru went to the hospital, my brother had just arrived from Switzerland. (By the way, it was Christmas Eve.) The Spanish doctors had told my brother, who is a doctor himself, in great detail about my present situation, which seemed quite hopeless, something between death and permanent coma.

At that point Guru obviously wanted to demonstrate his own point of view: he went to the lower edge of my bed and started concentrating on me. This had the effect that I sat up in my bed and started singing the word *pranam* (I bow) in a powerful voice for about five minutes. After that I lay down again and went on sleeping for one more month. I also had the great luck or grace, that my parents had an insurance policy which included bringing their sons back to Switzerland in a private emergency plane in case of a serious accident abroad.

The Swiss doctors were no less astonished than the Spanish ones, when they saw quite a hopeless case getting better and better in an inexplicable way.

However, it would be a lie to say that my mental capacities are just as they were before. My short-term memory is clearly reduced, which makes it impossible for me to work according to my training as an elementary school teacher. However I definitely do have the capacity to give meditation classes; I even have an increased intuitive ability and the capacity for more heart-to-heart contact.

So can you really speak of a handicap? In terms of money, yes.

In order to balance my reduced income, I moved down to Greece, a country with a lower cost of living, and also the country where I spent my last incarnation, as Guru told me later. Maybe that is the reason it was easier than I had expected to learn Greek, even though my memory was somewhat impaired.

Now you may ask yourself, why did I not speak directly about Guru's miracle, which is after all the point of this story, and why did I make such a long story about the before and after.

This is because to me a miracle makes sense only if it has some advantage for the soul's development, and it doesn't have any meaning if it is just for the astonishment of the mind and vital. I would say that the miracle which Guru performed in Spain belongs to the first category.

I forgot to mention what happened, right on my first meeting with Guru after the accident, when I was somehow returned to human consciousness. He gave me the name Mrittyunjoy, the soul who has conquered ignorance and death to please the Supreme in His own Way.

Needless to say, it was not me, but Guru himself who conquered ignorance and death to please the Supreme in His own Way, but I guess he needed some justification to give me a spiritual name.

SHAMITA
Vienna, Austria

In 1996 I was running a 100-km race. It was very, very hot – extremely and unbearably hot. I was running fast – maybe too fast for this hot and sunny day. During the race everything was quite normal. I just felt a little bit sick in the stomach, but this is not unusual when you are running long distances, so I did not take it seriously.

After finishing the race, I tried to relax in the medical tent, but I became more and more sick. When people asked me questions, my reactions became slower and slower, and my eyes bigger and bigger. My conscious awareness of what was going on became worse. They brought me to the hospital, because nobody really knew what was wrong with me. Seven hours after I had finished the race, my whole body started cramping and I lost consciousness. From that moment on I have no remembrance; I was in a coma.

Afterwards the doctors told me that I had something very unusual, called edema. Water from the body rises into the brain and the brain wants to expand, but because there is no room for it to expand, it stops functioning – which usually leads to death. I was in a coma for three days. They almost operated on my brain, but fortunately, I became better.

The doctors told my husband that there was hardly any chance that I would survive. Guru was informed immediately and said, "Everything will be fine. I am constantly with her. There will be no damage." And he was absolutely correct: I am now fine.

A few years later Guru said: "There was absolutely no chance. I brought her back from Heaven. I brought her back from God. It was a very serious hostile attack!"

For quite a long time I was told how much I should run every day. In the beginning it was not more than 8 km per day. After 2 years Guru allowed me to train for fast marathons but nothing more than that distance.

Guru: "I will tell you when you can run more!"

Finally after 16 years Guru gave me the information that I am again ready for long distance running.

PART III

LIVING AS A DISCIPLE OF SRI CHINMOY

CHAPTER 5

THE ETERNAL JOURNEY

*My physical death
Is not the end of my life –
I am an eternal journey.*

– Sri Chinmoy

PALYATI
*Alaska,
United States of America*

It was the summer of 1990. My mother had recently passed away and I was floating in a sea of confusion. She was my touchstone of my family life. She alone was the one I felt the most love from. Now she was gone.

I had been a meditator for a couple of years by then, but I taught myself and even though I now know I was meditating, I did not know for sure then.

A seeker of truth with a strong desire to grow spiritually I frequented a center that nurtured my needs for several years. The head of this center always told me not to get caught in the small stuff, the readings, the healings, but to keep focused on the Highest. I took the advice to heart.

It was at this center that I saw the small flyer, 'Learn to Meditate' and the event was free too. I registered. I needed to make sure I was meditating correctly as I thought that in order to truly meditate, one had to sit in the lotus position. There was no way I could do this.

Nayak from the Sri Chinmoy Centre in Seattle was the first of four to come to Anchorage, Alaska to give a series of four classes, one every two weeks. At the end of the class he asked if we wanted to see a video of Sri Chinmoy. I was enthralled.

Nayak might have been surprised when I phoned him at home later that week asking how I could 'sign up' as I put it and so started my disciple life.

How can gratitude ever end when my Guru has saved

me in many ways. In addition to saving my physical life more times than I can count on two hands, he has saved my vital from shock after shock, my mind from depression, my heart from abandonment. He has shown me unconditional love. There can be no end to gratitude even feebly expressed.

There were times in life when I was absolutely stunned, rendered speechless, my gut tight and aching, my heart shattered. In the safety of my home, with fists balled tight, I would scream until my throat was raw at some callous injustice. Then, with physical and vital sated, I would go to my meditation room and in the haven of my Himalayan cave, sit and cry to God. With emotion calmed, I would read Guru's writing. With mind slowly understanding and comforted by his words, finally, I could meditate.

As I write, I realize this is how I dealt with many things over the 17 years I have been blessed by being on Sri Chinmoy's path. What a revelation to define the process! In my meditation room I sought and found the solace to go on. In spite of depression, hurt, anger, disappointment, Guru never failed me. His light was there if I could be open to it.

The worst news came on October 11th, 2007. Guru entered into Mahasamadhi. In other words, he died, left the body. Fear and grief prevailing, when I arrived home from work, I went straight to my meditation room.

I spent the afternoon there, receiving and making phone calls to my friends about my arrangements for getting to New York for the Memorial Service and week of meditation. I had coffee with Guru in the form of his Transcendental Picture. I shared panic, grief and shock. I took comfort in the great invisible arms that hold me when my world is coming apart.

This is my relationship with my Guru. It is one of respect and honor, friendship and love, confidante and confessor, guidance and protection, mother and father. As some others, because of outer distance from Guru and other disciples, my relationship with him had to develop into an inner one of faith. I am grateful he stuck with me as my Guru and became my all.

Sri Chinmoy has offered me experiences I never thought nor dreamed. Foreign and domestic travel, a treasure-hunt style of spontaneity, sleeping side by side in a crowded room with my fellow disciples while working on a concert, public speaking, running around the United States, marathons and ultra marathons, attending events where famous musicians give an impromptu concert and famous politicians, dignitaries, royalty, sports figures or entertainers are present. He has rounded out my life in a variety of ways.

Now I and my brothers and sisters must continue without his physical presence. Judging by the palpable presence of his essence left here on earth, this should not be as difficult as we imagined. Even in my little room surrounded by the memorabilia, Sri Chinmoy's life and mission continue stronger than ever.

Guru, I remain eternally, your Palyati.

ABHINABHA
Amsterdam, The Netherlands

One never knows when the last time will come, but first times are remembered forever. Like first snow, they have that crystalline, spotless, pure quality, which never seems to wither, but rather increases its brilliance over time. I can remember my first day at school with surprising clarity (running into my mother's arms at the end of the day, feeling her pride, her love). I also remember my first day in secondary school (missing the opening speech by getting lost on our bicycles on our way there) and my first soccer match (losing 3-0, my best friend in tears). A first time is always magical.

And pure magic is what I remember from my first time in New York visiting Sri Chinmoy during August Celebrations. These memories are beautiful fragments of light, images framed in silver and gold, miniature documentaries of the soul.

I remember arriving at Aspiration-Ground in a blazing midday sun and Guru answering questions from disciples. The theme was humility and humiliation. I distinctly remember him saying it is not bad being humiliated once in a while, since it curbs the ego. The first words of wisdom I heard Guru speak on the court.

Of course I also remember that overwhelming aura of peace, which washed over you like a wave of silent ecstasy, endless and irresistible. I remember a flower-like fragrance, sweet, subtle, unearthly, emanating from that sacred place, driving the heart mad with joy. I remember laughter.

The first time I helped bringing in boxes of prasad stands out in my memory, since it was the first time Guru spoke to me directly, yet perhaps not in a way I had secretly hoped and longed for. My boxes were the last to be placed on the ground. In a silly and overzealous effort I decided to shift the other boxes around to make all the heaps look equal and orderly. His voice suddenly boomed out of infinite silence: "Oi, what are you doing? I liked it the way it was!" I, who had hoped for his high praise or an approving smile, wanted nothing more than to sink straight through the ground or to evaporate into thin air. Those options sadly unavailable, I stood rooted to the spot like a frightened rabbit and then sort of scuttled away. It's not bad being humiliated once in a while. Indeed. Cosmic consciousness was operating smoothly.

And so it always was around Sri Chinmoy. You had the feeling of being an eternal child, playing in an eternal garden under his loving eye, while at the same time all you needed to know about yourself, about your part in the game, was somehow communicated to you through a thousand different channels – and every time you recognized his voice. Such was his grace.

I remember playing soccer with the boys in the summer's heat. I remember intense play practices with an amateur crew showing its professionalism in its props, costumes and staging. I remember running the obligatory morning laps around Jamaica High and – o bliss – heaping warm muesli in a small paper bowl in Goose Pond Park afterwards. I remember a sunny afternoon on Aspiration-Ground when Guru had all the guards try a 'clean and press' from the ground with a 90-lb dumbbell. Excitement rippled through the crowd. Cute little games, which transported you back to your childhood days.

Everywhere I turned I felt the thrill of belonging to this family of souls, a unique gathering of spirits under his great wings. It was like coming home. The days were full of joy. The nights were full of peace. The mornings were full of freshness and newness. It felt like the world had just been born. Only when I got back home I truly and fully realized how magically beautiful it all had been. The real world stood before me like a roaring tiger. But I had felt the peace of the lion.

I remember a trip into Manhattan, all by myself. I felt obligate to pay the island a visit, if only to appease my parents and class mates that I had actually gone out and seen something of the real New York. So I did Wall Street, Central Park, Times Square, 5th Avenue.... There is a picture of me standing in front of the Manhattan skyline, the twin towers still looming in the back. It was 1999. Yet among the skyscrapers I felt empty and oddly out of place the whole time. When I got back to Queens I realized the sheer foolishness of going out to look for a speck of light, when I could have stayed to bathe in an eternal sun. It was the last time I traded the precincts of the tennis court for a touristy escapade. All you needed was there, between the dusty gravel and the white prayer flags flapping cheerfully in the breeze.

Until Sri Chinmoy left the body I paid 16 visits to his residence in Queens, New York. In my memory they epitomize a sun-drenched, endless afternoon, a spiritual and blissful tea-party with its ever-same and ever-changing patterns, a draught of the soul's nectar, an eternal day in Heaven.

I remember.

SUMANGALI
York, England

Is there such a thing as a junkophobe? That's me. I buy the same thing over and over because I keep throwing useful stuff away; I'm ruthless to the point of impracticality. I can't tolerate anything old, broken, unlovely, unclean, or out of place.

Then what is this old Cheese Doodles packet doing here? Cheap crinkly empty bag, garish primary print, 'Made with real cheese' blaring from the top, like that would make it okay. It's taped into a big silver book of handmade paper, Indian beads hand stitched onto the front. It sits beside seven others, now amongst my most precious possessions: one of raw silk in a rainbow weave and coloured pages, one embroidered with satin ribbons, one with my name across the face of a dog, and a felt-tip drawing of a bird.

Words are scrawled inside: rough shapes of words, the pen hurried or tired, the phrases hackneyed and dull, but this content has held me stunned over the last two days; compelling as an elysian dream remembered at daybreak.

These, my journals of the last ten years, have stayed mostly unopened. I wrote them for a future self I thought I would not meet for many years to come, never imagining my Master would leave his earthly frame for Heaven so soon.

I knew such apparent debris would turn to treasure then. The spent packets of blessed food from Sri Chinmoy's hand are now a link to another world which used to be my own; a world of outer instruction, more subtle, more powerful, more inwardly refined than I can even comprehend, let alone fit into the bounds of words. The path of the heart; the silent teaching; the sacred life of meditation; the unviolable bond between Guru and disciple.

Mostly these packets, photos, notes, bulging out of pages, are triggers to more abundant memories than those recorded. A concert ticket took me to the first time I saw Sri Chinmoy in person, Heathrow Airport 1997. In a bustle of artificial light and noise and movement, waiting for his arrival, I entered into one of the most profound meditations of my life. He passed by, looked into me with such surety and pure affection, I knew my life had found its home. Here at last was a teacher who could take me to God; a journey I knew I needed more than my own breath. His was the most familiar face I had ever seen, recognition flooded with sanctuary. Tears of relief followed me for twelve continuous hours.

Today I met with four others to meditate, the thirtieth day after Sri Chinmoy's Mahasamadhi, an official end of mourning. One of our little band was raised a Hindu, as was Sri Chinmoy, and told us that in India, family members take lotuses on such a day, to set them adrift in the Ganges with a prayer. Perhaps we could do the same as a symbolic mark of gratitude and respect.

We took golden roses with only stubs of stems to help them float. We walked a long way down the river Ouse, slipping on the cobbles in the damp of autumn, checking at intervals with each other if 'this' could be the 'right place'. Two lads, three girls, and one sleek white dog named Pearl, seemingly out for a weekend stroll.

Who would have thought such profundity would come to pass on a rotting jetty by a rowing club somewhere in North Yorkshire. In the space of moments, so many impulses rose up in me that I have not dared to feel these past days. It seemed we grew up all of a sudden. Orphaned, we had only each other then, with whom to carry the legacy of a sacred life into an unknown future, to offer to others what we have had the unimaginable boon of receiving.

I set the small bundle of softness on the wide mass of water and watched it bob away. It seemed to have its own light, glowing with a joy and purity I thought only Heaven could conceive, smiling and shining at the onset of an unknown journey; a warm light above the dark and changeable – on it, in it, yet apart from it. I touched my fingers in the water, then to my head and heart, making some unspoken promise to this beautiful city where I was raised: a sudden totality of love and oneness.

We parted, all but wordlessly, and I went home. I smiled to the homeless man selling magazines and gave him a pound – he works hard like a busker, all in joy and fun, to make others smile – and I saw myself in part in him. I smiled to the youth absorbed in a greasy paper of chips and scraps. I smiled to the aged lady struggling in pain and fear from the harbour of her own front door – I saw myself in part in her, and felt only love. I smiled to the big girls in skinny jeans, cursing and shouting; the lady in shades on an overcast day; the pub landlord at his back door in a dressing gown, ruddy from the night's excess; the sulking seven-year-old whingeing to her father for something vitally important.

Today I saw myself in part in them all. Or was it God?

TEJVAN
Oxford, England

The great Sufi poet Rumi writes of the experience of dying to be reborn.

*If you love me,
you won't just die once.
In every moment
you will die into me
to be reborn.*

– Mewlana Jalaluddin Rumi

What Rumi talks of in this instance is the death of the human ego. Through the death of the human ego we lose our false self and awaken to the Universal Consciousness. This is what he means by spiritual death and rebirth. Once we undergo this 'death', leaving the physical body can no longer hold fear.

Mahasamadhi is a term to describe a yogi's conscious exit from his body and return to the Universal Consciousness. A spiritual Master comes to teach: "You are not the body, but the immortal soul." Yet, when the Master leaves, the human in us tends to forget this immortal message, thinking of what we lose in the physical world. But, after a time, we need to remember the true nature of the Guru.

When we were introducing a new seeker to our Centre meditations, she made an interesting observation: "On the one hand you say the spiritual life is just as vivid and real now that Guru is not in the body. But, it also seems there were so many inspiring moments and stories when Guru was in the physical."

Both, of course, are true. Through meditation and prayer, you can feel the same consciousness, the same presence as when Guru was in the physical. But also, you do miss those moments of great spontaneity and inspiration when Guru was meditating, singing – or doing something completely new. Guru was constrained by nothing and could give a greater intensity to any meditation or experience. It was a most illumining experience, impossible to fully replicate.

Being in the physical presence of your Master is a great opportunity to make progress. But, close physical proximity can also be misleading. What matters is the spiritual life – our own consciousness and aspiration. I believe Guru once said that his best disciple was someone who had never even met him in the physical. Guru is no longer in the body, but the spiritual life still has the same joys, the same challenges, and the same intensity.

The funny thing is that when I joined the Centre in 1999, I wished I had been able to become his disciple much earlier. I felt, "If only I had joined Guru's path in the late 1960s, I would have had so much access to his physical presence and active life." Now, looking back, I feel I was lucky to have had just those few years. Though there was little external communication with Guru, I realise how many profound moments and life experiences I had meditating as his student.

But, right from the first week after Guru's passing, I really felt the fundamental aspect of the spiritual life was continuing. In essence, there was no change. I felt it was the same challenge of listening inwardly to Guru's guidance, the same challenge of quieting the mind and diving into the heart. I always felt Guru tried to teach us that his real Self was not constrained by the limits of his physical self. Guru had realised the highest consciousness, so now he is merely working and acting from a different room, not physically visible, but with the same inner presence and consciousness.

There are difficult moments, when you have to try and work out what Guru would have done or said. It would be so much easier to be able to ask the Master directly. I remember one occasion when I had an issue I really couldn't resolve. If Guru was in the physical I would have been able to write to him and get an answer, but that wasn't possible.

Guru said that if we want to know the answer to a question, we can inwardly ask it and then meditate with a perfectly silent mind for ten minutes. If we can do that, we will get the answer. The trouble is that when we have a real problem, we don't really feel capable of keeping the mind perfectly silent for ten minutes.

The question had been revolving around my mind for quite a while, and then I got the inspiration to write the question and place it on my shrine behind Guru's Transcendental Picture. I asked it with the attitude of a child; I really didn't know what was the best way. I didn't really try to meditate on it. There was no inner message; there was no flash of light. But, over the next week, a feeling grew of which was the best course of action. As time progressed, it grew increasingly clear. I forgot why I ever wanted to do the other option. It wasn't just receiving an answer, but receiving the inspiration to do the right thing without mental doubt.

When Guru was in the physical, taking prasad was a really special moment – a highlight of the evening. It was an opportunity to approach close to Guru's physical body and receive his blessings, both inner and outer. As you went to take prasad you would try your hardest to be in a devoted consciousness. In close proximity to Guru, you didn't want your mind cluttered with the usual rubbish thoughts. You wanted to cultivate gratitude and a divine attitude. If nothing else, I would repeat a mantra like 'Supreme'. After Guru's passing that magic seemed to dissipate. I remember one celebration, getting indigestion straight after eating prasad. The first time, I put it down to a dodgy Indian samosa, but when it happened the second night in a row, it made me reflect on my attitude for taking prasad. I realised how much I had lost from the days of Guru's physical presence. Prasad had become merely a chance to get some (hopefully) nice snack. The same devotion wasn't there. Perhaps it is just me mentally theorising, but the incident reminded me of how much prasad could mean when you took it with a devoted attitude. I resolved to always feel exactly as if Guru was there in the physical. It showed me how our inner attitude is the critical thing – not whether Guru is in the physical or not.

Since Guru's passing, little has fundamentally changed. I still get a lot from visiting Celebrations in New York, where Guru's presence permeates the environs in which he spent so many years. I would love to be able to have a physical conversation with Guru, and often wish that could happen. But, if anything, I feel closer to Guru now than when he was in the body. I feel very grateful for this incarnation and am just enjoying the experience of meditation and the spiritual life.

JAITRA
Auckland, New Zealand

"I'm really glad we came to this concert," she confided to her friend. "We were lucky to get in."

Still in her 20s, Greenwich Village hip with piercings and fashionably short, messy hair, she was as Sri Chinmoy might have described an Indian 'with an ultra-modern touch', yet here she was with 850 other New Yorkers to pay tribute to the India of tradition and yore, to spiritual Master Sri Chinmoy and his music; many more stranded without tickets outside. The concert yet to begin, the hall already full, they were indeed lucky to be inside.

In the darkened auditorium of the Skirball Centre, the discernible buzz of excitement is replaced by silence, curtained by darkness as master of ceremonies and student of Sri Chinmoy for some 30 years, Devashishu Torpy, begins to read a prepared introduction from spotlit corner of stage. This could be the beginning of any of Sri Chinmoy's Peace Concerts or Lifting Up The World ceremonies from the past ten years, except today is April 15th, 2008, six months after Sri Chinmoy's passing, and the man being introduced will not be taking the stage.

We are attending the very first Songs of the Soul concert, the first 'Tribute to the Music of Maestro Sri Chinmoy' as postured all over lower Manhattan, and body now departed, we are paying tribute to a spiritual Master's ever present soul.

A video is played, a brief outline of the Guru's in no way brief achievements, and there is an audible gasp as the possible to quantify, impossible to equate or understand raw, powerful, unbelievable numbers of Sri Chinmoy's lifetime scroll across the screen. 800 concerts just like this one, 1,600 books, 21,000 songs, 117,000 poems, 150,000 paintings and 16,000,000 bird drawings! None of these achievements are brand new or unknown – students of Sri Chinmoy have been proudly proclaiming to the world these astronomic, mortality-challenging figures for years, in press releases, faxes, newspaper articles and freely given meditation classes, and yet people in this darkened auditorium are saying with true wonder, as if for the first time, "Just who was this man?"

Sri Chinmoy is not yet known the world over, but it seems sure as the rising sun that he one day will, that the message, the light of this 21st Century spiritual luminary, will one day shine.

* * *

From the humblest of beginnings – an orphan at the age of 11, raised in a tiny East Bengal village and then a little known spiritual community in the southern Indian city of Pondicherry – Sri Chinmoy bestrode the world stage in every field he chose to draw, paint, write, compose, sing and perform upon.

This ceaselessly active spiritual Master and true Renaissance man would often relate how as a youth his only desire was to become a great athlete, but it is not every youth who achieves self-illumination or God-realisation at the age of 12, and it seems that God had greater plans for this one-time teenage decathlon champion:

> *My body desired to be*
> *A great runner.*
> *But God has made me*
> *A God-lover.*
>
> **– Sri Chinmoy**

In the very heart of democracy – America – and in the very heart of America and 20th Century heart of the world – New York – from the ages of 33 to 76 Sri Chinmoy practised and preached the democratic ideals of American sages and seers past. From his humble Queens, New York home, Sri Chinmoy embodied and expounded perfectly Ralph Waldo Emerson's 'Democracy of the Individual' and Walt Whitman's 'Democratic Vistas', but he did so always with sagacious eye fixed far beyond purple mountain majesties and enameled fruited plains, for Sri Chinmoy's was the vision of not just American but world democracy, a brotherhood and sisterhood without boundary or border, all of humanity united in what he termed a 'Oneness-Heart-Home', from sea to shining sea.

* * *

The concert continues, the Sri Chinmoy Bhajan Singers on stage, a women's music group formed by Sri Chinmoy himself, with members from over forty nations as if to perfectly illustrate the meditation-maestro's vision of world-oneness. They play to respectful silence, their multi-coloured saris like jewels against the regal purple backdrop that could be a window to heaven, and heaven seems not so far when it is beckoned by the Bhajan Singers' bejeweling, beatific tones. They finish to thunderous applause and leave the stage smiling, but seemingly bewildered, as if unsure of what to do in the face of a standing ovation.

I will not pass judgement on the musicianship of the next act, Gandharva Loka Orchestra, another ensemble of Sri Chinmoy's international students – although to these untrained ears they were superb – but I will pass compliment on their unity and power – what a perfect demonstration again of Sri Chinmoy's philosophy of oneness. Nearly 70 musicians and singers who do not normally perform together, thrown stage-wards with just a few days' practise, producing such a profound, transcendent result. The beauty and power of so many working together for a single goal is surely the true power and potential of the human soul!

Throughout the crowd, cellphones and cameras are visible as audience members not only watch and enjoy the concert but record it – for posterity or the immediate ephemera of internet posting.

Sri Chinmoy, the subject of this concert of dedication and tribute, may no longer be here, but he is present in spirit just as he always was, and many would say more strongly. The prevalent topic of the Sri Chinmoy Centre's April Celebrations in New York – the yearly commemoration of Sri Chinmoy's arrival in New York on April 13th, 1964 by his students – was how in this the first Celebrations without the meditation teacher's physical presence, many felt his protection and guidance even more powerfully. After all a Master of meditation is much, much more than just a human being – he is a Master of that of which we are singing tonight: the limitless, boundless, ultimately infinite human soul.

***

I first met Sri Chinmoy at another concert, thirteen years before. It was June 1995 and I was 20 years old, barely an adult and not really a man, yet in two decades on earth desperately prescient of the need for somebody to shape and inform the spiritual life I felt – unlike any person, occupation or thing – unmistakably destined to pursue.

It was my fortune to turn seriously to meditation as the answer to the open question that was my life just as a Sri Chinmoy Centre was founded in my city – Wellington, capital city of New Zealand – and only two months after becoming a member, as if reeled to shore by some master fisherman, Sri Chinmoy himself came to visit, giving a Peace Concert in Auckland, then meeting the Prime Minister of New Zealand in my home town.

My first memory of Sri Chinmoy was his arrival at Auckland Airport. An hour spent waiting for the plane to arrive and then suddenly, as though noise-cancelling headphones on, the crowded arrival lounge was no longer filled by cacophony of migrating human souls, and a 'presence' – a short, Indian man, only 5' 7", exactly the same height as myself, of medium build and latter middle age – walking past as if he was carrying the entire world. The room came alive by his being in it, brightened visibly, and for a moment it felt as if all the spheres in the heavens had paused, realigned themselves to the orbit of this suddenly hallowed arrival hall. Smiling, nodding, waving and blessing, he was gone within seconds, and the rest of my life had begun.

My first personal experience of Sri Chinmoy, first breath of the ever-shining love which would inflate, be the wind in sails of my just launched discipleship, came the very next day. Standing in a crowd of onlookers outside a vegetarian café dedicated to his spiritual philosophy, I struggled for a second glimpse of the man who was now the pole star and central mast of my lifeboat – and struggled against being swept away by an unruly swell of fellow students trying to do the same. Aghast at the unseemly jostling and pushing around me – fighting all as if for a few precious seats on a departing lifeboat – I retreated to a more secluded vantage point, island-haven of dignity and calm. "I don't need to jostle like a fan at a rock concert to see Sri Chinmoy," I told myself, pride somewhat ruffled, "a spiritual Master can see all inwardly, and despite the fact he may be looking anywhere but at me, that is where he truly will be found."

That is precisely where I first found Sri Chinmoy. Standing alone, on the side of an unremarkable city backstreet, jettisoned between rubbish bins and passing shoppers, barely able to see my spiritual teacher as he departed in the back seat of a car, I nonetheless felt him look at me, felt Sri Chinmoy glance inside me then through me, look right to the depths of my heart and soul even though I could not see his face. In a fleeting second, less time even than it took his car to pass, I felt accepted and embraced by a person who wordlessly understood every fibre of my being, understood every rhyme, reason, question and answer that might fill the pages of the book of my being and life – whether already written or yet to be – and was nothing other than love and compassion for all, for every single line.

I was not one who had a lot of outer contact with Sri Chinmoy – the number of times I spoke to him I can count on one, maybe two folded, prayerful hands, but Sri Chinmoy would have been first to say that the inner relationship between a spiritual Master and student is infinitely more important than that outer:

All real spiritual Masters teach meditation in silence. A genuine Master does not have to explain outwardly how to meditate or give you a specific form of meditation. He can simply meditate on you and his silent gaze will teach you how to meditate. Your soul will enter into his soul and bring the message, the knowledge of how to meditate, from his soul.

– **Sri Chinmoy**

In silence, from across oceans vast and with presence near, during regular, twice sometimes thrice-yearly visits to New York, Sri Chinmoy changed, radically transformed my life, turned me upside down and right ways up, as if darkest night into brightest day. Studying meditation with Sri Chinmoy was as though the book of my life was shelved, my life story completely rewritten – with his pen sketched anew.

Creativity, confidence, peace, poise, energy, strength inner and outer, wisdom and love – all of these things I now possess in quantities far greater than I once believed. It is as if the self before I began to practise meditation with Sri Chinmoy was a caricature; the self I am now a masterly self-portrait – a painting, or a song, of the soul.

JOGYATA
Auckland, New Zealand

To begin with, you can't help noticing how vivid and beautiful our Aspiration-Ground is. Physical spaces seem to interact so much with human consciousness, take on energy and light and livingness – here the devotion and caring of so many of the local disciples ahead of our arrival have created a sanctuary both tranquil and sheltering to the spirit. Within the grounds themselves – flanked by the great mass of vines and trees yellowing with fall – no-one is talking, not for the three days of these observances.

For three days and nights Aspiration-Ground will be open continuously, just as it was one year ago, and many will stay throughout these long hours, enchanted with the solitude and brimming silence.

Seated on a garden balustrade and majestic with his purple dhoti and meditative smile, Guru presides over everything in a centrepiece, a four-metre-high portrait. In a complicity of imagery, the garden theme of the photo flows out onto the stage – real flowers, great banks of pink roses, sections of identical garden wall, a profusion of plants, statues of Ganesha. Threaded strings and necklaces of flowers hang from the Temple entrance. On our first night a three-quarter moon shines perfectly above the amphitheatre of dark trees. And everywhere, candles and candlelit lanterns.

There is a hush in the air, a sense of possibility, as though at any moment something revelatory might come.... We are at the conjunction of a sacred occasion, hallowed ground, the energy generated by these hundreds of seeking souls. Cocooned in this haven of beauty and devotion, we strive for a deeper stillness, a renewal of aspiration. In the middle of the night the veil that separates us from those things we long for, those distant but remembered realities of spirit, seems almost translucent – a little effort more and some special dispensation of grace might come to bring a long-hoped-for epiphany. This is the place.

Each day repeats the same ceremonial themes. A gong, heraldic, strikes thirteen times and conches sound, triumphal as befits this salute to one of the greatest of great lives. And scores of tinkling simultaneous bells, all sweetness, sweetness. The sounds thrill the soul, proclamatory, seem to reach out to other co-existing worlds in invocation. Each day, too, we will sing together, trailing a little behind the Master's own recorded Invocation – I smile a little as he lingers on those long devotional notes, wringing out every little drop of God-love and still teaching us about soulfulness.

And each day, as well, our candle offering. In a long line we shuffle slowly forward, holding in our palms the votive candle that is at once the renewal of our discipleship and the offering of our soul's love. At night, down where Guru's physical lies, the 500 devotional candles flicker and shimmer, a pool of light like a far-off city, poignant and touching. Each tiny flame dances and sways, alive with our hopes or whispered prayers. At night a projection of our Guru's Transcendental Picture towers on a giant screen and there are wonderful long meditations. Remembering Guru's comment regarding meditation and the great secret of grace – "When the father is a multi-billionaire, why should the children have to work...?"

Each night Mridanga offers videos of Guru's life – his meditations, his activities and talks. By chance one has been filmed from almost exactly where I am sitting and in a bizarre juxtaposition of time past and time present I am sitting in Aspiration-Ground and watching a video from years ago that almost perfectly captures everything of here and now – same masses of flowers, candles, a stage of white trellises, statues and the Master's own portraits. Only Guru himself is missing from what we call the present – which might itself be an illusion – and I feel a thrill of surreal and vicarious anticipation (my time-past self?) as though at any moment he might again appear, sweeping around the court on his chariot.

How generous and thoughtful our New York family hosts – hot chai, assorted teas, trays of food appear around the clock. And they have built a stage against the back wall of the court beneath the steps – at intervals each day our songsters and poets and musicians perform. In the evenings the main Temple and court lights are turned off and candlelight and lanterns – fifty of these hang from walkway railings – create a haven's shadowed secrecy. We are each only dim figures, released by this soft half-light to our own deeper sincerity and private spaces. The candlelight mutes our setting, confers a curious timelessness – we are shuffling across a landscape that is history itself, impelled by our tribal memory of a lost enlightenment. Aspiration-Ground is returning us to the essence of life – we are seekers drawn together on the Great Quest to sing and pray and dream, released from all other banalities towards this single consummation.

Looking back at these wonderful October days, two impressions linger. One is of the after-midnight silence at Aspiration-Ground, its solemnity, portentousness, the unmistakable sense of being close to something. As though here, more than anywhere else in this vast world, a beckoning other realm is waiting for you – tonight, if you can summon your deepest meditation, you might pass through that portal to some lovely Beyond.

The second impression is of another silence, which has been telling us to listen more, to be patient, to not intervene or decide, and like a reed in the wind only to move and act and speak at the very last, responsive only to the currents of spirit. Letting everything in our lives work itself out without us, being intent instead on absorbing the Master's consciousness to best know and prepare for our tasks. As Guru aptly says:

> *Sometimes I must be silent,*
> *For that is the only way*
> *To know a little better,*
> *To think a little wiser,*
> *To become a little more perfect,*
> *To claim God a little sooner.*
>
> **– Sri Chinmoy**

CHAPTER 6

AN INNER CONNECTION

*If you want to maintain
A very close connection with your Master,
Here on earth and there in Heaven,
Your meditation will always be
Your direct line to him.*

– Sri Chinmoy

BIJON
Cambridge, England

I have much clearer memories of my early years than I do of the last few, but I feel blessed that so many of these involve Guru and our spiritual path.

My mother made a cot for me when I was born, which I still remember draped in sunshine yellow cloth, with a Transcendental Picture either end. Although I wasn't in Guru's physical presence most of the time, I had a strong feeling of him being around from all the photos and books scattered about the house. Guru's music was also a main feature, either on tape or sung by my mum. *Songs of the Soul* played in the morning would wake me up and Akasha would regulate my naps in the afternoon. All these things embody Guru's consciousness, and by knowing that, you really know Guru too. Some of us have had more opportunities to spend time with Guru in the outer world than others but we all have access to his consciousness and smile through his photos, music, writings and importantly for me, our imagination.

Each time I meditate in my car I try to picture a different image of Guru either in meditation, contemplation or action, or offering us his smile, etc. Some of my most special moments of meditation stem from these imagined blessings, which I feel are in fact real blessings that Guru is constantly offering us, although we may not always be aware of them.

When Guru spoke to us about our need to deepen our receptivity, I felt clearly that it applied to all of us and probably meant we have to work on something strong and deep that can't just be switched on at short notice. We might be in a good consciousness and bursting with happiness but, for me at least, I felt Guru was talking about a receptivity that comes only from a sustained inner cry and by connecting our life with his on a personal level. He has said he would love to do this on an outer level with all of his disciples, like watching the laundry go round with Sushumna. But it's not possible. There will be many disciples who have seen Guru little, if at all, so the more of Guru's consciousness that we can share with our brothers and sisters, the more Guru will be manifested through our daily actions and encounters.

I feel that every one of us is tremendously special, each with unique strengths, and are divine envoys of Guru for the rest of the world.

SHIVARAM
Toronto, Canada

In 1996 when visiting India, I went to see my relatives in Bangalore. Because of my interest in Indian astrology during my younger days, just for fun I accompanied a relative to see an astrologer. This particular system gives predictions not based on one's horoscope relating to one's date of birth, but formulates a horoscope just at that time using some divination technique.

After my astrologer was finished with my relative, I sat in front of him without any purpose in mind. He asked only for my name and the birth time star (known as *Nakshtraout,* of 27) under which I was born. He did his chants and procedures and without any prompting started to speak: "You see, in this world there are many Gurus who are guiding people. You have behind you a person who is the Guru of all the Gurus of the world. What more can I say?"

The fact that this man used such superlative terms about Guru without knowing anything about me except my name made me wonder. I felt that the brilliance of the sun is such that one hardly needs to open the eyes to know where the sun is.

PURNAKAMA
Winnipeg, Canada

This incident took place about two weeks after Guru's passing in 2007.

I had arrived back in Winnipeg after Guru's Mahasamadhi, and I don't think there was ever a lower point in my life. I was still in shock, exhausted, very sick with the flu, and after a long day of teaching, feeling the way I did, I know I looked like the dog's dinner. At that point I felt hopeless, alone and very depressed, barely making it through the seemingly long days.

I needed to go to the grocery store, so I stopped in after work, praying that I would not run into anyone I knew, as I did not want anyone to see me in that condition, and I was not in the mood to engage in idle conversation.

I was going down the aisles looking for the few things

that I needed when suddenly someone spoke to me as I was reading the ingredients on jars of salsa.

It was a man I had never met. He was small, looked rather like a gnome or a dwarf, and had a very sweet smile.

"Excuse me," he said. "I don't want to startle you or for you to think that I'm strange, but I can see auras around people, and you have the most incredible aura I've ever seen."

Silence.

I just stood there staring at this man. I looked and felt horrible, and here this man was telling me that I had an incredible aura surrounding me. I was sure that all he would be able to see around me at that point in time was a giant black cloud.

I found my voice and quietly asked, "What do you mean?"

He said, "I've been watching you as you walk around the store and you have light flowing out of you like a river. It's flowing to every person that you pass."

I stood there in silence once again trying to take in what this man had just said. He wasn't strange or crazy; he just spoke as if he were stating a fact.

I could feel tears welling up in my eyes. Seeing my tears the man was afraid that he had upset me, but I reassured him that indeed he had not. I explained that I had just lost someone very close to me and that my emotions were still very raw. I thanked him for his kind words and told him that I was grateful that he had stopped to speak to me.

He gave me his condolences, smiled, thanked me for spreading light, and went on his way.

Still holding back the tears, I quickly paid for my

items, then ran to my car, where the floodgates opened, and I sobbed uncontrollably for quite some time.

It took me a few days to process what had happened in the store. Was this man just some crackpot, or was he a messenger sent to soothe me in a time of desperate need?

I truly feel that he was a messenger. He showed me what we all have become, who we truly are as Guru's disciples. We are all vehicles of Guru's light on earth.

I believe that through this man Guru was showing me that we are not lost or alone. Guru may not be with us physically, but he is still inside our heart and our very life breath, now and forever.

UTTHAL
Ottawa, Canada

Shortly after accepting me as his 'true disciple' in October of 1972, Guru told me that for the meantime it wasn't safe for me to travel to New York to visit him, due to my status as a Vietnam War 'draft-dodger'. About a year and a half later, he said I could start coming across the border into the US to visit New York. That was just prior to the 1974 April Celebrations, which was my first occasion to visit New York as a disciple.

In May of 1976 I was on my way down with a car full of fellow Ottawa disciples to see Guru for Mother's Day. We arrived at the border at Thousand Islands early that Saturday morning and were all asked by the attendant officer for our ID. While I was not surprised, I was certainly apprehensive when we were asked to come inside and wait while they looked up our names in a registry. In all the times I had crossed the border, this had never happened before.

Shortly my group was told that they could leave, but that I would be staying. At that time Mukti, who was among us, called New York and asked that Guru be informed as soon as possible about what had happened. I was taken to a back room and told to wait – nothing was said of why I was being held, but I knew very well.

In July of 1969 I had been ordered to report for my pre-induction physical, which would have resulted in my immediate induction into the army, and in all likelihood being shipped off to the Vietnam War at the height of the conflagration. Instead I had fled to Sweden, where I was given humanitarian asylum. For failing to report as ordered, I was indicted, with a maximum possible penalty upon conviction of a $5,000 fine and/or five years in prison.

Within moments of being brought into the waiting room at the border station, where I sat alone, I turned inwardly to Guru and gave everything over to him – completely. Almost immediately there began a deluge of golden light. I'm not talking about a heavy mist or even a steady rain. No, it was a clearly visible monsoon downpour, accompanied by total peace and joy. Any fears I might have had were swept away by this golden light. I was in a timelessness place, but in a while an FBI agent arrived, accompanied by two burly state troopers. Imagine how intimidating their presence might have been, because at that time I weighed less than half what I now weigh – maybe 165 lb at the most.

When the FBI man approached me, I put out my hand and said, "Nice to meet you."

He replied, "I don't think you'll be so happy when you hear what I have to say," whereupon he read the indictment: The United States of America vs. 'me'.

Then the two state troopers came forward and were about to constrain me with big shiny chrome-plated handcuffs. Without thinking I said, "Please don't do that."

Immediately they stopped, looking at each other and at the FBI man with complete incredulity. At that point we all realised that this was not an ordinary day. By the time we reached the judge's office at his private law practice, it being Saturday, the FBI man had been transformed, as evidenced by his dismissal of the troopers.

"I could get into trouble for that," he said, "since you are in their custody until they bring you before the judge, but I didn't want the judge to have an unfavorable impression by seeing you with the police."

In turn, the judge treated me like his favorite nephew. To make a long story short, he released me under my own cognizance, with a promise to appear for trial in a month or so. After the judge called the bus station and learned that the last bus for Syracuse with a connection to New York City had just left, and after his efforts to find a young friend to drive me there, the FBI man took me up to a main road out of town to hitch-hike. He even gave me a legal folder and a red magic marker on which I wrote 'Syracuse'.

Not long after he dropped me off, a young couple pulled up, asking where I was headed. They were only going 10 miles south but said they'd take me up to the main highway where I'd stand a better chance of catching a ride. Moments later he turned to his wife, heavy with child and lying in the back behind a curtain, they whispered a few words and he turned saying they would drive me all the way to Syracuse – 120 miles out of their way! We pulled into the bus station just ahead of the bus I'd missed.

I arrived at Guru's house early the next morning – all showered and in whites – just ahead of the people in my car, whereupon Guru called me up and, smiling radiantly, gave me a most intense blessing, hands planted firmly upon my bowed head.

I did indeed appear as promised for my trial and was eventually sentenced to a 6-month probation, with the condition that I do community service during that time in Canada and send in a report of those activities at the end of each month.

When the probation officer asked whether there was some organization I had in mind, of course I said, "The Sri Chinmoy Centre." I believe I'm among only two or three disciples ever required by law to do selfless service.

When the venerable old white-haired judge sentenced me, the high-domed old courtroom in Auburn, New York, turned a shimmering gold and his face turned momentarily into Guru's countenance. As he spoke, I looked around. Everyone present – the stenographer, my defense lawyer, the district attorney and the probation officer – was overwhelmed, even to the point of tears, with sweet and transcendent emotion, as the judge pronounced: "In all my years as a judge, you are the finest young man to ever appear before me." So what could have been a most unpleasant episode in my life was changed into a series of wonderful inner and outer experiences – all due to Guru's grace. Throughout the day of my arrest, from the initial and overwhelming experience at the border to the young couple inexplicably driving me all the way to Syracuse, I knew what it felt like to be a saint, even if just for a day, and could feel the magical effect this had on everyone I encountered. But of course it was not of my doing; it was all due to Guru's concern, compassion and love, reflected in my light-flooded heart.

Months later Guru sent a message to me, saying that on that day at the border he had put an extremely powerful force on me, and it was the very first time that anyone had ever received his force 100%. For that great blessing, despite all my failings and shortcomings, I am divinely proud – both of myself and of Guru. I am proud of myself that I had the good sense to surrender as well as I could to Guru's grace and supremely proud of Guru that his compassion-light reached down and penetrated this 'body of clay'. Maybe that's why he later on gave me the name Utthal, meaning 'Indomitable Wave-Force', for it was the Supreme's Indomitable Wave-Force within me that I was lucky to have a tiny glimpse of that spring day in 1976.

Once several years later while visiting my divine enterprise, Bhakti Press, Guru asked me why I was unable to apply the considerable discipline I exhibited in my work to the task of losing weight.

After a long pause, thinking of no reasonable answer, I simply said, "Guru I love you," to which he replied, "I love you too. You belong to me, and that is why I can scold you." Those were the most precious words I have ever heard, and they will echo in the innermost depths of my heart forever. I have never lost faith that one day the Supreme will grant me the boon to harness the power of my Indomitable Wave-Force to please Guru in his own way by becoming once again trim and fit.

JOGYATA
Auckland, New Zealand

Guru often spoke about divine protection and over the years I've shifted from a new disciple's hesitation or disbelief to full-blown acceptance in my views on this interesting subject. With reason too. In 1990 I drove headlong into a concrete bridge column at 100 km an hour on the Auckland motorway – dressed in full clown regalia on my way to a children's birthday party – and with no seatbelt on. The wheels fell off, glass covered acres of highway, the engine ended up in the passenger's seat. Through a world of flying glass, spinning sky, the sounds of the car tearing itself to pieces, I could feel an irrational calm and a sense almost of God's Arms around me, a clear and tangible feeling. I crawled out of the wreckage, with not a scratch or bruise, so peaceful I could have given a spontaneous meditation class to the arriving medics, tow trucks and even a fire engine. My red foam clown hammer lay on the motorway, my box of tricks scattered all over. "You should be very, very dead," said an ambulance driver. My intactness astonished everybody.

In Malaysia I had a rendezvous with a bolt of lightning, a direct hit while crossing a road in the rain. Unconscious and stunned, I lay on the wet road, an electrocuted tourist, my eyes closed, a circle of solicitous villagers jabbering away and peering down at me. A full one minute before, I had a premonition that danger lurked and I was chanting a mantra silently for protection – clearly Somebody heard my invocation. That year many people were killed in this region by lightning strike – but I happily survived. These experiences hint at other forces in our lives where spirit and grace prevail over matter and logic – enough to nudge a sceptical mind along a new course.

Once, alone one evening in our house in Auckland, Subarata saw a very large man with a club trying to get in one of our windows – we had no telephone so instead she shouted at him, but then he tried to force a door. She sat at her shrine and prayed intensely for protection. Faith and belief and devotion are such powerful things! After some time she heard very clearly a voice saying to her, three times, "You are protected, you are protected, you are protected." Then the intruder went away. She was so excited and thrilled by this experience, all her fear vanished. She was so elated by the voice of her unseen guardian.

DINESH
Dortmund, Germany

In the early days at Pujaloy in summer 1997, I used to work with the hydraulic drill hammer. Because one day I got wounded with a cut in my arm, I could not drill for a day or two, as drilling creates not only a lot of noise but also a lot of dust.

So to avoid complications with my wound I decided to work down at the lowest level of the construction place. In those days we had a tube coming down from the top level. The workers there would throw the stones which we had broken out of the rock into the tube, which was some 10 metres long. The stones, which were approximately the size of a basketball, would run through the tube and come out at the lower end. There the worker would grab them and throw them further into a pit. From time to time a company would came to empty the pit with a digger.

The workers at the top would first fill a barrow with stones and then unload the barrow into the tube. Often they would just pick up the stones and throw them into the tube, but in order to be faster they would use the barrow. Because the barrow was larger in diameter than the tube, we created a kind of funnel to catch the stones that would otherwise miss the tube.

On one particular day I was working down at the lower end of the tube together with Pradyot. If we stood at the bottom, we had to be at some distance from the exit because the stones would rock the whole tube and then rush out of it at high speed.

All of a sudden, I was hit by a football-size stone, which had somehow missed the funnel at the top. So the stone jumped all the way down the hill and hit me at the back of my right thigh. I tell you, it was quite an impact! I wanted to continue working, but Pradyot did not allow it. He had seen the scene and was shocked because he thought I must have been injured. He immediately checked me over, only to discover that nothing had happened – not even a scratch was visible! If I had been standing just a little twisted to the right, that stone would have hit my knee or my shin and certainly would have caused a serious fracture. But I did not feel any pain. It just felt like someone had shaken me really hard.

Someone in the inner world definitely was holding a very big pillow to protect my leg. This Someone was making sure that I stood a little to the side just before the impact. And this same Someone even put a veil on my mind not to worry about it. However, Pradyot did not have this veil. He had seen the impact and was quite shocked, while I myself did not get a shock at all.

Many, many times Guru did this kind of thing to save not only our health but our lives too at Pujaloy. Otherwise some of us would have been seriously injured, and one or two would definitely already have gone to the other world. Often we were joking that in the morning when we started working, Guru must have been very aware, because so many near accidents happened. Of course, we had a few real accidents too, but nobody suffered lasting damage because Guru always used his protection power.

PRANIKA
New York,
United States of America

In 1972, having just turned 18 years old, I became Guru's disciple. I moved from my family home to an apartment with my sister and another disciple. Guru had warned us that this was the "year of destruction", and that we should be especially careful and pray for special protection. With the thrill of my new life before me, I prepared for my first breakfast in my new home.

Unexpectedly, as I screamed, "Supreme," my knife slipped from my hand and landed point down straight into my bare foot. Saying Guru's name, I pulled the knife free. Not a drop of blood, a mark or a speck of pain remained. This was the first protection-miracle of many that my Guru would so compassionately offer to my life.

SARVOSMI
Oxford, England

It was a cold February evening, and I was about to fly back to the UK from JFK airport. As soon as I walked into the departure lounge, I felt a strange restlessness, an uneasy energy. Looking around me, I saw a large number of US military personnel waiting for the United Airlines flight to London Heathrow. This was unusual, and certainly something that I had never encountered before. I boarded the flight still feeling a strange energy, a sense of foreboding. Immediately after I sat down, I discreetly took out the Transcendental Picture and began to meditate for protection.

The aircraft, a Boeing 747, took off smoothly and jetted skyward. We were climbing steadily, when somebody cried out, "OH MY GOD, THE WING IS ON FIRE!" I looked over to my right, and sure enough there were flames dancing from the wing. A cold numbing fear crept through me. We were totally helpless. I remember vividly, to this day, the wide unblinking eyes of my fellow passengers, frozen in silent terror. Without a moment's hesitation, I pulled out the Transcendental Picture and held it right in front of my face, high up for all to see. I prepared myself for death. Some women were starting to sob faintly. I prayed and prayed and prayed. I prayed with intensity that I had never experienced, before or since.

As suddenly as they had begun, the flames miraculously disappeared. Below on the runway we could see the fire engines and ambulances gathering.

Amazingly, we landed smoothly on one engine, without incident. The captain's voice came through the cabin speakers. He told us not to panic, that the fire was out and we were safe. His voice was shaking. We knew it was a close call. In quiet reflection, on my return home, I felt that the flight was destined for destruction, but by Guru's intercession I was saved. And the moral of this story – always, always, always carry a Transcendental Picture with you.

JAYALATA
Czech Republic

This is a story about a prayer for protection and how it worked. A few weeks ago I was cooking at Annam Brahma, frying bajjia, and the oil was very hot. At some point I got a little bit dizzy. I often pray for protection, just for a minute or even half a minute. While I was frying, I remembered that I should pray now, so I prayed a little bit for protection. Maybe a second after that, I wanted to take the bajjia out of the oil, but instead, I took a spoonful of oil and spilled it all over my hand.

The first thing I thought was, "O my God, I am going to be badly burned." I was waiting for the pain, but actually I did not feel anything. It felt just as if cold oil had spilled all over my hand, even though the oil was very hot. I immediately wiped the oil off my hand with paper towels and ran cold water over my hand. I was looking at my hand, and it wasn't even red – it was as if nothing had happened. It was amazing how my prayer had worked.

PARVATI
*New York,
United States of America*

One day I was doing service at an enterprise by myself. I had pulled out my brother's phone number to call him, but then got distracted. I was doing my work when the phone rang. It was Shephali calling from Guru's house. She said that Guru was looking for a particular disciple, whom I had unfortunately already taken to the airport. I heard Guru's voice in the background, and Shephali relayed a series of questions about various things. Then the question came, "How is your brother?" I told Shephali that I thought he was fine, and she relayed this to Guru. Guru then said, "Tell your brother that if he stops drinking for fifteen days, he can come to visit me." I was a little surprised and said, "I don't think drinking is a problem for him right now." Shephali told Guru this and he repeated, "Tell your brother that if he stops drinking for two weeks, he can come to see me." I said, "Wow, I guess Guru knows something that I don't."

When I hung up, I immediately called my brother and was very surprised when my stepfather answered the phone. I asked if my brother was there, and he said, "Oh, didn't your mother tell you? I'd better let you speak with her." Needless to say, my heart stopped. When my mother came to the phone, she explained that my brother was in the hospital; he had almost drunk himself to death.

It was obvious to me, in the one statement that Guru made to me on the phone earlier, that not only had Guru protected me from the shock of finding out about my brother without advance warning, but also that he knew about the situation and therefore his protection was already there. When I spoke to my brother, still in the hospital, he said that he had inwardly cried to Guru for help.

* * *

My mother was suffering from deep, deep depression. She and her husband had been fired from their job as hotel managers. I spoke to her several days after she was fired, and she seemed okay. But as the days passed she seemed to get more and more solemn, and she finally stopped taking my calls, always seeming to be asleep. In the last conversation I had had with her, she said that she had sent me her 'last will and testament', but that I shouldn't worry; she was just taking care of some business. I asked her point blank if she was considering suicide and she assured me she was not.

I sent a message to Guru that I was really worried. And once I received her will in the mail, I got frantic and kept trying to call her, but she wouldn't pick up the phone.

One night around 11 p.m., her husband called me and said that my mom was missing and he felt that he should call the beach patrol. (They were camped in their only home, a recreational vehicle, along a California beachfront.) At 1 a.m. he called back and said that the patrol had found my mother "unresponsive, in the surf, but alive," and they were going to take her to the emergency room. When I got the message to Guru, he suggested, "Can she not go?" I myself was not thinking so clearly or quickly, but suddenly doors flew open. Ashrita got me a ticket on a plane that was leaving in one hour, and on which I seemed to have gotten the only empty seat. Then once I got to the airport in California, I got the very last car at the rental place, after being told by six other rental agencies that they had no cars at all.

There are many, many miraculous stories attached to this story, but I will just tell one facet. On the second night that I was there, I received a call with a message from Guru. It was an exercise to perform while I was visiting my mother in the hospital:

"Imagine that you are breathing in and out at the same time as your mother. When she breathes in, feel that the Supreme has entered into her heart. Then feel that a beautiful white light is surrounding her. When she breathes out, feel that your own heart is growing larger and larger, and that you are taking away the wrong forces that have entered into her. Don't worry. I will take care of your life. It will be me who really takes the forces. You will not be affected."

I tried this exercise whenever she was sleeping or when she was conversing with my brother (yes, the same one whom Guru had saved just two years prior). I could really see this light surround her. If I had seen this light in any other circumstances, I would have thought that this person was a saint, it was that tangible.

As days went by, my mother communicated more, but she still would not eat, which concerned the doctors and nurses, nor did she show any sign of being interested in being alive. She had now been in the intensive care unit for four days, and they needed to move her out, ideally to a mental health hospital. But for various reasons, each time it seemed that she would get moved, something happened that would stop the transfer.

On the fourth day, my brother and I went to visit my

mother, but we were informed by the nurse that she did not want any visitors. Panicking, I called to give this message to Guru. Then, after several hours, she let us in. There was a lot of activity in the room. Apparently, one of her doctors had "called in a favour" to a doctor that she knew at another hospital – which had just one bed available. If they hurried, they might be able to get her in there. As we got excited, my mother suddenly started to show excitement, and even took a few bites of food to show her willingness. When she did a phone interview with the doctor at the new hospital, I heard her say, "Yes, I am willing to do whatever it takes," obviously in response to the doctor enquiring as to whether she was willing to get treatment.

The nurses worked frantically, trying to secure my mother's place in this new hospital. I watched in horror, however, as they couldn't successfully draw blood to do the required tests, and then as the records that they were faxing to the new hospital got jammed in the fax machine. The transfer, needless to say, did not happen that night.

Fortunately, when we returned the next morning, my mother had managed to maintain her enthusiasm. That afternoon she was transferred to a different hospital. In hindsight, the facility that everyone had been working so hard to get her into would have been almost two hours away from my brother's house; this one was just forty minutes away.

I had never been to a psychiatric hospital before and, while I tried to be cool and casual about it, when I left after visiting hours were over, I just started bawling uncontrollably. However, the miracle of transformation in my mother had already taken place, and she handled it amazingly well – she was thriving, in fact.

The next day, Guru's message was: "The darkest night has passed." When I told my mother this message that evening, her body jumped back as if a lightning bolt had struck her. She blinked back tears in her eyes and said, "Wow! That is so powerful!" Then I told her about the exercise Guru had given for me to do while she was in the intensive care unit. The next evening she told us this story: She was in a group session and the patients were talking about their fears. She explained that her fear was that she felt so fantastic(!) that she was worried that there was an inevitable crash around the corner. The therapist leading the session responded, "You know, it is funny, but I have been watching you and you just seem to have this light surrounding you." My mother laughed with embarrassment and said, "Oh, I must be sitting in the sunlight." The doctor said, "No, that's not it; it is something else. I think you will be fine."

And by Guru's grace, she is.

SUSHMITAM
Geelong, Australia

My father died at the age of 76, after 10 years of increasing ill health due to Parkinson's disease and a leukaemia-type blood disorder. He worked as a scientist for all of his adult life, at one of the main universities in Melbourne, where I grew up. One of my earliest memories is of visiting him at work and exploring the cyclotron (an atom splitting device) which he had designed for his doctoral thesis. It had a HUGE magnet about 3 times my size and a room full of wires and dials and things made of metal. A completely foreign world to the one I knew, which was at that time filled with soft toys.

Whilst Dad was, like most scientists, very focused on working out how the material world worked, he had a very philosphical bent of mind, and loved to ponder the 'big' issues of life. He could debate about the existence of God until the cows came home! He was a very refined man, with a love of classical music, very introverted by nature and rather self-contained. He loved exploring new fields of knowledge, and adored beauty. Mid-career he transferred much of his research energy into botany and the mathematics of plants, mostly because of his love of rhododendrons.

I became a student of Sri Chinmoy about 11 years before Dad left the body. On seeing me enamoured of sitting still for long periods appearing to do nothing, and noticing (for once!) that I seemed at times to be wearing an unusual garment (i.e. a sari), Dad enquired what it was I was doing. I attempted to explain, but was left with the feeling that he did not quite grasp what it was all about. "But I like my mind!" he said to me. He couldn't see any advantage whatsoever in taking a break from mental work!

A little while later though, he said to me, "I don't really know what this meditation is all about, but I just want you to know I am really proud of you for what you are doing." His pride stemmed I think, partly from the realisation that I was deeply exploring a territory so unknown to him, and also from the knowledge that I was to a certain extent going out on a limb as far as mainstream Australian culture went.

At around this time, my mother went to a work function with Dad and overheard a colleague ask him what I was doing with my life. Mentioning nothing about my professional life, Dad apparently said proudly, "Oh she's a disciple of Sri Chinmoy!"

Although outwardly it seemed that Dad didn't 'get it' as it were, inwardly, he was clearly responding to Guru more and more. A time came when he and Mum had to go into hospital for operations one after the other. At the time I offered to lend them about 5 of my favourite photos of Guru – a couple of them rather large. I explained that having photos of a spiritual Master would assist in healing and provide protection against any negative influences in the hospital. They both duly put the photos up and seemed to enjoy having them there. A month or so later I went to visit my parents and decided to retrieve the photos, which by that time had been placed strategically all around the house. I will never forget my father's face when he saw the collection of photos ready to return home with me. Usually not one to display emotion outwardly, he suddenly looked completely crestfallen, like a little boy who had lost his most beloved toy. I decided at that moment that I would be unable to take the photos and must give them to him. Before I could open my mouth, my mother came into the room, and on seeing the photos, said, "You can't take them back, we talk to him!" So that was that!

SURADHUNI
New York,
United States of America

About twenty years ago, when I was new on the path, I was going to visit my family at Christmas time. I took a taxi to LaGuardia Airport with a big suitcase full of my belongings and gifts for my family, but I had not considered that there would be heavy traffic for the holidays.

When we got to LaGuardia, the driver informed me that he could not get near the departures area in time for me to make my flight, so he dropped me off on the other side of the road. I would have to cross eight lanes of traffic with my heavy suitcase, and this was in the days before suitcases had wheels. I could not see how this was possible, and I was running out of time to make it to my flight.

As I stood there, I prayed: "Please help me, Guru. I am not able to get over to the terminal. I am afraid I am going to miss my flight." I looked over toward the terminal and just then I saw a tall, middle-aged man wearing a cowboy hat come out of the door at the lower level. He walked across the lanes of congested traffic and, I could hardly believe it, headed straight for me!

He came up to me and simply said, "May I help you?" I answered yes, that I was almost late for my flight. He easily picked up the bag, carried it through the correct set of doors (without even asking which airline I was taking) and took it up the escalator. At the top he handed my suitcase to me and I thanked him as profusely as I could manage through my astonishment. He turned around and melted into the crowd; I could not see where. He just disappeared!

When I returned home, I was telling one of the older disciples about my experience, and she told me about Guru's inner beings who help in times of need. Surely this was the only explanation for my helper.

CHAPTER 7

SERVICE

*Service
Is the secret
Of true happiness.*
– Sri Chinmoy

SIPRA
Adelaide, Australia

Sri Chinmoy manifests his spirituality and divinity in many ways – through his music, art, poetry, prose, meditation, athletics and weightlifting. He encourages his students to live in the world and serve our fellow human beings in whatever profession, creative endeavour or work that we take on.

In order to provide a happy work environment and a spiritual haven for the public, he asked some of his students to open small businesses. In the area of Queens where Sri Chinmoy lived there are restaurants, cafés, clothing stores, flower shops as well as laundries and barber shops managed and owned by his students. He called these small businesses 'divine enterprises'.

I first became familiar with a divine enterprise in Perth, Australia in 1974. This was the year I became Sri Chinmoy's disciple. A young couple purchased a small coffee lounge and transformed the untidy space into a sparkling vegetarian restaurant which they named 'Flame-Waves' in honour of a collection of poems and aphorisms that Sri Chinmoy had recently published. A meditation room was available behind the kitchen and the owners lived in rooms behind that.

When Sri Chinmoy visited Perth in 1976 he requested the meditation centre be in another location separate from the restaurant. This left several rooms in the building vacant which another member of the group decided to make into a bakery. This he called 'The Inner Smile Bakery'. I do not recollect ever tasting any of the bread or other goodies which were produced in this bakery and after a very short time the bakery was no more. The owners of Flame-Waves decided to use the space as extra seating for their patrons. So from a small operation of 20 seats in the front room, extra seating including a little fountain garden at the rear had the restaurant catering for 50+ people. On Friday nights customers lined up outside to get a seat.

When I visited New York in the 1970s I would often help out in the divine enterprises in the Queens area. Sri Chinmoy calls this selfless service – a very important component for any karma yogi. I served at Guru Health Foods as well as Divine Robe Supreme, and during a six month stay in New York Sri Chinmoy had me attached to Annam Brahma Restaurant. The owners of this restaurant were given the task of providing meals for Sri Chinmoy so I was very happy working in such a spiritually charged atmosphere. It was always such a difficult adjustment to make when I left New York and came back to Australia and had to take up a position once more in a state college.

When Sri Chinmoy came to Melbourne to give his first Peace Concert in Australia all his Australian students gathered there to receive our Guru's blessings. At that time Animesh, the leader of the Brisbane Sri Chinmoy Centre, was publishing a running magazine which was named *Runners: Oneness-World Harbingers*. Kishore, leader of the Melbourne Sri Chinmoy Centre, was working with the publisher of the country's premier running magazine – *Australian Runner*. This was the height of the running boom and Guru was very pleased with these two.

One morning I was standing in the lobby of the hotel

where Sri Chinmoy was staying. As he passed through he glanced over to me and said, "Why don't you publish a running magazine?" I responded that I did not want to compete with the other two boys. He then stated quite strongly, "Don't compete with them, compete with yourself!" I realized that Guru never says anything lightly and he was giving me the capacity to do the necessary.

The next day at breakfast in the hotel, Sri Chinmoy gave me specific guidelines regarding the number of pages, how often it should be published and how to get articles from disciples around the world. That day we flew out of Melbourne to visit Canberra. On the flight I was inspired with the cover of the in-flight magazine which was covered with blue sky and fluffy white clouds. I placed a picture of Guru running on the front of the magazine and presented it to Guru for his approval for the first cover. Guru liked the idea and wrote in his own handwriting the title for the magazine: *Runners: Joy-Discoverers of the Beyond*.

The first edition of *Runners: Joy-Discoverers of the Beyond* came out later in 1984. The first cover did feature Guru running through the clouds. The second edition displayed Guru with Olympian Carl Lewis. Soon after the magazine reached the stores I received a message from Guru that it was not necessary to have his picture on every edition. However, I could let him know what would appear on the cover of each edition. When the first edition appeared in newsagents I understood the spiritual concept of 'we are not the doers'. It was difficult to believe that I had in any way put this beautiful magazine together at all!

This was a period of very deep happiness and joy manifesting in this way. There were some issues with obtaining enough advertisements to pay for the printing and receiving enough articles. I sought stories on running injuries and their treatment from my chiropractor and a member of the Sri Chinmoy Centre in San Diego volunteered to supply articles on a runner's diet for each edition. Then Guru intervened and instructed various disciples around the world to write stories for our magazine. It then truly became an international running magazine. If the London Marathon was to be run soon, a phone call to London Centre to request someone to cover it and supply photos was made.

One disciple sent along an account of an ultramarathon race; however, it was almost unreadable. The spelling, grammar and syntax were so bad that it was difficult to make sense of the story. As our editorial policy was to include as many articles by disciples as possible, we corrected and rewrote the article, while attempting to preserve the essence of the author's account. The disciple was overjoyed at seeing the article in print.

Guru then instructed the disciple to continue sending stories and, in fact, fill up the magazine when we were lacking in articles. When I heard this, my heart sank! Later Guru detailed how the disciple was to do this. He was to attend track meets, go to airports etc. and interview famous runners. The tape of the interviews was then to be transcribed, edited and corrected by another disciple. In this way our magazine carried interviews of the highest caliber with top ranking athletes which made us the envy of many other running magazines. This experience helped me to understand that when a disciple has enthusiasm and willingness, then the Guru will provide the capacity.

During the two years that we published the magazine

I continued in my day job and would lay out the magazine on my kitchen table at night time. I found during this period of my life I required very little sleep. The one big problem was finding enough advertisements to pay for the printing. Eventually my debts became insurmountable and one of the printers sued me to recover the money we owed him. I let Guru know that I would be taken to court as a result of this debt. He asked me to give him the exact date and time that I would be appearing before the magistrate and hence the experience had me feeling Guru's presence so powerfully during the hearing. Very soon after this a disciple in our Centre had received a large inheritance from a relative and he very graciously gave me several thousand of the money that was owed.

I felt depressed that I had to stop publishing the magazine. Instead of feeling that this was an experience I could learn something from, I lapsed into the depth of feeling I had failed my Master in this most significant manifestation. A week or so later I received a phone call from Guru. He spoke to me most compassionately and requested that I remain happy. Ten minutes later Guru called again and spoke briefly and sternly. "I said be happy!" I realized how much I was torturing Guru with my grief and how important it is to obey the Master in his every request.

PRANIKA
New York,
United States of America

After one and a half years on the path, I began to consider going back to university. I left my work at one of the divine enterprises and began to clean houses to increase my savings, but I felt lost and miserable. As a solution, I decided to stop each day at noon and pray to the Supreme to show me how to be a more integral part of my Guru's mission. Not even one month later, Nishtha called to tell me that Guru wanted her to open a restaurant and me to work with her. I was shocked and surprised that this could possibly be the answer to my noon prayers.

After a few weeks of searching for a restaurant, Nishtha heard from Guru an 'all new plan': she would be the new owner of Annam Brahma. We were to open immediately!

For months I thought I was sent just to help Nishtha get started and soon Guru would reveal my real role, a job at the UN or whatever. One day while cooking at Annam Brahma, I gazed out the kitchen window, praying to Guru to help me. I felt a red thread holding me to my Guru's heart.

Shortly after that, Nishtha was labelling drinks for all the workers and without knowing why, she wrote the initial 'P' on my cup. A few days later I received my soul's name, and part of the meaning was "…the thread that links you to the Supreme. Without it there is no consciousness…"

SARAMA
New York,
United States of America

Shortly after I joined the Centre, one of the Manhattan disciples held a tag sale in her apartment to raise money for the Aum Centre, as we were then known. The sale raised over $300, which was quite successful, since there were only a few disciples at this point and only disciples (and seekers) donated and bought the sale items.

I suggested having a tag sale at my yoga centre, which was in a large house in Westchester. Guru liked the idea, so I solicited donations from my yoga students. They, and their wealthy families, responded generously. To make it more attractive we called it a 'bazaar' instead of a tag sale and we served homemade food.

Merchandise flowed in, everything from a mink coat to a blue sapphire ring, as well as lots of nice less-expensive items. By the end of the day we had quadrupled the amount raised in the Manhattan sale. Needless to say, Guru was delighted. He hinted that perhaps we could do it again soon.

A few months later we held our next bazaar. The well-known guitarist Mahavishnu John McLaughlin and his friend Larry Coryell came with their wives and gave a concert while volunteers brought all kinds of delectable prepared foods to sell. Guru was so happy with the results that he said, "Could you not have one every month?"

And so we did – one Sunday a month, with the help of quite a few yoga students, many of them former hippies who had become disciples. There were so many workers on bazaar day that we set up a cooking crew to prepare meals for everyone.

People worked on setting up and pricing items all day Saturday, the day before the bazaar. A few of us worked right through the night. If we sent someone out on a late errand, we had to check on him if he took too long, only to find him 'meditating' fast asleep in his car.

As for the pricing of the items for our sales, we were all pretty clueless. However, sometimes, looking over the prices that had been put on some items, my intuition would kick in and I would decide that this price had to be higher or lower – mostly higher, because everyone had the selfless tendency to give the stuff away.

One day I came across a long necklace of rough dark green beads on an ordinary piece of string. Someone had marked it 50¢, but I had a feeling that they might be semi-precious stones in the rough, so I changed the price to $4.50. At the end of the bazaar they were still there. Then, following another flash of my intuition (intuition is one meaning of my name, according to Guru), Rupantar offered to take them into the city to be appraised in one of the auction galleries. The beads turned out to be real jade and he came back with $1,300 for Guru!

It would be a boon to have my intuition work like that more often, but fortunately or unfortunately it is something sporadic, over which I have no control.

* * *

After a few months, the basement was loaded with so much merchandise that I said to Guru, "There is so much left-over stuff in my basement that one of the disciples could open a thrift shop and we'd have a steady income for the Centre." Guru's response was, "Wonderful idea,

Sarama. You will do it!"

As soon as I overcame the initial shock of being the 'lucky one', I went store-hunting. I found a little empty shop on Main Street in New Rochelle, just a few blocks from our house. It seemed like the ideal place, but I didn't see any heating system in the store. Well, there wasn't any, but the owner of the building said, "Don't worry about that. We'll put in a blower system before winter."

Everybody came to work at the new store. Both yoga students and disciples continued to do selfless service. Many of the newcomers eagerly welcomed the opportunity for regular selfless service.

The store had a rotating schedule of volunteers, mostly from among my local students, many of whom had also become members of the Sri Chinmoy Centre. One of the neighborhood kids also pitched in from time to time.

After a major transformation, the likes of which we have become accustomed to by now, inauguration day finally arrived, and we eagerly awaited Guru's announcement of the name of the store. He turned to me and said, "I hope you will like the name: 'I – Need – This – Store'. The 'I' in the name is the Supreme." I could think of nothing to say, as a thrill ran up my spine. I Need This Store was born!

A youngster who had been hovering about and helping us through all the construction was seeing Guru for the first time. He confided in me, "When I look at Sri Chinmoy, I feel as though my heart is being pulled out of my chest!" This young boy, who was about twelve years old, continued to spend a lot of time hanging out at the store after school. He was soaking up the 'good vibes'. I sometimes wonder what became of him.

Many of my students came from wealthy families who

often donated very expensive belongings to the store. There were items like a gold cross on a gold chain, gold rings and earrings and other valuables. We felt that those items should not be on the top of the counter, so we kept them in an open box on a shelf inside the counter, behind glass. If someone expressed interest in any of the items, we took the box out to show them what we had.

One of the volunteers didn't seem to realise that the expensive items were not on the counter for a good reason, so she decided they should be displayed more accessibly. Neighborhood kids used to come into the store quite often and one day, at closing time, the lady who was working in the store noticed a number of items missing from the box, which was on the counter.

The boy who had responded so deeply to Guru's presence said that he knew who had taken the missing items. He also said that this boy, when he stole things, always carried them on his person until he was able to unload them. He said that he might be able to get the rest of the boys to help get them back. I asked him to bring the boys to the pizza parlor next door for a little talk. We sat at a table and I explained the whole philosophy of karma to them.

They must have been convinced, because they went right out, jumped the boy and brought back all the stolen stuff. He still had it all with the exception of the gold cross and chain, which he had already unloaded. An interesting aside on the young thief was that he was apparently the son of a New Rochelle police officer.

When winter came it was more difficult to get volunteers to come into the store. The owner never did put in the heating system that he promised. I felt that his partner simply didn't want to spend the money. Our workers were catching cold and one even got pneumonia. Quite understandably, they were very reluctant to continue working there.

* * *

There were more and more Sri Chinmoy Centre activities in Queens, and Sunil and I were driving down from New Rochelle at 5:30 a.m. for six o'clock meditations with Guru. Sunil, who lived in my house, would drive and I would sit beside him, poking him with my elbow whenever I saw his head nodding.

One day in September, 1973, I received a phone call from Guru: "It is time for you to move to Queens. Kindly sell your house in New Rochelle and move I Need This Store to Queens also." The next day I put my house on the market and went to Queens to look for a new home.

* * *

In Queens, the store was soon relocated to Parsons Boulevard (which by now should be renamed 'Divine Enterprise Boulevard'!) in a store-front that had formerly been a butcher shop! The worst job of all was cleaning up a small room at the back, which was to become our jewelry room. It had been the room where they prepared the meat, and the meat hooks along the wall were surrounded by inch-deep layers of fat. Not a vegetarian paradise! I don't recall who were the stalwart souls who undertook that job, but it was done to a T-bone.

Children are usually sensitive to Guru's vibes. A couple of kids, a brother and sister, came after school and on weekends, hanging around and helping however they could, both before and after the store opened. Someone had made some button pins with Guru's picture on them. The little girl wore hers all the time. One day she showed up without it and told me that her mother always borrowed it for bingo night, because it brought her good luck!

There was a big basement below the store, very handy for sorting and storing new merchandise. I would stop by from time to time to see how things were going or if anything was needed. Once, as I was leaving, I remarked to the volunteer at the table, "It would be great to have a bell to signal someone downstairs when it gets busy upstairs." She heartily agreed. The store was big and it was quite impossible for one person to cover the three room-sized areas that needed to be watched. I returned to the store later and was greeted with a wide-eyed, "You won't believe this!" She said, "After you left, a man came to the door and gave me this." She held out a pair of bells, for upstairs and downstairs, along with all the wiring needed for connecting them. "He told me, 'Here, you need this.'"

One day the store received a little surprise package. Any package would have been a surprise, since I Need This Store didn't usually get any mail. The package contained a nice wallet, which I recognized as having been for sale in the store. No note enclosed. A guilty conscience redeemed?

People donated quite a few paintings. We did not price them very high, but one painting with a somewhat battered frame gave me a strange feeling that it might be worth something, so I priced it at $60. A disciple from Europe bought it. I guess he knew more about artwork than any of us did. The next time he came to Queens, he told us he had sold it for $400! Well, at least the money stayed in the family.

We also had a donation of a guitar from Mahavishnu John McLaughlin. It sold for what was a good price in those days. I've been told that now it would be worth at least ten times as much!

* * *

The years passed by – and the rent kept going up and up and up. Finally the owner of the building, who had probably amassed a nice sum of money from his job as head waiter in a fancy restaurant, said that he was taking the store back to open his own place. Guru asked me to find another site, but unfortunately rents had become astronomical by then. Reluctantly we decided that the era of I Need This Store had come to an end.

ARANYANI
New York,
United States of America

In 1981 my mother offered to give me money to start a business. I wrote to Guru and asked if it was the right thing for me to do. A few days later on a Saturday morning I was sleeping when I immediately awoke. I felt an inner urgency to go to the Jamaica High School Track where Guru played tennis. I rushed right over and Guru was already there.

When Guru finished playing tennis he sat in his chair. After a while he called me over. He had read my letter and liked the idea of me opening a divine enterprise. He told me to sell candy, chocolate and nuts. I could also sell newspapers if I wanted.

A few months later the enterprise opened. It was located on Parsons Boulevard by Hillside Avenue, just before the entrance to the 'F' train. It was a beautiful shop with sky wallpaper and green grass carpeting. Guru's pictures hung in the clouds.

On September 19th, a month after the store opened, Guru sent Databir out to buy prasad for the Jharna-Kala girls who were having a workshop that Saturday afternoon. Databir bought the prasad from my store and he told Guru that he had gotten it from me. Guru asked him, "Is she cheerful?" Databir said I was very cheerful. A little bit later Guru walked in! I was totally unprepared. Guru looked around the store for what seemed a long time. When I said to him, "Isn't it beautiful?" he looked lovingly at me but he was meditating and did not want to be disturbed. I remained silent.

Guru's chair finally came. At one point he had sat on the floor(!), and so did the Jharna-Kala girls, as well as many other disciples. Guru stayed for hours (I lost track of the time). He inaugurated the store and gave it the name 'Lakshmi Bhandar'. Guru said, "Lakshmi is the Mother of Beauty, Mother of Wealth, Mother of Satisfaction. Bhandar means store." He did a beautiful painting with magic marker and wrote a song for Lakshmi Bhandar. The words to the song are:

> *Lakshmi Bhandar ecstasy-store*
> *Amiya pathar oneness-shore.*
> *Rama Goddess bless more bless.*

(The word 'more' in the last line of the song is the Bengali word for 'me', though I believe Guru made a double entendre and meant both the Bengali and the

English meanings.)

Lakshmi Bhandar stayed open for four years. During that time I learned how to make truffles and other types of sweets. When the landlord sold the property the store had to close. Guru kindly allowed Lakshmi Bhandar to remain a divine enterprise as a prasad service. To this day I make prasad for Centre functions as well as for 'Sri Chinmoy: The Peace Meditation at the United Nations'.

TOSHALA
Auckland, New Zealand

In the first year of my PhD I became Sri Chinmoy's student. Prior to that I had completed a BSc, an MSc and had worked for a little over a year at MAF Technology (Ruakura) as a senior research associate.

It was at that time that I met and became closely involved in the study of what was to become my PhD research topic, which was looking at endocrine systems to ascertain aspects of the physiology of bone development in growing mammals. Thus I found myself armed with a new and exciting research topic and enrolled at the University of Waikato, with a prestigious scholarship from MAF Technology, in whose modern-ish laboratories I was to perform the research, and where I had allocated office space and access to a well-equipped scientific research library. *Brilliant!*

However, my family circumstances were in the throes of upheaval. All four of my grandparents, as well as my

Nana's mother (my great-grandmother) had just up and died and my uncle – a very wise and kind man to whom we all looked for guidance at this time – was stricken with leukaemia. Several months before he died he advised us to learn how to meditate. He said that, "Meditation brings you close to God!" So my mother and I both attended free meditation classes that were being offered as a community service by the Sri Chinmoy Centre. And we enjoyed them so much, we joined the Centre ourselves!

When my uncle died he left us to the guidance of the wise, kind and universal philosophy of Sri Chinmoy, with which we have been happy and safe for many years now. But I digress... this is really a story about my studies and how meditation augmented and ultimately completed my research.

Every Sunday afternoon for more than three years I would drive to Auckland from Hamilton (which took 1 hour and 47 minutes), attend meditation night at the Centre, and drive back late at night. Over these three years I also went to New York several times to attend Sri Chinmoy's special Celebrations, which were most fun-filled and fulfilling events. At this point I had better mention that these trips were much against my main PhD supervisor's advice and wishes! He felt that they were fruitless exercises and were distractions from the main focus of my life, which he felt was my budding scientific career. At one stage he called me into his office to rant at me about it! I calmly pointed out that these trips had not slowed my studies down, and I had also always met my work deadlines – and he had to agree! This was a small victory. I had noticed changes, though, with the passing of time. My focus shifting off my direct studies had side effects that I could never have imagined had I been outside of the situation. I found my perspective clarified and I became more liberal in my technical discussions and in decisions regarding my research directions – and I started coming across as a flexible and (*in some instances*) clever thinker! In short, my meditation life made me more philosophical, and as I was studying for a Doctorate of Philosophy degree, this was very useful.

However, the full meditation-derived benefits to my study came as the end of my research drew near early in 1994 when thesis writing (sketchily begun as research was carried out) began in earnest. For any research project (or degree involving one) there is not really any clear end, what with new avenues of research developing and suggesting themselves, as the main line of research grows and evolves. The project itself is usually not clearly set out at the beginning as, with progress, results determine further directions, in which way the study takes form. The end of a fruitful project like the one I was working on was when enough data had accumulated for a sizeable thesis. However, I had reached the end of the time for the research grant under the terms of the MAF scholarship, and I was also scheduled to go to New York for 12 days in April, which was one week away. I had worked hard to complete the comprehensive requirements for laboratory work so as to be at leisure to write the thesis intensively when I got back – freshly inspired – from overseas. How wrong could I be? My supervisor called me into his office (*uh oh*) and Laid Down The Law! He told me that if I went away at this point (when he felt I needed to focus for a few months on intensive thesis writing) my grant (already near the end) would be terminated and there would no longer be office space for me when I returned! (*Talk about a Drama King!*) His intention was to pressurise me to cancel my trip to New York so that I would not lose my 'Focus' on the project, in which MAF had a vested interest.

I was silent in that meeting, knowing that my whole career was on the line. On the line also was a post-doctoral fellow position at the University of West Virginia that I was negotiating for and which would be secured should I successfully finish my PhD within the next couple of months. Unknown to my supervisor I was also extremely reluctant to cancel my trip to New York – in fact, that was *not* an option. My sense of values had changed regarding what was important to me, and this *was*. What's more I viewed the trip as beneficial to myself personally, as well as to my work, in a way that I was not ready to impart to my supervisor, whose values were not the same. So I went home and prayed. Actually, I prayed really hard – a fervent and sincere prayer – asking for guidance and strength as I was about to forfeit everything I had ever worked for. If it was indeed God's Will then the whole PhD thesis would have to be written in less than a week (which is impossible!) or I would have to walk away from everything, here and now. (I was praying for the surrender and peace of mind to do this very thing for the thesis writing task *was actually* impossible.)

HOWEVER – and very suddenly – a Fire (for want of a better word) lit inside of me – *very intense, very concentrated*. I was drawn up as if by an unseen Hand and started to type frantically. I was focused and absolutely clear, fast and accurate, and the thesis started to form beneath my flying fingers. I filled up disks with information, correctly typed and formatted, and discussions and theories – as well as stored information from my brain – were lucidly and effortlessly discussed and retrieved. New concepts (that would never normally have occurred to me) were thrown about with ease and a comprehensive and complicated scientific document formed. Do not be deceived – this did not happen in a couple of hours – it happened over five days and five nights. Data and information were collated from MAF and the University and diagrams and photographic illustrations were also assembled from different places. All the time, *at every second*, my whole being was filled with the same unabated level of intensity and purpose that guided me – and in that short time, my thesis became *ready to submit*! The impossible had occurred. What should, by rights, have taken months instead took days. What is more, during this time (since the Fire took over) there was no sleep. I worked the whole time and there was no tiredness, even though I never lay down or rested for over 120 hours. Indeed, I felt refreshed! But it was as if I was just watching the whole procedure, fascinated. And here comes the icing on the cake – my supervisor was impressed by it and said that it was the best PhD thesis to have come out of his department to date! And some of the discussion points – he said also – were brilliant!

When I read the thesis myself a couple of months later (before my oral exams) I marvelled at the well-rounded and clever conclusions that had been drawn, the extrapolations from the information garnered during research were extraordinary and left me breathless. I *know* that I was not responsible for producing that superb piece of work. I just observed whilst it was being assembled. I am not being humble or modest when I say that I personally was not up to that standard scientifically – I am merely stating the truth. For some reason this work was meant to be done and – for want of a better description of proceedings – my being was just an instrument.

After my oral exams were successfully behind me and the PhD degree conferred, I then walked away from that particular career and embarked upon another. People ask how on earth I could become a café worker after doing top-level scientific research and that I must miss it... but no! I have never had a pang or looked back. The café I work in, The Blue Bird, is no ordinary place – it is a place that tries to offer a tiny bit of Sri Chinmoy's world to everyone who enters it. His music, philosophy and meditation can be heard, seen and felt in the ambience of spirituality that we try to create there.

The sudden loss of my close-knit and loving family no doubt changed my perspective on life, and my mother and I found comfort in the all-embracing philosophy of Sri Chinmoy. Everyone in the world is your brother or sister and there is a universal thread of unity and oneness in everyone and everything that is none other than God. This is God's Playground and He is always there, but unobserved. However, in your direst moments of absolute need, He may reveal Himself, and moments like that leave you changed forever. That there is disharmony amongst the people of the world means that there is much work to do. However small or menial my current work is, it does in a small part address the disharmony of the world, and this has been a more rewarding and fulfilling turn to my career than I can express.

* * *

The Kettledrum Café first opened its doors to the public on 15th March, 1995. Several months of hard work preceded this phenomenon, starting with finally summoning up the courage to tell my Dad that I was not going to be taking up an overseas post-doctoral fellowship after all but was instead going to walk away from my career and many years of training to open a café in Auckland. He just looked at me and said, "So do you need any appliances for this?" Just like that. No big deal.

Buoyed by Sri Chinmoy's encouragement, in August of 1994, to open a café representing the Sri Chinmoy Centre, I moved to Auckland from Hamilton and took a short business course, then obtained a hygiene certificate so that everything would be above board and 'proper'.

The next thing was the actual location of the shop and I decided on a small mall in Elliott Street initially because it was tiny and affordable. And, looking back, it was a good place to cut our teeth on and hone our skills, for although I was a keen amateur cooky-type and enthusiastic foodie, I had no idea how to run a business and had never worked in a café or restaurant before. Two very good friends, Subarata and Jogyata, chose all of the decorations, the crockery, tables and chairs, etc., whilst I organised (ergonomically, of course!), and decked out, the kitchen.

There are some rare and special people on this earth who are extremely generous, and even when they have nothing at all to call their own, they will still give you everything. Subarata only owned one (albeit battered!) pot, two plates and a fork and on the day before we opened, she walked into the Kettledrum kitchen with these in a box – she was donating her entire kitchen paraphernalia to the enterprise! She said that Jogyata and she would eat off napkins and takeaway plates from now on. Also when her sisters sent her any money from

Ireland, she would buy things for the café – things that would enhance the food display or could be used to decorate something. She really liked making things look cute.

We decorated the menu boards and we also recruited others to help us set up. The day before opening I cooked all day and all night. Then the Robert Harris representative turned up with our cappuccino machine, on which he gave us a quick demonstration. He made a cappuccino, took a sip, then offered the same cup for Subarata and myself to sample from. Very quickly Subarata said, "Oh, we only drink tea!" *Phew!*

So then we opened and the public swarmed in. We were very busy for that week as we had two stilt-walking clowns walking around outside on 1 metre stilts, handing out leaflets about The Kettledrum. They did a very good job. Since that fateful day we were open at the Elliott Street location for two and a half years. Sri Chinmoy came to visit us on 30th June 1995 – and liked it!

On 13th April 1997, Sri Chinmoy gave The Kettledrum the name The Blue Bird. The phrase, 'Blue Bird' is often used by poets to refer to the soul and Sri Chinmoy uses this avian metaphor in his own poetry.

This theme is also prevalent in Sri Chinmoy's art – he has drawn millions of birds in a series of drawings and paintings collectively called the 'Dream-Freedom-Peace-Birds', which represent the light and delight of the soul, and its flight to freedom and happiness. These have been displayed in many galleries and cities throughout the world. There is a very tiny selection of these on the walls of The Blue Bird.

Eventually the Elliott Street location became too small so we moved to bigger premises at 299 Dominion Road,

Mt Eden, which opened on 22nd July 1997. Again it was a team effort to set up – Subarata again as our interior decorator and purchasing officer.

Over the years we have changed and evolved – as has our menu! However, two things have remained constant: we all love spirituality and are avid foodies!

Sri Chinmoy came and visited us on the 30th of November, 2002 – and liked it! On that day he wrote a song for The Blue Bird. This has been recorded by the spiritual music group Shindhu on their CD *Shindhu 8*, which is one of the recordings of Sri Chinmoy's music that we play in the café to set a spiritual theme and to offer a little of Sri Chinmoy's beautiful and peaceful world to everyone who comes in.

The Blue Bird is one of the many International vegetarian cafés and restaurants owned and operated by the students of Sri Chinmoy. Each one has a distinctive name and atmosphere; they can be found in cities such as Christchurch, Melbourne, Adelaide, Brisbane, San Diego, San Francisco, Seattle, New York, Toronto, Ottawa, Halifax, Paris, Montpellier, Zurich... to name a few!

We believe that universal harmony begins in the heart of each individual and our goal is to nourish that harmony by offering delicious vegetarian food prepared in the spirit of love and oneness.

UTSAHI
Ottawa, Canada

*"My infinite light, delight and purity
Are being manifested here!"*

**– Sri Chinmoy,
during his visit to
The Garden of Light,
November 21st, 1999**

For many years, I had been dreaming of opening a divine enterprise. During my monthly visits to New York, I had adopted the habit of helping out at Guru Health Foods. Working with the boys there gave me lots of joy; plus I always found selfless service to be such a beautiful manifestation. When Guru found out that I was working there, he immediately suggested that I should open a health food store in Ottawa. Wow! What a challenge! Having worked there for some time by then, I kind of knew what it meant: so many products, about which you need to have knowledge, so many trends in health, natural living and healing, plus the staffing, the displays, not to mention the finances....

I started looking for a location in Ottawa. I was drawn to the Vanier area and learned that Hladini had had a health food store there in the 1980s. I continued to look for a suitable location. In addition, as I continued to work in Guru Health Foods, I became more attentive to customers' needs, trends in health food products and health care. I was getting ready!

I also visited angel shops whenever I had the occasion. I had always had a fascination for angels, ever since I was very young. My childhood dreams of Heaven always were comprised of two elements: angels and bicycles. Yes, bicycles – because we could not afford such a luxury when I was young. And angels because, in my Christian background, Heaven was full of angels singing, flying and gracefully dancing at the feet of God the Father, sitting on His Throne! Both my dreams have come true: I now have a bicycle, and in our Centre, angels are singing at every meditation.

But in 1998, all of a sudden, the health food store plan changed. The Supreme has His own Plans, I guess. In the same building as Prapti's Perfection-Satisfaction-Promise restaurant was a very small, messy, second-hand bookstore. And through Prapti, I had known for a while that the bookstore owner was struggling financially and considering letting go of his lease. Prapti pointed out to me that this location would have many advantages: it was in the same building as another divine enterprise, there were lots of students coming by, there was lots of other pedestrian traffic. This seemed like a unique project, where we could attract the student population into something divine. But what to put in this tiny spot? I was looking for signs, praying for God's Will to be manifested.

One curious sign was given to me while running in a remote area of Gatineau. At that time, I would run 10 km before going to work every morning. This was my training for the long runs: marathons, the 47-mile race, the 24-hour in Ottawa, the New Year's Self-Transcendence run, and a few others. That morning in May, 1998, I was running on a small dirt road, and what did I find on the side of the road? An angel! Yes, an angel figurine that happened to be there.... Was it a mere coincidence? Was it a sign from above? I picked up the angel and looked up to Heaven, full of gratitude, and smiled.

A wonderful idea materialized: an enterprise that would sell Guru's books and music, and spiritual merchandise, where we could sell angels and other spiritual statues, and where human angels would work selflessly. When this concept was presented to Guru, he loved it: people working selflessly in a store offering his message, his books, music and Jharna-Kala products.

And then the work started. The location had to be entirely renovated. A disciple from Montreal helped me plan the renovations. I had literally no money at the time, but with contributions from friends, I had set aside $5,000 for the project.

Then I got quite a shock: the estimate for renovations was more than $17,000! This was balanced by a wonderful surprise: the generosity of disciples. For example, to this day, I have never seen the renovation invoice... many disciples helped financially. Next, we needed a name. We had a friendly competition in our Centre, and disciples suggested approximately ten names. These were submitted to Guru. He listened to our suggestions, was silent for a minute, and then came up with his own name: The Garden of Light. What a beautiful name! What a gift! To this day, when we buy merchandise, we think about the name Guru gave the enterprise and ask ourselves: will this item bring light into his garden of light?

We opened on September 27th, 1999. The inventory was very small, but the staff and I were full of hope... Yasodhara, a retired school teacher, gave more than her full time and energy to the shop for two years. There were, at some point, 27 people working selflessly at The Garden of Light. Practically the entire Centre was involved, either working in the store itself or carrying out other responsibilities for the enterprise (accounting, scheduling, buying, etc.). Spiritually, it was a beautiful concept; financially, it was a great challenge and, as we all know, challenges are great opportunities to learn, to grow.

A few months later, on November 21st, 1999, Guru came to Ottawa for a concert. Of course, we had prepared The Garden of Light, hoping that he would come to visit. Our wish came true: he came and blessed the enterprise in such a beautiful way I can't even describe it. When he entered the store, he looked at me, silently, for several moments, meditating on me. Then he started looking around, and at some point picked up a pen, paused for a while, then wrote in our guest book:

My Soul's Infinite Blessings,
My Heart's Infinite Joys,
My Life's Infinite Gratitude.
Guru Sri Chinmoy

What a gift from our Guru! He continued looking around, and after 15-20 minutes, sat down and said: "Selfless service is the one hundred percent manifestation of my light and goal. It is the ideal way. In this place, you are doing exactly that. My infinite light, delight and purity are being manifested here." Approximately 300 disciples were outside, waiting for an opportunity to come in. They came in through Perfection-Satisfaction-Promise, and took prasad at Guru's feet while he was sitting inside The Garden of Light.

Over time, we were able to open a second location, next to the Peace Garden on Clarence Street. Eventually, we moved this store to Ottawa South, the area where our first divine enterprises were located in the 1970s. Some people will remember: Ananda Niketan (The Abode of Delight) – vegetarian restaurant and health food store – the health food store was famous for its Guru's Golden Granola, with a Transcendental Picture on the label; Saraswati Sopan (The Flight of Wisdom) – Vidura's Bookstore; and Bhakti Press – Utthal's printing shop. This second location on Bank Street offers more possibility in terms of space; plus, in the basement, we have a permanent exhibition of Guru's Jharna-Kala artwork.

With The Garden of Light stores came lots of new challenges, possibilities and opportunities: what and where to buy, how to manage a divine enterprise, how to offer to the community some spiritual opportunities, through classes, informal discussions, meeting with seekers, etc. In this way, our enterprise, as well as selling products, offers an oasis of peace where people can come and browse through a book, listen to spiritual music, experiment on a singing bowl or two. One woman expressed it this way in our guest book: "Every time I come to Ottawa from Maniwaki (more than one hour away), I go and eat at Perfection-Satisfaction-Promise and then I come here, to The Garden of Light and bathe in its atmosphere. After this, I have enough of the city and head back home."

I'm so fortunate that, through my work, I participate in conferences the world over. So whenever I travel to Tunisia, Turkey, Myanmar, China, India and other countries, I take some time to shop, and then I can bring home unique gifts to sell in the enterprise. Once, while at a conference in Chennai, I made a little detour to Kathmandu, and there I realized that there were many opportunities, both for my spiritual edification as well as for our business. Since this initial three-day detour, I have made many more trips to Nepal. This lovely land, with its soulful inhabitants, is a very spiritual place. I have met many people there who have become close friends and not merely business partners. Now when I visit, it's not mainly for shopping; it's more to be with my fellows, my sisters and brothers. Also, I have attended the Sri Chinmoy Centre in Kathmandu so often that I now consider it my second spiritual home. Of course, I do some shopping on the side, and love to give classes there, as well.

The dream of becoming a wholesale distributor had been in my mind for a while; it became a reality in August 2013, when we started the Pure Himalaya Distribution enterprise under Gautami's expert vision and abilities. From now on, going shopping in Nepal has become even more important, since we have to supply both the stores and the distribution business. I never expected that doing a little selfless service in Guru Health Foods would bring all these consequences. For the guardian angel found while running, for Guru's suggestion that I open an enterprise, for the innumerable occasions to serve, and for thousands of other reasons, this song of Guru's is so appropriate:

Life is beautiful,
Life is bountiful
Only when
God's Grace guides.
– Sri Chinmoy

VIJALI
*Rhode Island,
United States of America*

Almost from the beginning, Guru had me selling his Jharna-Kala cards and gifts. One day he called me to his house and said, "Please sell Jharna-Kala in Manhattan."

In those days, the book of samples was so big that it almost dragged on the sidewalk! I was not familiar with Manhattan, but I soon learned my way around the stationery stores. I then continued to sell in Rhode Island as well.

I decided one day to take Jharna-Kala on the road. Along with a New York Jharna-Kala girl, I set out on the road with the hope of driving as far as possible throughout the States. We drove as far as Texas, stopping along the way at book shops and stationery stores. We were not successful in making sales, but we felt we had at least spread some of Guru's light. We travelled through the Bible Belt most of the way – a very interesting experience!

We would stop at motels at night and then get back on the road the next day. I drove the whole day and was most happy to have a competent map-reader along with me, directing me the entire way. Our trip lasted a week – a very pleasant week.

Guru requested me to go to Texas for a stationery show one year. At least Jharna-Kala was being seen by people!

When the company started to attend the stationery shows in Manhattan, Guru asked me to help with selling in the booth. This I continued to do for as long as the company participated at the yearly stationery show.

* * *

In 1980 I decided to look for a house close to the then 'tennis court' – today's Aspiration-Ground. I ran into the owner of the house Vyakulata now owns and asked him if he was thinking of selling his house. He said yes, and we negotiated a price. A few weeks later the man told me he had decided not to sell. Guru was surprised at the man's change of plans and encouraged me to look for another house. As I walked down 85th Avenue, I saw a man sitting on the porch of his house. I asked if he wanted to sell it, and he replied, "Maybe." His wife was home and he invited me to see the house. When I left, I gave him my card and phone number and asked him to call me if he made a decision.

A few weeks later he called and told me he wanted to sell the house. With the house in that location, electricity could now be provided for the court, as well as access to water.

Not too long after the purchase of the house, the home that housed Jharna-Kala items was sold and the Jharna-Kala Card Company needed a storage place for their products. Later my house became a meeting place for the girls working on Jharna-Kala. The girls met there weekly for many years.

Guru visited the house often when the girls had their workshops. He would stop in to give prasad to the workers and meditate with them. Guru blessed the house shortly after I purchased it.

SULOCHANA
New York,
United States of America

The divine enterprise was interesting!

Before I went to work in Manhattan, every day I used to come to the court. Guru was at the court every morning. Before I went to the subway, just for five minutes I meditated a little bit and then I would go to my job.

One day Guru sent Pulak to tell me that he wanted to talk to me. At the end of the tennis court, near Guru's entrance, I was waiting. I had a 10:00 appointment at work. I was very conscientious about my job always; I had held it for eighteen years. I knew the customers were waiting for me. But I waited until Guru called me. Then he said, "I want you to open a divine enterprise."

I said, "Yes, Guru." That was it! I ran to work.

Managing a beauty salon was not my kind of job, because I did not do pedicures or manicures. I am an aesthetician, so I did facials, waxing and eyelash tinting. That was all – just those three things. I liked my job in Manhattan. Who would come here to Jamaica?

We should have more faith in our Master if he asks something. I never was thinking about opening a divine enterprise next to the tennis court. I went to Union Turnpike, because there were big beauty salons there, but I did not find any place. I thought: all right, I went looking for a place, but I do not have to do anything because I did not find a place.

One day while I was with a customer in Manhattan, a phone call came. He never said, "This is Guru." He just started to talk. He said, "Why don't you do what I am asking you to do?"

I said, "Yes, Guru." I shifted from one foot to the other, because Guru was talking about the enterprise. I had stopped trying; I was not looking for it any more. But Guru inwardly knew that this particular place was empty, which I did not know. Then I said, "Yes, Guru, I will do it."

I talked to Pranika and she said, "Well, this place is empty." It used to be a gambling place. I talked to the owner and I rented it. I gave a down payment and then I opened the door and went inside by myself. I sat down in the middle of the room and started to cry, because it was terrible! It was a mess! And it was dark. They had dark curtains over the window and dark wood panelling. There was a big roulette table at the front, and in the little room, another roulette table. Oh, it was terrible!

I asked the boys to wallpaper it, but nobody wanted to do it! Then I said, "Guru asked me – I'm going to do it myself!"

After finishing my job in Manhattan, at six o'clock I went over there and started wallpapering. I got nice wallpaper; I chose it myself and put it up by myself. It was very nice.

The ceiling was nice. The little room I painted, then the woodwork, and the floor. I did not have a car, but I went to Jamaica Avenue where there was a big linoleum place. I bought linoleum and with big scissors cut it to just the size of the room. It was a whitish colour, like cream, so everything looked very clean. And then it was ready.

I opened up the place and in February I said to my manager in Manhattan, "I will take my vacation right now." I was clever! My mind did not really a hundred percent trust Guru. It was afraid of the whole thing.

The day I opened the divine enterprise, I did an eyebrow waxing for $3 – that was it for the whole day! I said to myself, "Oh God! In Manhattan they are waiting for me at my job, and I am here."

I went back to my boss and said, "I cannot work full time any more – only four days."

For ten years I worked seven days a week. Three days a week the enterprise was open. For quite a while, Snehashila was there to answer the telephone.

Guru came not very long after I opened – in July. In the corner I had a kind of partial wall, and I made an area with a little round table and a chair covered with a white sari. Guru sat there, and many disciples came. I do not know which day it was exactly, but there were beautiful flowers. It was summertime, when the lilies were opening.

Guru went into deep meditation, and then he suddenly asked who had paper and a pen. I think Nilima had them, and she gave them to him. Then Guru wrote down on the paper 'God's Beauty' and my spiritual name, and he said, "Do not open it now." That was how I got my spiritual name. I wanted to get it so badly when I became a disciple!

I was crying for my spiritual name, and I did not know what I should do to get it! Finally I figured out that I had to run for it. That was why I wanted to run. I did long-distance running, everything, but no name! When Sudhahota became a disciple, I remember that Guru said he wanted to get a spiritual name. Narada brought him, and Guru said, "Bring me a chair." Guru meditated on him and gave him a spiritual name right away. He composed a spiritual song for him, and I was singing that song in oneness. I said, "I am Sudhahota!" So I had oneness! I was singing the song that he composed for Sudhahota. But I still did not have my name.

Five years went by, and then I got my name and the divine enterprise. Why? Because I obeyed Guru. He was asking me to do it. Financially I was all right. I made good money in Manhattan, so it was comfortable for me. I dressed up every day, wearing nice things. We could not work in sandals; we needed nice shoes. I did like that, and it was easy for me. And because my husband had had a business, I knew everything that goes with it. I really did not think of having a divine enterprise, but Guru told me to do it, so I obeyed him and opened it.

In the beginning, I still had financial issues. I had the mortgage on the house. I never wanted to go to Guru and say, "Guru, I cannot pay the mortgage." I always worked with my hands, so that was how it was.

I should, at the very beginning, have had that absolute faith in the Master. If the Master says something, it is going to be all right – positive, positive! I am a worrying type by nature, because of everything that I went through in my life. But even now, why do I not give up God's Beauty? Because Guru asked me to do it.

Now also I try to live the philosophy, when my body is unfortunately not the same. I am working many times in pain. I have to come home and lie down, but I do not feel sorry for myself. Everybody does that! I do not like to eat until I rest a little bit. I turn on the TV and then fall asleep. Sometimes I eat my food at about 8:00 at night, because I am so tired when I come home that I really do not want to eat then. But I never asked Guru how long to continue with the divine enterprise. With running, he said to continue until it is unbearable. So I always say, "I can do it longer, I can do it longer."

CHAPTER 8

SELF-TRANSCENDENCE

Individual self-transcendence
Collectively inspires
Humanity at large.

– Sri Chinmoy

SULOCHANA
New York,
United States of America

Running – that is very interesting! I was a young disciple. We were at Progress-Promise, and Guru said, "Stand up, those who want to run the New York City Marathon!" Right away I stood up.

Guru did not ask how old I was, but he asked, "How much do you run?"

At that time, after Guru had taken me back in the Centre and I was working at Annam Brahma again once a week, I was still living in Manhattan, and I used to train along the East River."

I said, "Guru, at the most I run 15 or 16 miles. Guru said, "It is not a joke – that is not enough."

I sat down right away and I thought the floor would open underneath me, because all around me were young disciples who were going to run. I was older, because I was about 47 or 48 years old when I became Guru's disciple. And Guru said the marathon was not a joke.

Then, whenever I came to Annam Brahma, I used to train. I liked to train where I knew how far a mile was. I ran on 150th Street until the end, and then back again, but not down the hill. One time we had a race there. That was how I knew my mileage, and that was how Guru trained me inwardly. But outwardly he never asked me to run. That was how I started. The next year, by God's Grace, I ran the New York City Marathon.

Guru had some meetings in Annam Brahma, sometimes on Sunday mornings. Once Guru made an announcement: "I would like to have in different Centres, once a month, a marathon. It will be in different Centres, not in the same Centre."

I said to myself, "I would like to do a marathon once a month." I told this to a boy who used to massage Guru's feet, and he told Guru. Guru said it was all right, so that was how it started. For the whole year I signed myself up for a marathon once a month. The first one was in Montreal – with snow blowing, and ice everywhere.

I finished the marathon in Montreal, by God's Grace. I was able to finish in the high snow and ice. Lots of snow was coming down, and the wind was blowing.

Usually I never used to eat during a marathon. I would just drink a little bit. In the New York City Marathon, even after 13 miles sometimes I did not drink – just after that, which was not so good. My stomach cannot hold so much water. Later on I tried to drink, but I would spit the water out from my mouth. I could not swallow it, so I had to be careful.

The second marathon was in Ottawa. It was almost the same. Everything was icy – it was difficult, but I still finished that marathon.

I think the third marathon was in Chicago. I went to Chicago. I saw the lake, but I thought it was the ocean! It was March, and the weather was good – not too hot, not too cold – so I finished and I had a very good time. That was my best marathon. It was 4 hours and maybe 20 or 30 minutes.

After that was, I think, Australia. I asked Guru, because I really did not know if I should go there. I did not have vacation from my job. I would have to just go there, run the marathon and fly back, but the flying time was very long.

Guru had a 24-hour race somewhere – in Connecticut, I think, around a track. That was a certified course. I asked Guru, "Can I run the marathon in Connecticut?" Guru said, "Fine." So, instead of Australia, I ran in Connecticut.

That was how it started.

I finished the marathon on the track and took off my shoes and my socks, and then I saw Cahit Yeter. Cahit and others were also running around, so I thought, all right, others are running, so I could do a little bit more. Then I changed my socks, put on the same shoes, went back and started to run with the others, but not fast. I reached, I think, 70 miles. Then I had to go to the medical area. I sat on the bed and right away I just collapsed and went to sleep.

Guru came in the morning. He saw my name on the scoreboard, saw '70 miles' and heard that I was not running any more. The disciples came over to me and said, "Guru is here! Come out!"

Somehow I got out of the bed. I was hardly able to stand on my feet, because I had never run that much! Then I put on my shoes. I saw that people were still going around the track, and I thought, okay, maybe I will walk around a little bit. And what happened? Suddenly the energy came to me, and I just started to race. I did about 3 more miles, like that, fast! When I started I was hardly able to walk, so that was Guru's miracle.

Guru never said anything. But after that, I did many New York City Marathons, as others also did. When the first 5 or 7-day race came up, for that I asked Guru. But before that, Guru decided to have an international 1,000-mile race, and I entered it. I did not do 700 miles first. Right away I went to the 1,000-mile race, because there was nothing less. Suprabha and I were the only women. I have a picture of it. I remember Siggy Bauer, who came, I think, from New Zealand. He was in it, and Cahit Yeter and others.

I had experience in marathons, but not really in longer races. The runners started teaching me, sometimes with a few words – I should eat, or something like that. Unfortunately my training was not enough, so I got shin splints in both legs. A chiropractor said I had to stop; I could not run any more. They bandaged my legs and I had to put them up. But I had vacation from my job, and I had left everything behind. What could I do now? The race was not over, so I did not want to go back to my job. I still was in the race, so I started to walk slowly. I learned later that you really can continue, but very slowly, and the shin splints go away after a while. You do not have to quit. I know a boy who just stopped and never ran again, because it was painful. But I was kind of a trouper!

I did not complete 700 miles in that 1,000-mile race. The head of the Sri Chinmoy Marathon Team at that time said, "Well, she is a tough cookie! But she can never finish the 700." He was wrong!

The next year Guru decided to have 1,300 miles, 1,000 miles and 700 miles. I asked Guru at that time which race I should enter, and he sent the message, "700." I always asked Guru. In the 700-mile race, shin splints came, but only in one leg.

I attempted 700 miles a third time, in Flushing Meadows. Everybody finished, and I was the last one.

I did not touch any sugar during this race, and no coffee or tea. I was absolutely very clean in my body. But the last night, when I was about to finish, I started to see nightmares – not really nightmares, but hallucinations.

I saw a train running beside me, and then I saw a big woman's face on the pavement.

I went to the medical area, and right away three people were working on me – one on my head, one on my middle and one on my legs. It was only for a short time, because I could not rest for long – I had to finish!

I finished, by God's Grace. I said, "I finished," but I mean that Guru finished in and through me! Then Suprabha came and put the wreath on my head. Suddenly, we saw Guru's car. At that time I just felt he was holding my hand. Guru has that story about two sons: the father is holding one son's hand and the other son is holding the father's hand. The second son falls into the pond. I felt that Guru was holding my hand. He did not say anything, but I knew that he had come out for me, because I was the last one to finish. That was a big thing for me. I felt Guru was holding my hand for the rest of my life.

The other thing about my running is that I wanted to do it, but Guru inspired me. He gave me the energy and everything else. One time I asked Guru outwardly, when I was in intense pain during a long-distance race, "Guru, how long should I run?" Guru said, "Until the pain is unbearable." That was his answer. I always said to myself, "A little bit longer, a little bit. I still can take it. Still I can run a little bit longer." And I finished the race! After that I never stopped. I could have stopped if I wanted to, but I did not.

That was my experience with Guru. I had many other experiences because of my running, by God's Grace. My feeling is that Guru put me there for the younger disciples who thought they could not finish. They would say, "She is old. If she runs, we can also do it."

More people started to do long-distance races, but not every one of them was able to finish 700 miles, for certain reasons. I was just an instrument. Guru chose me, because I wanted to do it and I liked it. Even nowadays it is in my blood. I do not really meditate so much, because I always have to go out to do my mileage. Nowadays I have to walk slowly, but I have to go out. This is how Guru trained me over the years. He made me feel that perhaps I am able to do more.

VIJALI
Rhode Island,
United States of America

Oh yes, the running world! When I discovered Guru was having disciples run every day, I panicked! I was not a runner, and as a matter of fact I had never been a runner. Even as a child I could not run. I was always the one behind everyone else whenever we raced. I had chronic bronchitis for many years, with less breathing capacity than my friends. A walker, however, I was. I could walk for hours with much ease.

I remember how Guru would have 2-mile races on weekends and during Celebrations. I did participate, but of course I was the last one to finish.

One Celebration Guru scheduled a 7-mile race in Flushing Meadows Park. I had twisted my ankle earlier that day, but went ahead to the park to cheer the runners on. When Guru walked by me, he said, "Run!" So I started the race with everyone else on a slightly sprained ankle. It was a challenge and a great learning experience. I discovered that if I put my foot on the ground a certain way, the pain lessened. It became a game for me, placing the foot to the ground without having pain. Then, because of course I was behind everyone else in the race, I suddenly found that I was lost! I did not know which way to go. I was inwardly saying, "Guru, I need your help." All of a sudden I noticed a disciple who was not running the race walking a short distance away. I got his attention and he kindly told me which way I should go.

Just a few miles away from the finish line, I ran into one of the Japanese disciples. We were both very happy to find one another. We ran and walked the rest of the way together. As we approached the finish line we held hands and finished together. Guru had stayed until we finished. He was smiling, but the race officials, who were perhaps tired of waiting for the slower than the slowest runner of all time, could not appreciate it!

My ankle actually felt much better!

* * *

When Guru lifted 200 pounds, he asked who would like to run 200 miles in honour of his lift. Several people stood up, including me. Guru laughed and said, "What, you?" I thought to myself, "I am being silly!" So I decided to go to the race and help count the runners' laps.

When I arrived at the park, I entered the counters' booth only to be asked to please leave! As I left the booth, I found myself standing in line with the runners, posing with Guru for a picture. One of the run officials said, "Vijali, that's only for the runners." Then, someone in the back of the line said, "She is doing it!" So I stayed in line and started the 4-day run along with the others.

I have to say it was all joy! I loved it from beginning to end. I would have moments of pure joy and moments of serious concentration. I was fortunate that Sanatan would drive me home in the evening so that I could sit in a tub and sleep for a few hours. He would then come to pick me up and drive me back to the park. Guru would come to the run several times a day to cheer us on and give prasad.

* * *

One day Guru said to me, "Vijali, if you don't want to come back into this world you must run a marathon, because I have done it." I wondered if Guru had his fingers crossed when he said it! Nevertheless, I felt I had to one day run a marathon.

In 1988, we were meeting in Progress-Promise the night before the New York City Marathon. I always sat in the back of the room and Guru came into the hall from the back. As he walked by me he said, "What, you are not running?" Oh my! I had no number, and I was not prepared! But I felt I had to find a way to get a number. Then the head of the Sri Chinmoy Marathon Team made an announcement that he had a few extra numbers. Quickly I ran out of the hall and said to him, "I need a number." He replied rather roughly, "What! No, no, not you." I told him that Guru wanted me to run and had asked me why I was not running. Very reluctantly he handed me a number.

The next morning I joined the rest of the disciples on the bus to Staten Island. My Lord, I had never seen so many people, all waiting at the starting point! I had decided to walk and not run.

Finally I started (and of course everyone was passing me). I suddenly started to have pain in my hip. I was born with a deformed hip, and at that moment it started to hurt me badly. I discovered that if I jogged the pain went away, so I jogged for the next few miles.

I would be pain-free for a while and then the pain would return and I would think, "I will not make it, I will have to stop." As soon as I had this thought, the pain would go away. This kept happening for several miles. By the time I reached 18 miles, there was no way I would consider stopping. I thought I would make it in about 7:30.

Oh my, I did not expect what was coming! I *hit the wall*, big time. When I finally reached the park, I was barely putting one foot in front of the other.

I suddenly realised I was alone in the park and I was not feeling safe. Once again I inwardly said, "Guru, I don't feel safe all by myself in Central Park." At that moment one of the race workers showed up driving a tractor and asked if I was OK. I answered yes, but I did not like being alone in the park. He told me he would drive alongside me until we reached the finish line. He did, and I was ever grateful to him for staying with me.

Yes, I did my marathon (the first and last New York City Marathon for me). I am grateful for the experience – both painful and joyful. I am happy I finished, even if it took me 9:05:18.

The only other marathon I ran was the one on 150th Street. I did not finish it by the cut-off, but I was pleased I had only a few miles left to go when Guru stopped the run.

I did do the 12-hour walk several times, until one year I felt inwardly I did not need to walk it anymore. After that I helped out at the races as a counter for many years.

STACEY
Auckland, New Zealand

In 2006 Guru made an announcement after the Self-Transcendence Marathon in Rockland State Park that he would like to hold another marathon for his elite running students in April, open to all of his students around the world who can run his fastest marathon time – 3:55:07 – or under.

When I heard this – after finishing in a respectable 5:25 – it totally thrilled me! To be able to cheer on the best runners in our spiritual family and watch them compete in this gruelling but spiritually rewarding event... I couldn't wait!

April came around and I spent 4 hours cheering my throat dry and clapping my hands raw. Every time I saw the runners I got an inner thrill; I had to keep myself from bursting into tears at the finish. For anyone who knows me, you will know that I am not a 'cry at the drop of a hat' kind of girl.

Fast-forward a year and a half, and I am at our annual Joy Weekend in Christchurch; it is on the same weekend as the Christchurch Marathon. I had been kind of training for it, not really following a programme, just doing a few runs during the week, a long run in the weekend, and a few speed work sessions with my flatmate. She had been complaining about how hard her 200m repeats were, so I did a few weeks with her. It was that whole 'misery loves company' kind of thing. Can't say they were pleasant days running, or that I could really function for the rest of the day, but I did them, flatmate duty over.

Anyway, back to the Christchurch Marathon. I had made a pact with myself that if I could do under 4:15 for the marathon, then I should train properly and try and break 4 hours. If it was over 4:15 I would start training for the 24-hour race. My best time before this race was 4:40, a few years ago. Both prospects were daunting for me, the commitment and determination needed to follow a programme and the need to push myself to the limit was something I was lacking. But in the spirit of self-transcendence, I would give it a try.

The day was perfect, the gun went off and we slowly made our way to the start line. I had one of the best races in my life, the first half was fantastic, it got a bit horrible at 25 km, but with 10 km left I perked up, just repeating, "It's less than an hour, it's less than an hour, it's less than an hour." And miracle of miracles – *I did 4:03!* I crossed the finish line with a mix of joy and disbelief; if it wasn't such a well-marshalled course with absolutely no way of going off course I would have believed that I inadvertently cheated. But no, I did that time all on my own steam.

My friend Pip was at the finish, deep in the crowd of supporters screaming, "Oh my God you are so fast!" All I could say in response was, "*I know*," grinning ear to ear.

A few weeks after the euphoria of the race was subsiding I started to think about the promise I had made. I was trying to prepare myself for the task ahead. Guru has written so much on running and self-transcendence. One book that I pored over was *The Inner Runner and the Outer Runner*. I found a few quotes that struck a chord so I wrote them out and put them on the back of my door. I then found a programme that was titled 'Under 4 Hour Marathon', well yep that was my goal, it looked achievable so up that went on my door. Come November my training started, with the Taranaki Marathon my goal race to break 4 hours. That was a mere one month before the April Marathon I was trying to qualify for.

I became dedicated and determined: my one goal was to give it my all. That meant after 11 hours of working, Toshala would run with me on Tuesday nights, because it was dark by the time we left work, pushing me along when all I wanted to do was close my eyes and go to sleep. Well, I would close my eyes for longer than I normally needed to blink on those runs, but never fear, I stayed upright. Another friend would run home with me after our shift at the Blue Bird Café at 9 p.m. on a Friday night, rain, hail or gale force winds! Then there was the speedwork! You see, I don't have that athletic marathon-runner look about me, my running style is not the best and when I am tired or not concentrating I go into an old man hunch. So hill sprints, 1-mile repeats and 200, 400 and 800s were done. But, to make sure I did them to the best of my ability, it was usually in a public place, so that I would try and look like I knew what I was doing. Looking at me, though – which a lot of people walking by did – you would have thought, oh, that poor girl is just starting to run; oh well, it will get easier as she gets fitter. A strange way of using my ego to go faster and smashing my ego all at the same time!

My speedwork was getting slower, my long runs were getting harder and harder to do, my mantra at home became: "I am so tired." I never seemed to get enough to eat, but I kept going. Writing this, I can't believe I had that determination.

But 16 weeks later and race day has finally arrived,

it is a point-to-point course, starting at the base of the mountain and finishing at the beach. Running downhill, now that must mean a fast course right? The whole gravity thing, I will be flying down! Yeah right. As any runner will know – which I did know in the back of my mind, I just tried to ignore it – running downhill is hard on your old body, especially the quads.

The first half was great, this was where most of the downhill was, so, yes, I was flying, doing an excellent time, I think I hit halfway at about 1:52, well within my time frame to break 4 hours; but as the second half started, my quads decided to let me know just how much they didn't like the downhill; and as the kms progressed my legs screamed and slowed and I started to get worried. My flatmate – a sub 3-hour marathoner – had told me, that when it gets painful just push through it, as it won't last.

Well, hello, you could have let me know that you meant it would stop when I stopped running! Runners started passing me and encouraging me. They were telling me I was nearly there, with sympathetic smiles, which I was grateful for. Any word of encouragement I was greedily eating up to get me through this pain. When there were 10 km to go, my flatmates were screaming at me to speed up and not slow down! A little hard-nosed encouragement was definitely what the doctor ordered, so I gritted my teeth and pushed on. With 3 km to go, I was surrendered to whatever the fates give, my body was just hanging in there and I knew I would make it to the finish, no matter what.

As I turned into the park with about 300m to go, I could hear my friend screaming, "Sprint or you won't make it!" Let me tell you she has some lungs on her when she wants to use them, and a way of saying it that in my exhausted state all I could do was obey, and off I sprinted.... Well I started to run a lot faster, don't think you could ever call it a sprint.

But it worked, I made it... only just... but I made it in 3:54:11, scraping into the Invitational Marathon by 56 seconds. I just stood there in disbelief and gratitude.

And then I tried to move.

I had stopped, so my leg muscles decided that meant they could pack up and leave me for a while! So along with my hunch – that I had perfected over the last 21.1 km – I now had a shuffle to go with it. Grinning in a post-marathon daze, I slowly shuffled my way to my Dad's waiting car.

April 14th rolls around – the start of the Invitational Marathon. I know where I will come in the pack – last or close to it – but I don't care. I am here, running the marathon that gave me such an inner thrill. I am running with the elite runners of our spiritual family, me, a person who only two years ago clocked a 5:25 marathon.

One aphorism by Guru that I always tried to remember during my training and running was:

> *We are all truly unlimited,*
> *If we only dare to try*
> *And have faith.*
> **– Sri Chinmoy**

I dare to try.

SMARANA
Vienna, Austria

Why run 3,100 miles? Very often I have been asked: why am I doing such a long race? This is not a question that you can answer in a few words; it needs a lot of background description.

First of all I love any kinds of sports and I started running when I was 6 years old. Running is so simple; you just need your running shoes, running trousers and a shirt. When I was 10 years old, I did my first half marathon, just for myself. I was never really a very fast runner, but I liked the movement, the challenge and the feeling of satisfaction after the training. So I was running with no real goal, but for the satisfaction of running and feeling fit itself.

Things changed rapidly when I got in touch with Sri Chinmoy, who became my spiritual mentor. A major part of Sri Chinmoy's philosophy is 'self-transcendence' in every walk of life – that is to say, whatever you do, you can improve and you can go one step further, transcending your previous achievement. That was and still is something that strikes me and inspires me in everything; to go beyond yesterday's achievement.

Many restrictions are creations of the limited mind and we think this and that is not possible. Once we try it, we find that it is not only possible but also attainable – if we believe in it and cultivate patience. Ashrita Furman is a shining example of self-transcendence in action. Ashrita has set more than 100 Guinness records and he is still going on.

I think every runner has at one point had the dream to finish a marathon. In the beginning it is a far-fetched dream, but as you start training, it becomes more and more a reality. Then the big day is coming, you are standing at the starting line and... hours later you cross the finish line and you are in ecstasy, you did it; a mental barrier has been lifted.

Years back many people thought the marathon runners to be a crazy folk and now see 30,000 participants in the New York Marathon; marathon running has become something honorable. After I did my first marathon, I heard about a 700-mile race in New York and I was thrilled about the idea. The problem was that I thought that I did not have the capacity to do it, but there was a voice in me that inspired me to try it and I finished it.

Gradually I improved my stamina and my mental capacity to run the 3,100-mile race. Who would have thought that one day I would run such a distance? With patience and determination and grace, is there anything that is impossible?

The Self-Transcendence 3,100-Mile Race, as it is called, is a very special race in many ways and on different levels. It comprehends:

the eternity of our progress in life
the challenge of life
the endurance we need for our life
the patience for achieving something
the mental poise we need in every situation of our life
the positive mind helpfulness...

What makes this race so special for me is that you can learn so much about yourself in a relatively short time. The distance of 3,100 miles has to be done in 51 days; that makes 60.7 miles per day.

Everything gets very intense in this race. For 51 days you have to be very focused and endure rain, heat, humidity, injuries and lack of sleep. You are really pushing the limits and you can learn day by day, how to tackle problems in a better way.

Here at this point I have to say that the longer the race is, the fitter your mind has to be. You can create so much energy when your mind is cheerful and poised. When your thoughts are running amok and are becoming negative, you are losing your energy and you are just seeing negative reasons to continue. At this point meditation is very helpful, it helps you to control your mind and gives it a positive momentum.

At a 100-km race in Vienna a friend of mine was running. He had already done 70 km and he felt quite fresh, when his wife came and told him, "You look tired, you will not be able to finish the race." Sure enough, 5 km later he had to quit; the power of the mind.

During the race it is like a roller coaster; you have your ups and downs, but if you continue you are creating the experience that even after a very long tunnel you are going to see light again, you just have to hang in, look for the positive and you will be rewarded.

Is that not the same as in the day-to-day life? There are days we do not want to go out of the house, life seems like a barren field. So here in the race you get plenty of opportunity to practise this experience and overcome it again and again. After such a race so many problems seem to be negligible, non-existent. I simply love the opportunity to get this intense training of problem-solving drills.

At the race you can not back off; you are confronted with the problems and you have to find a solution, or it will haunt you the next day and the following day. In normal life you go and watch a movie or do something else to escape of the problem. Not there – 'Face the problems and solve them!' is the motto.

You have to start the 3,100 miles with your first step and many are to be followed. If you always think of the whole race, your mind can not take it, so you have to break it into smaller portions, laps, hours, days... so it becomes digestible.

In our life if we think of everything that we have to do, then it looks like an impossible task, so we also have to start with the first task, the second... until everything is done.

Is this race not a great teacher for our life?

Sri Chinmoy took a very personal interest in this race and came nearly every day to encourage the runners. Every time he came I felt my spirit lifted and it gave me additional physical power.

Al Howie was an ultra-running legend in the 80s and after a 1,300-mile race, organised by the Sri Chinmoy Marathon Team, he said, "Every time I am coming here and I am running a race, I am leaving as a better person."

Yes, that is why I am also running this race – to become a better person.

RATHIN
Canberra, Australia

When I was growing up I was pretty lazy. My dad was often telling me off for "lolling around on my bed reading comics", instead of engaging in more active, outdoorsy pursuits. I couldn't understand what his problem was. What could be better than lying down and reading comics? I devoured anything I could get my hands on. *Spiderman*, *Batman*, *the Phantom*, *Atari Force*, *Garfield*, *Andy Capp*, *The Wizard of Id*, *Archie*, *Richie Rich*, *Casper the Friendly Ghost*, *2000 AD*, *Whizzer and Chips*, *Buster*; there was nothing I would not read.

Before long I was attempting to draw my own comic strips. School provided ample opportunity to practise. It's pretty hard to catch a kid doing something unauthorised when he's sitting there quietly with pencil in hand. I thought I was pretty good until I got to high school. Suddenly there were at least half a dozen boys in my year who could draw better than me. By this stage I was completely disinterested in any scholastic pursuits. I changed high schools, but kept drawing.

Somehow, despite my terrible marks, I managed to get into a university art course. I didn't fare much better though academically. I never stopped drawing – I was just drawing the wrong things! Yep, more comics. This surprisingly paid off at the end of my first year: I won the editorial cartooning competition in the local newspaper. I beat at least one full-time commercial artist whose work had been on postage stamps. My prize was $500 in art supplies, which provided me with enough acrylics, inks, gouache, oils, and watercolours to get through the rest of university. Or, it would have been enough, if I had have applied myself.

In the last year, we were told that we had the whole year to produce five or six assignments that would make up the bulk of our assessment. I knew I would never get it all done. I was just too slack. Besides, my other interest was trying to play the electric guitar in an indie rock band. I was going to be famous. What did I need an art degree for?

After failing uni, I went on to fail at being in a rock band. It really is a long way to the top, if you want to rock and roll. Especially if you spend all your time hanging out in record shops instead of practising. Somewhere along the way I discovered the Sri Chinmoy Centre and meditation. Having gotten a glimpse at something a little more fulfilling in life, I devoted more and more time to it, until I left the band. When I looked round the practice room and realised I was the only one without piercings, tattoos, or coloured hair, I deduced that perhaps my boat was sailing in a different direction.

As a result of being a member of the Sri Chinmoy Centre, I have run the longest race in the world, the Self-Transcendence 3,100-Mile Race, four times. Now I work six days a week in a busy vegetarian café. Every other weekend there is a sports event to help out at. Sometimes I wonder: Is this karma? Have I been so busy these last few years to make up for how lazy I used to be? Well, it's certainly not a curse. Being lazy is a pretty empty existence. There's nothing great about sleeping in until the crack of noon – or beyond. So if it's karma, I can only surmise that it is of the good variety.

TEJVAN
Oxford, England

At school, I remember always coming last in a cross-country running race. It was pretty dispiriting to come last. I put it down to bad genes and quickly retired from running around muddy school fields. I did like cycling, but never got into racing – I wouldn't want the experience of coming last again. With my first tentative self-exploration into spirituality, I came to the conclusion that competitive sport must be bad because it was all about name, fame and ego. So I gave up any interest in competing, but when I joined Sri Chinmoy's path, I was surprised to learn that he himself was a great sportsman and encouraged his students to take part in running and other sports. Sri Chinmoy also had great admiration for sportsmen; he saw their athletic discipline as being a step along a spiritual path of self-improvement and self-transcendence.

As a new disciple, I tried running with great eagerness. But, it left me with a very bad knee injury, which prevented me from doing any sport for about three years. When the knee finally healed, I gingerly got back into cycling, thinking it would be better for my knee. After a year of just riding the bike, I thought, "Why not enter some races?" To my surprise, I found myself doing quite well, and soon I was winning a few local time trials (cycle races against the clock). In British time trials, a large portion of the field are often veterans, people over 40. So when you come 1st out of 120, it's not always quite as impressive as it sounds, but nevertheless, it is still very nice to win and I really enjoyed competing with myself and trying to get fitter.

After starting to race in 2004, I finished 4th in the national 100-mile time trial (2005) and finished in the top 10 in the national hill climb championship nearly every year from 2005 to 2012. Finally, in 2013, at the age of 36 I won the national hill climb championship, which had been a big target for me. One interesting thing is that around 2007, Guru had mentioned to a few people that, "Tejvan is our cycling champion." I wasn't sure if Guru was just saying nice things or whether he saw possibilities. Anyway, several years later, it came true on an outer level; winning a national title was a real highlight.

After the first year of cycling for a local club, I wanted to race for the Sri Chinmoy Cycling Team, so we asked Guru about setting up a team and he replied, "Very good." Actually, as most disciples were into running, in the beginning it was a pretty small club, and in the UK I was the main rider. But, I got an added joy for riding for the Sri Chinmoy Cycling Team. Recently the team has grown, as more of Sri Chinmoy's students have got into cycling.

When competing for the Sri Chinmoy CT, it is surprising to find how many people have heard about Sri Chinmoy in some form. The most common way is through running. But, with other cases it might be through music, or some other way. I remember bumping into one schoolboy at a race in Lancashire. He had been learning about Sri Chinmoy – he knew that Sri Chinmoy was a poet, humanitarian and "had met some famous people." The schoolboy was trying to work out why a poet would have his own cycling team. I tried to briefly explain, though I think at the time I was probably more concentrated on the upcoming race.

Time trials are a great sport because you can always compete against yourself – trying to beat your own personal bests. It also requires great focus, concentration and discipline. With competing in time trials, I do try to implement some of the teachings Sri Chinmoy gives for athletes. One visualisation he gives is to feel that you are just an instrument, and there is a power cycling in and through you.

I also see cycling as a good practice for remaining concentrated and focused – a quality you develop and need in meditation. Another important aspect of preparing for cycle races is the power of positive visualisation. This is a technique we use in meditation – to visualise peace or infinity. But, for cycling, I try to visualise a very good performance, riding at the peak of my potential with a silent mind.

Another important race for me was the national hill climb championship in 2014. I was trying to retain the title, but the hill was shorter, so didn't suit me quite as well. I still prepared really well and on the day came 4th. It is sometimes said that 4th is a disappointing place to finish. But, in the race, I had a really good experience. There was no mind, no thought, just tremendous intensity. I learnt from that race that sport can be very fulfilling even if you don't win. Finishing 4th was just as important as winning the previous year.

In New York, Sri Chinmoy founded the world's longest footrace – the annual Self-Transcendence 3,100-Mile Race. Needless to say, it is an epic race – runners must cover an average of 60 miles a day over a period of 50 or so days. It is very much a pioneering event, stretching commonly held notions of what is possible in long-distance running. Sri Chinmoy took a great interest in the race, visiting it every day when he was in New York. On one occasion, he told the runners words to the effect that, if they smiled more, they would be able to run faster. Again, it struck me as a surprising approach. Obviously you can't be a champion cyclist just by smiling. But, to be inwardly happy and positive does make a big difference in both training and racing.

One teaching of Sri Chinmoy's that made a lasting impression on me was his advice that the real key to training is the consciousness with which we train. In other words it is not just about miles, heart rates and power meters, but if we can be fully concentrated, aware and inwardly happy, then the training will be much more effective. Sometimes, you can have a training session and half your mind is elsewhere, roaming around. I try to avoid this and have a very specific frame of mind and training target.

* * *

Spiritual philosophy teaches us to be detached from the result of our actions. Sri Chinmoy writes that the right attitude is to take victory and defeat in the same spirit.

> *Who is the winner? Not he who wins, but he who has established his cheerful oneness with the result, which is an experience in the form of failure or success, a journey forward or a journey backward.*
> **– Sri Chinmoy**

When racing I try to bear this in mind. But, as well as taking victory or defeat in the right spirit, I still like very much to win. I feel the secret is to concentrate on your own performance – to race to your potential, to strive for greater efforts and speed and not worry about others. If we are competing with ourselves, then it is a spiritual discipline. If we are only concerned about winning, we start focusing on other competitors and just try to beat them. In a way this dissipates our energy because we are worrying about others getting faster, etc.

In racing, mental preparation also plays a key role. The first step is to concentrate on a positive visualisation of doing well. This is not a visualisation of seeing yourself at the top of the results board, but a visualisation of doing the best possible race. When racing, it is also very important to have the right motivation, enthusiasm and concentration. When racing, as much as possible, I try to keep the mind quiet and blank. In a short intense race, such as a hill climb, this is quite possible. It is a very striking experience when the body is numb with pain, fighting every signal to slow down, and you are just experiencing this mixture of sensation and mental quiet. The effort needs to be so intense that thinking random thoughts feels as if you are dissipating your precious energy.

When you can race at that intensity, being completely detached from thoughts, you feel you are giving your best performance. Some of my most disappointing results come when the mind gets distracted and I start thinking and doubting myself.

I wouldn't say racing with a clear mind is like meditation. There is a great pain in the body and part of you is screaming for it to end, but it feels that with a silent mind you can maximise your limited energy; it also feels like an exhilarating experience – at least when you collapse over the finish line.

For longer races, keeping a completely quiet mind is not possible. In long time trials, e.g. 100-mile TT, it becomes quite easy for the mind to start wandering. In these kinds of races, I may inwardly repeat a mantra (sacred word) or concentrate on visualisation techniques.

On one of the few occasions Sri Chinmoy spoke to me, it was about cycling. He took an interest in my races and liked to see the results of the races I did.

Sri Chinmoy was involved in so many multifarious activities during his 76 years on earth, that it is perhaps not surprising that he also tried his hand at cycling. In the 1970s, Sri Chinmoy and other members of the Sri Chinmoy Centre took part in a 24-hour cycle race around Central Park, New York. For a few weeks before the race, Guru would go with disciples to practise cycling in Flushing Meadows Park. Being relatively untrained, he didn't find cycling easy, but with great determination he completed three 24-hour races. After his last cycling 24-hour race in 1979, Guru increasingly focused on long-distance running, completing several marathons and ultra-marathons.

In one sense, Guru didn't have to be involved in so many different activities. But, I feel he was trying to show that spirituality could be applied to any aspect of life. It was certainly inspiring to know Guru had tried cycling with great enthusiasm.

ASHRITA
New York
United States of America

It was an ambitious plan and it actually worked – well, almost! Since I was scheduled to go overseas for a few weeks in September, the plan was to attempt 4 Guinness world records in 4 different countries in less than a month. And to make it even more exciting, if I succeeded, the 4th record would mark my 100th, the culmination of more than 25 years of record-breaking that began with 27,000 jumping jacks way back in 1979! Looking back on it, there was no compelling reason to try to reach so quickly, but the mad scramble made it ever so much more fun!

* * *

The first of the 4 attempts would take place at the end of August right here in the USA, New York, to be specific. This would be a team effort involving a bunch of my friends who are almost as over the top as I am! While flipping through the 2005 Guinness Book, the candle-lighting record caught my eye. The record was for the most simultaneously lit candles on a cake: 12,432 to be exact. Since my meditation teacher's 74th birthday was coming up in a few weeks, I figured it would be cool to present Sri Chinmoy with an historic 27,000-candle blazing tribute! However, unlike the previous record holders who crammed all their candles onto a 6-foot cake and ended up with a giant bonfire, I wanted our cake to have 27,000 individual flames. After some experimentation, I quickly realized that this would be a massive project requiring a cake 3 feet wide and 47 feet long, and 50 fearless guys with blowtorches to ignite it!

The hours of practicing were crucial. We discovered that we would only have about one minute to light all the candles and no more than another 60 seconds for the official counters and videographers to do their job before the candles melted down. We also determined which brand of candles burned the longest (they have to be traditional birthday candles), the most efficient way to set up the candles, and even the best type of footwear to use. (Once the lighting starts, within seconds a river of melted wax begins streaming off the cake onto the ground and the guys quickly learned that wearing sandals was hazardous to one's health!)

I also learned the hard way about fire extinguishers. People kept warning me that I should be worried about the fire getting out of control, so I bought a fire extinguisher and decided to test it out a couple of hours before the attempt. The birthday festivities are held in a small park in Jamaica, Queens, and were already underway. I was on the outskirts, along with a few other people who were waiting to get in. My friend Satyajit was sitting about 15 feet away, meditating quietly with his eyes closed. I was sure he was safe when I pointed the extinguisher in his direction and lightly depressed the release lever. Oh, my God! To my disbelief, a huge white burst of powder emerged from the hose and was headed straight for the tranquil Satyajit, who had no idea what was about to hit him. I froze in horror. By the time I yelled my friend's name to warn him, it was too late – he was already invisible, engulfed in the unstoppable cloud. Fortunately, after a quick trip home for a shower, he was fine, but my friends banned me from ever touching the fire extinguisher again! The actual attempt went well. The 50 guys were lined up on both sides of the cake with their blowtorches turned on high. The intensity was palpable. I gave the signal to start and within 70 seconds, amidst the cheers of over a thousand bystanders, the cake was fully ablaze. A few unlit patches of candles remained and, to his credit, my pal Virendra braved the fierce heat and made several kamikaze lunges to successfully complete the cake, burning off parts of his eyebrows in the process!

Sri Chinmoy offered his deepest gratitude for our presentation, and then it was time to blow out the cake – a task easier said than done. Eventually we got most of the flames extinguished except for a small section which raged out of control. We were about to call for the fire extinguisher, but Aryavan realized that the guys who were blowing from the opposite side of the cake were actually fanning the 3-foot high flames. Once we curbed their enthusiasm, we managed to get the fire out. You could almost hear the collective sigh of relief. The Guinness rules state that the cake has to be eaten, so afterwards, a crew peeled off the hardened wax coating, re-iced the cake and everyone enjoyed a piece of the delicious, although admittedly slightly waxy, record-breaking pastry! So far, so good – #97 was a glorious success.

* * *

Exactly a week later, Sri Chinmoy began a concert tour dedicated to world harmony that would bring him to Cambodia on September 5th and then continue on to Switzerland and Germany. I was fortunate to be able to join him on the trip and I hoped his performances would energize me in my quest to break 3 more records in 3 countries while on the tour. My plan was to go for #98 in Cambodia, fly from Switzerland to Italy to break #99, and then take off for England at the end of the tour to attempt the big 1-0-0. So, a day after the 20-hour flight to Cambodia, my friend Udar and I took a quick side trip over to the famous ancient temple complex of Angkor Wat. Here I would attempt to break the record for the most turns with a jump rope in a minute while bouncing on a pogo stick. I hoped to better the 156 jumps that I did in front of the Old Faithful geyser at Yellowstone National Park in September 2004.

I had been to Angkor Wat before, but it was even more spectacular than I remembered and also much hotter! Udar set up the video camera on a tripod, our official witness took control of the stopwatch and, after several attempts, I was thrilled to reach 170 jumps. The record was achieved – or so I thought! You see, to validate this particular record the count on Udar's mechanical counter had to agree with the count on the videotape. There was a problem – Udar apparently had missed a few jumps, so we would have to attempt the record all over again!

I was drenched with sweat, my quadriceps felt like Jello, and I was feeling drained, but then something happened that really turned things around. A middle-aged Australian couple came over to inquire what we were up to. As soon as we explained, the wife, presumably noticing that I was overheated, suddenly and spontaneously unscrewed the top off her bottle of water and, without saying a word, poured its contents over my head! It both cooled me off and gave us all a lift! After I stopped laughing, I was able to do 173 jumps in a minute, and this time the video confirmed that it was a new world record!

* * *

Following an inspiring concert by Sri Chinmoy in Cambodia, the tour headed off to Zurich, Switzerland, but I took a detour to Pisa, Italy, where I met up with my co-conspirators, Bipin and Sanjaya. It had long been a dream of mine to break the milk crate balancing record at the Leaning Tower of Pisa. I could just see in my mind's eye an awesome photo of a tower of 22 milk crates stacked up on my chin next to the world-renowned architectural mishap. Someone had just surpassed the milk crate record I had held for several years, so it was the perfect time to try to get it back. Unfortunately, I had my own mishap at Pisa! The area I was assigned to, as stipulated by the permit, was severely sloped, and the angle affected the mechanics of my balancing. Although I gave it my best, I could only manage to keep the stack of crates balanced for 8 seconds, a mere 2 seconds short of the mandatory 10 seconds required by Guinness. The ironic part of the story is that instead of the photo I had imagined, Reuters Press Agency got a spectacular shot of me dropping the crates which appeared in newspapers all over the world!

* * *

Before leaving Pisa, I promised myself that I would return next year and make another attempt, but in the meantime, I rejoined the tour in Zurich, one record short. Very uncharacteristically for me, I had a contingency plan. When I left New York, I had packed a regulation pool cue. There was a record for running a mile while continuously balancing a pool cue on one's finger in 7 minutes and 24 seconds. Although I had practiced this event in the past, it had been quite a while ago. Still, I decided to give it a try. Within 24 hours, my buddy Hutashan got permission for me to use the world-class Letzigrund Track, and he also rounded up the required number of reputable witnesses. Although I felt a bit sluggish, and nearly lost balance of the cue on the final turn, I managed to run a 7-minute and 6-second mile to clinch record #99! Of course, Guinness would have to verify the last 3 records, but barring any unforeseen problems, I was now within 10 days of making my dream to go after record #100 in London a reality!

* * *

Just before I left for London, I got the good news and the bad news. The good news was that all the record attempts to date had been officially accepted. The bad news was that Guinness had been unable to get permission for me to break the giant hula hoop record at the Eye and instead, arranged for me to go for the century mark on live national TV. I dislike attempting records on live TV because there is much more pressure – it is unforgiving. On live TV you only get one chance to succeed and if you mess up, you are history; whereas when a show is taped, you can make several attempts until you get it right. Even so, I was excited.

I was booked to attempt the giant hula hoop record on the popular Richard and Judy Show. Being an ignorant American, I had never heard of the program, but I soon discovered firsthand that it was popular because when I told the scowling immigration lady at London Heathrow airport about my purpose for visiting England, her eyes lit up, and she actually smiled at me!

I didn't have to be at the studio until the afternoon, so I called some of my British friends, including Devashishu, to check on the giant hula hoop that I would be using on the show. Devashishu had attended Sri Chinmoy's birthday celebration in New York and had transported the disassembled hoop back home with him to England. This new hoop was 16 feet in diameter, more than a foot larger than the hula hoop I had used to set the previous record. The larger the hoop gets, the more wobbly it becomes, and the more energy and skill it takes to meet the Guinness requirement of rotating the aluminum ring at least 3 times around one's waist without the hoop touching the ground. I had managed 7 revolutions of the new hula hoop in practice just before leaving for the tour, but that was 3 weeks ago. I was desperate to practice, especially considering that I would only have one chance to bring home the prize.

I thought it would be fun to hold the practice at a London landmark and, after some discussion, my friends and I decided that Trafalgar Square would be the ideal location. However, as soon as we pulled up to the Square in our unmarked white van and began to assemble the hoop, we realized we had been a tad optimistic, because the police immediately converged on us and unceremoniously kicked us out! Undaunted, we drove over to Hyde Park and quickly riveted the hoop together, hoping not to be noticed. Of course, it's hard not to notice half a dozen guys putting together a hula hoop the size of a small house, but the Park police were too amused to chase us away! Bipin and I then carried the hoop across one of the busiest intersections in London to the Marble Arch and, after several unsuccessful attempts, I was able to do 8 revolutions of the monster metal circle in front of the famous Arch. I was exhausted, but ready to finally meet Richard and Judy!

The actual attempt was slotted to take place in the parking lot outside of the studio, a fine location as long as it didn't rain. Of course, by the time the director called for a rehearsal, it was raining cats and dogs, but I agreed to give it a whirl anyway. I had never practiced in the rain and soon discovered why. The rain makes everything slippery and you need good traction to overcome the inertia of the heavy hula hoop. Anyway, I finally got the hoop spinning and then something really unprecedented happened. Suddenly, the hoop flew off my body and over my head, and went sailing like a giant flying saucer through the air! I was in shock, and so were the cameramen who were in the line of fire. Luckily, the errant hula hoop veered off to the left and crashed into a fence, leaving all unharmed.

The time for the live performance had finally arrived and I was blessed with good fortune. The rain stopped in the nick of time and both Richard and Judy turned out to be delightful people. I said a silent prayer and gathered all my strength to give the hoop a mighty spin. I think everyone on the show was worried that the hula hoop would become airborne again (the cameramen had relocated to the roof of the studio!), but I was able to keep it down to earth. The Guinness judge, Sue Morisson, was on hand and I could hear her counting aloud as the gigantic hoop circled my body and bruised my ribs - "one, two, three –" Halfway through the fourth revolution the hoop scraped the ground, ending the attempt; but as I had completed the required 3 revolutions, Sue announced, "It's official, a new Guinness record, congratulations Ashrita on your 100th world record!" Sue handed me a certificate commemorating the occasion, and Richard and Judy were beaming.

I didn't find out until after the show when we disassembled the hoop that, as a result of the crash into the fence, several of the rivets holding the hoop together had been damaged. During the attempt, the hula hoop did feel wobblier, but I thought it was just my imagination. My heart was full of gratitude to my meditation teacher who, I am convinced, not only gave me some inner help for this event, but inspired and encouraged me every step of the way. Of course, the journey is far from over – as of this writing I've broken 3 more records – one while holding a small dog! As Sri Chinmoy so aptly says:

> *There is only*
> *One perfect road*
> *And*
> *That road is ahead of*
> *You,*
> *Always ahead of*
> *You.*
>
> **– Sri Chinmoy**

* * *

The word 'adventure' conjures up images of the African Serengeti or the Amazon rainforest. I am fortunate to have had my share of such adventures – pogo stick jumping in Antarctica and juggling underwater with sharks in an aquarium in Malaysia, to name a few. But adventures don't necessarily have to be in exotic places. With the right attitude, you can have an adventure in your own backyard or, as in this case, at a nearby zoo!

I do like to find an appropriate backdrop for my record attempts. It's part of the fun, but at the end of 2006 I was extremely busy with work and couldn't spare the time to go to a faraway place. I wanted to attempt two records – the first... juggling three balls for the most number of catches while hanging upside down; and, the second... crawling the fastest mile. One of my friends suggested the Beardsley Zoo in Connecticut, which is less than two hours away from my house. I'm an animal lover, and it sounded like a lot of fun, so my friends and I piled into a car and visited the charming zoo.

I found a flat course on grass for the crawling mile, but I really got excited when I saw the tiger cage. On the outside of the cage was a post from which I could attach a bar to hang and juggle. I think the tiger liked the idea because when I approached the cage, he came to the fence and stood up on his hind legs. "Wow", I thought, "either this guy really likes me or else he's thinking what a tasty meal I would make!"

Of course, I still needed permission which is often not immediately forthcoming from the authorities. Fortunately, the zoo management couldn't have been more encouraging (about the record attempts, not about the tiger eating me!) and we set up a date for the following week.

On the appointed day, I decided to do the juggling record first. The tiger cage drew quite a crowd of the usual zoo-visiting kids and parents, but the record attempt brought some reporters as well. I was pretty nervous because upside down juggling requires intense concentration, and I was concerned that all the people might divert my attention.

I hopped up onto the bar, focused and began my

record attempt. I had not anticipated all the noise from the watchers. Even the tiger seemed put off by all the commotion as he retreated to the far corner of his cage! Concentration was difficult and at about 150 catches, one of the balls fell to the ground. Ugh. To perform this record, you hang by your ankles and bend your torso up to toss the balls skyward. The record at 197 continuous catches doesn't sound like much, but after a short time your abs fatigue and ache, and your throws tend to become erratic. It takes unwavering concentration to keep the balls from flying out of reach.

I was concerned because the stress on the abs is such that you can only make a couple of attempts before your abs turn totally to jelly. I rested a few minutes and tried a second time, but again, I came up short. My adventure was becoming an adventure in embarrassment!

I announced to the disappointed crowd that I might try again after the crawling record depending on how I felt. However, I knew from experience, that a third juggling attempt was unlikely because the crawling record is also very ab-intensive. If anything, my already fatigued stomach muscles would be in even worse shape after crawling for a mile.

Anyway, I knew I needed 'inner recovery' from my failed attempts so I meditated for a minute on my spiritual teacher, Sri Chinmoy. I was suddenly flooded with energy! I approached the starting line of the crawling mile determined not to fail. At the starter's "Go!" I became a crawling fool! The timers announced my split times in disbelief. I was so concentrated that I didn't even notice a dog on the course who seemed to be perplexed by this unrecognized four-legged creature huffing and puffing towards him!

My time for the mile was 24 minutes 44 seconds, more than 4½ minutes better than the previous record! My abs were sore, but fortunately my inner focus from my meditation was still with me and I was eager to try the juggling record again. The television reporter could see that I was tired and told me it wasn't necessary to try again because he already had a good story. I thanked him for his concern, but explained that this wasn't about the show – it was about the challenge!

I waved to the tiger, struggled up onto the bar on his cage, and began juggling. It was amazing... everything became effortless. I was able to manage 251 catches and, when I landed back on terra firma, I surprised myself by letting out a resounding whoop. Across the zoo, visitors must have wondered at this new and strange call... the call of the joyful, juggling, crawling, *homo crazylius*, who just had a wonderful adventure in self-transcendence at his local zoo!

VASANTI
Heidelberg, Germany

On September 9th, 1985, by Guru's grace I became the first disciple and member of the Sri Chinmoy Marathon Team to swim the English Channel. (Adhirata from New York made it one day later, in a much faster time; his pilot had wanted to wait another day for even better weather conditions.) For me, it was a very, very special experience. I could feel the inner and outer support and oneness of so many disciples. And, as I was told, Guru was sitting for most of the time at home, meditating on my swim and constantly trying to get information on how I was doing.

I was blessed with an extremely easy swim. When I stepped into the cold Channel waters at Shakespeare Beach at 7 a.m., after only 4½ months of serious preparation and a lot of waiting due to bad weather, I was eager to swim and full of confidence that I would make it. 6 hours into the swim, when I had reached the middle of the Channel and could see both shorelines, I had the firm conviction that on the inner plane, it was already done – it just had to be executed outwardly. I felt carried by a wave of joy and bliss most of the time – once the first 2 hours had passed, when my mind was still a bit restless. Around 12 hours, however, the cross-current set in and it was slowly getting dark. Previously I could not imagine swimming in the dark. I would never have dared to get into pitch black, unknown water at night. Now, with the gradual transition into night, I felt extremely comfortable.

12 hours was the longest I had swum in training – so now the real self-transcendence started. This inspired me and gave me extra joy and motivation.

I enjoyed the star-strewn sky above me each time I took a breath. And when I looked down into the black water – where earlier I had enjoyed watching the dance of the rays of sunlight – I started to see bright light once again. In the midst of the darkness, Guru's trancelike face, his Transcendental Picture, appeared. Because of the unpredictable strong cross-current, I ended up having to swim for 5 more hours, but it did not matter to me. At each feed stop I was told, "Only 1 or 2 more hours," over and over. For those peaceful hours, I was swimming into the light of the Transcendental Picture, into Guru's

KARTEEK
Edinburgh, Scotland

Adverse weather conditions one summer meant that my channel swim attempt had to be aborted after about four hours. That was of course the outer excuse as the sea was indeed quite rough but it was also a convenient excuse to stop. The pilot kindly agreed that he could take me a few days later when the sea state might be more favourable and he would just ask me to contribute to the fuel that had been used that day. I thought it would be heaven to be out of the torment but very soon I felt deflated and that I had given up far too easily.

I subsequently concluded that this barrier at the three to five hour point was the key one to push through. At this stage you can feel at your most miserable and the prospect of endless further hours going through more of the same turmoil can be overwhelming. However, if you can overcome this hurdle most of the mental and physical difficulties seem to evaporate remarkably quickly. It may still be quite a long haul to the end but you settle into a rhythm and feel much more relaxed.

This time round, though, having got stuck at the four hour point, I was totally discouraged and really quite determined that this should be the end of swimming for some time. I was resolute that nothing anybody could say would change my mind.

Each year I would inform Guru through Ashrita of the upcoming channel plans and the night before the swim he would always be informed of the exact starting time. This of course was a tremendous solace and undoubtedly the energy behind the whole swim each time. After a successful crossing Ashrita would often call back with a special message from Guru expressing his pride and blessings.

This time I certainly wasn't expecting any message so it was a surprise to get a call from Shephali in Annam Brahma later that evening. Up until that point, and in the years to follow it would always be Ashrita who called me, so this was something very unexpected. She said she had a short message from Guru saying that he sent all his love and blessings and was very happy that I was planning to go again later in the week. Of course, given my mood, my mind was all set to rebel against the very thought of going back out there, but after recounting the message to me she added that Guru had "the sweetest smile".

Something about this smile completely captivated me. The smile was in fact the message and it had the power to change things completely. It was as if Guru was completely at one with what I had been going through and although it was a severe test, it was an age-old hurdle to be conquered. Looking back I now see how the unusual route that the message took to get to me was also the only way the 'smile' could have been communicated over such a long distance.

Suddenly I felt totally energised and found a new way to visualise the challenge. At a certain point around four hours into the swim a scary sea monster was going to appear and my mission was to chop off its ugly head. Like a hero in a myth entrusted with a task, I was the one responsible for saving the community from this beast and now instead of being full of dread I relished the prospect of getting going and completing the job. Then I imagined that I was to be the lead in an army of very powerful swimmers. I felt that with this huge army accompanying me, the monster wouldn't stand a chance.

It wasn't long before the seas had calmed down and I was back out there again. Despite less than perfect conditions, throughout the day I had a strong determination and never felt like giving up. In the evening, darkness set in quite quickly and with it a bright yellow moon rising over the French shore. I remember streams of bright phosphorescence every time I moved my hands through the water and thinking how beautiful it all seemed.

For what seemed like an eternity the lights on the coast didn't get any nearer. Finally, after more than sixteen hours swimming, I felt the wonderful sensation of sand under my hands. Just the thought of that special smile of Guru's had carried me across the Channel.

TRISHAKASH
Kingston, Canada

One year, when I was about 54 years old, I went with Guru on a Peace Concert trip to Germany, and at one of the evening functions, I came in right at the end of the function when prasad was being given by Guru. I was not aware of any previous conversations with Guru in the room, so when I went up to take prasad, I didn't know what Guru meant when he said to me, "What about you, Vince?"

And I said, "What about me, what, Guru?"

And Guru said, "What about you swimming the Channel?"

And I replied, "Maybe in some other incarnation, Guru."

Guru simply said, "When you have the capacity, don't wait for the future." That was all I needed to hear from my Master, as he knew my capacity and destiny better than I did. So began my Channel swimming experience, which ranks right up there as one of the most significant and beautiful happenings of my life with Guru.

One of the most special times of my life was spent in training to swim the Channel. I loved the challenge and the discipline of the daily 3-hour swims in a pool, which increased to 7 to ten 10 closer to the event. I enjoyed the advice and inspiration of my swim coach, Trevor Tiffany, and the other disciples who were also Channel swimmers. I loved the meditative rhythm of being in the water for so long. It was such an opportunity to really get into a 'zone' in which you could go far beyond the mind and become one with the endless flow of the universe. This is really true of any ultra-distance sport. Chanting while swimming was a great help!

Guru's song 'I Must Never Give Up' applies to my Channel experiences, as the saga continued for 3 wonderful years, which I thoroughly enjoyed! After the first year of training, I lasted only 5 hours in the 57-degree water. I was really too thin at 6' 3" and 165 pounds to bear the cold, and as a result I got hypothermia. When you swim the Channel you are only allowed to grease yourself with a layer of lanolin and paraffin to protect you from the cold, as no wetsuits are allowed.

The next year of training included the challenge of gaining 30 pounds or so – no mean feat when you are exercising as much as I was. Thanks to an insane dietary regimen that included pouring whipping cream on cereal and eating myself 'under the table', I made it to 195 pounds and headed to Dover for my second attempt. This second time, while training in the Dover waters, I tripped on rocks while entering, and broke a rib. If something is not meant to be, it just doesn't happen!

In the third year of training my long swims took place in a lake at our cottage. The cottagers said they didn't need an alarm clock because they could hear the slap of my arms hitting the quiet morning waters at about 5:30 a.m. They loved me, at that early hour, I'm sure! Sometimes the loons joined me in my swim. What a beautiful, sweet experience it was! Also, I enjoyed a couple of long swims with Adhiratha at Lake Ronkonkoma in New York State.

Finally, after year 3 of perfecting my training regime and enjoying the physical and spiritual discipline, I did it! I really did it! The Supreme swam in and through me for 15 hours and 50 minutes from the shores of Dover to Calais, France. I chanted the whole way. I drank a concoction of maple syrup, aspirin, and other secret ingredients that even I cannot remember! My boat pilot, who accompanied me for all of my swims, was Dave White. I am eternally grateful for his professional navigation and for his friendship and that of his wife, who was the official Channel Swimming Association observer. I was especially grateful when I learned that the reason the whole crew at one point was standing on the side of the boat with poles raised was to fight off the large fish, 'rays' that were once seen following me! Thank you, Supreme and Dave, for that one!

The final feat of self-transcendence was that when I finally reached the shores of Calais, elated but exhausted 15 and some hours later, it was too rough and too shallow for the boat to pick me up. I had to put one hand in front of the other and swim back to the boat. That was the longest 1 km that I ever swam in my life!

Thank you, Guru, for swimming in and through me and allowing me the honor of being the oldest known Canadian to swim the English Channel – a record that has held for 20 years. Guru knew that swimming the Channel would be one of the highlights of my entire life. The greatest highlight of my life was meeting Guru!

Later, Guru honored me with a beautiful trophy.

CHAPTER 9

MEDITATION AND TRANSFORMATION

*Each time
I sleeplessly, soulfully
And self-givingly meditate,
I add my soul's dream-beauty
And my heart's reality-joy
To my life's
Transformation-perfection.*

– Sri Chinmoy

SHISHIR
Winnipeg, Canada

I believe it was on my first Christmas Trip that this transpired. I remember spending enchanting hours with Guru amidst palm trees and coconuts in beautiful warm weather. One day we were outside near the ocean in a sheltered area. I would estimate there were about sixty or seventy of us there. Guru suddenly said he wanted to speak to the people who gave meditation classes and called them forward. "Come, sit," he said as they moved towards him and sat in front of him. I had recently started giving meditation classes but I did not go forward. I am not sure why. Maybe it was because I thought Guru was going to praise the class givers and as I had just started giving classes, I did not consider myself yet worthy of this praise. Moreover, I did not consider myself to be in the same category as the regular course givers who all seemed to be older disciples and much more senior than I was. I also think, though this may be hard to believe, that I was a bit shy to go forward. I was very much in awe of Guru.

After they shuffled forward and sat down, Guru looked at them with perfect love. It was a long gaze of silent, deep affection that also conveyed his pride in these stalwart souls. I thought Guru was going to say how good they were and how grateful he was for their efforts: What he said was completely different. I cannot remember the opening remarks, but I have never forgotten the main message.

This is the gist of it: "So, you are the ones," Guru said.

"You give the meditation classes. You think you are so good. You think you are so eloquent. You teach them to meditate. You teach them nothing! Their souls teach them to meditate. Their souls teach them to meditate. Their souls teach them to meditate."

Guru kept repeating that last sentence again and again: "Their souls teach them to meditate." He said it many times, as if it was a message of utmost importance that they simply had to absorb.

Though I was standing at the back rather than sitting at the front, I have never forgotten Guru's words and often think he was saying them for my benefit. The message is so profound. We are not doers, only instruments. Meditation is mystical: we cannot really teach it. Each soul, the Divinity within each person, guides that person to the meditation technique that is best for them. We only share. Their souls teach them to meditate – to commune with God. And it is imperative we always remember that and approach our task with utmost humility. Utmost humility! We cannot imagine how immensely fortunate and blessed we are to have this incredible opportunity to share our Guru's light and teachings with others. We are the lucky ones.

MAHIRUHA
*Chicago,
United States of America*

When I returned from the World Harmony Run one year, I cleaned out my room throwing out lots of useless junk – old clothes, broken alarm clocks and sentimental keepsakes that had long lost their value to me. I also took a long-planned trip to Germany and caught up on my correspondence and launched *Inspiration-Letters* with the help of my friends. The energy that I got from running across the country for world harmony and peace I applied at home. That six-week long running adventure was actually a kind of meditation that uplifted me and transformed my life.

Meditation isn't just sitting with folded hands in front of our shrines. We can turn every action of our lives into a kind of meditation. But I still think our daily practice is essential to maintain equanimity. When we consecrate a little time each day to reflection and prayer, I think we eventually get sharper, more discriminating and more careful. We can tell the real and the true from the false and the flaky.

Carl Sagan once said something like that it is through human beings that the universe is aware of its own existence. I like this idea, that through our spiritual search and growth we can offer the whole world more self-awareness. That's a great motivation.

I love Cezanne and Beethoven so much because they created art that reflects a deep spiritual awareness. They both slaved and struggled to get exactly the right effect, the right shade of color or tone, so as to be totally authentic to their own inner voice. Would that more artists could follow their example!

I'm really grateful to Sri Chinmoy for his clear and simple teachings about meditation. He writes that meditation is a totally normal practice and can help us to become stronger and happier people.

I began to meditate not only to find God but also to become a better writer. Meditation has enabled me to write in a more natural and spontaneous style. Interestingly enough, I find that I can meditate and write at the same time, to a certain extent. I mean, after ten years of practice in meditation, I've learned how to put that equanimity, poise and profundity to good use in many fields, and especially in creative expression.

In his immortal introduction to the English edition of *Gitanjali* by Rabindranath Tagore, William Butler Yeats writes: "We write long books where no page perhaps has any quality to make writing a pleasure, being confident in some general design, just as we fight and make money and fill our heads with politics – all dull things in the doing – while Mr. Tagore, like the Indian civilization itself, has been content to discover the soul and surrender himself to its spontaneity."

Meditation is a key to a more beautiful and fulfilling life. There's no end to our self-discovery. If our aims in life are high and elevating, then why should our lives also not be beautiful and fulfilling? Meditation is a good and practical way of living your dream and making your dearest hopes come true in the here and now.

NAYAK
Seattle,
United States of America

I am out here 2,000 miles from home on a job to help workers lead a better life. But what I wanted to say is that coming into an empty hotel room after traveling on a plane in public circumstances for hours and hours, I felt a kind of desolation. A very nice Indian man who owns this motel drove the shuttle that picked me up from the airport and has already offered to cook me eggs for breakfast. That's good, I have something to look forward to.

Coming into that hotel room, I felt a kind of deep loneliness that I could easily have boiled away with some useless TV (or worse than useless TV). Recently I talked about getting to know God and the gratitude that I feel to Sri Chinmoy for giving me the big picture (G-O-D). That is relevant here, because when I come out of my context in Seattle, when I leave my nice house with pictures of Sri Chinmoy smiling, when I leave behind the bird drawings and the books by my Guru lining the shelves, a lot of cues about spiritual life are gone, and the support system all has to come from within. Within is sometimes there and sometimes not, so the quest can be quite desert-like rather than dessert-like at times.

So where is this all leading? I sat down in my nice hotel room (that Indian owner has done an excellent job on this place), I sat down on the floor leaning against the generically nice couch, I sat with Sri Chinmoy's meditation picture in front of me – a picture that he personally handed to me (and to many others) during a

Christmas Trip – I sat with the TV just a few feet away over there, and a towel was draped over it to prevent me from even thinking about turning it on, and I just cried and cried in loneliness for the Supreme. Where are You, God? That is what I felt in this nice but nowhere place. I also felt tremendous pressure to go and rip that towel off the TV and anesthetize my mind with its desired input of entertaining junk.

Well, I meditated for about a half-hour, and it did its magic. The TV god did not grab me, no. I felt that even my tears were a presence of Him (and Her). I felt, "This is going to be okay." My quest to discover my Friend, God, my Protector, God, my All, God – that continues.

Now, the funny thing is, if I want to go watch TV now, if I want to see what the rest of humanity is doing, if I want to see what moronic stuff, what humor, is out there, well, that's fine.

So, what do we learn from this? We learn (well, I learn), that if the God touch is there then whatever we do has that God-touch. We also learn that if you call to God, He comes, She comes, It comes, They All come. That's nice. I like that.

JOGYATA
Auckland, New Zealand

In my early years of exploring meditation and the little known subject of reincarnation, I came across a rather discouraging description of the long passage of time the soul supposedly takes from its very earliest entry into the earth arena until its full blossoming in God-realization. Imagine, said the words of an old Indian text, a beautiful white bird flying to a large lake once every several thousand years and taking away a single drop of water in its beak – the length of time it takes for the bird to empty the lake is a description – metaphorical of course – of how long it takes for this journey to be concluded, for realization or self-blossoming to be won.

A rather bleak thought! But encouragingly, it did add the further comment that for those who have a curiosity or an awakening interest in spirituality, the lake is almost empty and the long journey of the soul is not in front of us but already behind us.

Guru had a rather more encouraging view of all this, and saw will power and intense aspiration as the key forces that govern the time we will take to achieve that final yoga or union with God... "We are our own fate-makers." It is in fact we who decide how long our journey will take, not a pre-determined destiny. Sri Aurobindo concurs: "Fate can be changed by an unchanging will."

Guru saw every kind of spiritual quest as something precious, every faltering effort at meditation a step towards illumination, each truth seeker an awakening soul setting forth... and laid out very clear guidelines that would add velocity and direction to our journey. Like the map of a beckoning new world, he plotted out the requisite steps for us to take, offered us guidance in our great search for happiness, and helped us navigate the challenging perils and shoals of our lives. He filled us with courage and purpose.

It is always a joy to share these key steps and the essentials of meditation with seekers in our workshops around the world – and to pass on to them the view held by all the great teachers, that they have each reached a very special point in their life journey. God has tapped them on the shoulder… 'wake up!' Yes we are meditating because our souls are responding to a call from God, from the universe. In the image of the bird and the receding waters of the lake, the long journey is now largely over, the goal almost won.

* * *

One of the recurring themes in the writings and legacies of the great spiritual teachers all the way down through time is the accent they each place on the preciousness of a human incarnation, especially one in which there is some kind of spiritual awakening. One of India's teachers spoke of only three real miracles – the rarity of a human birth in this infinitely vast cosmos with its endless possibilities of life; a human incarnation characterized by spiritual awakening and interest; and the culmination of these in finding your path and your realized teacher, the Guru.

One of the things that always interests me about meditation is the feeling of close-by discoveries, a sense of being near to a sudden insight or an understanding that can make your life different. Or a veil that could part to show you something, making you happier or closer to

God, a little enlightenment experience that could come suddenly like a rainbow in your day. They seem to be a gift rather than an achievement, and though they rarely come, even the promise of them lifts your heart.

As my own years multiply I find meditation to be more of an abandonment to God than anything, perhaps recognizing that after a lifetime of struggles and strivings we haven't really got the foggiest about anything, and that we can't really reach the loftiest heights on our own. After so many years, after all the meditation practice and self-discovering and immersion in a path, there is a humbling sense of our littleness. Yet Guru encourages this feeling of being a child – and to having a child's innocence, purity, sweetness, simplicity, its helpless dependence on the loving parent.

In a world full of outer enchantments and endless distractions, the great light, beauty and purpose of the human soul becomes lost to us, covered over just as easily as a single cloud can hide the power of the sun. But Guru's path brings back to us, keeps close to us the sense of our sacred purpose; and encouragement, reassurance; the promise of joy and delight; the nearness of God. Our teacher has mapped out a lovely guidebook for those embarking upon the eternal journey, an exemplar and wayfarer pointing our own way back home.

* * *

A deep meditation is one of the most beautiful and fulfilling of all possible experiences. Once we have learnt how to find our way into that desireless inner stillness that is always there inside us, our life can never be the same. Here in the sanctuary of the heart, free of time and the burdens of the mind, everything is clear, everything is already done. Out of this silence comes wisdom, understanding and delight.

In many ways Guru taught us to take our practice of meditation out into the everyday aspects of our life – karma yoga – train ourselves to sustain the meditative feeling as long as possible. Walking through a park, sitting on a bus, waiting for somebody, travelling to the next moments of our life, learning to string these moments of calm together as a necklace of day-long happiness moments.

A wave rider makes the effort to reach and finally catch the wave that will carry him ashore... the student of meditation also strives in his practice and eventually his own slow awakening grows into a wave of spirit that sweeps him beyond thought and technique. He finds and rides the forgotten ocean of joy that has always been there inside him. This is why we need to commit to regular practice, the accumulation of all the tiny breakthrough moments; and to have patience and discipline, to find and catch the rising wave.

At first, the experience of meditation itself relies upon environment and some combination of time, place, correct technique. But then it goes beyond these needs. We begin to realize that while our increasing moments of 'success' have been possible through some combination of factors – a workshop we attended, group practice, a new exercise we tried or inspiring music – in reality they merely reconnected us with our deeper self, and that 'self' is always there inside us, wherever we are.

Guru wanted us to understand our own capacity to uplift and serve the world, reminding us that 'every human being is a very special dream of God'. And that meditation will take us past our identification with our body, thoughts, personality to a deeper understanding of our ultimately God-like nature. The space in our lives where we put aside the burdens and preoccupations of the day's dramas, silence our thoughts, venture past the many attachments and distractions of the mind to a growing stillness, this space allows us to rediscover the very source of all our creative, intuitive, spiritual capacities. The closer we move towards this 'intelligence of silence', our 'inner pilot', the more perfect our outer lives become.

Meditation comes easily today, sitting on the grass in a park in Auckland under a wide blue summer sky, a sky of such startling clarity and endless transparency as to illumine things and gather close the silhouettes of far-off, familiar mountains. There is this lovely sense of stepping outside of the story of one's life into a state of just 'being', at rest in the here and now, a lovely inner space of pure consciousness. Over in the western corner of the park the tai-chi practitioners are also touching the lives of passers-by and strollers, their calm and gentle movements reminding of other realities beyond the ordinary. And I remember Sri Chinmoy's words, reminding us that we co-create this world and that:

> *Just one smile*
> *From my gratitude-heart*
> *Immensely increases*
> *The beauty of the universe.*
>
> **– Sri Chinmoy**

* * *

Spiritual progress is always tested in the proving ground of everyday life and our maturing is always examined there. To be peaceful during a deep meditation is one thing, but how peaceful will you be when someone is rude to you? To be filled with loving-kindness on a friend's birthday is fine, but can you still see the divinity in someone who has just stolen your car?

One of the truly illumining things we can observe in the company of spiritual Masters is how they respond to the everyday challenges and problems of life. The passing hours in their company are our schoolroom and each situation with the teacher illustrates an important lesson – how to be happy or detached, or what is the right conduct or response in a certain situation.

Many of our most significant and enduring lessons have been taught in this way. I remember, in one very random example, in a six-day race in New York how one of the competitors endlessly complained about everyone and everything, finding fault everywhere. A foot blister had worsened and become infected and as he found his number two race position slipping back to number five, then sixth, his mood worsened and he demanded stronger and stronger painkillers, then prescription medicines to mask the pain and keep going in the race. At a certain point, when the race officials feared serious injury could result and refused his request for further pain suppressants, our competitor became extremely bitter and complaining.

Guru was consulted and simply said, "The nature of the scorpion is to sting, the nature of the Supreme is to be compassionate." It was a simple thing to say but it put everything into a perspective that carried the calming and soothing feeling that deep truth always brings. Our competitor was caught by the force of his own nature but God's nature is to be compassionate – and our challenge as spiritual seekers is to respond in this same way.

Guru reminded us that compassion does not mean excessive leniency or indulgence – instead it endows us with a sympathetic identification and kindness, empowers us also with detachment and the understanding that everything is just God's game, that He is enjoying His own unfolding in every human being.

SUSHUMNA
London, England

One evening in London I visited a friend of very long standing. She was not a disciple but a very good person, and I was very fond of her.

When I arrived she was not at all well. She was very unhappy and crying. Her circumstances were indeed very difficult. Nothing I said could ease her distress. In the end I said, "Well, Betty, the only thing I believe could help you – my Guru's power and love – you don't believe in. So you sit down in that chair – don't try to do anything, just sit there – and I will sit in this chair and meditate on my Guru's picture." This she did and I took out a very small Transcendental Picture that I had in my purse.

I had not been a disciple very long and I did not have much faith in my meditation. In fact I was not sure that I could meditate at all. I just looked at Guru's picture. In a very short time, maybe only two or three minutes, she jumped up, her face shining with relief, saying, "It's gone, it's gone! I'm all right – Oh, it's so wonderful!"

Exactly what had gone I never asked. Obviously some

hostile force had been tormenting her. Sadly, her very conventional mind never allowed her to come to Guru, but she was always grateful, and I have never forgotten.

As a result of this, sometimes when I am travelling on the Underground (subway) and I see someone looking quite sad and worried, I take out Guru's picture and look at it for a few minutes. I quite often see that person relax and sometimes give a little smile to themselves, and I know that Guru's light has touched them. Then I think of Betty and our experience together.

TEJVAN
Oxford, England

In a good meditation, you have a better feeling about yourself, other people and the world. Sometimes you may fear a particular situation, or you are annoyed with someone. After a good meditation, the solution has invariably presented itself. Nothing has changed; only you have a different consciousness – a different perspective. When we are in the mind, the ego is to the fore, so we are often nursing feelings of wounded pride, insecurity or jealousy. But, meditation takes us out of this mental disequilibrium. In the heart, we don't have these negative thoughts. We are just happy with ourselves as we are; naturally we feel more charitable towards others. We empathise with the failings of others rather than being judgmental and critical. When we are in a good consciousness it is much easier to offer goodwill to others.

I have to admit that at the start of the spiritual life, one of the great attractions was the idea of entering into some vague samadhi trance, to lose consciousness of the body and see the universe in its reality of delight.

However, after ten years of meditating, I realise that such states are the end of a very long spiritual journey. Yet, there have been a couple of times when, unexpectedly, I felt a very different consciousness, a very powerful experience and vivid realisation that there is something much vaster and deeper than the ordinary human consciousness.

One experience was this feeling of tremendous peace. Previously, I had associated peace with a nice feeling of relaxation or something like that. But, this was quite different. It was a feeling of peace associated with great joy. It felt like this peace belonged to everybody. It wasn't something I was experiencing on my own. It was simply a consciousness that everybody had deep inside them. The only thing I wanted to do with this peace was to feel grateful and share it with everyone; I didn't want to exclude anyone. Everyone is part of this experience. There was also a feeling that this wasn't a new experience; it was something I always had, but now had just remembered and I couldn't work out why I had forgotten it. There was also a sense of being really alive, like I had really woken up and life was much more vivid and real than ever before. Inwardly, I was begging for this consciousness to remain forever; nothing could approach it; all the name and fame and possible worldly enjoyments were as nothing compared to this experience. You would gladly lead the most ascetic life if it could be maintained. The last thing I remember is that I felt like I was making absolutely no effort. It was like something was meditating in and through me. Often, when you meditate, you feel it is you who are making a great personal effort. But, actually, when you meditate really well, you feel like you aren't doing anything! This is one of the paradoxes of meditation.

* * *

When I started the spiritual life, I felt at times progress was effortless. There were beautiful, sublime meditations; everything was going so well the mind would start to mentally count the years before God-realisation. Then after the most sublime moments of meditation, the next day, you could be shocked by your own weaknesses and frailties coming to the fore. For no good reason or from the smallest of incidents, you could feel negative emotions such as frustration and pride looming over your mind. You might develop ill feeling towards a certain person; the mind creates images of wounded pride. Before you know it, you can get caught up in the thought-trains of the mind, and it can become difficult to get off. Even when you mentally rationalise your emotions and know them to be wrong, the emotion may persist – as if it is something coming from outside you. It takes away all your joy and you wonder what went wrong. One moment, you feel you're making great progress, the next you feel you've made hardly any progress at all.

At such times, meditation can actually be difficult. It is like the mind or vital (emotional aspect of our being) is too strong for your limited willpower, and you feel you are fighting a losing battle.

Such moments are an inevitability of life and the attempt to transform human nature. Perhaps, following a spiritual life we feel these negative moments more keenly.

After experiencing real, sublime peace, it is even more painful and shocking when you are overwhelmed by the opposite qualities. You almost feel guilty for losing so much. Yet, though it is human nature to have setbacks, you feel the spiritual life gives you the tools to overcome it. You learn that the mind doesn't have to be the master. There is always a choice of what to feel and what to experience. On innumerable occasions, you experience a situation where a short meditation or reading can transform your consciousness – enabling you to throw off what is bothering you. In a relatively short time, you see everything from a very different perspective.

Sometimes problems only dissolve when you realise you can't fix them on your own. The mind goes round in circles trying to solve the problem, but often just magnifies it. It is a relief to feel you are offering the problem to Guru, to the Supreme. Outwardly, I never told Guru about any issue, but inwardly I would meditate on his Transcendental Picture to try and resolve problems or ask questions.

I feel Guru knows human nature in all its multifarious aspects. Guru identified with his disciples – not just their success but also their failures and weaknesses. When we suffered, he took this on himself to throw it off. Just one quick glance from Guru could take away a seemingly intractable problem. This happened quite a few times.

When we think of other people, it is often their faults and weaknesses that spring to the fore. It is so difficult for the mind to be tolerant and see the best in others. Sri Chinmoy was once asked how he looked upon his disciples. His answer was quite revealing. In his highest meditation, he does not see us like we would. Guru said he saw a stream of consciousness – it was the beauty of our own souls that he saw in us. To Guru, the outer human nature was only a shadow of the real self, which was all-illumining and all-beautiful.

> *So when I see someone, immediately I see the divine aspect inside them. After realisation, you see everything as divinity. That is why I say that God sees you as another God. As soon as you look in a mirror or at another person, you see the physical body. But when I see someone, the magnetic pull is immediately to the highest divinity of the person.*
>
> **– Sri Chinmoy**

This is something not so easy to understand. But, when I get frustrated with others, I try to imagine how Guru sees others.

It is one thing to know that the Divine resides within, but it is another to bring it to the fore. Swami Vivekananda said transforming human nature was like straightening the tail of a dog; as soon as it was straightened it would curl back. Both the seeker and the spiritual Master, certainly need great patience. But, through all his years in the West with his spiritual children, Guru never gave up. He always kept trying and striving to change our human nature.

Despite all the miracles of Guru's weightlifting, his innumerable poems, musical performances and art work, I feel his supreme achievement was to strive selflessly and tirelessly for the transformation of his disciples. Is there any more difficult task than the transformation of human nature?

MAHIRUHA
Chicago,
United States of America

As someone who lived very close in the Master's physical proximity, I knew Sri Chinmoy very well, and saw him at least twice a week for years and years. But I hardly ever spoke with him. I did not have the kind of close, intimate relationship that some other people had on the outer plane. Of course, by meditating with him so many times, I had the most important connection one can have with any Master, and that is a meeting of minds and of souls. Guru says that this very mixing of consciousness is the essence of meditation. In other words, the Master doesn't have to give outer instructions on how to meditate. You simply sit in front of the Master, and the Master's silent gaze teaches you the ins and outs of meditation. Your soul enters into his soul and learns how proper meditation is done.

To be honest, I am a little bit embarrassed to be using loaded terms like 'soul' because what do I know about the soul? I am just a beginner in the spiritual life; even after twenty years of meditation, I am still just at the very early stages of spiritual self-discovery. But I can claim that, at times, I have felt deep joy and purity, and so those few experiences make me feel that the soul exists. Sometimes I just like repeating the word 'soul' many, many times. I feel a deep thrill when I say that word with a prayerful attitude.

When I sat in class, listening to my philosophy professor lecture, I felt all my cares and worries wash away from me in a torrent of light and peace. Dominick really had something. I once showed Guru a poem I had written about this man, and Guru told me that my experiences with him were absolutely real.

When I sat in Guru's presence, the experience of light and joy was infinitely, infinitely more palpable and capacious. I am not putting Dominick down, of course! How many people after all, radiate light and joy in a way that irreverent, arrogant college freshmen like me could actually feel?

I came to the spiritual path out of sheer luck, or maybe sheer Grace. I had some inner experiences of these subtle, mysterious realities, and those experiences made me hungry to learn more about the spiritual life and the nature of God. But if those realities had never tapped me on the shoulder and said, "Hey, dummy! We're here! Higher light is real!" then I wouldn't have seen anything unusual or special either in Dominick or in Sri Chinmoy. People need some kind of preparation before they can recognize real spiritual figures. The name of that preparation is sheer, unconditional Grace.

These recollections are just my way of saying "thank you" to that Grace that, by some combination of miracles, raised me from a state of awkward and confused brokenness to one of peace, joy, confidence and satisfaction. I am not what I was. By praying and meditating I have found out that my possibilities and hopes are unlimited in all directions. A greater gift than that I cannot imagine.

ARUNA
Augsburg, Germany

How Sri Chinmoy answers children's questions is fantastic. It is simple and totally understandable, and that is how I remember it from my childhood. Nothing was ever 'not understood'. Everything always made perfect sense, because I was always told the truth in a very simple way, as you can only tell a child. And I still feel the same way now that I am 28 years old! Whenever I had the opportunity to ask Sri Chinmoy something and expected a grand complex answer, he replied in the simplest possible way, that totally makes sense when you hear it. It blows your mind away! – and you ask yourself, "Why didn't I think of that myself before?!"

When I was 2½ years old, my parents took me along for the first time to Sri Chinmoy's birthday celebrations in New York, so I met him for the first time. I do not remember so much from those early years, but for me, the most important thing is that I do not remember a life without Sri Chinmoy and his guidance and love.

During my entire childhood and teenage years, and now in my adult life, I have always felt protected somehow, inwardly and outwardly. My parents raised me as Sri Chinmoy advises parents to raise a child – although I think they did it intuitively, led by God, because they themselves were still children, and still are, more than me sometimes.

They were there for me at every moment. They showered me with love, guidance, compassion, forgiveness (especially my mother), oneness. They taught me the results of their own spirituality, not always consciously, but through their behaviour, and many more things....

I am most grateful to them for loving the spiritual Aruna more than the ordinary person Aruna, for that is the ultimate love of a parent, the only real love.

Sure, there were some hard times in my life – growing up isn't always easy – but whatever happened, I always knew it will be taken care of, it will turn out okay, it is for the best. I never lost my faith completely. And it always turned out fine. And I know in every life situation my teacher Sri Chinmoy was present, watching me, guiding me, showing me the right way.

Now when I think back, I had a great childhood – I still do! We travel a lot, getting to know the world, widening our view. I've always had great friends I know I can trust who share the same interest in spirituality; I always feel protected, safe and happy among my friends at Sri Chinmoy Centre, which is like an extended family.

When I look at some children or teenagers who do not have spirituality, and see how lost they are, how sad, how confused, how rude they are, what language they use, how they treat others, I feel grateful that I was able to live a life like mine.

My gratitude to Sri Chinmoy for blessing me with such a great life.

HARITA
Auckland, New Zealand

Before consciously embarking on my spiritual journey, for some time I primarily identified myself as a feminist. I studied feminist studies at university and read many books and articles by well-known feminists. I knew the cause was significant and justified, and greatly admired these brave and strong women.

My challenge was that the more I immersed myself in the world of feminism, the more agitated and upset I became. My search for an ideal of freedom and liberation through feminist values left me feeling frustrated and disheartened by the world around me. In the struggle for equal rights in a male-dominated society, it became increasingly apparent that if there was light at the end of this tunnel, it was a very long tunnel.

I am not deprecating feminism, but rather seeking to share how my own spiritual awakening expanded and clarified my identity as a woman, and showed me a way forward that worked for me. I now see that my views were limited by my mental perceptions and judgements. My adopted values were not from within myself, but founded primarily on what other people wrote, said and did. I learned that to change the world the best thing I can do is to start with myself.

I am deeply grateful that I became Sri Chinmoy's disciple. At first the idea of having a male spiritual teacher was challenging, however this concern soon became unsubstantiated as I felt a new reality dawn in my life. I learned that the freedom and strength we all yearn for can only be found within ourselves. I soon experienced for myself that meditating on my heart centre inspired, strengthened and empowered me in a true and lasting way.

Living a spiritual life has enabled me to connect with my deeper nature. Nowadays I am not usually disturbed if I am discriminated against, because I feel my own value powerfully within. I know that I am only responsible for my behaviour and not that of others. I have a greater love and understanding of the world and myself. I get much satisfaction from sincerely striving to identify with the inherent goodness in all people.

Perhaps some people are afraid of spirituality, consequently they try to discount its value rather than try it, or at least attempt to gain any deeper understanding of it. Feminine qualities like purity, compassion, sweetness and humility are given little value in our modern society, and yet when we see them, how beautiful and powerful they are! When we feel them within ourselves, how strong and happy we feel!

Sri Chinmoy's philosophy has no gender-based discrimination. As a spiritual teacher, it seems likely that, more than any of the great teachers before him, he encouraged women to come to the fore in all aspects of human endeavour, from sports to business to creativity, and most especially, spirituality. He taught me to nurture and be proud of my feminine qualities, and bring them into everything I do. He also taught me to understand and respect the difference between women and men. We each have a significant role to perform here on earth, in our own ways.

In the past men were given more of a chance to develop spiritually, but now I believe that in the West women have equal opportunity, and the qualities we bring to modern society are increasingly important. I am well aware that in many parts of the world women are still denied basic equal rights. This makes me super grateful and increasingly committed to making the most of the opportunities I have.

I find increasing strength and significance in my role as a spiritual woman. This inspires me to encourage and find ways for all women to express and unify the strength they have within themselves, not only for their own happiness, but also for the resulting progress of humanity. I have learned that we get true strength when we see strong qualities in others and, instead of separating ourselves by being jealous or insecure, consciously become one with them.

From ancient times until the present day there have been an increasing number of inspirational women whose spirituality has enabled them to overcome all kinds of obstacles and do remarkably good and great things. Some that come to mind are Joan of Arc, Mother Teresa, Sister Nivedita, Anandamayi Ma, Maya Angelou, Oprah Winfrey and Malala Yousafzai. Of course there are countless incredible women who we will never hear of whose faith and spirituality has, and continues to, profoundly impact the world we live in.

Sri Chinmoy always encouraged us to bring forward the unique light of our own soul, the Supreme representative within us all. I once heard him say, "Every soul is so precious." He was, and continues to be, an unconditionally loving and deeply inspiring teacher and friend to me. I feel most fortunate to live in this beautiful world, to be part of a spiritual community, and to have the aspiration to strive every day to live in union with the Universal laws of truth, peace and oneness.

SHARANI
Rhode Island,
United States of America

I slowed the car to a stop under the shade of a tree on the residential street lined with houses that were typical for this Jamaica, Queens NY neighborhood. It was a perfect spring morning with sunny skies, trees awash in blossoms and flowers blooming everywhere within the well-manicured yards. I was about to attend a group meditation with students of spiritual teacher Sri Chinmoy. Because I myself am a long-time student of Sri Chinmoy, I undoubtedly qualify as an old-timer at many of the activities of the Sri Chinmoy Centre held in this Queens neighborhood. Yet I walked up to the house with a sense of anticipation for what the morning would offer at this gathering comprised mostly of new students of Sri Chinmoy. My eagerness stemmed from the fact that I had not attended a meditation meeting at this first floor apartment, now transformed into a spiritual oasis, since the fall of 2005. That first and only visit found me delighting in a social gathering filled with games, food, meditation, singing and video watching – affectionately termed a 'Joy Day' by Sri Chinmoy.

Today I came as a guest for their regular Sunday morning group meditation. Upon arrival, the foyer inside the front door sparkled with neatness. Gleaming white cubbies lined the wall to hold our shoes in the tidiest of fashion. Then I walked in the door and was instantly mesmerized by the elegance of this apartment turned meditation mecca. The walls themselves and everything inside seemed to sing a cheerful and harmonious tune for the onlooker. Light blue carpet and furnishings created a peaceful aura and several striking framed photographs on the wall of Sri Chinmoy in a serene gaze added to the meditative atmosphere.

In the main room established and decorated for meditation, the shrine table for candles and flowers perched underneath a large window draped with sheer white curtains. The sunlight streamed in through the window creating a symbolic reminder that we would seek inner light during our meditation together.

Just past the area for meditation is the kitchen and a small art gallery of sorts that had been created with numerous abstract paintings by Sri Chinmoy arranged on the walls. The paintings offered a palette of cheerful primary colours combined in harmonious fashion inside similarly colorful frames. Beyond that a library of numerous spiritual books could be found and another smaller room currently in a state of remodeling but seemingly also intended for group meditation.

Once I finished looking around, I joined in the flurry of activity to prepare for the meeting. Cuttings of flowers from the yard were brought inside and vases were emptied and arranged for adornment of the meditation shrine table. Candleholders were diligently emptied of old wax. The shrine cloth was whisked off the table and a new fresh one was quickly in place. A row of candles inside exquisite votive holders were lit and flickered in welcome.

I was put to work washing cherries for prasad. We would take this prasad, an Indian word for blessed food, at the conclusion of our meditation. As additional people arrived, so too came more food for prasad. Pastries were artfully arranged on platters. Oranges scored for easy peeling. Together we hand-lettered invitations on artsy note-cards to announce an inaugural book discussion meeting of the group later that week.

By the conclusion of these preparations, this already beautiful and inviting atmosphere now additionally glistened with the care, concern and dedication permeating every loving touch of readiness. When we finally sat on chairs and cushions on the floor to begin the meeting (which themselves were also elegant yet simple), I felt as if the intensity and dedication of these shared preparations set the stage for a meditation all the more cherished as a special and sacred inner journey.

Our meeting included reading aloud, group chanting of mantric words such as *Aum*, silent meditation, walking meditation, meditating upon a short video of Sri Chinmoy himself in meditation, and singing. Afterwards we took prasad and shared news and conversation.

This small gathering impressed me deeply. Humble and heartfelt, it inspired me in the core of my being. In the space of only a couple of hours, I felt as if my inner existence had risen to the surface and been sumptuously fed in a realm of beauty, simplicity and harmony.

From the outside this miracle haven looks like an ordinary house on an ordinary street. Inside a doorway to the soul waits to be discovered. Reaching and passing through that doorway is quickened by the treasure chest of soul-stirring tools found in Sri Chinmoy's contributions as an author, teacher, musician and artist coupled with the peace-elevating interior décor. By the time I left this shared meditation, a tangible and palpable sense of spirit pervaded my awareness. My soul, previously hidden underneath the ordinary routine, entwined itself in the forefront of my consciousness. I left feeling like spirit is the main fabric of life – not just in theory but in concrete and current reality.

I find this transformation to be nothing less than a miracle, even if eventually tarnished by the return to my daily outer-world responsibilities. Inside this house on a regular-looking street, I mingled with people from diverse ethnic and religious backgrounds (representing the Ukraine, Scotland, Guyana, Bangladesh, India and America) in a spirit of harmony and community. And this despite meeting half of them for the first time on that day. Breaking the bread of spirit together melted away our differences and fed our souls. No wonder the name of this meditation group is called 'The Oneness-Heart-Centre'.

This quality of unity is a central tenet of Sri Chinmoy's teachings and the ease in which we shared the gift of spirit across cultures, age, religion and race proved to me it is attainable. Remembering the beloved holiday movie, I contend that 34th Street in New York is not the only place to find miracles. In New York, miracles can also easily be found on none other than this humble street in Jamaica, Queens. I found a miracle there and hope you find your own miracles on any street address anywhere across the globe simply through cultivating the purity, beauty, simplicity and peace inside the ever miraculous meditation.

GLOSSARY

ASPIRATION-GROUND
The outdoor meditation area in Queens, New York, where Sri Chinmoy used to meet with his disciples and guests. It was once a tennis court, where Sri Chinmoy would play tennis in the daytime, and later where he would practise weightlifting. It continues to be a sacred place of meditation for disciples and guests from around the world. Sri Chinmoy's samadhi is located at Aspiration-Ground.

CELEBRATIONS
There are two major Celebrations each year. The first is around April 13th. This is to mark Sri Chinmoy's arrival in the West, April 13th, 1964, and the beginning of his mission in the West. The other major Celebration is August 27th, to celebrate his birthday. There is now also the observance of Sri Chinmoy's Mahasamadhi around October 11th. Celebrations are an opportunity to spend time at Aspiration-Ground, mixing with other disciples, meditating, singing, running and enjoying other activities.

CHRISTMAS TRIPS
Each winter Sri Chinmoy would leave New York, to spend time in various countries with some of his disciples. In addition to daily meditations and functions, there would usually be public events such as concerts and meetings to honour local dignitaries. Since Sri Chinmoy's Mahasamadhi, his disciples still enjoy similar trips to different locations each year.

DIVINE ENTERPRISES
Enterprises independently owned and run by Sri Chinmoy's disciples. There are many divine enterprises around the world – primarily cafés, restaurants and shops – dedicated to serving the public in a peaceful and uplifting environment.

GOD-REALISATION
Also known as self-realisation, this is the ultimate goal of meditation – a state of conscious oneness with the Supreme.

JOY DAYS
In addition to twice-weekly meditations at local Centres, Sri Chinmoy encouraged his disciples to meet in larger groups on occasional weekends – all those from an entire country, several countries, or a smaller region. Joy Days often include sports, games and other innocent entertainment, as well as meditation and soulful performances.

MAHASAMADHI
A term used to describe a yogi's final departure from his earthly body. A yogi who has realised the highest consciousness has the ability to choose his time of exit and will go when his play on earth is finished. It is considered misleading to talk of a spiritual Master's death, because he or she has merely entered into the soul's world and soul's consciousness.

PRASAD
Blessed food traditionally given out by spiritual Masters or after spiritual worship. Often it is a simple fruit, but Sri Chinmoy liked to give out generous prasads. He

said that if taken with the right devoted attitude, prasad is much more than just physical food; it also contains a spiritual energy.

SAMADHI
A state of very high meditation or trance. There are three stages of samadhi: *Savikalpa samadhi*, *Nirvikalpa samadhi* and *Sahaja samadhi*. In this last state the person is constantly in the highest transcendental consciousness even whilst moving in everyday life. In other traditions, other terms like *Nirvana* may be used to describe types of samadhi. Ultimately, it is an experience that far transcends the mind, and so cannot be described or understood by the intellect. The term samadhi can also be used to refer to the sacred place where a yogi's earthly frame is interred.

SELFLESS SERVICE
Serving without seeking reward is a common practice across a wide range of spiritual paths. According to Sri Chinmoy's teachings, selfless service goes hand in hand with meditation. It encourages oneness with those around us, rather retreating from the world.

SUPREME
Supreme is a term Sri Chinmoy uses to refer to God. Sri Chinmoy says he prefers the term Supreme to God, because it expresses an ever-expanding consciousness, whereas in the West, God often evokes images of a static consciousness.

TRANSCENDENTAL PICTURE
A photograph taken of Sri Chinmoy in a very high state of meditation. Sri Chinmoy's disciples meditate on this picture in order to identify with the universal consciousness it embodies.

YOGA
A Sanskrit word meaning union with God, union with one's own highest Self. There are different types of yoga: *Karma Yoga* (action), *Jnana Yoga* (wisdom), *Bhakti Yoga* (devotion). The most common type of yoga in the West is *Hatha Yoga* – the yoga of physical postures. This is mainly a preparatory stage for the other yogas and is not indispensable to realising God.

NOTES

Page 8, paragraph 5, quote from:
AUM, Vol. 1, No. 2, September 27, 1965
Boro Park Printers, 1965

Page 11, aphorism from:
Twenty-Seven Thousand Aspiration-Plants, Part 10,
Agni Press, 1983

Page 35, quote from:
Reincarnation and Evolution, Agni Press, 1977

Page 40, aphorism from:
Ten Thousand Flower-Flames, Part 2, Agni Press, 1979

Page 61, aphorism from:
207 Flower-Flames, Agni Press, 1985

Page 106, quote from:
Compassion-Sea and Satisfaction-Waves,
Agni Press, 1992

Page 134, paragraph 1, aphorism from:
Ten Thousand Flower-Flames, Part 70,
Agni Press, 1983

Page 134, paragraph 2, aphorism from:
Seventy-Seven Thousand Service-Trees, Part 20,
Agni Press, 2001

Page 150, aphorism from:
Ten Thousand Flower-Flames, Part 17, Agni Press, 1981

Page 162, aphorism from:
Twenty-Seven Thousand Aspiration-Plants, Part 56,
Agni Press, 1984

Page 164, aphorism from:
Meditations: Food for the Soul, Agni Press, 1970

Page 165, poem from:
My Flute, Agni Press, 1972

Page 183, quote from:
Entertainment Versus Enlightenment, Agni Press, 1973

Page 190, aphorism from:
Four Hundred Gratitude-Flower-Hearts, Agni Press, 1979

Page 194, quote from:
My Consulate Years, Agni Press, 1996

Page 225, aphorism from:
Twenty-Seven Thousand Aspiration-Plants, Part 92,
Agni Press, 1984

Page 232, song from:
Supreme, Teach Me How to Cry, Agni Press, 1975

Page 300, prayer from:
My Race-Prayers, Part 2, Agni Press, 2006

Page 311, aphorism from:
Seventy-Seven Thousand Service-Trees, Part 28,
Agni Press, 2002

Page 337, aphorism from:
Ten Thousand Flower-Flames, Part 84, Agni Press, 1983

Page 355, quote from:
Earth's Cry Meets Heaven's Smile, Part 2,
Agni Press, 1974

Page 364, aphorism from:
*My Christmas–New Year–Vacation Aspiration-Prayers,
Part 52*, Agni Press, 2007

Page 382, excerpt from:
The Golden Boat, Part 8, Agni Press, 1974

Page 386, quote from:
The Master and the Disciple, Agni Press, 1985

Page 390, aphorism from:
Transcendence-Perfection, Agni Press, 1977

Page 391, aphorism from:
Ten Thousand Flower-Flames, Part 75, Agni Press, 1983

Page 417, aphorism from:
Seventy-Seven Thousand Service-Trees, Part 33,
Agni Press, 2003

Page 447, aphorism from:
Seventy-Seven Thousand Service-Trees, Part 46,
Agni Press, 2006

Page 455, aphorism from:
Seventy-Seven Thousand Service-Trees, Part 13,
Agni Press, 1999

Page 470, aphorism from:
Aspiration-Body, Illumination-Soul, Part 1,
Agni Press, 1993

Page 480, quote from:
Everest-Aspiration, Part 3, Agni Press, 1977

Page 491, aphorism from:
My Fifty Gratitude-Summers, Agni Press, 1981

Page 503, aphorism from:
Twenty-Seven Thousand Aspiration-Plants, Part 176
Agni Press, 1993

Page 515, aphorism from:
Twenty-Seven Thousand Aspiration-Plants, Part 179,
Agni Press, 1993

Page 522, quote from:
My Heart-Melody, Agni Press, 1994

INDEX OF AUTHORS

Abhinabha	13, 370
Adarini	16
Adesh	20
Adhiratha	295
Agraha	339
Ajita	24
Anandashru	26
Animesh	229
Antaranga	29, 343
Apaga	325
Aranyani	36, 431
Arpan	323
Arthada	316
Aruna	525
Ashrita	38, 483
Bhashini	40, 333
Bijon	393
Bipin	243
Chidananda	233, 280
Databir	55
Devaki	57
Devashishu	313
Devavira	62
Dhanu	66
Dinesh	403
Dodula	81
Eshana	85
Harita	527
Ishani	87
Jaitra	89, 380

Jana	94
Jayalata	407
Jogyata	104, 288, 387, 402, 511
Kanan	319
Karteek	496
Kodanda	298
Lotika	355
Magdalena	107
Mahanidhi	207
Mahiruha	507, 523
Medhyata	111
Mridula	114
Mrittyunjoy	357
Nayak	303, 509
Palyati	367
Pankaja	124
Parvati	408
Pierre	127
Pipasa	132
Prachar	237, 300
Pradeep	134
Prakhara	141
Pramodan	308
Pranika	405, 424
Pratul	144
Priyavadin	306
Pulak	250
Purabi	148
Purnahuti	153
Purnakama	159, 395
Rathin	475
Saral	162
Sarama	166, 336, 425
Sarvosmi	406

Shaivya	335
Shamita	361
Sharanagata	333
Sharani	168, 530
Shilpa	334
Shirini	173
Shishir	505
Shivaram	177, 394
Sipra	181, 322, 419
Smarana	471
Stacey	466
Sujantra	184
Sulochana	450, 457
Sumangali	186, 373
Suradhuni	415
Sushmitam	412
Sushumna	190, 227, 320, 517
Sutushti	194
Tanima	321
Tejvan	198, 376, 477, 518
Tirtha	205
Toshala	433
Trishakash	498
Unmilan	256
Upasevana	207
Utsahi	442
Utthal	397
Vajra	212
Vasanti	494
Venu	217
Vidagdha	341
Vidura	315
Vijali	448, 462

www.ingramcontent.com/pod-product-compliance
Lightning Source LLC
Chambersburg PA
CBHW050523300426
44113CB00012B/1933